2009/10

The
Educational
Grants
Directory

Alan French and
Jessica Carver

DIRECTORY OF SOCIAL CHANGE

Published by
Directory of Social Change
24 Stephenson Way
London NW1 2DP
Tel. 08450 77 77 07; Fax 020 7391 4804
Email publications@dsc.org.uk
www.dsc.org.uk
from whom further copies and a full books catalogue are available.

Directory of Social Change is a Registered Charity no. 800517

First published 1988
Second edition 1992
Third edition 1994
Fourth edition 1996
Fifth edition 1998
Sixth edition 2000
Seventh edition 2002
Eighth edition 2004
Ninth edition 2006
Tenth edition 2009

ISBN-13 978 1 906294 31 1

British Library Cataloguing in Publication Data
A catalogue record for this book is available from the British Library

Cover design by Keith Shaw
Text designed by Gabriel Kerne
Typeset by Marlinzo Services, Frome
Printed and bound by Page Bros., Norwich

Other Directory of Social Change departments in London:
    08450 77 77 07

Directory of Social Change Northern Office:
    Federation House, Hope Street, Liverpool L1 9BW
    Courses and conferences 08450 77 77 07
    Policy & Research 0151 708 0136

CONTENTS

INTRODUCTION

Welcome to the tenth edition of *The Educational Grants Directory*. The main focus of the guide is to provide a comprehensive list of sources of non-statutory help for people in education who are in financial need. All levels of education are covered up to and including first degree level. This edition contains information on over 1,400 grant-making trusts, which together distribute over £61 million in grants. Over 20 trusts are included in this guide for the first time. Also new in this edition is an increased focus on funding for gap year students and overseas voluntary work.

During 2008, we saw the beginnings of a global recession, the scale of which has not been seen for many generations, if ever. This will undoubtedly have an impact on people at all levels of education – particularly vulnerable are low-income families already struggling to meet needs not covered by the state. In previous editions of this guide we have highlighted the struggle many families have to meet school uniforms costs, which can run into hundreds of pounds a year. A 2008 poll carried out on behalf of Barnardo's and Citizens Advice found that almost three quarters of parents were put under additional stress because of these costs.

Alongside the economic crisis, rising student debt has continued to make the headlines, with higher education students finding themselves getting deeper into debt as state support for them drops still further. One survey conducted in 2008 predicted that 2010 graduates could leave university with debts amounting to over £17,000.

Many students undertake work to assist with their living costs and fees, although many have to turn to other sources of funding to ease the financial burden that a university education now presents. It is often students with children of their own or those from low-income backgrounds who leave their university education because they can not afford to continue, and for them the limited help available from grant-making trusts will continue to be crucial. Some trusts offer small grants to help with tuition fees, others offer scholarships based on their own, often strict, criteria; however, there is always stiff competition for the limited funds available.

Trusts can meet needs ranging from school clothing and books for schoolchildren to equipment and materials for people starting work. Individuals are more likely to be helped with extras like these, rather than with fees or living expenses. Funding to enable people with few qualifications to re-enter education is also popular, as is support for informal educational opportunities involved with music and other arts (see *How can trusts help?* on page 5).

About this guide

Which trusts are included?

Those that give:

- at least £500 a year in education grants to students (most give considerably more)
- grants for up to and including first degree level
- grants based on need rather than merely academic performance
- grants to students of more than one school or college.

Not those that give:

- grants solely for postgraduate study
- awards or scholarships for academic excellence, except where these appear to be particularly relevant to people in need.

Many of the trusts support individuals for non-educational causes as well. These are all included in the sister guide to this book, *The Guide to Grants for Individuals in Need*. Some trusts support organisations such as schools or educational charities. Entries in this guide concentrate only on trusts' educational grants to individuals.

How trusts are ordered in the guide

National section

National trusts are classified according to:

- **need**, for example, independent & boarding schools, illness/disabilities and overseas students page 17

- **occupation**, of parent or applicant page 51
- **subject**, being studied page 65

To find relevant trusts, individuals should initially use the flow chart on page 10, or go to the index on page 287.

Local sections

Local sections start on page 93; see page 89 for how to use these sections.

Supporting information

The guide also contains:

- a basic guide to the statutory entitlements and support for people in education (page 263)
- information on company sponsorships and career development loans (page 271)
- a guide to funding for gap year students and overseas voluntary work (page 273)
- a description of some of the options available for boarding and independent school education (particularly state maintained boarding schools) (page 275)
- a list of education authorities (page 279)
- sources of further information and advice (page 285).

How trusts can help

Most trusts in this guide can only give supplementary help.

Trusts typically help with the cost of books, small-scale fees such as GCSE and A-level exam fees and supplementary awards. It is very rare for a trust to fund fees and maintenance throughout an individual's academic career.

Creative use of the resources available in this guide can, however, have far-reaching effects on an individual's education.

Grants are usually given for one of the following purposes:

- to enable individuals to study at any educational establishment (including for study or training of a professional, technical or vocational nature) – these grants are usually for fees or to buy books or equipment

- to help with the cost of travel for educational purposes (for example, field studies or visits to museums)

- to help with extracurricular activities that are aimed at the physical and social development of the individual (such as outdoor centres or voluntary work overseas).

Loans of money, such as for buying musical instruments, can also be made.

Schoolchildren

Children who come from families that have severe financial needs can miss out on educational benefits such as books or school outings. This often puts the child at a social as well as an educational disadvantage to his or her peers. Grants from trusts do not address the causes of such situations, but they do help to redress some of the balance.

Grants can be made, for instance, for:

- children who struggle academically but have potential in extracurricular activities (for example, grants for musical instruments or sports equipment that could help them to develop their potential in those areas)

- children with learning difficulties who may be helped with grants towards extra lessons

- children with disabilities, who may be able to get grants for equipment related to their disabilities not otherwise available from statutory sources.

Many such grants will be for less than £100, but make a great difference to those concerned.

Students in further and higher education

Student loans now constitute the main source of funding for students and the demand for trust grants and other non-statutory sources of funding is higher than ever. Trust funds can help to relieve some of the debt students face, by making grants for:

- childcare costs

- books, equipment and materials

- travel, such as fieldwork or during gap years

- fees.

People starting work or apprentices

Many of the older educational trusts were originally set up to give grants to apprentices or to those 'entering a trade or profession'. These days, this means that grants are made to school-leavers and people leaving further or higher education who are starting work.

Grants can be awarded to buy tools and equipment to help people in their trade; for example, arts materials, clothing or books/manuals. This can be extremely valuable to people who have student loans to repay.

Help with getting support

Which trusts should I apply to?

Applications should not be made to trusts that clearly state the applicant is not eligible to receive a grant.

Trusts usually have very tight restrictions on who they can make grants to. These are usually set through legally defined criteria that cannot be altered. Eligibility can depend on various factors such as birthplace or parental occupation, as well as more obscure criteria such as surname. More commonly it is a matter of family background and where you were born or now live.

Trusts in this guide are listed thematically (parental occupation, geographical area of benefit and so on). This is also done to emphasise that individuals should not apply to those trusts which clearly state that they would *not* be eligible to receive a grant. Individuals who do contact such trusts waste their own money and annoy trustees, who either feel obliged to reply (using their trust's money) or, as we would recommend, put the letter straight in the bin.

Before approaching trusts for grants

Before approaching trusts for grants, always enquire after any other possible sources of funds. Several trusts make this a prerequisite for considering applications.

Parents or students should first ask the school, college or university concerned whether they offer any financial help. Many have at least some funds for cases of need, even though they may not be publicised.

Other possible sources of funding are included in more detail at the back of the guide.

Approaching trusts

When you have found relevant trusts that may be worth looking into further (see *How to use this guide*, page 9), read the entries through carefully. Many trusts have several criteria that potential applicants must meet. Some trusts publish guidelines to assist applicants. If so, get hold of them before making an application, along with an application form if there is one.

Some trusts welcome an initial telephone call from the individual or a third party, to enquire whether the application is suitable. Many of the correspondents for local trusts, however, administer the trust in their free time from home and may not be available during the day.

How to make an application on page 11 goes into these issues in more detail.

How trusts work

Applications should not be made to trusts that clearly state the applicant is not eligible to receive a grant.

A trust can only make grants for the purposes outlined in its objects, defined when the trust is formed. One or two trusts in this guide are restricted to making grants to inhabitants of relatively wealthy parishes and appear to have great difficulty finding individuals in need of financial support.

Most trusts, however, receive a constant flow of applications for worthy causes. Where the objects of the trust permit it, we would like to see an increase in trusts forming clear policies on who they do support, targeting those most in need, across a range of academic abilities, stages of education and types of need – from paying for school trips for schoolchildren to supporting the childcare costs of mature students on vocational courses.

The effectiveness of grant-making trusts

While some trusts, particularly national ones, produce clear guidelines, others (especially local trusts) do not. Based on our experience of researching this publication over the past 20 years we would like to make some suggestions as to ways in which trusts giving grants to individuals, particularly local trusts, could seek to encourage greater fairness in funding:

- Local trusts could seek to expand their resources to meet new or more widespread needs.

- If trustees can only meet twice a year, they should aim to cover the peak periods. Although educational needs arise throughout the year, there are obvious peak times, notably around November (when people have started their course and have a much clearer idea of how much money they need) and May (when people are running out of money at the end of the academic year).

- Trusts should also aim to ensure that needs can be met as rapidly as possible; for example, by empowering the clerk or a small number of trustees to make payments up to a certain limit (say £100).
- Trusts should ensure they are very well known in their area of benefit.

We recommend that each trust (depending on its eligibility restrictions) writes to at least the following: all welfare agencies (especially Citizens Advice); all community centres and other public meeting points; and the offices of the relevant education authority.

Great Giving Campaign

DSC exists to help voluntary and community organisations achieve positive social change. We campaign on a number of issues that we feel will advance this aim. In 2008 we launched our Great Giving Campaign, which originates from our principle of Responsible Giving. We want to support and help develop best practice among grant-making organisations. The campaign encompasses four areas:
(1) understanding the funding landscape;
(2) funding for campaigning;
(3) transparency; and (4) ineligible applications.

Although the campaign relates mainly to grant-making charities that support organisations, some of the principles extend to the trusts covered in this publication.

We believe that funders have a responsibility to understand the environment they are operating in. At present there is little information about where money is going and what is being supported. Providing a clearer picture will enable better planning and decision making from funders and policy makers, as well as contributing to the growing body of knowledge about the sector.

We know that most funders receive more applications for funding than they can award. We also know that a significant proportion of those applications are ineligible. In some cases the fault lies with the information provided by the funder, and in some cases the fault lies with the interpretation of that information by the applicant. We plan to use our ongoing research process to assess and quantify the level of wasted effort that occurs on both parts as a result of ineligible applications. This will help to build a picture of the most and least oversubscribed funders. We hope this information will drive future recommendations for both funders and applicants.

Full information of the Great Giving Campaign can be found at our website (http://www.dsc.org.uk/ NewsandInformation/ PolicyandCampaigning).

Acknowledgements

We are extremely grateful to the many trust officers and others who have helped compile this guide. To name them all would be impossible. We made every effort to ensure that the entries were correct. Where possible, drafts were sent to individual trusts and any corrections were noted and incorporated. However, the text and any mistakes within it remain ours rather than theirs.

A request for further information

The research for this book was done as fully and carefully as we were able, but there will be relevant charities that we have missed and some of the information will be incomplete or will become out of date.

If you come across omissions or mistakes in this guide, please let us know by calling or emailing the research department at the Directory of Social Change (0151 708 0136; email: research@dsc.org.uk) so that they can be rectified in future editions.

How to use this GUIDE

Below is a typical trust entry, showing the format we have used to present the information obtained from each of the trusts.

On the following page is a flowchart. We recommend that you follow the order indicated on the flow chart to look at each section of the guide and find trusts that are relevant to you.

Individuals should initially look at the charities that give nationally, firstly in the section classified by occupation of parent. Once you have found any charities in that section we advise you to look in the section classified by subject, followed by the section classified by need. Individuals should then look in the local section of the guide, which relates to where they live, or at any other areas with which they have a connection.

Eligibility

This states who is eligible to apply for a grant. It can include restrictions on age, family circumstances, occupation of parent, subject to be studied, stage of education, ethnic origin, or place of residence.

Exclusions

This field gives information on what the trust will not fund.

Annual grant total

This shows the total amount of money given in grants to individuals in the last financial year for which there were figures available. Other financial information may be given where relevant.

Correspondent

The main person to contact, nominated by the trustees. Often the correspondent is the trust's solicitors or accountants, who may just pass applications on to the trustees and therefore will not be able to help with telephone enquiries.

The Fictitious Trust

Eligibility: Children or young people up to 25 years of age who are in need. Preference is given to children of single parent families and/or those who come from a disadvantaged or unstable family background.

Types of grants: Small one-off grants, to assist in cases of short-term need. The trust gives grants for a wide range of needs, including school uniform, books, equipment and educational trips in the UK and abroad. The maximum grant is £250.

Exclusions: No grants for school/college or university fees.

Annual grant total: 140 grants totalled £25,000 in 2008.

Applications: On a form available from the correspondent, submitted either directly by the individual or by the parent or guardian for those under 18. Applications are considered in January, April, July and October.

Correspondent: Mrs I M Helpful, Charities Administrator, 7 Pleasant Road, London SN0 0ZZ (020 7123 4567; Fax: 020 7123 4568).

Other information: The trust also gives relief-in-need grants to individuals.

Types of grants

Specifies whether the trust gives one-off or recurrent grants, the size of grants given and what grants are actually given for; for example, school uniform, travel to school or another educational establishment, living expenses, college fees, tools or instruments, books and so on.

Applications

Including how to apply, who should make the application (i.e. the individual or a third party) and when to submit an application.

Other information

This contains miscellaneous further information about the trust.

How to identify sources of help
Quick reference flowchart

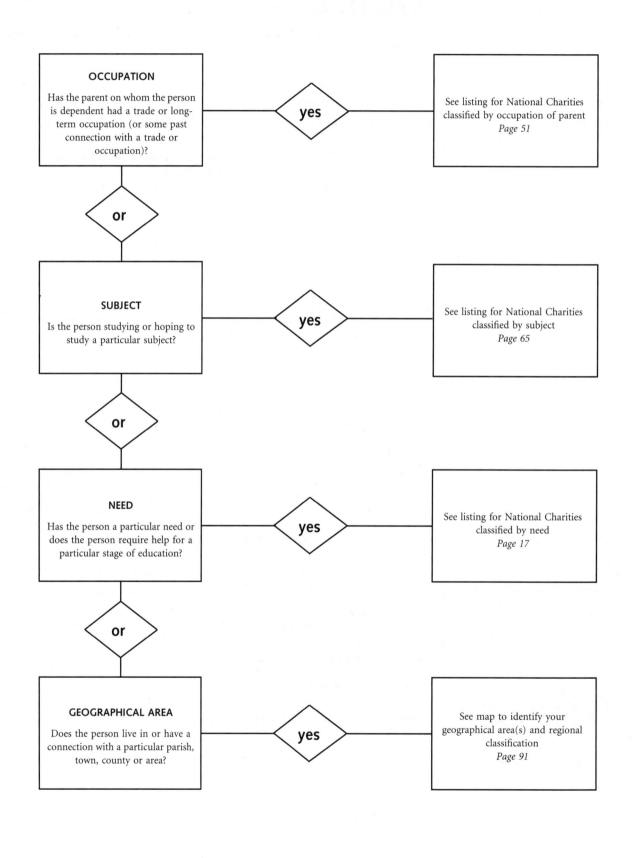

OCCUPATION

Has the parent on whom the person is dependent had a trade or long-term occupation (or some past connection with a trade or occupation)?

→ **yes** → See listing for National Charities classified by occupation of parent
Page 51

or

SUBJECT

Is the person studying or hoping to study a particular subject?

→ **yes** → See listing for National Charities classified by subject
Page 65

or

NEED

Has the person a particular need or does the person require help for a particular stage of education?

→ **yes** → See listing for National Charities classified by need
Page 17

or

GEOGRAPHICAL AREA

Does the person live in or have a connection with a particular parish, town, county or area?

→ **yes** → See map to identify your geographical area(s) and regional classification
Page 91

How to make an Application

In general, applicants should:

1. Exhaust other sources of funds

All sources of statutory funding should have been applied for and/or received before applying to a charity. Applications, therefore, should include details of these sources and any refusals. Where statutory funding has been received, but is inadequate, an explanation that this is the case should be made. A supporting reference from a relevant agency may also be helpful.

Educational establishments should also have been approached to see if they have any funds or can give a reduction in fees.

2. Give details of any unforeseen circumstances

Where relevant, try and show how the circumstances you are now in could not have been foreseen (for example, illness, family difficulties, loss of job and so on). In general, charities are reluctant to help people who start a course knowing that they have not got the money to complete it.

3. Ask for a suitable amount

Ask for an amount that the trust is able to give. Most trust grants are under £300, and local charities often give much less. If a trust only makes small grants, try asking for help with books, travel, childcare expenses and such like, and apply for fees elsewhere.

4. Give clear, honest details about any savings, capital or compensation

Most trustees will consider the applicant's savings when they are awarding a grant, although sometimes this does not need to affect trustees' calculations. In circumstances where you are certain that your savings are not relevant to grant calculations, you should explain this in the application.

5. Tailor the application to suit the particular charity

For example, if someone is applying to a trade charity on behalf of a child whose father had lengthy service in that particular trade, then a detailed description (and, where possible, supporting documentation) of the father's service would be highly relevant. If an application for the same child was being made to a local charity on another occasion, it would not.

6. Remember each charity has different deadlines for applications

Some charities can consider applications throughout the year; others may meet monthly, quarterly or just once a year. Very urgent applications can sometimes be considered between the main meetings. Where trusts have provided us with information about their deadlines, we have included it in the entries.

7. Mention applications to other charities

Explain that other charities are being approached, when this is the case, and state that any surplus money raised will be returned.

8. Make sure the appropriate person submits the application

Some trusts specify that they wish the application to be made directly by the individual and others request that the application is submitted via a third party; for example, a professional such as a teacher or educational welfare officer, or a parent/guardian.

9. Offer to supply references

For example, from a teacher, college tutor and/or another independent person. If the individual is disabled or has medical needs then a report from a doctor would be necessary.

10. Complete the trust's application form if there is one

Each entry in this guide should state if there is an application form available and how to obtain it.

On the next page is a general purpose application form. It can be photocopied and used whenever convenient and should enable applicants to state clearly the basic information required by most trusts. Alternatively, it can be used as a checklist of points to include in a letter. For notes on using the form see page 14.

11. Be honest and realistic, not moralising and emotional

Too many applications try to morally bribe trustees into supporting the application, or launch tirades against the current political regime. It is best to confine your application to clear and simple statements of fact.

12. Be as concise as possible and provide sufficient detail

Give as much relevant information as possible, in the most precise way. For example, 'place of birth' is sometimes answered with Great Britain, but if the trust only gives grants in Liverpool, to answer 'Great Britain' is not detailed enough and the application will be delayed pending further information. Applications are dealt with in the strictest confidence.

13. Write neatly and clearly; do not use jargon

Do not make it difficult for trustees to understand your application, they often have a lot of applications to read.

Please see page 14 for notes on the application form template.

Application form template

PURPOSE FOR WHICH GRANT IS SOUGHT	AMOUNT SOUGHT FROM £ THIS APPLICATION

APPLICANT (Name) Address Telephone no.	Occupation/School
Date of birth	Age Place of birth
Nationality	Religion (if any)

☐ Single   ☐ Married   ☐ Divorced   ☐ Partnered   ☐ Separated   ☐ Widow/er

FAMILY DETAILS: Name	Age	Occupation/School
Parents/ Partner	....	....
Brothers/Sisters/ Children.............................	....	....
....	....	....
....	....	....
Others (specify)........................	....	....

INCOME (weekly)	£	p	EXPENDITURE (weekly – *excluding course fees*)	£	p
Father's/husband's wage	....		Rent/mortgage	....	
Mother's/wife's wage	....		Council tax	....	
Partner's wage	....		Water rate	....	
Income Support	....		Electricity	....	
Job seekers allowance	....		Gas	....	
Child benefit	....		Other fuel	....	
Family Credit	....		Insurance	....	
Attendance allowance	....		Fares/travel	....	
Disability living allowance	....		Household expenses (food,		
Housing benefit	....		laundry etc).	....	
Maintenance payments	....		Clothing	....	
Pensions	....		School dinners	....	
Other income (specify)................	....		Childcare fees	....	
....	....		HP commitments	....	
....	....		Telephone	....	
....	....		TV rental	....	
			TV licence		
			Other expenditure (specify)..........	....	
			....	....	
			....	....	
			....	....	

TOTAL WEEKLY INCOME £ _____   **TOTAL WEEKLY EXPENDITURE** £ _____

NAME OF SCHOOL/COLLEGE/UNIVERSITY:

Address

COURSE:

Is the course ☐ full-time? ☐ part-time?

Date of starting course:

Date of finishing course:

NAME OF LOCAL EDUCATION AUTHORITY:

Have you applied for a grant? ☐ YES ☐ NO

What was the outcome of the application?

Give details of any other grants or scholarships awarded:

Have you applied to your school/college/university for help? ☐ YES ☐ NO

What was the outcome of the application?

Have you applied to any other trusts? ☐ YES ☐ NO

What was the outcome of the application?

Have you applied for any loans? ☐ YES ☐ NO

What was the outcome of the application?

HOW MUCH ARE YOUR SCHOOL/COLLEGE FEES?

£

Have they been paid in full? ☐ YES ☐ NO

If NO, please give details:

Other costs (e.g. books, clothing, equipment, travel etc.):

How much money do you need to complete the course? £

EXAMINATIONS PASSED & OTHER QUALIFICATIONS

PREVIOUS EMPLOYMENT (with dates)

ANY OTHER RELEVANT INFORMATION (*please continue on separate sheet if necessary*)

Signature:

Date:

Notes: application form template

1. Because this form is designed to be useful to the wide range of people who apply for education grants, not all the information asked for will be relevant to every application. If, for example, an applicant is not in receipt of state benefits, or does not have credit debts, he/she should write 'N/A' (not applicable) in the box or line in question.

2. If, similarly, you do not have answers for all the questions at the time of applying – for example, if you have applied to other trusts and are still waiting for a reply – you should write 'Pending' under the question 'Have you written to any other trusts? What was the outcome of the application?'.

3. The first page is relevant to all applications; the second page is only relevant to people applying for school or college fees. If you are applying for clothing or books for a schoolchild then it may be worth filling out only the first page of the form and submitting a covering letter outlining the reasons for the application.

4. Filling out the weekly income and expenditure parts of the form can be worrying or even distressing. Expenditure when itemised in this way is usually far higher than people expect. It is probably worth filling out this form with the help of a trained welfare rights worker.

5. You should always keep a copy of the completed form in case the trust has a specific query.

6. This form should not be used when the trust has its own form that must be completed.

National and General Sources of Help

The entries in this section are arranged in three groups classified by need, occupation of parent (or applicant) and subject. Generally, trusts which occur in the second and third classification are not listed in the first, which is reserved for more general trusts. However, they may have been cross referenced where appropriate.

The breakdown aims to make it easy to identify trusts which might be of relevance and as such as have attempted to make the terms as specific as possible. In doing so, there will be some cross-over between categories as, for instance, mature university students could identify trusts in the 'Adult & continuing education' and 'further & higher education' sections, with various other categories possibly being relevant dependent on personal circumstances. There were, however, a number of trusts which did not fall into any specific category and these have been listed at the front of the guide.

The trusts are arranged alphabetically within each category. Readers are warned not to use these lists by themselves as a guide to sources of money. Each main entry must also be read carefully because in most cases there will be further specific requirements to be met. The trusts in each category tend to be in contact with each other, and any applicant who just writes to them all, regardless of their particular policies, will meet with limited sympathy.

Classification by subject

NATIONAL CHARITIES CLASSIFIED BY NEED

Lawrence Atwell's Charity

Eligibility: Young people who have reached the age of 16 but who are under 27 at the date of application. Assistance will not be given to applicants whose parents' joint income exceeds £25,000 a year, plus £2,750 for each other dependent child under 18 years, nor to individuals with full LEA (or other) awards for fees and additional maintenance funding available to them, in the form of grants or loans. Applicants must be British citizens or refugees with indefinite leave to remain. Only students undertaking vocational training will be considered for funding.

Types of grants: The charity was founded over 400 years ago (1588) to 'set poor people upon work'. Grants are made for books, fees, travel, living costs and childcare. Grants can include those towards the cost of an apprentice's tools as well. In general, need as much as merit is taken into account when deciding to make grants.

Grants are usually one-off or recurrent and range from £200 to £3,000. Grants can be made for courses lasting more than one year. If the applicant is on a 2 or 3-year course, he/she may be asked to re-apply before the start of each year. If the applicant's costs are very high, they will be expected to show how they intend to raise the funds needed. The trustees will not make an award if they feel that finances are not feasible. Loans are rarely made.

Exclusions: Grants are not made for: study abroad; expeditions in the UK or abroad for any reason; intercalated degrees; clinical years of study (where LEA/NHS funding is in place) or electives; research, PhD degrees or non-vocational masters; business ventures; those already qualified for work; computer equipment (unless studying IT); students on dance or drama courses which are not accredited by the National Council for Drama Training or the Council for Dance Education and Training; students of music who have already had a year of postgraduate study (excluding voice students); students studying for A levels, GCSEs and GNVQs; and students seeking to help cover debts or loans that have already been taken out.

Annual grant total: In 2006/07 the trust had assets of £17 million and an income of £523,000. Grants totalling £562,000 were awarded to 274 applicants. The average size of grant has also increased to £2,100 (£1,800 in 2004/05). The majority of recipients received grants towards their tuition fees and maintenance costs whilst undertaking study. Support was also given towards the purchase of equipment, tools and instruments.

Applications: On a form available from the correspondent to be submitted directly by the individual. Guidelines for applicants, the application form, explanatory notes and a family finance form are also available to download from the charity's website www.skinnershall.co.uk/lawrenceatwell.htm.

Applications require proof of age and nationality, evidence of parental income and the support of two referees, which will be taken up in writing. Applications are considered in every month. The charity recommends that applications should be made as early as possible and to bear in mind that August, September and October are their busiest months. For courses finishing in June/July, the deadline for applications is Easter.

Correspondent: Gemma Garret, Atwell Administrator, The Skinners' Company, Skinners' Hall, 8 Dowgate Hill, London EC4R 2SP (020 7213 0561; Fax: 020 7236 5629; email: atwell@skinners.org.uk; website: www.skinnershall.co.uk/lawrence_atwell.htm)

The Alfred Bourne Trust

Eligibility: Students aged under 30, who have lived in the UK for at least two years, are not in receipt of a mandatory grant and are in need for one course year only.

Types of grants: A general UK fund for students under 30, this fund only awards grants totalling £1,000 in any one year.

Because funding is limited for applicants to be successful they are likely to be in their final year of GCSE, A level or a first degree and to have specific funding difficulties.

Annual grant total: About £1,000 is available each year for individuals.

Applications: In writing to the correspondent, enclosing an sae.

Correspondent: J Kidd, Director, Maybrook House, Godstone Road, Caterham, Surrey CR3 6RE (01883 331177; email: britforeign@aol.com; website: www.bfss.org.uk)

The Coffey Charitable Trust

Eligibility: People in need in the UK.

Types of grants: One-off and recurrent grants according to need.

Annual grant total: In 2006/07 the trust had an income of £6,300 and a total expenditure of £3,700.

Applications: The trust has previously stated that funds are fully committed.

Correspondent: C H Green, 24 Portman Gardens, Uxbridge, Middlesex, UB10 9NT

Other information: This trust also makes grants to organisations.

Conservative and Unionist Agents' Benevolent Association

Eligibility: Children of deceased Conservative or Unionist Agents or Women Organisers.

Types of grants: One off and recurrent grants according to need. Recent grants have been given for books, equipment, instruments and fees for school children.

Annual grant total: In 2006/07 the association had assets of £2.5 million and an income of £92,000. Grants were made to individuals totalling £39,000.

Applications: Initial telephone calls are welcomed and application forms are available on request. Applications can be made either directly by the individual or their parent/guardian, or through a member of the management committee or local serving agent. All beneficiaries are allocated a 'visiting agent'.

Correspondent: Mrs S Smith, Conservative Party Central Office, Millbank Tower, 30 Millbank, London SW1P 4DP (020 7984 8172; email: sally.smith@conservatives.com)

The Gillian Diamond Charitable Fund

Eligibility: People in need in the UK and developing countries.

Types of grants: One-off cash grants in the range of £100 and £300. Grants are given to schoolchildren, mature students, people with special educational needs and overseas students, including those for books and equipment/instruments.

Exclusions: Grants are not paid for fees or debts. No loans are made.

Annual grant total: In 2007/08 the fund had both an income and expenditure of around £11,000. Previously, the fund has dedicated approximately 50% of its expenditure to grants.

Applications: In writing to the correspondent to be submitted either directly by the individual or a family member, through an organisation such as Citizens Advice or school or through a third party such as a social worker or teacher. Applications are considered on an ongoing basis.

Correspondent: Gillian Diamond, PO Box 49849, London, NW5 9AJ (020 7485 6522; Fax: 020 7482 1384)

Other information: Grants are also made to organisations.

The Fenton Trust

Eligibility: 'British-born subjects who are dependants of a member of the professional classes and are undergoing a course of education or training approved by the trustees; or poor members of the professional or middle class.'

Types of grants: Grants are one-off and range between £100 and £500. They are only intended to be supplementary, therefore applicants are only considered if they are in the final year of a course and if they have managed to raise almost the whole amount needed, or if they encounter unexpected difficulty. Grants can go to students and mature students for help with costs of books, fees, living expenses, travel and childcare.

Exclusions: Grants are not given towards postgraduate study.

Annual grant total: In 2006/07 the trust had an income of £21,000 and a total expenditure of £25,000.

Applications: On a form available from the correspondent, to be submitted directly by the individual and supported by an academic reference. Trustees meet monthly.

Correspondent: Ms Fiona Macgillivray, Educational Grants Advisory Service, Grants Service Family Action, 501–505 Kingsland Road, Dalston, London E8 4AU (020 7254 6251; Fax: 020 7249 5443; email: grants.enquiry@ family-action.co.uk; website: www. familyaction.org.uk)

The General Federation of Trade Unions Educational Trust

Eligibility: Members of a trade union. Grants will only be considered for the subjects of economic history and theory; industrial law; and the history and principles of industrial relations.

Types of grants: Full-time and part-time students undertaking a course nominated by the recipient's trade union receive a grant of up to £150 (full-time), £50 (part-time) or £100 (Open University). Open University students will be supported after completing the first year. Grants may be paid annually.

Annual grant total: In 2006 the trust had assets of £3 million and an income of £1 million. Grants are given to around 15 individuals totalling about £1,500 annually.

Applications: A nomination form is available from the correspondent and must be signed by the general secretary from the applicant's trade union. Applications are considered quarterly. Proof of trade union membership may be required. Forms signed by lay representatives and local officials are not valid.

Correspondent: Michael Bradley, Secretary, GFTU Educational Trust, Central House, Upper Woburn Place, London WC1H 0HY (020 7387 2578; Fax: 020 7383 0820; email: gftuhq@gftu. org.uk; website: www.gftu.org.uk)

The Eleanor Hamilton Educational Trust

Eligibility: Priority is given to children who are either in their second year of GCSEs or their second year at A level. Consideration is also given to students (under 30) who are dyslexic or have other special needs and are estranged from their parents.

Types of grants: One-off grants in the range of £100 and £500 towards fees for schoolchildren and people with special educational needs and towards living expenses for college student, undergraduates, vocational students and people with special educational needs.

Annual grant total: In 2006 the trust had assets of £5 million and an income of £173,000. Educational grants to individuals totalled £116,000.

Applications: On a form available form the correspondent at any time.

Correspondent: The Trustees, 62 Park Lane, Norwich NR2 3EF (01603 614945)

Other information: The trust also gives to organisations (£10,000, 2007).

The Leverhulme Trade Charities Trust

Eligibility: Undergraduates who are in need and are the dependants of people who have been employed for at least five years as commercial travellers, chemists (members of the Royal Pharmaceutical Society) or grocers. This includes the offspring, spouses, widows and widowers of such people.

Types of grants: Grants of up to £3,000 a year to full-time first degree students for needs such as tuition fees, books, travel costs and accommodation. Grants can be one-off or last for the duration of the course.

Annual grant total: In 2007 grants were made to 59 undergraduates (from 60 applications). Grants paid totalled £471,000. A further £1.1 million was given in grants to organisations.

Applications: Undergraduate applications must be made through their university rather than directly by the individual, with the grants paid to the institutions to pass through to the successful applicants. The deadlines for the trust receiving the completed applications are 1 March and 1 November, with decisions made and funds available by the end of the month. Potential applicants should contact their student support services department for details of how to apply.

Correspondent: The Secretary, 1 Pemberton Row, London EC4A 3BG (020 7822 5227; website: www.leverhulme-trade.org.uk)

P & M Lovell Charitable Settlement

Eligibility: People in education who are in need.

Types of grants: One-off grants of £50 to £500.

Annual grant total: About £500 to individuals.

Applications: In writing to the correspondent.

Correspondent: c/o Mike Haynes, KPMG, 100 Temple Street, Bristol BS1 6AG (0117 905 4000; Fax: 0117 905 4065)

Other information: Grants are also made to organisations.

Moody Charitable Trust

Eligibility: Students in need in the UK.

Types of grants: One-off and recurrent grants according to need.

Annual grant total: About £10,000, mostly to organisations.

Applications: In writing to the correspondent.

Correspondent: T J Mines, Thomas David, Orchard House, 5 The Orchard, Hertford SG14 3HQ

The Noon Foundation

Eligibility: People in education.

Types of grants: One-off and recurrent grants according to need.

Annual grant total: In 2006 the foundation had assets of £3.7 million, an income of £146,000 and a total expenditure of £87,000. During the year the foundation made grants to institutions totalling £69,000.

Applications: On a form available from the foundation. All enquires should be made by email or by post enclosing an sae.

Correspondent: The Trustees, 25 Queen Anne's Gate, St James' Park, London SW1H 9BU (email: grants@noongroup.co.uk)

The Osborne Charitable Trust

Eligibility: People in education in the UK and overseas.

Types of grants: One-off and recurrent grants according to need and one-off grants in kind. Grants are given to schoolchildren for equipment/instruments and special needs education for fees and equipment/instruments.

Exclusions: No grants for religious or political purposes.

Annual grant total: In 2006/07 the trust had an income of £24,000 and a total expenditure of £38,000. Grants are made to organisations and individuals.

Applications: This trust does not respond to unsolicited applications.

Correspondent: Jet Eaton, 57 Osborne Villas, Hove, East Sussex BN3 2RA

The Tim Rice Charitable Trust

Eligibility: People in need in the UK on academic or cultural courses.

Types of grants: One-off and recurrent grants of up to £1,000, but typically around £500 each. Grants can be for the costs of music and sport, school fees and for other educational purposes.

Annual grant total: In 2006/07 the trust had an income of £259,000 and made grants totalling £225,000 mostly to organisations but including about £2,000 to individuals.

Applications: In writing to the correspondent.

Correspondent: Mrs E Heinink, Trustee, Ivy House, 31 The Terrace, Barnes, London SW13 0NR (020 7580 7313)

Scarr-Hall Memorial Trust

Eligibility: People in education in the UK.

Types of grants: One-off grants according to need, usually in the range of £100 and £500.

Annual grant total: About £10,000.

Applications: In writing to the correspondent.

Correspondent: Mrs D Thorley, Baker Tilley, Festival Way, Stoke-on-Trent, Staffordshire, ST1 5BB

Southdown Trust

Eligibility: Individual ventures of general educational benefit.

Types of grants: One-off and recurrent grants and loans ranging from £20 to £1,000. Grants are to 'support individual ventures of general educational benefit'. Previously grants have been made, for example, to fund a teaching assistant at a primary school, and to provide a scholarship for a university student.

Exclusions: No grants are made for art, dance, sociology, theatre, law, journalism, counselling, media studies, PhDs or materials.

Annual grant total: In 2006/07 the trust had assets of £1.1 million and an income of £72,000. Grants totalled £38,000 of which £20,000 went to individuals in 123 grants.

Applications: In writing to the correspondent enclosing full information and an sae. Applications should be made directly by the individual.

Correspondent: J G Wyatt, 'Holmbush', 64 High Street, Findon, West Sussex BN14 0SY

The Stanley Stein Charitable Trust

Eligibility: People under the age of 21 who are in need.

Types of grants: One-off and recurrent grants according to need.

Annual grant total: In 2006/07 the trust had assets of £697,000, an income of £28,000 and made grants for welfare and educational purposes totalling £17,000.

Applications: In writing to the correspondent.

Correspondent: The Trustees, Berg Kaprow Lewis LLP, 35 Ballards Lane, London, N3 1XW

The Vardy Foundation

Eligibility: People in need in who live in the UK.

Types of grants: One-off and recurrent grants according to need.

Annual grant total: In 2006/07 the trust had assets of £23 million and an income of £1.2 million. Grants to 38 individuals for education and welfare purposes totalled £102,000.

Applications: In writing to the correspondent.

Correspondent: The Chair of the Trustees, Venture House, Aykley Heads, Durham, DH1 5TS (0191 374 4744; website: www.vardyfoundation.com)

Other information: Grants are also made to organisations (£1.5 million in 2006/07).

The Wingate Scholarships

Eligibility: People aged 24 or over on 1 September in the current year who are citizens of the UK, or another Commonwealth country, Ireland or Israel; or citizens of the EU who have been resident in UK for at least three years. Applicants must be living in the UK at the time of application. Applicants must satisfy the scholarship committee that they need financial support to undertake the work projected and, where relevant, show good reason why Research Council, British Academy or major agency support cannot be expected.

Types of grants: Wingate Scholarships are awarded to individuals of great potential or proven excellence who need financial support to undertake pioneering or original work of intellectual, scientific, artistic, social or environmental value, and to outstandingly talented musicians for advanced training. The work to be undertaken may or may not be in the context of a higher degree.

They are designed to help with costs of a specified project which may last up to three years, including grants for living expenses/fees, study or travel abroad and overseas students studying in the UK. Grants average about £6,500 each and the maximum available in any one year is £10,000.

Exclusions: Awards are not made for medical research, taught courses, including those at art, drama or business schools or those leading to professional qualifications or for electives.

Fine artists are not eligible for Wingate Scholarships, but those engaged in art history, craft or other related research can apply.

Annual grant total: In 2006/07 the foundation had assets of £14 million and an income of £452,000. A total of £412,000 was distributed from the scholarship fund. In 2006/07 there were 478 applications, 99 people were interviewed and 42 scholarships were awarded.

Applications: More detailed information and application forms will be sent on written request to the correspondent. A large A4 sae should be enclosed. Alternatively, application forms and information are available on the website. Applications should be submitted between 1 October and 1 February for consideration in March/April. Interviews of shortlisted candidates are carried out in London in May.

Correspondent: Faith Clark, Administrator, QABC, 28 Broadway, London, SW1H 9JX (clark@wingate.org.uk; website: www.wingatescholarships.org.uk)

Mrs Wingfield's Charitable Trust

Eligibility: People who are in need. Individuals in Shropshire have priority over the rest of the country.

Types of grants: Grants are given to schoolchildren, further and higher education students, vocational students, mature students and people with special educational needs, including those towards the cost of uniforms/clothing, fees, books and equipment/instruments.

Annual grant total: In 2006/07 the trust had assets of £798,000, which generated an income of £19,000. Charitable expenditure totalled £13,000.

Applications: In writing to the correspondent, directly by the individual. Cases are considered at regular meetings of the trustees. Refusals are not always acknowledged due to the cost involved. If a reply is required, please enclose an sae.

Correspondent: Helen Thomas, Dyke Yaxley, 1 Brassey Road, Old Potts Way, Shrewsbury SY3 7FA (01743 241281)

S C Witting Trust

Eligibility: Schoolchildren under 15, undergraduates and mature students who live England.

Types of grants: One-off grants are made for uniforms/clothing, books and equipment/instruments.

Exclusions: No grants towards debts or loans.

Annual grant total: In 2007 the trust had assets of £4.3 million and an income of £1.6 million. Grants were made to individuals totalling £17,000. Grants are made for both educational and welfare purposes.

Applications: In writing to the correspondent, through a third party such as a social worker or teacher including a short case history, reason for need and the amount required. University students must have a letter of support indicating financial need. Unsuccessful applications are not acknowledged unless an sae is included.

Correspondent: The Administrator, Friends House, 173 Euston Road, London NW1 2BJ

Other information: Grants were also made to organisations totalling £61,000.

The Zobel Charitable Trust

Eligibility: People in education in the UK, particularly in the Christian field.

Types of grants: One-off and recurrent grants according to need.

Annual grant total: About £1,500 a year.

Applications: This trust does its own research and does not always respond to unsolicited applications.

Correspondent: S D Scott, Tenison House, Tweedy Road, Bromley, Kent BR1 3NF

Other information: Grants are also made to organisations.

Adult & continuing education

The Adult Education Bursary Scheme

Eligibility: People over 19, attending full-time courses of at least one year of liberal adult education at one of the following residential colleges: Coleg Harlech, Harlech, Wales; Fircroft College, Birmingham; Hillcroft College, Surbiton, London; Newbattle Abbey, Dalkeith; Northern College, Barnsley; and Ruskin College, Oxford. Applicants must have been offered a place on certificate and diploma courses at one of the colleges, and have been recommended for a bursary.

Types of grants: These colleges offer to relatively small numbers each year the opportunity of full-time university-type education in the broad field of social sciences and liberal studies. Students accepted by the colleges for one year courses are normally eligible for the bursaries covered by this scheme. These cover tuition fees and a maintenance grant and dependants' allowances. Grants for travel of over £80 a year are considered for the journey between the home and the residential college, or daily travel fees for students living at home during term-time. Grants are also available to students who are disabled, including:

- a special equipment allowance of up to £4,795 towards buying, leasing or repairing special equipment
- a non-medical personal helpers' allowance of up to £12,135 for non-medical helpers such as lip-readers or note-takers
- a general disabled students' allowance of up to £1,605 towards items such as printer inks, disks, Braille paper and so on to supplement other grants.

Annual grant total: Grants total about £250,000 each year.

Applications: Most of the colleges have an annual intake of students each September or October, with some offering intakes in January or April. Intending applicants should write initially to the college of their choice for a guideline to applying. Their addresses are listed above. English and Welsh students' application forms will be allocated by the college once they have been accepted on the course.

English and Welsh students wishing to study in Coleg Harlech should contact: The Student Grant Officer, Coleg Harlech, Harlech, Gwynedd LL46 2PU.

Correspondent: Christine Francis, Awards Officer, Adult Education Bursaries, c/o Ruskin College, Walton Street, Oxford OX1 2HE (01865 554331; Fax: 01865 556362; email: awards@ruskin. ac.uk)

Other information: The addresses of the colleges are as follows:

Coleg Harlech, Harlech, Gwynedd LL46 2PU (01766 780363).

Fircroft College, 1018 Bristol Road, Selly Oak, Birmingham B29 6LH (0121 472 0116).

Hillcroft College, South Bank, Surbiton, Surrey KT6 6DF (020 8399 2688).

Newbattle Abbey College, Dalkeith, Midlothian EH22 3LL (0131 663 1921).

Northern College, Wentworth Castle, Stainborough, Barnsley, South Yorkshire S75 3ET (01226 776000).

Ruskin College, Walton Street, Oxford OX1 2HE (01865 554331).

The Gilchrist Educational Trust

Eligibility: Two categories of tertiary level students are eligible for consideration:

(i) Those who have made proper provision to fund a degree or higher education course but find themselves facing unexpected financial difficulties which may prevent the completion of it. Applicants will normally be in the last year of the course.

(ii) Those who, as part of their degree course, are required to spend a short period studying in another country. Examples are the fieldwork necessary for a thesis or dissertation, or medical students' elective periods study.

Types of grants: Grants are modest and are given once only. Adult Study Grants are up to £1,000. Travel Study Grants are up to £500.

Exclusions: Assistance cannot be offered to the following: part-time students; those seeking funds to enable them to take up a place on a course; students seeking help in meeting the cost of maintaining dependents; students who have (as part of a course) to spend all or most of a academic year studying in another country; those wishing to go abroad under the auspices of independent travel, exploratory or educational projects.

Annual grant total: In 2007/08 the trust had assets of £1.8 million and an income of £99,000. Grants to individuals totalled £36,000, which was given equally in Adult Study Grants and Travel Study Grants to 65 applicants.

Applications: There is no application form. In response to an initial enquiry, the trust sends a sheet listing the information required to enable an application to be considered. They can be submitted at any time of the year.

Correspondent: The Secretary, 13 Brookfield Avenue, Larkfield, Aylesford, ME20 6RU (01903 746723; email: gilchrist. et@blueyonder.co.uk; website: www. gilchristgrants.org.uk)

Other information: This is a small trust with limited funds; grants have to be very modest and applicants are expected to be seeking help from other sources as well. A large number of applications are received each year, but only a few students can be helped.

The trust also gives to organisations (£26,000 in 2007/08).

The Sure Foundation *see entry on page 42*

The Sure Foundation *see entry on page 42*

Correspondent: The Trustees, Hobbs Green Farm, Odell, Bedfordshire MK43 7AB

Business start-up & apprentices/ vocational training

The Oli Bennett Charitable Trust

Eligibility: Young people between 18 and 30, who are self-employed and are UK residents.

Types of grants: Grants in the range of £1,000 and £1,500 for people starting up their own businesses.

Annual grant total: In 2006/07 the trust had an income of £11,000 and a total expenditure of £9,000.

Applications: Application forms are available on the trust's website. Applications are considered every three months. A business plan is required to assess the viability of the idea.

Correspondent: Mrs B J Bennett, 'Camelot', Penn Street, Amersham, Buckinghamshire HP7 0PY (01494 717 702; email: info@olibennett. org.uk; website: www.olibennett.org.uk)

Other information: The trust was set up in memory of Oli Bennett, who died in the September 11 2001 attacks in New York.

The N & P Hartley Memorial Trust

Eligibility: Priority is firstly given to those living in West Yorkshire, secondly to individuals living in the north of England and thirdly to those elsewhere in the UK and overseas.

Types of grants: One-off grants for vocational training for vocational employment.

Exclusions: No support is given to animal rights or welfare.

Annual grant total: In 2006/07 the trust had assets of £796,000 and an income of £37,000. Grants to individuals totalled £5,200 and were given solely for medical care facilities.

Applications: In writing to the correspondent, preferably through a social worker, Citizens Advice or other welfare agency, for consideration twice yearly. Re-applications from previous beneficiaries are welcomed.

Correspondent: J E Kirman, Trustee, Arabesque House, Monks Cross Drive, Huntington, York YO32 9GW (01904 464100)

Other information: Grants are mainly made to organisations (£141,000 in 2006/07).

The Prince's Trust

Eligibility: Young people between the ages of 14 to 30, some further restrictions lie within different projects, see type of grants section. The Prince's Trust works with individuals who have experienced difficulties at school, have been in trouble with the law, are long-term unemployed or have been in care.

Types of grants: The Prince's Trust aims to change the lives of young people, helping them to develop confidence in themselves, learn new skills and get practical and financial support.

In 2006/07 the trust helped over 40,000 individuals. Around 5,500 of these young people were awarded cash grants and funding to develop their skills and employability, and help devise and deliver their own community projects. Cash grants and funding are available in the following forms:

- The Business Programme provides low-interest loans and grants to 18 to 30 year olds who wish to start their own business. To be eligible for this programme, applicants must be either unemployed or working less than 16 hours a week and have limited access to any other sources of funding.

- Development Awards are offered between £50 and £500 for young people aged 14 to 25 to help facilitate education or training or to secure employment.

- Group awards are also given to groups of young people who want to set up their own projects that will benefit their local communities.

Annual grant total: In 2006/07 the trust had assets of £36 million, an income of £45 million and a total expenditure of £41 million. Approximately £1.4 million was given in grants to individuals.

Applications: An online contact form is available on each of the trust's programmes on its website, or freephone 0800 842 842.

Correspondent: Ms Nicola Brentnall, Secretary, 18 Park Square East, London NW1 4LH (020 7543 7480; Freephone: 0800 842 842 - for details of how to apply; Fax: 020 7543 1300; email: nicola. brentnall@princes-trust.org.uk; website: www.princes-trust.org.uk)

The Thomas Wall Trust

Eligibility: UK nationals in financial need, who wish to undertake educational studies which are vocational, short courses of professional training, or in a broad sense are concerned with social service and which will lead to paid employment.

Types of grants: One-off grants, up to £1,000, to supplement assistance from other sources. The trustees also need to be satisfied that the cost of the course is reasonable and that the intended result cannot be equally well obtained at less cost.

Both full-time and vocational part-time courses are considered for support.

Exclusions: Grants are not given: to those who qualify for support from the Student Loan Company for undergraduate study; for travel, study or work experience abroad; for elective periods or intercalated courses; for attendance at conferences; for research or study for higher degrees by research; or to schoolchildren.

Annual grant total: In 2006/07 the trust had assets of £3.1 million and an income of £97,000. Grants were made to 39 individuals totalling £38,000.

Applications: Applications can be made online at the trust's website. Applications are considered from January until September, or until funds run out. Only successful applicants will be notified by the trust. All information on the trust is available on its website.

Correspondent: The Directors, PO Box 52781, London EC2P 2UT (website: www. thomaswalltrust.org.uk)

Other information: Grants are also given to charitable organisations in the field of education and social welfare, especially small ones or those of a pioneering nature (£31,000 in 2006/07).

Carers

The Princess Royal Trust for Carers

Eligibility: Unpaid carers in the UK, especially those who live near a Princess Royal Trust for Carers Centre.

Types of grants: One-off grants towards educational bursaries.

Annual grant total: About 650 grants are made each year.

Applications: Applications are made via your local Princess Royal Trust for Carers Centre.

Correspondent: The Clerk, Unit 14, Bourne Court, Southend Road, Woodford Green, Essex, IG8 8HD (0844 800 4361; email: info@carers.org; website: www. carers.org)

Children & young people

The French Huguenot Church of London Charitable Trust

Eligibility: Young people, usually in secondary or higher education, but applications for younger children can be considered. For all categories, where there are two or more claimants of equal merit, the trustees have the following order of priority:

(a) people who, or whose parents are, members of the Church

(b) people of French Protestant descent

(c) other people as trustees think fit.

Grants can be given for the education of:

(i) children of members of the church

(ii) French Protestant children attending French schools in London

(iii) those under 25 of proven French Protestant descent

(iv) girls at schools of the Girls' Public Day School Trust and the Church Schools Company Ltd

(v) boys at selected independent day schools

(vi) choristers at schools of the Choir Schools Association

(vii) people under 25 for individual projects, at home or abroad.

Types of grants: (i) Bursaries at the schools mentioned above; these do not usually exceed the value of one term's fees. (ii) Project grants [as in (vii) above]; these do not usually exceed £250 and may be less.

Annual grant total: In 2007 the trust had assets of £11 million and an income of £387,000. A total of £101,000 was given in grants and bursaries to support 55 individuals at schools and colleges. A further 18 young people were awarded grants to help towards costs of overseas projects totalling approximately £3,000.

Applications: Applications for categories (i) and (ii) above should be made to the Secretary of the Consistory, 8–9 Soho Square, London W1V 5DD. Correspondence regarding categories (iii)

and (vii) should be sent to the correspondent. Applications for categories (iv), (v) and (vi) should be sent to the head of the school concerned, mentioning the applicant's connection (if any) with the French Protestant Church.

Correspondent: Mrs Danielle Ford, Haysmacintyre, Fairfax House, 15 Fulwood Place, London, WC1V 6AY (020 7969 5591; Fax: 020 7222 3480; email: dford@haysmacintyre.com)

Other information: The trust also awards an annual scholarship for Huguenot Research at the Institution of Historical Research at the University of London, and has endowed an annual scholarship to support students under 25 wishing to undertake projects relevant to modern Europe (Peter Kirk Memorial Fund).

The trust also gives to organisations.

The William Gibbs Trust

Eligibility: Young people in education who are of British nationality.

Types of grants: One-off and recurrent grants according to need.

Annual grant total: In 2006 the trust had both an income and a total expenditure of around £11,000.

Applications: This trust states that it does not respond to unsolicited applications as the funds are already allocated. Any enquiries should be made in writing.

Correspondent: Mrs A Johnson, Mrs A Johnson, 40 Bathwick Hill, Bath, BA2 6LD

The Glebe Charitable Trust

Eligibility: Children and young people up to the age of 18 who have a disability or are disadvantaged in addition to being in financial need. Please note that financial need alone is not sufficient.

Types of grants: One-off grants in the range of £250 to £2,000. Although some grants are made for individual children, the trust prefers to give to registered charities and organisations which give practical help to children living with disabilities or other disadvantages.

Exclusions: Grants are not made for school or university fees, building programmes, gap year activities or for dyslexia.

Annual grant total: In 2007 the trust had assets of £370,000 and an income of £20,000. Grants were made totalling £15,000, of which £3,000 was given in grants to individuals.

Applications: The trust has previously stated that it receives applications beyond its capacities both administrative and financial. The trustees have therefore taken the reluctant decision that they can no longer consider unsolicited applications from either charities or individuals. Its current policy is to make grants to organisations known to the trustees, which

give practical help to children with disabilities or who are disadvantaged in some way.

Small grants are given to known schools and other organisations in Zimbabwe for individual children but the trustees have continued with their policy of not assisting any UK individuals with school fees.

Correspondent: The Secretary, PO Box 38078, London, SW19

Professional Classes' Aid Council

Eligibility: The dependants of people with a professional background who are in need.

Types of grants: One-off and recurrent grants are usually given each term to help children from low income families and students whose expected funding has broken down since starting essential courses. Grants may also be awarded for school uniforms, essential school trips and help with school fees for children who are in the middle of their GCSE's or A levels when their parents' financial circumstances worsen.

Annual grant total: In 2007 the trust had assets of £2.8 million and an income of £140,000. Educational grants were made to 64 individuals totalling £25,000.

Applications: On a form available from the correspondent, to be submitted either by the individual, or via a third party such as a social worker, Citizens Advice or other welfare agency.

Correspondent: Miss Nerina Inkson, 10 St Christopher's Place, London W1U 1HZ (020 7935 0641)

Other information: Grants are also made for welfare purposes.

Red House Youth Projects Trust

Eligibility: Young people between the ages of 10 and 21 who are resident in Norfolk.

Types of grants: Grants do not normally exceed £500.

Annual grant total: In 2006/07 the charity had assets of £847,000 and an income of £27,000. No grants were made to individuals during the year. Grants to organisations totalled £18,000.

Applications: In writing to the correspondent. Grants are considered four times a year in March, July, October and December.

Correspondent: The Grants Administrator, 12 Spruce Avenue, Ormesby, Great Yarmouth, Norfolk, NR29 3RY (01493 731976; email: admin@ redhouseyouthprojects.co.uk; website: www.redhouseyouthprojects.co. uk)

Dr M Clare Roberts Memorial Fund

Eligibility: Children and young people in the UK looking to expand their 'educational horizons'.

Types of grants: Provision of facilities, equipment or financial assistance.

Annual grant total: About £1,000.

Applications: In writing to the correspondent.

Correspondent: Sarah Roberts-Penn, 52 Stubbington Way, Fair Oak, Eastleigh, Hampshire, SO50 7LR

The T A K Turton Charitable Trust

Eligibility: Students in the final year of GCSE or A level courses, where a sudden loss of parental income would mean they are unable to complete the course.

Types of grants: Grants are from between £500 and £2,500.

Annual grant total: In 2007 the trust had an income of £17,000 and a total expenditure of £12,000.

Applications: Applications should be submitted through a school, college or educational welfare agency at any time. They must be sent to the following address: Joint Educational Trust, 6–8 Fenchurch Buildings, London EC3M 5HT (020 3217 1100).

Correspondent: Mrs R M Fullerton, 47 Lynwood Road, London, W5 1JQ

Further & higher education

The Follett Trust

Eligibility: Students in higher education.

Types of grants: One-off and recurrent grants according to need.

Annual grant total: In 2006/07 the trust had assets of £23,000 and an income of £92,000. Grants to individuals totalled £19,000, of which £16,000 was given for educational purposes.

Applications: The trust states, 'A high proportion of applicants come to the attention of the trustees through personal knowledge and contact rather than by written application. Where the trustees find it impossible to make a donation they rarely respond to the applicant unless a stamped addressed envelope is provided'.

Correspondent: M D Follett, 17 Chescombe Road, Yatton, Bristol BS49 4EE (01934 838337)

The Gen Foundation

Eligibility: Postgraduates and students in further education studying modern languages, music, art and natural sciences. Usually only people who live in the UK or Japan are considered. Applications that promote cultural exchange between Japan and the UK are given priority.

Types of grants: One-off grants of approximately £3,000, past subjects of award have included photography, Islamic art, translation, modern Japanese literature, food bioscience, Japanese style music, piano, Japanese cultural studies, optical sensory, furniture design and molecular biology.

Annual grant total: In 2006 the foundation had assets of £1.2 million and an income of £56,000 and gave grants to eight individuals totalling £15,000

Applications: On a form available from the correspondent. Applications should include an essay proposal.

Correspondent: Masanori Wada, The Gen Foundation, 45 Old Bond Street, London W1S 4DN (020 7495 5564; Fax: 020 7495 4450; email: info@ genfoundation.org.uk; website: www. genfoundation.org.uk)

George Heim Memorial Trust

Eligibility: People aged under 30 who are in further education.

Types of grants: Grants range from £100 to £1,000.

Annual grant total: In 2006/07 the trust had an income of £1,900 and a total expenditure of £1,200.

Applications: In writing to the correspondent.

Correspondent: Paul Heim, Wearne Wyche, Picts Hill, Langport, Somerset TA10 9AA

The Hockerill Educational Foundation

Eligibility: The trust gives widely for causes related to religious education, which are broken down into the following categories:

- Students and teaching assistants taking teaching qualifications, or first degrees leading to teaching
- Teachers, teaching assistants and others in an educational capacity seeking professional development through full-time or part-time courses
- Those undertaking research related to the practice of Religious Education in schools or further education
- Students taking other first degree courses, or courses in further education
- Others involved in teaching and leading in voluntary, non-statutory education, including those concerned with adult and Christian education.

Types of grants: Grants of £500 to £2,000 are available for students in further/higher education for help with fees, books, living expenses and travel.

Exclusions: No grants to schoolchildren, those studying for Christian ministry or mission unless continuing in teaching, and for visits, study or conferences abroad, gap year activities, courses in counselling, therapy or social work, or for courses leading specifically to non-teaching careers such as medicine, law or accountancy. Grants are no longer made to overseas students.

Annual grant total: In 2006/07 grants totalling £37,000 were made to 54 individuals, of which 45 were given for training in education, 8 were given for students taking higher degrees or diplomas in education and one was given for a student preparing for overseas education.

Applications: On a form available from the correspondent, to be returned by 1 March.

Correspondent: Colin Broomfield, 16 Hagsdell Road, Hertford SG13 8AG (01992 303053; Fax: 01992 425950; email: hockerill.trust@ntlworld.com)

Other information: The charity states that the majority of annual funding is committed to long-term projects or activities in education, but funding is also given to other projects, namely:

- Training and support for the church's educational work in the dioceses of Chelmsford and St Albans
- Research, development and support grants to organisations in the field of Religious Education.

The Humanitarian Trust

Eligibility: British citizens and overseas students under 30 years old on a recognised course of study in the UK and who hold a basic grant for the course.

Types of grants: Grants of £200 are available to graduates and postgraduates and are awarded for 'academic subjects only', and top up fees.

Exclusions: No grants for domestic expenses such as childcare, overseas courses, fieldwork or travel, theatre, music, journalism or art, drama, sociology, youth work or sports.

Annual grant total: In 2006/07 the trust had assets of £4.3 million and an income of £106,000. No grants were made to individuals in the year.

Applications: In writing to the correspondent including a cv, income and expenses and total shortfall and two references (from course tutor and head of department).

Correspondent: Mrs M Myers, 27 St James's Place, London SW1A 1NR

Other information: The trust gives mainly to organisations (£72,000 in 2006/07).

Helena Kennedy Foundation

Eligibility: Students attending a further education college in the UK who are progressing to university education and who may be disadvantaged in some way. Applicants must be intending to undertake a higher diploma or undergraduate degree for the first time

Types of grants: One-off bursaries of £1,000.

Annual grant total: In 2006/07 the foundation had assets of £308,000 and an income of £204,000. Student bursaries totalled £62,000.

Applications: Applicants are encouraged to visit the website www.hkf.org.uk, or send a short email to enquire about eligibility criteria. The application deadline is the end of April.

Correspondent: Rachel Watters, Development & Fundraising Officer, Helena Kennedy Foundation, The Mansion, Bletchley Park, Bletchley, Milton Keynes, MK3 6EB (01908 363452; email: admin@hkf.org.uk; website: www.hkf.org.uk)

The Sidney Perry Foundation

Eligibility: The trust aims primarily to help first degree students. Students must be younger than 35 when the course starts. Eligible foreign students studying in Britain can also apply. Postgraduates may also receive support (see under Types of grants).

Types of grants: One-off and recurrent grants with the maximum award of £800 reserved for exceptional cases. Grants are usually towards books and equipment/instruments. Applicants can reapply in further years.

Distance learning, correspondence, part-time and short-term courses may be considered according to circumstances, in particular open university engineering courses.

Exclusions: The foundation is unable to assist: students in the first year of a (three or four year) first degree; medical students during their first year if medicine is their second degree; medical students during elective periods and intercalated courses; any second degree courses where the grade in the first degree finals was lower than a 2:1; second degree courses, unrelated to first degrees, unless they are a necessary part of professional training such as medicine or dentistry; expeditions overseas; cases where a full LEA funding has been awarded; GCSE and A level courses; students on Access, ESOL, HNC, HND, BTEC, GNVQ and NVQ Levels 1–4 and foundation courses.

Annual grant total: In 2006 the trust had assets of £4.7 million and an income of £180,000. Grants totalled £126,000 and were made to 230 individuals, with the average level of grant being £500.

Applications: Applications can be made at any time on official forms available from the correspondent and directly by the individual. Incomplete forms will be disregarded. Enclosure of an sae would be appreciated. 'Students are expected to have a confirmed placement at college and have the bulk of their funding before approaching the foundation. We will not contact referees on an applicant's behalf: candidates should ensure an academic reference (not a photocopy) is included'. Previous beneficiaries of grants should include details of the previous grant i.e. amount of grant, year received and grant number.

Correspondent: Mrs L A Owens, Secretary, PO Box 2924, Faringdon SN7 7YJ (email: sidneyperryfound@cs.com)

Other information: The foundation is unable to deal with student debt or financial problems needing a speedy resolution.

The Wilfred Maurice Plevins Charity

Eligibility: Sixth form students, who are children of professional men or women, whose education or career training has been prejudiced by financial misfortunes not of their own making. The father is required to be or have been a member of a professional institute or association having disciplinary control over members in the event of professional misconduct. This includes commissioned members of the armed forces.

Types of grants: Preference is currently given to A level students. Grants are made on an annual or short-term basis with a discretionary maximum of half-fees.

Exclusions: Grants are not given for first degree courses or in circumstances where parents were not in a position to fund the fees when entering the child for the school.

Annual grant total: In 2006/07 the charity had assets of £3.5 million and an income of £98,000. The sum of £92,000 was paid in grants to individuals.

Applications: In writing to the correspondent including full financial details of parents (capital and income), full details of other awards, grants, scholarships, and so on, and school reports. Applications should be submitted by the applicant's parents, normally by 31 March for the following September.

Correspondent: The Trustees, c/o Chantrey Vellacott, Prospect House, 58 Queens Road, Reading, Berkshire RG1 4RP

Other information: The correspondent also administers the Thornton-Smith Young People's Trust (see separate entry).

Shell Personal Development Awards

Eligibility: Students not yet in the final year of a university course.

Types of grants: One-off grants of £500 to help towards developing a talent in sport, music or performance art. Grants are also available towards expedition costs and learning a language or another skill.

Annual grant total: About £30,000 is available each year for grants to 60 individuals.

Applications: More information is available from the Shell website.

Correspondent: Shell Recruitment, Shell UK Limited, Shell Centre, London, SE1 7NA (website: www.shell.com/home/content/careers/)

UNIAID Foundation

Eligibility: Higher education students and prospective students experiencing extreme financial hardship.

Types of grants: Support towards the financial challenges of higher education by provision of accommodation bursaries. One-off in kind grants are made.

Exclusions: No grants for postgraduate study.

Annual grant total: About 60 students are helped each year.

Applications: Application forms can be found on the foundation's website to be submitted directly by the individual. Also see the website for full guidelines.

Correspondent: The Administrator, CAN Mezzanine, Downstream Building, 1 London Bridge, SE1 9BG (website: www.uniaid.org.uk/bursaries)

Williamson Memorial Trust

Eligibility: Students on first degree courses.

Types of grants: Grants of not more than £200 a year are made to people not known to the trustees for help with books, fees, living expenses and study or travel abroad. Grants limited to £200 a year to overseas students; the trust is not able to make a more significant contribution towards the higher fees and living expenses that overseas student incur. Grants are rarely made for student exchange or postgraduate study.

Annual grant total: In 2007/08 the trust had an income of £9,400 and a total expenditure of £8,500. Grants are made for education and welfare purposes.

Applications: Due to a reduction of its funds and the instability of its income, the trust regrets that very few new applications will be considered to ensure it can meet its existing commitments. Support will generally only be given to cases known personally to the trustees and to those individuals the trust has existing commitments with.

Correspondent: C P Williamson, 6 Windmill Close, Ashington, West Sussex, RH20 3LG

Gap years/ voluntary work overseas

The Melanie Akroyd Trust

Eligibility: Young people aged 22 to 27 living in the UK.

Types of grants: Travel scholarships for educational or personal development purposes, up to a maximum of £1,500. The applicant must begin their journey alone and will have to demonstrate that (i) they have been earning their own living for some years, (ii) that there are no financial resources available to them from their family which could go towards the trip, and (iii) that they have earned and saved funds for the trip which are equal to the funds which the trust will provide. Candidates' trips must cover a period of at least six months and must be in developing countries.

Annual grant total: In 2006/07 the trust had an income of £1,700 and a total expenditure of £1,300.

Applications: This trust does not accept unsolicited applications.

Correspondent: R M Tasher, Trustee, 9 Cambrian Place, Llandidloes, Powys, SY18 6BX (07711 178 162; email: robert.tasher@btinternet.com)

John Allatt's Educational Foundation *see entry on page 175*

Correspondent: Clerk to the Trustees, The Old Vicarage, Atcham, Shrewsbury SY5 6QE (01743 761598; email: caney@dsl.pipex.com)

Lady Allen of Hurtwood Memorial Trust *see entry on page 46*

Correspondent: Mrs Caroline Richards, Hon. Secretary, 89 Thurleigh Road, London, SW12 8TY

The Alvechurch Grammar School Endowment *see entry on page 187187*

Correspondent: David Gardiner, 18 Tanglewood Close, Blackwell,

Bromsgrove, Worcestershire B60 1BU (0121 445 3522)

Angus Educational Trust *see entry on page 100*

Correspondent: The Clerk, Education Offices, County Buildings, Forfar, Angus DD8 3WE (01307 473212)

The Arrol Trust

Eligibility: Young people aged 16 to 25.

Types of grants: Grants are given to people wishing to broaden their horizons through travel in the UK or overseas for gap years and educational trips.

Exclusions: No grants are made for course fees or other educational expenses.

Annual grant total: In 2007/08 the trust had an income of £8,700.

Applications: Application forms may be obtained from the correspondent and must be supported by a reference from the applicant's teacher or employer. Applicants must be willing to attend an interview with the trustees and be willing to report back on the completion of their trip.

Correspondent: C S Kennedy, Lindsays, Caledonian Exchange, 19a Canning Street, Edinburgh, EH3 8HE (0131 229 1212)

The Barnabas Trust *see entry on page 84*

Correspondent: Mrs Doris Edwards, 63 Wolsey Drive, Walton-on-Thames, Surrey KT12 3BB (01932 220622)

Jim Bishop Memorial Fund

Eligibility: People under 19 who wish to participate in any adventure activity.

Types of grants: Grants of between £50 and £150.

Exclusions: University expeditions will not be supported.

Annual grant total: Previously £2,000.

Applications: On a form available from the correspondent, or as a download from the Young Explorers' Trust website. Applications are considered in late February.

Correspondent: Maggie Brown, c/o Young Explorers Trust, 10 Larch Close, Bingham, Nottinghamshire NG13 8GW (email: grants@theyet.org; website: www.theyet.org)

The Challenger Trust Bursary Scheme

Eligibility: Young people taking part in overseas expeditions whose family or financial circumstances have changed dramatically, preventing them from continuing with their project.

Types of grants: 'The Trust offers bursaries to young people who have signed up for an overseas expedition experience and subsequently suffer a significant change in family circumstances and finances which will prevent them from continuing with this opportunity. These may arise from parental separation, job loss, illness or bereavement. Preference is given to those who demonstrate their determination to succeed despite such adversity'

These are 30 bursaries are available each year, and these will be awarded to the most deserving applicants. Bursaries are awarded to young people whose personal situations have genuinely changed, perhaps due to parental separation or bereavement in the family, and who are able to demonstrate their determination to succeed against adversity.

Previously the trust has supported young people taking part in expeditions with the British Schools Exploring Society, World Challenge and Yorkshire Schools Exploring Society. Applications will be considered on behalf of any approved organisation that promotes personal development through outdoor education.

Annual grant total: The trust gives around 30 bursaries per year of £250 and £500 each

Applications: Applications are considered once a year at the end of May and successful applicants will be notified by mid-June. Application forms and guidelines can be downloaded from the trust's website.

Correspondent: Jo Stocks, Trust Development Manager, The Challenger Trust, 4th Floor, Black Arrow House, 2 Chandos Road, London, NW10 6NF (020 8728 7356; email: enquiries@challengertrust.org; website: www.challengertrust.org/bursary.html)

The Church Burgesses Educational Foundation *see entry on page 129*

Correspondent: G J Smallman, Church Burgesses Educational Foundation, 3rd Floor Fountain Precinct, Balm Green, Sheffield, S1 2JA (0114 267 5596; Fax: 0114 267 3176)

Churchill University Scholarships Trust for Scotland

Eligibility: Students in Scotland.

Types of grants: Grants are given for one-off educational projects of benefit to the community, for example, medical electives or voluntary work overseas in a student's gap year or holiday.

Exclusions: Grants are not made for any other educational needs, such as course fees, books or living expenses.

Annual grant total: In 2006/07 the trust had an income of £25,000.

Applications: In writing to the correspondent.

Correspondent: Kenneth MacRae, McLeish Carswell, 29 St Vincent Place, Glasgow G1 2DT (0141 248 4134)

The Roger & Sarah Bancroft Clark Charitable Trust *see entry on page 82*

Correspondent: Lynette Cooper, K P M G, 100 Temple Street, Bristol, BS1 6AG (0117 9054694; Fax: 0117 9054065; email: lynette.cooper@clarks.com)

The Cross Trust *see entry on page 96*

Correspondent: Mrs Dorothy Shaw, Assistant Secretary, 25 South Methven Street, Perth PH1 5ES (01738 620451; Fax: 01738 631155; email: Crosstrust@ mccash.co.uk; website: www.thecrosstrust. org.uk/)

Crowthorne Trust

Eligibility: People in need who live in the parishes of Crowthorne, Finchampstead, Sandhurst and Wokingham Without. These parishes are all in Berkshire. Preference is given to applicants under 25.

Types of grants: Grants are towards the spiritual, moral, mental and physical well-being of recipients. Previously grants have been awarded for a wide range of overseas gap year projects, outward bound expeditions and school trips.

Annual grant total: In 2006/07 the trust had an income of £19,000 and a total expenditure of £14,000. The trust awards grants usually totalling around £15,000 a year to individuals.

Applications: In writing to the correspondent from whom an application form may be obtained. Meetings are held three times a year, although in urgent cases applications can be considered between meetings.

Correspondent: The Hon. Secretary, Wellington College, Crowthorne, Berkshire RG45 7PU (email: adtr@wellingtoncollege. org.uk; website: www.wellingtoncoll. demon.co.uk/ctrust/)

Other information: The trust also gives £5,000 a year to local youth organisations.

Frank Denning Memorial Charity *see entry on page 255*

Correspondent: Gerry Hudson, Assistant Honorary Secretary, Democratic and Legal Services Division, Policy and Corporate Services Department, London Borough of Croydon, Taberner House, Park Lane, Croydon CR9 3JS (020 8726 6000; email: gerry.hudson@croydon.gov.uk; website: www.croydon.gov.uk)

The David Finnie & Alan Emery Charitable Trust

Eligibility: People between the ages of 18 and 25 who are in need and are permanently resident in the UK and are of British nationality.

Types of grants: Grants of £500 to £3,000 are given towards education, personal achievement and development.

Exclusions: No grants where alternative funding was or should be made available by other agencies, government or otherwise. No support for: loans and non-specific cash sums; expeditions, conference attendance and seminars; general cases of hardship falling outside the stated criteria; requests for holiday trips, family reunions and the like; debts of any kind; house removal or funeral expenses; TV, car and animal licences; nursing and/or residential care fees (including for people who are homeless); furniture and fixtures, treatment that should be provided by the NHS; overseas funding; religious purposes; building work of any kind; wheelchairs; or pushchairs.

Annual grant total: In 2006/07 the trust had assets of £2.3 million which generated an income of £82,000. Grants were made to 36 individuals totalling £49,000 with a further £28,000 given to organisations.

Applications: Initially, in writing to the correspondent. Applications can be submitted directly by the individual or through a social worker, Citizens Advice, other welfare agency or other third party. They are considered in April and October each year, and, if successful, an application form is forwarded for completion.

Correspondent: John A Buck, 4 De Grosmont Close, Abergavenny, Monmouthshire NP7 9JN (01873 851048)

Reg Gilbert International Youth Friendship Trust (GIFT)

Eligibility: UK residents who are aged 14 to 25 and are visiting a developing country on a trip lasting at least four weeks. Applicants must be unable to afford the cost, be planning to live with an indigenous family in the host country as an ordinary member of the family, and be aiming to develop friendship. The trust stresses that there must be an indigenous homestay element within the programme to be eligible for any funding.

Types of grants: The aim of the trust is to help with the personal development of young people by assisting them in gaining firsthand experience of a different culture, thereby developing friendships with, and an understanding of, people of that culture. The more applicants can show they will have a clear association with indigenous people, the more likely they are to get a bursary.

Bursaries range between £100 and £300.

Exclusions: No grants for proposals leading to academic or vocational qualifications.

Annual grant total: In 2006/07 the trust had an income of £4,500 and a total expenditure of £3,300.

Applications: Potential applicants who will be living with an indigenous family in a developing country should send an outline proposal. An application form and guidelines will then be sent out. Please enclose an sae.

Applications are considered in November and June.

Correspondent: Reg Gilbert, 67 Nunney Road, Frome, Somerset BA11 4LE

The Mary Grave Trust *see entry on page 140*

Correspondent: The Secretary, Cumbria Community Foundation, Dovenby Hall, Dovenby, Cockermouth, CA13 0PN (01900 825760; email: enquiries@ cumbriafoundation.org)

Hazel's Footprints

Eligibility: Young people from the UK and Europe who want to take part in voluntary projects abroad. Proposed projects must be of an educational nature, i.e. teaching, community development work, and should last no less than six months.

Types of grants: The trust gives funding to people of any age who want to take part in voluntary work abroad but are struggling to cover the whole costs themselves.

Annual grant total: In 2006/07 the trust had an income of £47,000. Expenditure in grants can vary from year to year, and the trust aims to help on average 15 to 20 individuals per year.

Applications: On a form from the website. Grants are awarded three times a year in November, early May and June.

Applications can be considered throughout the year, however grants are usually awarded on a mostly first-come-first-served basis.

Correspondent: The Clerk, Hazel's Footprints Trust, Legerwood, Earlston, Berwickshire, TD4 6AS (01896 849677; Fax: 01896 849677; email: info@ hazelsfootprints.org; website: www. hazelsfootprints.org)

Other information: The trust also makes annual donations to the Otjikondo village school in Namibia and other educational establishments in need in developing countries.

The Hertfordshire Educational Foundation *see entry on page 225*

Correspondent: The Secretary, c/o Finance Accountancy Group, 3rd Floor, North West Block, County Hall, Hertford, Herts,

SG13 8DN (01992 588525; website: www. hersdirect.org/hef)

The Holywood Trust *see entry on page 106*

Correspondent: Richard Lye, Trust Administrator, Mount St Michael, Craigs Road, Dumfries DG1 4UT (01387 269176; Fax: 01387 269175; email: funds@ holywood-trust.org.uk; website: www. holywood-trust.org.uk)

The Leadership Trust Foundation

Eligibility: Young people, primarily those aged 16 to 25, living within 25 miles of the trust's office who are undertaking activities designed to enhance their personal development and leadership training with an established and recognised charity.

Types of grants: Grants are given to individuals embarking on activities with Raleigh International, Duke of Edinburgh's Award, GAP, British Schools Expedition Society, Jubilee Sailing Trust, Global Young Leaders Conference and so on.

Annual grant total: In 2007 the foundation had net assets of £6.7 million and an income of £3.6 million. Grants totalled £141,000, of which £1,250 went to individuals.

Applications: Initially in writing to the correspondent, who will then send an application form to relevant applicants. Completed forms are considered quarterly.

Correspondent: The Grants Department, The Leadership Trust, Weston Under Penyard, Ross-on-Wye, Herefordshire HR9 7YH (email: grant.making@ leadership.org.uk; website: www. leadership.org.uk)

The Milly Apthorp Charitable Trust *see entry on page 253*

Correspondent: Secretary, Iveco House, Station Road, Watford, WD17 1SR (01923224411)

The New Durlston Trust *see entry on page 42*

Correspondent: N A H Pool, Trustee, Anchor Cottage, 98 Reading Road South, Fleet, Hampshire, GU52 7UA

The Claude and Margaret Pike Charity

Eligibility: Students who live in Devon between the ages of 16 and 21. They should either be at or between school and university.

Types of grants: 70 to 80 grants are given each year for gap year 'overseas ventures' organised by Raleigh International, Sail Training Association and so on.

Annual grant total: The trust is allocated income each year from The Claude and Margaret Pike Woodlands Trust. About £25,000 is available each year to give in grants to individuals.

Applications: In writing to the correspondent.

Correspondent: J D Pike, Trustee, Dunderdale Lawn, Penshurst Road, Newton Abbot, Devon TQ12 1EN (01626 354404)

Roger and Miriam Pilkington Charitable Trust

Eligibility: Grants are given to 'enterprising' people aged 18 to 25, particularly those who are undertaking imaginative projects abroad which could be said to broaden horizons, giving them experiences which they may not otherwise have; increase awareness of other cultures and ways of living; or help them understand something of social problems outside their immediate environment. Suitable projects include British Schools Exploring Society, Raleigh International, Project T and Trek Aid.

Types of grants: Donations are usually in the range of £300 to £500.

Exclusions: The trustees favour making awards for medical electives and VSO projects. The trustees do not take on responsibilities which are properly those of the education authorities. Long-term funding is not given.

Annual grant total: In 2006/07 the trust had an income of £38,000. There were nine individual grants made totalling £3,700.

Applications: In writing, directly by the individual to the correspondent at any time, for consideration in March and August. All grants are contingent on the applicant raising a significant proportion of the funds through their own efforts.

Correspondent: The Clerk, c/o Brabners Chaffe Street, 1 Dale Street, Liverpool L2 2ET

Other information: Grants are also made to schools.

The Prince Philip Trust Fund *see entry on page 212*

Correspondent: Kevin M McGarry, Secretary, 10 Cadogan Close, Holyport, Maidenhead, Berkshire SL6 2JS (01628 639577; email: kmmcgarry@aol. com)

Provincial Insurance Company Trust for Bolton

Eligibility: People who live in Bolton Metropolitan Borough.

Types of grants: Grants are mainly one-off and are for between £100 and £1,000.

Grants are not made for relief-in-need, but are given to individuals towards character

development and 'helping others', for example, Operation Raleigh, Health Projects Abroad.

Exclusions: No grants to students or recent ex-students of Bolton School, building works, commercial ventures or for personal loans.

Annual grant total: About £25,000 to organisations and individuals.

Applications: On a form available from the correspondent. Applications are usually considered in March/April and September/October and should be submitted at least two to four weeks before those meetings.

Correspondent: Mrs S Riley, Taylors Farm, Back Lane, Heath Charnock, Chorley, Lancashire, PR6 9DN

Other information: The trust also makes grants to organisations.

The Sir Philip Reckitt Educational Trust Fund

Eligibility: People in full-time education who live in Kingston-upon-Hull, the East Riding of Yorkshire, or the county of Norfolk.

Types of grants: Grants are given towards educational travel such as Raleigh International, working in the developing world, outward bound type courses and so on. Travel must be connected with the extracurricular projects of the course. Grants can also be used to help with residence and attendance at conferences, lectures and short educational courses.

Exclusions: Awards will not normally be made to persons under the age of 14 on the date of travel.

Annual grant total: In 2006 the trust had assets of £899,000 and an income of £34,000. Grants totalled £20,000.

Applications: Applications can only be made using the trust's official forms which can be completed online at its website. Postal applications can be made using forms available on request or by downloading a printable version.

Contacts:

Kingston-upon-Hull, the East Riding of Yorkshire – The Trustees, Sir Philip Reckitt Educational Trust, Rollits, Wilberforce Court, High Street, Hull HU1 1JY (email: hull@spret.org).

Norfolk – The Trustees, Sir Philip Reckitt Educational Trust, c/o Mrs J. Pickering, 99 Yarmouth Road, Ellingham, Bungay NR35 2PH (email: jpickering@spretrust. freeserve.co.uk).

Correspondent: The Trustees, Charity's principal address:, Wilberforce Court, High Street, Hull, HU1 1YJ (website: www. spret.org/)

The Saint George's Trust see entry on page 42

Correspondent: The Bursar, St Edward's House, 22 Great College Street, London SW1P 3QA

Shell Personal Development Awards see entry on page 24

Correspondent: Shell Recruitment, Shell UK Limited, Shell Centre, London, SE1 7NA (website: www.shell.com/home/content/careers/)

The Bassil Shippam and Alsford Charitable Trust

Eligibility: Students in need who live in West Sussex.

Types of grants: One-off grants for projects undertaken voluntarily, such as gap year activities, for example, Operation Raleigh.

Exclusions: No grants for expenses related to academic courses.

Annual grant total: In 2006/07 it had assets of £4.1 million and an income of £160,000. Grants were made totalling £148,000, mostly to organisations.

Applications: In writing to the correspondent, for consideration at any time. Applications should indicate the nature and location of the project and should give as much notice as possible.

Correspondent: S A E MacFarlane, Trustee Administrator, Messrs Thomas Eggar, The Corn Exchange, Baffins Lane, Chichester, West Sussex PO19 1GE (01243 786111)

W W Spooner Charitable Trust

Eligibility: Young people who are taking part in voluntary overseas projects and expeditions, with a preference for those living in Yorkshire – especially West Yorkshire.

Types of grants: One-off and recurrent grants towards voluntary work overseas.

Annual grant total: In 2006/07 grants totalled almost £100,000 and were broken down as follows: Wordsworth Trust Projects (£471,000); hard core grants and donations (£37,000); and single appeals (£16,000).

Applications: In writing to the correspondent by the end of March, July or October.

Correspondent: M H Broughton, Tree Tops, Main Street, Hawksworth, Leeds, LS20 8NX

The Sydney Stewart Memorial Trust

Eligibility: People in Northern Ireland taking part in voluntary projects in the developing world. Preference is given to individuals going to the Indian sub-continent.

Types of grants: One-off grants of £150 for projects lasting up to 3 months and up to £350 for longer projects.

Exclusions: Grants are not given to people going away for less than one month.

Annual grant total: Grants usually total about £2,000 each year.

Applications: On a form available from the correspondent or to download from the website. Applications are usually considered once a year.

Correspondent: Grants Officer, Voluntary Service Bureau, 34 Shaftesbury Square, Belfast BT2 7DB (028 9020 0850; Fax: 028 9020 0860; email: info@vsb.org.uk; website: www.vsb.org.uk/)

Other information: The trust was established in honour of Sydney Stewart who was Director of Voluntary Service Belfast, an active member of War on Want and a frequent organiser of projects in India. In addition to making grants to individual volunteers, the trust also distributes funding to groups (of 5 or more people) who are organising a common voluntary activity in the developing world. Around £6,000 was available in 2008.

The Erik Sutherland Gap Year Trust

Eligibility: Young people living in the UK

Types of grants: Grants for young people who wish to take a gap year or take part in voluntary work overseas before entering higher education.

Annual grant total: In 2006 the trust had an income of £28,000. Several awards are given each year to individuals.

Applications: On a form available from the correspondent.

Correspondent: Viki Sutherland, Erik's Gap Year Trust, Torren, Clencoe, Argyll, PH49 4HX, Scotland (01855 811 207; Fax: 01855 811 338; email: info@eriks-gap-year-trust.com; website: www.eriks-gap-year-trust.com)

The Harry Tee Young People Foundation see entry on page 212

Correspondent: The Secretary, Civic Offices, Civic Centre, Reading RG1 7TD

The Vandervell Foundation

Eligibility: Medical students and other gap year students.

Types of grants: One-off grants averaging £300 to £500 towards students taking medical electives and gap year projects.

Exclusions: Grants are not made where the foundation already makes a major grant directly to the organisation, such as Raleigh International.

Annual grant total: In 2006 the trust had an income of £373,000 and made 768 grants to individuals totalling £237,000.

Applications: In writing to the correspondent, enclosing a CV and a budget. Trustees meet about every fortnight to consider applications from individuals.

Correspondent: Sheila Lawler, Bridge House, 181 Queen Victoria Street, London EC4V 4DZ

Other information: Grants are also made to organisations.

Warwick Apprenticing Charities see entry on page 181

Correspondent: C R E Houghton, Clerk, Moore and Tibbits, Solicitors, 34 High Street, Warwick CV34 4BE

Illness & disability

The British Association of Health Services in Higher Education Student Disability Assistance Fund

Eligibility: Students in an institution of higher education who are wholly or mainly engaged in a course of study. The study must have been affected by illness, accident or disability and grants are only given to help students who need extra assistance due to this problem. No grants to people under the age of 18.

Types of grants: Grants are generally given to first degree students, although postgraduates can be funded. Items of equipment to aid study such as computers, software, special chairs and other aids to study have been purchased through previous grants, and funding can also be used towards extra travel, books or instrument expenses. The trust gives one-off grants of up to £500.

Exclusions: Grants are not given towards living expenses, taxes, examination fees, costs of medical treatment and medical equipment unless specific to study problems.

Annual grant total: In 2006/07 the trust had an income of £12,000 and a total expenditure of £15,000.

Applications: Further details and application forms are available from the correspondent and online via the website. Applications can be submitted directly by the individual or by a relevant third party, for example, RNIB, RNID and social workers. The trust also requires a reference from the applicant's tutor and a doctor's letter, stating the area of disability or problem due to illness or accident.

Applications should be made in triplicate; an sae is preferred. No telephone contact is possible. Deadlines for applications to be considered are 1 March, 1 June and 1 November. BAHSHE expects students to apply for the Disabled Student's Allowance before applying to the SDAF. Students who are disabled but not entitled to receive DSA are more likely to be awarded a grant by the SDAF than students who do receive DSA.

Correspondent: Dr K. Cockerill, 35 Hazlewood Road, Bush Hill Park, Enfield EN1 1JG (website: www.bahshe. demon.co.uk)

David Hyman Charitable Trust

Eligibility: University students, under 25 years of age, who are severely disabled (wheelchair bound) or blind.

Types of grants: One-off grants of up to £200, depending on circumstances. Grants can be towards university fees, books and equipment.

Annual grant total: In 2006/07 the trust had both an income and a total expenditure of approximately £1,000.

Applications: In writing to the correspondent with full proof of disability and educational opportunity.

Correspondent: David Hyman, 101 Flood Street, London SW3 5TD

The MFPA Trust Fund for the Training Of Handicapped Children in the Arts

Eligibility: Children with physical or mental disabilities living in the UK between the ages of 5 and 18.

Types of grants: One-off and recurrent grants towards participation in painting, music, or drama, for example, books, educational outings and school fees. The maximum grant available is £5,000.

Annual grant total: In 2006/07 grants to children totalled £42,000.

Applications: In writing to the correspondent for consideration throughout the year. Applications can be made directly by the individual or through a third party such as their school, college or educational welfare agency.

Applications should enclose a letter explaining their needs and a doctor's letter confirming disability.

Correspondent: T Yendell, Trustee, 90 London Road, Holybourne, Alton, Hampshire, GU34 4EL

The National Association for Colitis and Crohn's Disease

Eligibility: People in need aged between 15 and 25, who have ulcerative colitis,

Crohn's Disease or related inflammatory bowel diseases.

Types of grants: One-off grants of up to £300 to meet special needs which have arisen as a direct result of illness. For example, funding has been given for books and other materials, tuition fees, maintenance expenses, travel passes and computer equipment.

Annual grant total: In 2007 the association had both an income and expenditure of £1.9 million. Grants were made to over 100 individuals totalling £7,000.

Applications: On a form available from the correspondent or to download from the website. The form has two extra sections, one which should be completed by a doctor to confirm the individual's illness and one to be filled in by a social worker (or health visitor, district nurse or CAB advisor). Completed applications should be sent to the personal grants fund secretary at: PO Box 334, St Albans, Herts AL1 2WA. Applications are considered every 6 to 8 weeks.

Correspondent: Julia Devereux, N A C C, 4 Beaumont House, Beaumont Works, Sutton Road, St. Albans AL1 5HH (01727 759654 or 01727 830038 (main switchboard); Fax: 01727 759654; email: julia.devereux@nacc.org.uk; website: www.nacc.org.uk)

Other information: Grants are also made for welfare purposes. However, the association's main role is provide information and advice to people living with IBD.

The Silverwood Trust

Eligibility: Children and young people of school age with physical or learning disabilities.

Types of grants: One-off or small recurrent grants according to need. (Normally restricted to people known to the trustees.)

Exclusions: No grants for computers or school fees.

Annual grant total: Around £1,000 is given each year in educational grants.

Applications: In writing to the correspondent.

Correspondent: J N Shergold, Trustee, 35 Orchard Grove, New Milton, Hampshire BH25 6NZ

The Snowdon Award Scheme

Eligibility: Physically disabled students (including sensory disabilities) who are in or about to enter further or higher education or training in the UK and because of their disability have financial needs which are not met elsewhere.

Types of grants: Grants are given towards costs which cannot be met in full from statutory sources, including: human help such as sign language interpreters or

people to take notes; computer equipment; adapted or additional accommodation; travel costs; mobility equipment; and other costs which relate solely to disability. Grants are normally between £250 and £2,000.

Annual grant total: In 2006/07 the trust had assets of £786,000, an income of £184,000 and a total expenditure of £231,000. Grants were made totalling £164,000. About 100 grants are awarded each year.

Applications: Application forms are available from the trust's website, along with full guidance notes or by contacting the trust directly. The closing date for completed applications is 31 May for consideration in July; late applications will be accepted until 31 August for consideration in October, funds permitting.

Correspondent: The Administrator, Unit 18, Oakhurst Business Park, Wilberforce Way, Southwater, West Sussex, RH13 9RT (01403 732899; email: info@snowdon awardscheme.org.uk; website: www. snowdonawardscheme.org.uk)

Student Disability Assistance Fund (formerly British Students Educational Assistance Fund)

Eligibility: Students engaged in a course of study, in any subject, at a higher or postgraduate level, who are affected by illness, disease, injury or physical infirmity. Priority will be given to those who are not eligible for funding from LEAs. Mature students can also be supported. The fund expects students to apply for the Disabled Students' Allowance before applying.

Types of grants: One-off grants of up to £500 towards educational aids made necessary by the student's disability, for example special computer equipment, extra travel costs for those with mobility problems, cost of note-takers or signers and other special equipment.

Exclusions: Grants will not be made for the payment of fees or general living expenses.

Annual grant total: In 2006/07 the fund had an income of £11,000 and a total expenditure of £15,000.

Applications: An application form can be requested by email or can be downloaded from the fund's website. Preferably it should be submitted directly by the individual with a letter of support from a tutor/member of disability staff/ disability adviser and a doctor's letter confirming illness or disability. Deadlines for applications are 1 March, 1 June and 1 November.

Correspondent: c/o Sandra Furmston, Administrative Secretary, BAHSHE Office, 35 Hazlewood Road, Bush Hill Park, Enfield EN1 1JG (020 8482 2412; email: s.furmston@mdx.ac.uk; website: www.bahshe.demon.co.uk)

Illness & disability – Blindness

Gardner's Trust for the Blind

Eligibility: Registered blind or partially-sighted people who live in England and Wales.

Types of grants: Grants are mainly for computer equipment, music equipment or course fees.

Exclusions: No grants for loan repayments.

Annual grant total: In 2006/07 the trust had assets of £2.5 million and an income of £96,000. Grants to individuals totalled £52,000, through which £19,000 was given in education, trade and music grants. The trust also supported 57 pensioners with grants totalling £28,000 and gave a further £5,000 in general welfare grants.

Applications: In writing to the correspondent. Applications can be submitted either directly by the individual or by a third party, but they must also be supported by a third party who can confirm the disability and that the grant is needed. They are considered in March, June, September and December and should be submitted at least three weeks before the meeting.

Correspondent: Angela Stewart, 117 Charterhouse Street, London EC1M 6PN (020 7253 3757)

Other information: The trust also gave a block grant of £5,000 to the Royal College of Music to help meet the educational costs of visually impaired students studying music.

The Webster and Davidson Educational Trust

Eligibility: People who are blind or partially sighted studying music at secondary school, or at further or higher education. Applicants must be resident or normally resident in Britain. Preference will be given to those living in Dundee, Tayside or Scotland.

Types of grants: Each bursary awarded will normally be tenable for one year, but may be renewed at the discretion of the governing body.

Exclusions: The bursary is not intended to take the place of or supplement Scottish Students' Allowances or other awards derived from public funds.

Annual grant total: In 2007 the trust had a total income of £9,300. Previously £1,000 has been awarded in grants to individuals.

Applications: Application forms are available from the correspondent.

Correspondent: The Trustees, c/o Thorntons Solicitors, Whitehall House, 33 Yeaman Shore, Dundee DD1 4BJ

Illness & disability – Cancer

CLIC Sargent (formerly Sargent Cancer Care for Children)

Eligibility: Children and young people under the age of 21 living in the UK who have cancer or have been under treatment in the past six months.

Types of grants: Grants of up to £170 to alleviate crises or help with the quality of life of the child and/or family during treatment. Exceptional grants of up to £400 may be issued where no other support is available.

Annual grant total: Previously the charity made 25 educational grants totalling £6,000. Grants are also made for welfare purposes.

Applications: On a form, to be completed by the CLIC Sargent Care Professional working with the family.

Correspondent: Grants Department, 161 Hammersmith Road, London W6 8SG (020 8752 2800; website: www.clicsargent.org.uk)

Other information: The charity also provides respite holidays. Details of grants holidays and other services are available from the CLIC Sargent Care Professional.

Illness & disability – Deafness

The Peter Greenwood Memorial Trust for Deaf People

Eligibility: Post-school (over 16) students living in England and Wales who are deaf or whose hearing is impaired and who live in England and Wales. Grants are tenable for any higher or further education course or training and mature students and post-graduates can also be supported.

Types of grants: Grants of under £200 towards books, videos, software and equipment that cannot be provided from other sources.

Annual grant total: Around £2,000 to £3,000 is distributed in grants annually

Applications: On a form available from the correspondent, to be received before 1 October, together with a letter from a sponsor who can verify the applicant's deafness and need. Late applications will not be considered.

Correspondent: Nicola Storey, Bursary Secretary, Bursary Secretary, Westbrook Building, Great Horton Road, Bradford, BD7 1AY (01274 436414 (voice) and 01274 433223 (text); website: www.pgmtrust.org.uk)

Other information: Applicants are requested to ask their LEA for assistance before contacting the trust as they often offer special help to deaf students.

The National Deaf Children's Society

Eligibility: Deaf children between the ages of 4 and 18 who are in full-time education.

Types of grants: The society has a limited fund that is able to provide equipment to deaf children that will support their educational or social development. This excludes equipment that would normally be provided by the education, health or social services. Only one grant per family is allowed.

Annual grant total: In 2006/07 the society gave £25,000 in grants to individuals.

Applications: On a form available as a download from the society's website. The application form includes an income declaration section. Support from relevant professionals, such as social workers, teachers of the deaf, IT teacher and so on is necessary. Evidence of the child's type and level of deafness is required.

Correspondent: The Fund Coordinator, 15 Dufferin Street, London EC1Y 8UR (Freephone family information and helpline: 0808 800 8880 voice & text; Fax: 020 7251 5020; email: helpline@ndcs.org.uk; website: www.ndcs.org.uk)

Other information: The society also runs the Blue Peter Loan Scheme, which loans out radio aids, environmental aids and other equipment for children to access in the comfort of their own homes.

Illness & disability – Dyslexia

Dyslexia Action

Eligibility: In practice, school-aged children living in England and Wales who have dyslexia and are from families on a low income.

Types of grants: Grants are made for assessments and for specific periods of tuition based on educational needs related to dyslexia. Grants for assessments are for about £300 each; grants for one term's tuition are for about £500, totalling about £3,000 for six terms' tuition. A contribution from the individual's family is required at a minimum of £25 for an assessment and £5 a week for tuition.

The majority of bursary-funded pupils attend the nationwide centres of Dyslexia Action for 1.5 or 2 hours multi-sensory tuition each week during the academic year.

Exclusions: Applicants from families where joint annual income is in excess of £22,000 will not be considered without evidence of exceptional circumstances.

Annual grant total: In 2006/07 the fund had assets of £1.6 million and an income of £7.6 million. Grants have previously totalled around £200,000 and the fund currently supports 250 individuals.

Applications: In writing via the Dyslexia Action Centre (network of centres throughout England and Wales), at which the applicant wishes to have assessment/tuition. Applications are considered by the Bursary Allocations Committee three times a year (one meeting each academic term). Grants are awarded on the basis of educational need. Applicants for grants for assessments should indicate difficulties experienced and family income; applicants for tuition grants should indicate family income and severity of dyslexia – a full educational psychologist's assessment is required.

Please note that whilst a bursary is awarded to an individual, the payment of fees for assessment or tuition is made directly to the consulting psychologist or Dyslexia Action.

Correspondent: The Administration Manager, Park House, Wick Road, Egham, Surrey TW20 0HH (01784 222330; Fax: 01784 222333; email: info@dyslexiaaction.org.uk; website: www.dyslexiaaction.org.uk)

Illness & disability – Meningitis

Meningitis Trust

Eligibility: People in need who have meningitis or who are disabled as a result of meningitis.

Types of grants: One-off and recurrent grants are given towards equipment, re-education and special training, such as sign language lessons.

Annual grant total: In 2006/07 the trust had net assets totalling £1.9 million and an

income of £3.3 million. Grants for educational and welfare purposes were made to over 100 families totalling £138,000.

Applications: On a form available from the correspondent. An initial telephone call to the grants coordinator Tracy Lewendon on 01453 769043 or the 24-hour helpline on 0800 028 18 28 to discuss the application process is welcomed.

Applications should be submitted through a third party and are reviewed on a monthly basis.

Correspondent: Tracy Lewendon, Fern House, Bath Road, Stroud GL5 3TJ (01453 769043; Fax: 01453 768001; email: info@meningitis-trust.org; website: www.meningitis-trust.org)

Other information: The trust runs a 'family day' for children who have meningitis and their families. The day includes arts, crafts and music for children and gives parents an opportunity to meet the trust's staff and other families. The trust also supports a range of professional counselling, home visits, therapy and information services.

Illness & disability – Renal

The British Kidney Patient Association

Eligibility: Renal patients of UK nationality. The association covers all renal patients, whether on dialysis or not.

Types of grants: Grants to help with the cost of books and materials, computers, board and lodgings, university and college fees and educational trips in the UK and overseas.

Exclusions: The association will not pay loans, court fines or bills already paid.

Annual grant total: In 2007 the trust had assets of £33 million and an income of £2.4 million. The trust gave £1.6 million in grants, of which £299,000 went to individuals.

Applications: Via a social worker or medical staff on a form available from the correspondent, or which can be downloaded from the BKPA website. Applications are considered on an ongoing basis.

Correspondent: Mrs Elizabeth Ward, BKPA, Bordon, Hampshire GU35 9JZ (01420 472021/2; Fax: 01420 475831; website: www.britishkidney-pa.co.uk)

Illness & disability – Special educational needs

The Royal Eastern Counties Schools Limited

Eligibility: People under 25 with special educational needs, particularly those with emotional and behavioural difficulties. Preference is given to people living in Essex, Suffolk, Norfolk, Cambridgeshire and Hertfordshire.

Types of grants: One-off grants are given to people with special educational needs for uniforms/clothing, fees, study/travel overseas, equipment/instruments, maintenance/living costs and educational outings in the UK.

Exclusions: Normally no grants are made for recurring costs.

Annual grant total: In 2006/07 the charity had an income of £111,000 and a total expenditure of £125,000. Grants are made to organisations and individuals.

Applications: Application forms can be obtained from the correspondent. Applications should normally be submitted during October for consideration between November and March, although urgent applications can be considered at other times. Applications should be made through an organisation. Unsuccessful applicants will not be informed unless an sae is provided.

Correspondent: A H Corin, Secretary, Brook Farm, Wet Lane, Boxted, Colchester, Essex CO4 5TN

Independent & boarding schools

The Athlone Trust

Eligibility: Adopted children under the age of 18 who are in need.

Types of grants: The trust gives grants for school fees, but not for people at college or university. Occasionally one-off grants are given to help with the cost of education essentials for schoolchildren.

Annual grant total: In 2007 the trust had an income of £7,200 and a total expenditure of £7,500. Grants totalled about £6,000.

Applications: In writing to the correspondent. Applications should be submitted by the applicant's parents and are usually considered in May and November.

Correspondent: Peter Canney, Stoakes Cottage, Hastingleigh, Ashford, Kent, TN25 5HG (01233 750216)

The Frank Buttle Trust – School Fees Grants Scheme

Eligibility: Children and young people with acute needs that cannot in practice be met within the state education system. The following groups are eligible to apply: adopted children and young people; children and young people cared for by grandparents, other relatives or friends; children and young people from single parent families; children and young people of secondary school age; and, children and young people with two carers, where one is severely incapacitated through illness or disability, or is terminally ill. In the majority of cases, help is given during the secondary phase of education.

Types of grants: 'Two forms of assistance are given:

- 'Help with fees at a boarding school – Assistance is given when it is impossible for the fundamental social and personal needs of the child or young person to be met fully within the home. Such a situation may arise either because of the nature of the needs of the child or young person or because of the age or ill-health of those responsible for providing a home for the child or young person.
- 'Help with day fees – Assistance with fees as a day pupil is only offered when serious loss of self-esteem, suicidal tendencies or chronic school phobia has resulted from the failure of the state system to meet the needs of the child or young person, or to protect them from damaging situations, such as bullying.'

Exclusions: The trust does not assist: children or young people with two able bodied carers/adults in the home; children or young people who are looked after by a local authority or Health and Social Care Trust in Northern Ireland; children or young people who do not have settled status in the UK or who are normally resident abroad; and, children or young people whose parental preference is for a particular type of education.

Annual grant total: In 2007/08 the School Fees Grants Scheme distributed 371 grants totalling £767,000.

Applications: In writing, through a statutory agency or voluntary organisation that is capable of assessing the needs of the child and that can also administer a grant on behalf of the trust; where no such organisation exists, the trust will discuss alternative arrangements. Applications should include the facts of the case,

highlighting the problems or misfortune experienced by the child. Eligible applicants will be sent an application form which will be considered monthly.

Applications should be directed to the trust's offices as follows:

For applicants in England: The Frank Buttle Trust, Audley House, 13 Palace Street, London SW1E 5HX (020 7828 7311; email: info@buttletrust.org).

For applicants in Wales: The Frank Buttle Trust, PO Box 7, Rhayader, Powys LD6 5WB (01597 870060; email: wales@buttletrust.org).

For applicants in Scotland: The Frank Buttle Trust, PO Box 5075, Renfrewshire G78 4WA (01597 870060; email: scotland@buttletrust.org).

For applicants in Northern Ireland: The Frank Buttle Trust, PO Box 484, Belfast BT6 0YA (02890 641164; email nireland@buttletrust.org).

Correspondent: The Director, Audley House, 13 Palace Street, London SW1E 5HX (020 7828 7311; Fax: 020 7828 4724; email: info@ buttletrust.org; website: www.buttletrust. org)

Other information: The trust was founded by the Revd W F Buttle in 1953. The trust publishes useful notes for the guidance of social agencies or others applying for a Buttle Trust grant.

Grants are also made for welfare purposes.

The Emmott Foundation Limited

Eligibility: Young people aged 16 to 18 starting or completing sixth form education, whose parents have experienced unforeseen hardship from death, illness, divorce, redundancy and so on.

Types of grants: Grants are given to enable children to start or complete A level courses at independent day or boarding schools and at maintained sector boarding schools. Applicants should usually expect to go to university or other higher educational establishment. Grants are usually of between £400 and £1,000 per term.

The trust states that unless there are mitigating circumstances, a majority of A and A* grades are expected at GCSE. Grants are also only usually considered if the school is willing to make a significant contribution towards the applicant's fees.

Grants are subject to regular review of academic progress and confirmation that the family's financial resources have not materially changed.

Annual grant total: In 2006/07 the trust had assets of £9.7 million and an income of £640,000. Grants of an educational nature came to £399,000, with £360,000 given directly to individuals for sixth-form fee assistance.

Applications: Application forms are sent to individuals if there is the possibility of a grant being made. Except in cases of extreme emergency, all requests should be received by the end of November for grants to be made for the following September. The trustees meet in March and June to consider applications.

Correspondent: Guy Dodd, Education Officer, Brill, Tregew Road, Flushing, Falmouth, Cornwall TR11 5TF (01326 375383; email: emmott foundation@btopenworld.com)

Other information: This trust also gives the following annual grants to organisations:

- £8,500 to higher educational establishments specialising in agriculture
- £25,000 to the Combined Trusts Scholarships Trust
- £5,000 to the Arkwright Scholarship Trust for Design and Technology.

The Fishmongers' Company's Charitable Trust

Eligibility: Children/young people up to 19 years of age in need of a sum of money to complete schooling. Preference is given to children of single-parent families and/or those with a learning difficulty or disability, or those who come from a disadvantaged or unstable family background.

Types of grants: Small, one-off grants to assist in cases of short-term need. The company gives assistance with school fees. The maximum grant is £1,800.

Exclusions: No grants for further/higher education.

Annual grant total: In 2006 the trust had assets of £9.6 million and an income of £1.1 million. Grants given for educational purposes totalled £540,000, with £40,000 given directly to individuals and a further £32,000 given for fishery-related educational purposes.

Applications: On a form available from the correspondent, to be submitted directly by the individual or by the parent or guardian for those under 18.

Correspondent: The Clerk, Fishmongers' Hall, London Bridge, London EC4R 9EL (Fax: 020 7929 1389; email: clerk@fishhall. co.uk; website: www.fishhall.co.uk)

Other information: The company also gives to organisations for welfare, environment and heritage causes and administers Gresham's School in Norfolk, a fee-paying public school.

Joint Educational Trust

Eligibility: Children aged between 7 and 13 who are dealing with problems at home, are at risk, are likely to benefit from a place in an independent school and whose families cannot meet the financial demands of this.

Types of grants: Grants of free and reduced fee places at an independent school are awarded. They may also provide grants if there is a shortfall in funding. Grants are for £500 a term.

Grants in the past have been awarded to allow two young boys in a custody battle to be educated in a boarding school while their father worked away from home and for a young girl whose sister was disabled and prone to violent acts, and whose mother had cancer, to get the support she needed.

'The Joint Education Trust helps children who have suffered tragedy or trauma at home or are at risk in some way. JET enables these children to attend independent schools where they have a real chance of making a new start.'

Exclusions: The trust states it will not help in cases of financial difficulty or learning need alone – there must also be a social need.

Annual grant total: In 2006 the trust had assets of an income of £220,000 and a total expenditure of £276,000. Grants were made to 154 children totalling £151,000.

Applications: On a form available from the correspondent. Applications are considered in March, June and October, and can be submitted by the individual, through a social worker, the individual's school or educational welfare agency, or a third party such as a doctor or minister of religion, at any time.

Correspondent: Mrs Julie Burns, 6 Lovat Lane, London EC3R 8DT (020 7283 3445; Fax: 020 7283 3446; email: admin@ jetcharity.org; website: www.jetcharity.org)

Other information: The trust also administers grants to individuals through four other charitable institutions.

The Lloyd Foundation

Eligibility: The children (between 5 and 25 years old) of British citizens where the family are necessarily living/working overseas.

Types of grants: Grants ranging between £300 and £3,000 a year to enable such children to attend the nearest English-medium school. Where no such school exists the foundation may give some help with fees for a school in the UK. Grants for schoolchildren, further/higher education and special educational needs are for educational expenses, such as fees, books, equipment and living expenses.

Exclusions: No help can be given for children under the age of five or for those taking postgraduate courses.

Annual grant total: About £100,000.

Applications: On a form available from the correspondent, to be submitted directly by the individual or through a third party. Applications are considered quarterly.

Correspondent: The Secretary, Fairway, Round Oak View, Tillington, Herefordshire HR4 8EQ (01432 760409; Fax: 01432 760409)

The McAlpine Educational Endowments Ltd

Eligibility: Schoolchildren aged 13 to 18 who are in need.

Types of grants: Grants of up to £1,800 a year, mainly towards the cost of independent school fees for children of academic ability, sound character and leadership potential who, for reasons of financial hardship, would otherwise have to leave the school. Grants are paid each term while the child is at school (subject to an annual review) and are limited to children attending 10 schools selected by the trustees.

Exclusions: There are no grants for students at college or university, nor for people at specialist schools (such as ballet or music schools, or schools for children with learning difficulties).

Annual grant total: Grants total about £3,500, given to individuals and organisations.

Applications: In writing to the correspondent. Applications must be submitted through one of the 10 schools where applicants are supported by the trust but, because of the long-term nature of the trust's commitments, very few new grants can be considered each year. Applications are considered during the summer before the new academic year. A list of the schools involved is available from the correspondent.

Correspondent: G L Prain, Eaton Court, Maylands Avenue, Hemel Hempstead, Hertfordshire, HP2 7TR

The Ogden Trust

Eligibility: Academically gifted young people in the areas of science and maths who wish to attend a selection of independent secondary schools at sixth form level. Grants are also made to undergraduates. Applicants must be British.

Types of grants: (i) Educational scholarships covering at least 50% of school fees, paid half by the trust and matched by the school, which is a condition of their participation. The bursaries fund the pupils through the two years of their A-levels. (ii) Undergraduate scholarships of £1,500 per annum for up to four years of undergraduate study and are payable in two annual instalments (October and February).

Annual grant total: In 2006/07 the trust had assets of £33 million and an income of £259,000. There were 36 bursary grants made totalling £299,000, 19 scholarships totalling £79,000 and 67 general grants totalling £485,000.

Applications: The sixth form scholarships operate through schools associated with the trust, a list of which can be found on its website. The list is not closed and new schools may submit candidates.

Undergraduate scholarships are only open to specific categories of candidate. See the trust's website for further details.

Correspondent: Tim Simmons, Hughes Hall, Wollaston Road, Cambridge CB1 2EW (01223 518164; email: ogdentrust@hughes.cam.ac.uk; website: www.ogdentrust.com)

The Reedham Trust

Eligibility: Children aged up to 16 who, due to the death, disability or absence of one or both of their parents (whether natural or through adoption) or of their own disablement or other domestic or personal circumstances, are in need of boarding care. Help will continue after the age of 16 only in exceptional circumstances.

The trust does not support day pupils or children of two-parent families, unless one or both parents are totally incapacitated in some way.

Grants are only given where there is a social need for boarding, not an educational need. Assistance is only available where the Local Educational Authority has no statutory duty to help.

Types of grants: Grants towards boarding fees, of up to £2,000 per year.

Annual grant total: In 2006/07 the trust had assets of £6.9 million and an income of £376,000. Total expenditure was £391,000, with grants being awarded to individuals totalling £269,000.

Applications: On a form available from the Caseworker. Guidelines are available from the correspondent. Applications may be submitted directly by the individual, a parent/guardian, through the applicant's school or an educational welfare agency. They are considered throughout the year. Applications need confirmation from a professional that boarding school education is in the best interests of the applicant.

Correspondent: Jean Watkins, Trust Secretary, The Lodge, 23 Old Lodge Lane, Purley, Surrey CR8 4DJ (020 8660 1461; email: info@reedham-trust.org.uk; website: www.reedham-trust.org.uk)

Royal Wanstead Children's Foundation

Eligibility: Children aged 11 to 18 years whose home circumstances make boarding essential. 'The main criterion is a lack of parental care, where no other suitable care is available. This situation can arise through:

● death or permanent absence of one or both parents

- chronic and enduring mental or physical ill health of a parent
- a parent who can no longer meet the daily needs of a child
- disability of a sibling of sufficient severity to affect the care and normal development of other children within the family
- abandonment or abuse of a child.'

Grants are restricted to children living within the UK and in respect of schools also situated in the UK.

Types of grants: Grants towards school fees.

Emphasis is on boarding need rather than on educational need. The foundation does not discriminate between state and independent education and where a place is secured at a state boarding school, the foundation is prepared to consider help with the boarding element of the fees if necessary.

Annual grant total: In 2007/08 the foundation had assets of £21 million and an income of £643,000. During the year grants were made to 262 individuals totalling £796,000.

Applications: On a form available from the foundation. Initial enquiries can be made to the correspondent.

Correspondent: Julie Burns, CEO, Sandy Lane, Cobham, Surrey KT11 2ES (01932 868622; Fax: 01932 866420; email: ceo@royalwanstead.org.uk; website: www.royalwanstead.org.uk/)

The Thornton-Smith Young People's Trust

Eligibility: Children of above average ability already attending fee-paying public schools and whose parents have experienced an adverse change in financial circumstances. Currently the trustees only support sixth formers studying A levels.

Types of grants: Grants follow a means test of the parental resources and are paid per term, subject to reasonable progress. The average award is up to half the total fees. Preference is given to short-term applications primarily in relation to A levels.

Grants are not given for first degree courses or in circumstances where parents were not in a position to fund the fees when entering the child for the school.

Annual grant total: In 2006/07 the trust had assets of £5.6 million and an income of £158,000. The sum of £127,000 was given in grants to individuals.

Applications: In writing to the correspondent, including details of education and parents' financial situation. If an applicant is considered eligible further inquiries are made. Applications are normally considered by 31 March to commence in September.

Correspondent: The Trustees, c/o Chantrey Vellacott, Prospect House, 58 Queens Road, Reading, Berkshire RG1 4RP

Other information: The correspondent also administers The Wilfred Maurice Plevins Charity (see separate entry).

Orders

The Journal Children's Fund (in conjunction with the Royal Antediluvian Order of Buffaloes)

Eligibility: 'The education and preferment of orphan or necessitous children of deceased members of the Royal Antediluvian Order of Buffaloes Grand Lodge of England.' The fund's activities extend worldwide.

Types of grants: Help with the cost of books, clothing and other essentials for schoolchildren. Grants may also be available for those at college or university who are eligible.

Annual grant total: In 2006 the trust had assets of £319,000 and an income of £64,000. Grants totalled £35,000.

Applications: Initial enquiries regarding assistance can only be made through the individual's branch of attendance.

Correspondent: Stuart Steele, Grant Secretary, RAOB GLE Trust Corporation, Grove House, Skipton Road, Harrogate, North Yorkshire HG1 4LA (01423 502438; email: hq@raobgle.org.uk; website: www.raobgle.org.uk)

Royal Masonic Trust for Girls and Boys

Eligibility: Generally the children of Freemasons. The objects of the trust are to relieve poverty and to advance education. Those eligible for assistance are the children of any age (including adopted children, step-children and children of the family) of Freemasons under the United Grand Lodge of England who are considered to be in need of such help.

The trust also has power, provided sufficient funds are available, to help children who are not the offspring of a Freemason. Such assistance is usually only given by way of grants to other children's charities.

Types of grants: Any necessary kind of assistance. The children concerned are usually, but not always, in state education. Help with the costs of a boarding education can only be given if there is a specific and demonstrable boarding need. Grants can go towards school uniforms, school clothing, books, educational outings, maintenance costs, living expenses, childcare and study or travel overseas.

Exclusions: No grants are available for student exchanges.

Annual grant total: In 2007 the trust had an income of £6.6 million and a total expenditure of almost £8 million. During the year the trust supported 1,801 children and young people in schools, colleges and universities through its various schemes, bursaries and subsidiary funds. Previously grants to individuals have totalled over £1 million.

Applications: Applications should be made in the first instance to the nearest Masonic authority or, where that is not known, a preliminary enquiry may be addressed to the correspondent.

Correspondent: Mr Leslie Hutchinson, Freemasons' Hall, 60 Great Queen Street, London WC2B 5AZ (020 7405 2644; email: info@rmtgb.org; website: www.rmtgb.org)

Overseas students (by place of origin)

British Government & British Council Award Schemes – Scholarships for Overseas Students & Trainees

Eligibility: Specified foreign nationals resident outside of the UK.

Types of grants: There are various awards/schemes. The following two scholarships may be awarded to undergraduates:

(i) DFID Shared Scholarship Scheme

Eligibility: Students from developing Commonwealth countries who are of high academic calibre and intend studying subjects of developmental relevance but who are unable to support their studies in Britain. Normally under 35 years of age; they must be able to speak English fluently.

No grants to people who are employed by their government or by an international organisation.

Types of grants: Awards are for taught courses at postgraduate level. Very exceptionally, awards for undergraduate study may be made available where the course of training satisfies the conditions of the scheme but is not available in the student's own country or at a nearby regional institution.

Applications for awards should be made directly to the participating British institutions. These usually vary from year to year, as can each institution's individual closing date for receipt of applications. A revised list of institutions is normally available from December onwards from the Association of Commonwealth Universities, the Department for International Development, and British High Commissions and British Council representatives in the Commonwealth countries concerned.

Applicants must be resident in a developing Commonwealth country at the time of application and, if successful, are required to return there on completion of their awards.

Further details are available from the correspondent.

(ii) Commonwealth Scholarships and Fellowship Plan (CSFP)

Eligibility: People who live in either a Commonwealth country or a British dependent territory.

Types of Grants: The scholarships are normally for postgraduate study or research, so applicants must have a university degree or equivalent qualification. If there are no undergraduate courses in a particular subject in a country or regional university, it may sometimes be possible to apply to do a first degree course under this scheme.

Grants are for one to three years and usually cover the cost of travel, tuition fees and living expenses. In some cases additional allowances may be available for help with books or clothes. An allowance may be paid to help with the cost of maintaining a spouse.

Applications for awards should be made through the Commonwealth Scholarship Agency in the individual's home country. Agency addresses are listed in the 'Commonwealth Universities Yearbook', available from the address below. If you are already in the UK the ACU can help you with general information concerning the scheme, but it cannot issue application forms to international students.

Further details from the correspondent.

Other postgraduate awards include:

British Chevening Scholarships, British Council Fellowship Programmes, Overseas Research Students Awards Scheme and Royal Society Fellowships.

Correspondent: The Association of Commonwealth Universities, Woburn House, 20-24 Tavistock Square, London WC1H 9HF (website: www.acu.ac.uk)

The British Institute of Archaeology at Ankara see entry on page 81

Correspondent: Gina Coulthard, 10 Carlton House Terrace, London SW1Y 5AH (020 7969 5204; Fax: 020 7969 5401; email: biaa@britac.ac.uk; website: www.biaa.ac.uk)

Churches Commission on Overseas Students: Hardship Fund

Eligibility: Full-time students from developing countries attending British or Irish institutions for first-degree or postgraduate studies lasting a minimum of one academic year, who are within six months of completing their course but face unexpected financial problems. They are required to confirm their intention to return to their home country immediately after their course.

Types of grants: Grants are typically £500 but do not exceed £800; the same person is not funded twice.

Exclusions: The fund will not consider students from industrialised countries, asylum seekers or refugees, or those whose studies relate to arms manufacture or experimentation on live animals.

Annual grant total: Grants are made to individuals each year totalling about £150,000.

Applications: Initial enquiries should be made to the grants secretary and should contain basic information about the student, particularly related to eligibility. Applicants should be able to show that with the help of a small grant, they will be able to complete their course. Application documents are sent to those who appear likely to meet the criteria. The hardship fund committee decides on grants three times a year, in February (for studies finishing April-July), June (for August-November) and October (for December-March).

Correspondent: David Philpot, Grants Secretary, 121 George Street, Edinburgh EH2 4YH (0131 225 5722 ext 300; email: dphilpot@cofscotland.org.uk)

Ruth Hayman Trust

Eligibility: Adults (aged over 16) who live in the UK and who speak a language other than English as their first language. In practice, most beneficiaries are refugees and asylum seekers.

Types of grants: One-off and recurrent grants ranging from £20 to £300. First priority is given to tuition and examination fees, but small grants can also be made towards books and materials. Grants towards travel costs are also made to people who have disabilities.

Exclusions: No grants to overseas students for fees, higher degrees, or for childcare or living costs.

Annual grant total: In 2006/07 the trust had an income of £7,400 and a total expenditure of £18,000. The trust gave grants to approximately 200 applicants totalling £17,000.

Applications: On a form available from the correspondent on request either by letter or email. Applications are considered

in June, September, December and March. Deadlines for applications are posted on the trust's website. Applicants must provide a reference.

Correspondent: The Trustees, PO Box 17685, London N6 6WD (email: trustee@ruthhaymantrust.com; website: www.ruthhaymantrust.com)

The Nora Henry Trust

Eligibility: Students from any country with a preference for students from developing countries who are studying subjects which will be of use when the student returns to that country.

Types of grants: One-off grants usually ranging from £100 to £200 can be given towards books, fees, living expenses, travel and childcare.

Exclusions: No grants for study or travel overseas for British students, or for student exchanges.

Annual grant total: In 2006/07, the trust had an income of £52,000 and total expenditure of £43,000.

Applications: On a form available from the correspondent. Applications should be submitted directly by the individual and supported by an academic referee. They are considered all year round.

Correspondent: Ms Fiona Macgillivray, Educational Grants Advisory Service, Family Welfare Association, 501–505 Kingsland Road, Dalston, London E8 4AU (020 7254 6251; email: grants.enquiry@fwa.org.uk; website: www.fwa.org.uk)

The Professor D G Montefiore Trust

Eligibility: Students from developing countries, principally those undertaking postgraduate medical work in the UK before returning to their own countries. Asylum seekers who need retraining in this country at any level, from language courses to medical exams.

Types of grants: Normally grants are in the form of single payments in time for the start of the academic year and can be for up to £500.

Annual grant total: About £9,000 is given in grants.

Applications: Applications must be made through the university or college and provide details of how all other costs, including living expenses, are going to be met. Applications from individuals will not be considered without confirmation from the university including references and CVs. Applications are considered monthly.

Correspondent: Miss Jean M Bogaardt, 17 Market Street, Crewkerne, Somerset, TA18 7JU (01460 74401)

Other information: The trust prefers all correspondence to be received in writing.

The Nurses Association of Jamaica (NAJ) (UK) *see entry on page 83*

Correspondent: NAJ (UK), PO Box 1270, Croydon, Surrey CR9 3DA (email: info@najuk.org; website: www.najuk.org)

Prisoners of Conscience Appeal Fund

Eligibility: Prisoners of conscience and/or their families, who have suffered persecution for their beliefs. The fact that the person is seeking asylum or has been a victim of civil war is not sufficient grounds in itself.

Types of grants: Mainly one off grants of about £350 each for travel, resources, equipment, vocational conversion courses and re-qualification costs.

Exclusions: No support is given to people who have used or advocated violence or supported a violent organisation.

Annual grant total: In 2007 bursaries were awarded to post-graduate students amounting to £45,000.

Applications: Application forms are available from the correspondent and should be submitted through an approved agency on behalf of the individual. Applications should include evidence of identification of the applicant and of costs.

Correspondent: The Grants Officer, PO Box 61044, London SE1 1UP (020 7407 6644; email: grantsofficer@prisonersofconscience.org; website: www.prisonersofconscience.org)

Other information: The fund was initially established in 1962 as the relief arm of Amnesty International, but is now a charity in its own right.

The Mary Trevelyan Fund

Eligibility: Students from developing countries studying in London. Students must be in their final year of study and intend to return home on completion of their course. Preference is given where the institution is a member of International Students House.

Types of grants: Grants of up to £1,000 are available to those who experience difficulties due to unexpected financial hardship.

Exclusions: Students with outstanding tuition fees will not generally be considered

Annual grant total: About £15,000, between 15 and 20 individuals are supported each year.

Applications: On an application form available from the correspondent. Applications can be submitted directly by the individual or through a social worker, Citizens Advice or other welfare agency at any time. The trust states that an application will have a greater chance of success if it is supported by the student's own college/university advice or welfare service.

Correspondent: The Welfare Service, International Students House, 229 Great Portland Street, London W1W 5PN (website: www.ish.org.uk)

Overseas students (by place of origin) – Africa

The Africa Educational Trust

Eligibility: Students of African descent. Most of the trust's work is carried out in Africa.

Types of grants: (i) Full-time and part-time scholarships

The trust currently has extremely limited funds therefore enquiries regarding both full-time and part-time scholarships must be made before application.

(ii) Emergency small grants for students from Africa

Candidates for the small emergency grants programme should be in the final few months of their course and need a small amount of money to enable them to complete the course. The average grant under this programme is £350. Applicants should be studying in the UK and hold a student's visa.

The trust is also usually able to provide a number of small grants each year with funds received from donors and individuals. The availability, criteria and restrictions for these vary from fund to fund.

Annual grant total: In 2006/07 the trust had assets of £1.5 million and an income of £2.4 million. Out of a total expenditure of £1.9 million, grants were made to individuals in the UK amounting to £57,000.

Applications: Candidates can contact the trust for information concerning its programmes at any time during the year.

Correspondent: Ms J Landymore, Africa Education Trust, 18 Hand Court, London, WC1V 6JF (0207 831 3283; Fax: 020 7379 0090; email: j.landymore@africaeducationaltrust.org; website: www.africaeducationaltrust.org)

Other information: The trust also offers a free educational advice service to migrants and refugees with an African background.

Overseas students (by place of origin) – Armenia

The Armenian General Benevolent Union London Trust

Eligibility: Children of an Armenian parent(s) studying recognised undergraduate or postgraduate courses in British universities or educational institutions, including specific vocational courses. Preference is given for courses in Armenian studies or subjects which may benefit the Armenian community.

Types of grants: Student loans are normally for educational fees, otherwise, a contribution can be made towards the cost of books or some maintenance costs. All loans are interest free and subject to a maximum set by the trustees reflecting the current income available. Student grants are occasionally given to Armenians with significant financial hardship or for refugees in the UK.

Special grants are available for people to attain Armenian university education or to pursue Armenian studies at university.

Annual grant total: In 2006 the trust had assets of £3.8 million, and income of £89,000 and a total expenditure of £31,000. Grants were given to 8 students totalling £17,500.

Applications: On a form available from the correspondent, to be submitted by 15 June each year.

Correspondent: The Chair, c/o Student Loans Committee, 25 Cheniston Gardens, London W8 6TG

Other information: Support is also given to Armenian schools, nurseries and cultural groups in the UK and overseas, usually towards running costs for Armenian language, history and culture classes. Occasionally welfare grants can be given to people in need.

The Armenian Relief Society of Great Britain Trust

Eligibility: Poor, sick or bereaved Armenians, worldwide.

Types of grants: One-off and recurrent grants of £150 are available.

Annual grant total: In 2006/07 the trust had an income of £56,000 and a total expenditure of £47,000. Grants were made during the year totalling £27,000 to Armenian organisations. No grants were made to individuals.

Applications: In writing to the correspondent.

Correspondent: Mrs Matilda Megerdichian, 180 Great West Road, Hounslow, TW5 9AR (020 8570 2268; Fax: 020 8723 8948)

The Benlian Trust

Eligibility: Children of Armenian fathers; applicants must be members of the Armenian Church studying at universities in Great Britain.

Types of grants: Grants for people studying on undergraduate degree courses and apprenticeships. Grants may also be given to help with the cost of articles, but otherwise priority is given to undergraduates.

Annual grant total: In 2006/07 the trust had net assets of £1.5 million, an income of £150,000, with a total expenditure of £167,000. The Trustees granted £97,000 towards the fees and living expenses of 40 students studying at various colleges and universities in England.

Applications: On a form available from the correspondent, completed applications must be returned before 30 April.

Correspondent: S Ovanessoff, Administrator, 15 Elm Crescent, Ealing, London W5 3JW (020 8567 1210; Fax: 020 8567 1210)

The Mihran Essefian Charitable Trust

Eligibility: University students of Armenian origin studying in Armenia. Help can also been given to Armenian university students in the UK.

Types of grants: Scholarship grants are made ranging from £100 to £4,500.

Annual grant total: In 2006/07 the trust had assets of £1.7 million and an income of £95,000. Grants totalling £54,000 were given to nearly 800 students, mainly in Armenia and to two studying in the UK.

Applications: In writing to the correspondent by 30 April each year.

Correspondent: Stephen Ovanessoff, Administrator, 15 Elm Crescent, Ealing, London W5 3JW (020 8567 1210)

Other information: Grants are also given to organisations (£13,000).

Overseas students (by place of origin) – Asia

The Bestway Foundation

Eligibility: Higher education students who are of Indian, Pakistani, Bangladeshi or Sri Lankan origin.

Types of grants: One-off and recurrent grants according to need.

Annual grant total: In 2006/07 the trust had assets of £4.2 million and a total income of £931,000. A total of £296,000 was given in grants to 22 individuals.

Applications: In writing to the correspondent enclosing an sae. Applications are considered in March/April. Initial enquiries should be made in writing.

Correspondent: A K Bhatti, Bestway Cash & Carry Ltd, 2 Abbey Road, Park Royal, London NW10 7BW (email: zulfikaur. wajid-hasan@bestway.co.uk; website: www. bestwaygroup.com/default. aspx?id=382988)

The Hammond Trust

Eligibility: Students from Asia between the ages of 18 and 45, who are studying in the UK. Grants are available to students whose studies are at risk of being affected by unexpected financial difficulties, to enable them stay in the UK to finish their course of education. Applicants must be in their final six months of study for a degree, diploma or other professional qualification at a recognised institution. Preference will be given to those following a course of study that will be of benefit to the applicant's own country. Applicants are expected to make every effort to meet their commitments from their own resources

Types of grants: One-off and recurrent grants, generally of £500.

Exclusions: Grants will not be awarded for help with tuition fees.

Annual grant total: In 2006/07 the trust had an income of £5,600 and a total expenditure of £3,600. Grants of about £500 are usually awarded to around 10 individuals.

Applications: On an application form available from the correspondent. The course tutor or supervisor must give a report on the applicant in part B of the application form which must be sent through the academic institution's authority and be endorsed with the official stamp.

Correspondent: International Student Services Unit, British Council, Bridgewater

House, 58 Whitworth Street, Manchester M1 6BB (0161 957 7279)

Overseas students (by place of origin) – Australia

The Britain-Australia Society Education Trust

Eligibility: Individuals 18 or under (usually of secondary school age) living in the UK who have a connection with Australia.

Types of grants: Grants contributing towards the expenses (but not fares) of educational projects leading to better British-Australian understanding. Grants are also given to schoolchildren for uniforms/clothing, fees, study/travel overseas and books. Grants range from between £250 to £500.

Annual grant total: In 2006/07 the trust had an income of £1,700.

Applications: In writing to the correspondent, including details of the funding required. The deadline for applications is 31 March for consideration through May.

Correspondent: The Trustees of the Education Trust, The Britain-Australia Society, Swire House, 59 Buckingham Gate, London SW1E 6AJ (020 7630 1075; Fax: 020 7828 2260; email: natdir@britain-australia.org.uk; website: www.britain-australia.org.uk)

Overseas students (by place of origin) – Belgium

The Royal Belgian Benevolent Society

Eligibility: Belgian students who are living/studying in Britain and are in need.

Types of grants: One-off grants of £500 to £2,000 towards the costs of further/higher education and postgraduate study.

Annual grant total: In 2007 the society had an income of £9,000 and a total expenditure of £7,000.

Applications: On a form available from the correspondent, submitted directly by the individual.

Correspondent: The Chair, Anglo-Belgian Club, c/o 60 Knightsbridge, London SW1X 7LF

Overseas students (by place of origin) – British Commonwealth

The Sir Ernest Cassel Educational Trust: Mountbatten Memorial Grants

Eligibility: Overseas students from Commonwealth countries studying in the UK who are in the final year of their studies and are experiencing unforeseen financial difficulties. Grants are only given to students in higher education (at college or university) in the UK.

Types of grants: Grants of £200 to £500 for living or general expenses.

Exclusions: Overseas students who are UK-registered for fees purposes are not eligible; applicants must have paid course fees as an overseas student. Grants are not given for the actual course fees themselves.

Annual grant total: In 2006/07 the trust had an income of £61,000 and a total expenditure of £59,000. Grants made to individuals totalled £30,000.

Applications: The grants are administered by 10 universities and institutions on behalf of the trust. Potential applicants should consult their student welfare officer for further details. Students at universities and institutions not included in the scheme may also apply through their student welfare officers to the address below

Correspondent: David Constable, 199 West Malvern Road, Malvern, Worcestershire WR14 4BB (01684 572437)

Other information: Grants are also made to organisations.

Overseas students (by place of origin) – Canada

The Canadian Centennial Scholarship Fund

Eligibility: Canadian post-secondary school students studying in the UK, who are planning to return to Canada after studying and both in need and of high academic ability. Preference is given to students taking courses which are 'of relevance to Canada'.

Students must already be enrolled in a UK educational institution before applying for a grant.

Types of grants: One-off grants of £500 to £2,500 for fees, study or travel abroad, books, maintenance and living expenses.

Annual grant total: In 2006/07 the trust had an income of £24,000 and a total expenditure of £30,000. Grants were made to 17 students.

Applications: Further information and application forms are also available from the fund's website. Applications must be received, with references, by 15 March. Interviews for those shortlisted are the first week of June and scholarships are paid out in late September.

Correspondent: Mrs Julia Montgomery, Chair, Canadian Women's Club, 1 Grosvenor Square, London W1K 4AB (020 7258 6344; email: info@canadianwomenlondon.org; website: www.canadianscholarshipfund.co.uk)

Overseas students (by place of origin) – Costa Rica

Ronaldo Falconer Charitable Trust

Eligibility: Further and higher education Costa Rican students, including mature students, who are studying in the UK, with a preference for technical courses.

Types of grants: Scholarships and bursaries.

Annual grant total: In 2006/07 the trust had an income of £5,600 and a total expenditure of £32,000. Grants have previously totalled about £50,000.

Applications: In writing to the correspondent. Applications are considered in September or October.

Correspondent: The Manager, NatWest Trust and Estate Services, 153 Preston Road, Brighton BN1 6BD (01273 545064; Fax: 01273 545075)

Overseas students (by place of origin) – Czech Rebublic

The Anglo-Czech Educational Fund

Eligibility: Students from the Czech Republic who wish to study primarily in the UK, USA and European countries.

Types of grants: Grant and loans.

Annual grant total: In 2006/07 the fund had an income of £57,000 and a total expenditure of £12,000.

Applications: In writing to the correspondent.

Correspondent: Paul Sheils, Moon Bever Solicitors, 24-25 Bloomsbury Square, London, WC1A 2PL

Overseas students (by place of origin) – Egypt

Egyptian Community Association in the United Kingdom

Eligibility: People in need who are Egyptian or of Egyptian origin and are living in or visiting the UK.

Types of grants: One-off and recurrent grants towards course fees, clothing, books, and so on.

Annual grant total: Grants usually total around £500 per year.

Applications: In writing to the correspondent.

Correspondent: Dr Wafik Moustafa, Chair, 100 Redcliffe Gardens, London, SW10 9HH (020 7244 8925)

Other information: The association arranges seminars and national and religious celebrations, as well as offering other services. It also gives grants to individuals for general welfare purposes.

Overseas students (by place of origin) – Greece

The Schilizzi Foundation

Eligibility: Greek nationals pursuing an undergraduate degree course or vocational training in Great Britain where there is a real need for financial assistance. Priority is given to students in their final year of study and second year students will only be considered in exceptional circumstances.

Types of grants: One-off grants ranging from £250 to £2,000, awarded in cases of hardship or special need during the final year of study for books, fees and living expenses. Other cases will be considered only in exceptional circumstances of serious or unforeseen hardship. (Major scholarships for further education in the UK are also awarded to selected students; no direct applications will be considered.)

Exclusions: Postgraduates are not eligible for funding.

Annual grant total: In 2006/07 the trust had assets of £1.8 million, an income of £67,000 and made grants totalling £51,000.

Applications: On a form available from the secretary. Applications can be submitted directly by the individual or a parent/guardian, or through an organisation such as a school or an educational welfare agency. They are considered up to 1 April in the final year, although earlier applications are preferred.

Correspondent: The Secretary, Rowan, Turweston, Brackley, Northamptonshire NN13 5JX (email: schilizzifoundation@ tiscali.co.uk; website: www.schilizzi foundation.org.uk)

Overseas students (by place of origin) – India

The Northbrook Society

Eligibility: Nationals of India who are studying in the UK and returning to India to related employment.

Types of grants: One-off grants ranging between £250 and £750 to students in further and higher education, including mature students, towards books, fees and living expenses.

Annual grant total: About £8,000.

Applications: In writing to the correspondent directly by the individual. The applicant must provide evidence of a return to India on completion of the course, and a reference from a supervisor or tutor.

Correspondent: Ms B Weller, Secretary, Northbrook Society, 37 Neatherd Road, Dereham, Norfolk, NR20 4AU

The Charles Wallace India Trust

Eligibility: People of Indian nationality and citizenship, aged between 25 to 38, normally resident in India and intending to return to India at the end of their study. Certain short-term awards are available for people aged between 25 to 45.

Types of grants: Only in the arts and humanities, with particular emphasis on fine arts, music, theatre, crafts and design, conservation of historical buildings and materials, anthropology, the preservation of archives, letters, history and the history of ideas.

Most awards are at postgraduate level to supplement other sources of funding or constitute completion of study awards for those whose scholarships have run out. A limited number of post-doctoral or post-professional research grants are awarded.

Exclusions: Studies relating to economic development or leading to professional legal, business or administrative qualifications are not considered.

Annual grant total: In 2006/07 the trust has net assets of £6.2 million. The trust had an income of £240,000 and a total expenditure of £253,000, from which scholarships were made to individuals totalling £194,000.

Applications: In writing to the correspondent. Detailed information and application forms can be downloaded from the website

Correspondent: The Trustees, c/o The British Council, 10 Spring Gardens, London SW1A 2BN (website: www. wallace-trusts.org.uk/)

Other information: There are separate, smaller Charles Wallace Trusts for Bangladesh, Burma and Pakistan. All of the trusts are registered charities in the UK with separate and independent boards of trustees. The registered address for all of them is: The British Council, 10 Spring Gardens, London SW1A 2BN.

Overseas students (by place of origin) – Poland

The Jeremi Kroliczewski Educational Trust

Eligibility: Polish students under 25 who are in education and live in England or Wales. The trust has previously stated that all funds are fully committed years in advance.

Annual grant total: In 2007/08 the trust had both an income and a total expenditure of around £8,000.

Applications: The trust states that all funds are fully committed.

Correspondent: Simeon Emmanuel Arnold, Solicitor, 37–38 Haven Green, Ealing, London W5 2NX (email: sarnold@ montaguelambert.com)

Overseas students (by place of origin) – Turkey

Hazel Heughan Educational Trust

Eligibility: Students and academics in further, higher or postgraduate education who usually live in Turkey and are from poor backgrounds.

Types of grants: One-off and recurrent grants towards education at university, and for trips to the UK (usually Edinburgh) to further studies in the English language and, if possible, gain work experience. This can include grants for travel expenses, books, equipment and instruments, fees and maintenance and living expenses.

Annual grant total: In 2006/07 the trust had an income of £8,700.

Applications: In writing to the correspondent at any time, for consideration usually in May and November. Applications should be submitted by a third party.

Correspondent: The Trustees, 14 Camus Avenue, Edinburgh EH10 6QT

Prisoners/ex-offenders

The Aldo Trust

Eligibility: People in need who are being held in detention pending their trial or after their conviction. The applicant must still be serving the sentence. Applicants must have less than £25 in private cash.

Types of grants: Education grants of £10 to help with items such as books, course fees, equipment, audio/visual and other training equipment and tools for employment. Those eligible can only receive one grant a year.

Annual grant total: In 2006 the trust had assets of £907,000 and an income of £29,000. The trust had a total expenditure of £33,000, of which £23,000 was given in grants.

Applications: On a form available from the correspondent. Applications must be made through prison service personnel (for example, probation, chaplaincy, education), and should include the name and number of the prisoner, age, length of sentence and expected date of release. No applications direct from prisoners will be considered. Applicants may apply once only in each twelve-month period, and applications are considered monthly.

Correspondent: c/o NACRO, Coast Cottage, 90 Coast Road, West Mersea, Colchester, CO5 8LS (01206 383809; Fax: 01206 383809; email: owenwheatley@ btinternet.com)

Other information: NACRO also offers a fund for people on probation; see separate entry in this guide.

The Longford Trust

Eligibility: Ex-prisoners undertaking higher education courses to degree level. (Eligibility remains open for up to five years after release.) Applicants must be at a UK university or equivalent UK institute.

Types of grants: Scholarships are worth a maximum of £5,000 per annum, extendable for up to three years on receipt of suitable reports of academic progress. Grants are intended to cover both the cost of tuition fees on higher education courses and offer a contribution to living expenses

for books, course material and basic sustenance.

Exclusions: No grants for postgraduate study.

Annual grant total: In 2006 the trust had an income of £56,000 with scholarship costs totalling £11,000.

Applications: Application forms can be downloaded from the trust's website, or are available by contacting the trust in writing. Applications for courses beginning in the September of any year must be made by the start of June in that year.

Correspondent: Peter Stanford, 42 Callcott Road, London, NW6 7EA (website: www.longfordtrust.org)

Other information: The trust also administers the Patrick Pakenham Educational Awards, for ex-prisoners wishing to study law to degree level.

The National Association for the Care & Resettlement of Offenders (NACRO)

Eligibility: Ex-offenders and their partners and families.

Types of grants: One-off grants of up to £100 for study and employment training fees, course materials, work wear and tools required for training.

Young offenders, aged under 30 years, can also be supported towards expenses associated with education and training. Most of these grants are one-off and for up to £100, but support can also be given for successive years for a two or three-year course.

Annual grant total: Grants usually total around £50,000 per year.

Applications: Either directly by the individual or through a probation service, social service department, Citizens Advice or registered charity. Applications are considered every two months.

Correspondent: Finance Director, 169 Clapham Road, London SW9 0PU (020 7840 6431; Fax: 020 7840 6720; website: www.nacro.org.uk)

The Prisoners' Education Trust

Eligibility: Prisoners aged 18 and above who are in custody in England and Wales and still have at least six months of their sentence to serve.

Types of grants: Grants to pay fees for distance learning and resettlement courses, including Open University courses (funded by contract from DIUS), A level, GCSE and vocational qualifications, including both accredited and non-accredited courses.

Annual grant total: In 2007 grants totalled £453,000.

Applications: Applications should be submitted on a form available from the trust or through a prison education department, for consideration monthly.

Initial telephone enquiries are welcome. Endorsement by a prison education manager is essential.

Correspondent: The Director, Ground Floor, Wandle House, Riverside Drive, Mitcham, Surrey CR4 4BU (020 8648 7760; Fax: 020 8648 7762; email: info@ prisonerseducation.org.uk; website: www. prisonerseducation.org.uk)

The Royal London Society

Eligibility: Offenders, both before and after discharge from prison, their families and young people 'at risk' (that is young people under a supervision order or who have come to the attention of the police). Grants are only made to people living or serving a sentence in the London area.

Types of grants: One-off grants that will help lead to employment in the immediate future or within the next six months. Donations may be made for training, work clothing, tools and equipment and travel expenses.

Exclusions: Grants are not given for books, university courses, clothing, maintenance/ living expenses or debts.

Annual grant total: In 2006 the society had assets of £1.1 million, an income of £92,000 and a total expenditure of £121,000. There were 53 grants made totalling £50,000.

Applications: On a form available from the correspondent. An authority, such as a welfare agency or probation officer, must support all applications; grants are made through that authority (not directly to the beneficiary). Applications are considered in March, June, September and December.

Correspondent: The Secretary, 71a Knightsbridge, London, SW1 7RB

SACRO Trust

Eligibility: Ex-offenders in Scotland who are in need.

Types of grants: Grants are usually to a maximum of £150, including those for fees, driving lessons, books and equipment.

Exclusions: No grants are made where financial help from other sources is available.

Annual grant total: Grants usually total around £10,000 per year.

Applications: On a form available from the correspondent. Applications can only be accepted if they are made through a local authority, voluntary sector worker, health visitor or so on. They are considered every two months. No payment can be made directly to an individual by the trust; payment will be made to the organisation making the application. Other sources of funding should be sought before applying to the trust.

Applications for grants up to £200 can be made at any time, although assessments are made quarterly; applications for larger sums will be considered at two trustees' meetings held in June and December.

Correspondent: Trust Fund Administrator, 1 Broughton Market, Edinburgh EH3 6NU (0131 624 7258; Fax: 0131 624 7269; website: www.sacro. org.uk)

The Paul Stephenson Memorial Trust

Eligibility: People who have served at least two years of imprisonment and are near the end of their sentence or have been released recently.

Types of grants: One-off grants of up to £100 for tools for work or assistance with college fees.

Exclusions: Grants are not given for recreational activities, setting up small businesses or becoming self employed, or for existing debts.

Annual grant total: Previously the trust had an income of £1,800 and a total expenditure of £300. More up-to-date information was unavailable.

Applications: On a form available from the correspondent, which must be submitted via a probation officer, prison education officer or voluntary associate. Applicants should mention other trusts or organisations that have been applied to and other grants promised or received, including any statutory grants. Trustees usually meet twice a year.

Correspondent: Pauline Austin, The New Bridge, 27A Medway Street, London SW3 2BD

Refugees

Aid for Jewish Refugees

Eligibility: Refugees and in particular Jewish refugees living in the UK.

Types of grants: Grants may be spent on vocational training courses, fees, books and equipment for any future career.

Annual grant total: In 2006/07 the trust had an income of £1,600 and a total expenditure of £6,000.

Applications: In writing to the correspondent.

Correspondent: Henry Jonas, Flat 17 Greenleaf Court, 17 Oakleigh Park North, Whetstone, London N20 9AQ (020 8445 1694)

The Airey Neave Trust

Eligibility: Refugees or those with exceptional leave to remain in this country.

Types of grants: Grants of £1,000 to £1,500 towards English language classes

and help towards the cost of postgraduate courses or research.

Exclusions: Grants are not given to asylum seekers, overseas students or British citizens.

Annual grant total: In 2006/07 the trust had an income of £47,000 and made grants totalling £30,000.

Applications: In writing to the correspondent. Applications should be submitted before the end of April for consideration in July. They can be submitted either directly by the individual or through the British Refugee Council or other related bodies.

Correspondent: Hannah Scott, PO Box 36800, 40 Bernard Street, London WC1N 1WJ (020 7833 4440; email: schnn8@aol.com, hanthoc@aol.com; website: www.aireyneavetrust.org.uk)

Ruth Hayman Trust *see entry on page 35*

Correspondent: The Trustees, PO Box 17685, London N6 6WD (email: trustee@ruthhaymantrust.com; website: www.ruthhaymantrust.com)

Prisoners of Conscience Appeal Fund see entry on page 36

Correspondent: The Grants Officer, PO Box 61044, London SE1 1UP (020 7407 6644; email: grantsofficer@prisonersofconscience.org; website: www.prisonersofconscience.org)

The Russian Refugees Aid Society

Eligibility: Refugees and asylum seekers from the area that was formerly the Russian Empire and their families who are in need, and now live in Great Britain.

Types of grants: One-off grants, usually around £50. Grants are awarded for books and equipment/instruments.

Schoolchildren can also receive grants towards the cost of uniform. Grants are particularly given for English language courses.

Annual grant total: In 2007 the trust had net assets of £1.4 million and an income of £116,000. Out of a total expenditure £115,000, grants totalled £86,000.

Applications: In writing to the correspondent. Applications can be submitted directly by the individual or through the individual's school, college or an educational welfare agency. Applicants must show proof that they have applied to the Home Office for asylum. They are considered at any time.

Correspondent: Barbara Irvine, Room G03, Britannia House, 11 Glenthorne Road, Hammersmith, London, W6 0LH (020 8735 6511)

Religion – Christian

The Alexis Trust

Eligibility: Members of the Christian faith.

Types of grants: Grants of between £50 and £100 are available, mostly for Christian-based activities.

Annual grant total: In 2006/07 the trust had an income of £36,000 and total expenditure of £38,000 of which £6,000 was given in grants to individuals. A further £29,000 was given in grants to institutions.

Applications: In writing to the correspondent.

Correspondent: Prof. D W Vere, 14 Broadfield Way, Buckhurst Hill, Essex IG9 5AG

Other information: The grants given to individuals are usually from the surplus funds from the grants to organisations. Applicants should contact the correspondent for further information before making an application.

The Britland Trust

Eligibility: People involved in the advancement of Christianity, mission work and Christian education and training.

Types of grants: One-off and recurrent grants according to need.

Annual grant total: In 2006 the trust had an income of just £248 and a total expenditure of £7,000. It would appear that the trust may be winding down, as income and expenditure levels have reduced over the past few years.

Applications: In writing to the correspondent.

Correspondent: J M P Colman, Trustee, 20 Henderson Road, Wandsworth, London SW18 3RR (email: jcolman@lineone.net)

Other information: The trust also gives to organisations.

Medical Service Ministries

Eligibility: 'Committed Christians' of any nationality who wish to train in basic healthcare, or gain an additional medical qualification in order to help the group or community they are working with. Applicants must be sponsored by a recognised Christian society or community.

Types of grants: Grants towards the costs of training.

Exclusions: No support for basic professional medical training, for example courses leading to qualification as a doctor, nurse, midwife, dentist, and so on.

Annual grant total: In 2006/07 the trust had an income of £9,000 and a total expenditure of £14,000.

Applications: Applicants should contact the trust giving a brief outline of the work they are, or will be, involved in, together with brief details of the sort of training envisaged.

Correspondent: The Trustees, PO Box 13, Newton Abbot TQ13 9WZ (email: resources.msm@btopenworld.com; website: www.preachandheal.org.uk)

Other information: Training courses for groups may also be considered.

The New Durlston Trust

Eligibility: Students undertaking gap year projects or youth work in conjunction with Christian charities.

Types of grants: One-off grants of around £100 each.

Annual grant total: In 2006/07 it had assets of £82,000 and an income of £27,000. Grants were made totalling £33,000, mostly to organisations.

Applications: In writing to the correspondent, including confirmation from the charity that the applicant will be working with. They are considered every three to four months.

Correspondent: N A H Pool, Trustee, Anchor Cottage, 98 Reading Road South, Fleet, Hampshire, GU52 7UA

The Podde Trust

Eligibility: Individuals involved in Christian work in the UK and overseas.

Types of grants: One-off and recurrent grants.

Annual grant total: In 2006/07 the trust has an income of £31,000. There were 26 grants to individuals totalling £8,000.

Applications: In writing to the correspondent: please note, the trust states that it has very limited resources, and those it does have are mostly already committed. Requests from new applicants therefore have very little chance of success.

Correspondent: P B Godfrey, 68 Green Lane, Hucclecote, Gloucester GL3 3QX (01452 613563)

Other information: Organisations involved in Christian work are also supported.

The Stewardship Trust Ripon

Eligibility: People connected with Christian causes living in the UK, with a preference for Yorkshire.

Types of grants: One-off and recurrent grants, for example, for training in Christian ministry.

Annual grant total: In 2006/07 the trust had an income of £20,000 and an expenditure of £16,000.

Applications: In writing to the correspondent. The trust's funds are usually fully committed and new applications are only considered if there is 'extreme need'.

Correspondent: W B Metcalf, Chair, Hutton Hill, Hutton Bank, Ripon, North Yorkshire, HG4 5DT (01765 602887)

The Sure Foundation

Eligibility: Christians seeking to share their faith in the UK or overseas and people needing a new start in employment, such as ex-offenders. Preference is given to those training to promote Christian work and faith.

Types of grants: Grants in the range of £50 to £200 are given towards training for various aspects of Christian ministry and to people restarting work for equipment, tools and so on.

Exclusions: Grants are not made to individuals with previous vocational or professional qualifications or for higher education.

Annual grant total: About £2,000.

Applications: In writing to the correspondent directly from the individual. References are considered helpful when assessing applications.

Applications are considered in February, May, August and November.

Correspondent: The Trustees, Hobbs Green Farm, Odell, Bedfordshire MK43 7AB

Religion – Church of England

The Saint George's Trust

Eligibility: People involved in work 'for the furtherance of the Church of England and churches in communion with her'.

Types of grants: Grants are small, one-off and made towards a specific project or theological course, e.g. young people undertaking voluntary Christian work abroad and clergymen planning special work during a sabbatical.

Exclusions: Restoration projects or any long-term financial support.

Annual grant total: About £15,000 to £18,000 is given in grants each year.

Applications: In writing to the correspondent, giving details of the project, its likely cost and with a note of any funds available towards it. An sae is required for a reply.

Correspondent: The Bursar, St Edward's House, 22 Great College Street, London SW1P 3QA

Religion – Huguenot

Charities in connection with the Society of St Onge & Angoumois

Eligibility: Young people aged 16 to 25 who live in the UK, with preference for those who are descended from French Protestants (Huguenot) and in particular those who have at any time lived in the province of St Onge and Angoumois in France, who are in need, and who are preparing for, entering upon or engaged in any profession, trade or service.

Types of grants: One-off grants to enable beneficiaries to train for a trade or occupation in order to help them to advance in life or earn their living. Grants are only given on proof of purchase, for example, for books, equipment, daily travel and clothing for people on a training course, and for books, equipment and daily travel for students in further or higher education. Grants range from £100 to £400.

Exclusions: No grants to foreign students studying in the UK.

Annual grant total: About £1,500.

Applications: On a form available from Mr A Squire, 26 Blaisdon, Weston-super-Mare, Somerset, BS22 8BN. Applications should be submitted directly by the individual or by a parent or guardian. They are considered in April and May.

Correspondent: Mrs P J Lane-Gilbert, Flat 19, Amberley Court, Angell Road, London SW9 7HL

Religion – Jewish

The Anglo Jewish Association

Eligibility: Jewish students studying a full-time course at a UK university, regardless of nation of origin, who are in need.

Types of grants: Grants ranging between £500 and £3,000 a year for students at either undergraduate or postgraduate level.

Annual grant total: In 2006 the trust had assets of £292,000 and an income of £143,000. A total of £131,000 was given for educational purposes.

Applications: On a form available from the correspondent in January, or from the website, to be submitted by 30 April. Applications must include academic references, a CV and details of the applicant's personal history.

Scholarships are for one academic year and individuals may apply for the part or the whole of an additional academic year by submitting another complete application, prior to the closing date for the relevant year. The award of a second, third or fourth scholarship is not automatic.

Correspondent: Ms J Samuel, Suite 4, 107 Gloucester Place, London W1U 6BY (020 7486 5155; email: info@anglojewish. co.uk; website: www.anglojewish.co.uk)

Finnart House School Trust

Eligibility: Jewish children and young people aged over 14 years who are in need. Bursaries and scholarships are for those with ability, who, because of family circumstances, may otherwise be unable to achieve their potential.

Types of grants: Bursaries are awarded through schools. Awards may be made regularly each term, or may be one-off. Grants range between £100 and £1,500. Scholarships are awarded for higher education until the completion of the course and range up to £5,000 a year.

Exclusions: Only members of the Jewish faith can be supported.

Annual grant total: In 2006/07 the trust had assets of £4.8 million, which generated an income of £181,000. Finnart scholarships were awarded to 13 individuals totalling £104,000.

Applications: Bursaries are awarded via schools. Scholarship applications are made by the individual on a form available from the correspondent, to be submitted by April.

Correspondent: Peter Shaw, Clerk to the Trustees, PO Box 603, Edgware, Middlesex, HA8 4EQ (020 3209 6006; email: info@finnart.org; website: www. finnart.org)

Other information: This trust also makes grants for relief-in-need purposes and to organisations which work with children and young people of the Jewish faith who are in need.

Gur Trust

Eligibility: People connected to the Jewish faith in the UK.

Types of grants: One-off and recurrent grants according to need.

Annual grant total: In 2006/07 grants were made totalling £25,000. Grants are made to both individuals and organisations.

Applications: 'Funds are raised by the trustees. All calls for help are carefully considered and help is given according to circumstances and funds then available.'

Correspondent: The Trustees, 5 Windus Road, London, N16 6UT (020 8880 8910)

The Jewish Widows & Students Aid Trust

Eligibility: Jewish students from the UK, France, the Commonwealth and Israel who are aged 10 to 30 years old. Grants are also given to widows with young children.

Types of grants: Mainly interest-free loans ranging from £250 to £1,000. Awards are made on the basis of academic excellence and need. Students can be given grants towards fees, living expenses, books or travel. On occasions grants can also be given to schoolchildren.

Annual grant total: In 2007/08 the trust had assets of £642,000 and an income of £68,000. Grants to 25 students totalled £32,000.

Applications: In writing to the correspondent requesting an application form, including a cv and confirmation of acceptance at an educational establishment. Applications should be submitted directly by the individual to be considered at any time.

Correspondent: Alan Philipp, 5 Raeburn Close, London, NW11 6UG (020 8349 7199)

The Charities of Moses Lara

Eligibility: Spanish and Portuguese Jews, born in wedlock and living in the UK. There may be a preference for people whose principal place of worship is a Sephardi Synagogue.

Types of grants: Help with the cost of books, clothing and other essentials for college and university students. Preference may be given to those promoting the study of texts and so on of Judaism involving the Rabbinic Law. The trust also assists residents in Beth Holim (Wembley).

Annual grant total: In 2006/07 the trust had an income of £18,000 and a total expenditure of about £13,000.

Applications: In writing to the correspondent.

Correspondent: The Secretary, Spanish & Portuguese Synagogue, 2 Ashworth Road, London, W9 1JY

The Montpellier Trust

Eligibility: People in education connected to the Orthodox Jewish faith.

Types of grants: Grants given according to need.

Annual grant total: In 2006/07 the trust had an income and a total expenditure of £11,000.

Applications: In writing to the correspondent.

Correspondent: Michael Allweis, 7 Montpellier Mews, Salford, M7 4ZW

The Spanish & Portuguese Jews Children's Fund

Eligibility: People under 26 who are in need and are Sephardi Jews or are accustomed to congregate with them.

Types of grants: One-off and recurrent grants for schoolchildren and people in further and higher education.

Annual grant total: In 2006/07 there were 32 grants made for educational purposes totalling £22,000.

Applications: In writing to the correspondent. Applications are considered twice a year, and are to be submitted by 31 March or 30 September.

Correspondent: H Miller, Secretary, Spanish & Portuguese Jews Congregation, 2 Ashworth Road, London W9 1JY

The Benjamin Winegarten Charitable Trust

Eligibility: People involved in the advancement of the Jewish religion and religious education.

Types of grants: One-off and recurrent grants according to need.

Annual grant total: In 2006/07 the trust had assets of £586,000, an income of £152,000 and made grants totalling £108,000 of which £8,000 went to individuals.

Applications: In writing to the correspondent.

Correspondent: B A Winegarten, 25 St Andrew's Grove, London, N16 5NF (020 8800 6669)

Religion – Protestant

William and Mary Hart Foundation

Eligibility: Baptist Christians under the age of 25. Preference shall be given to persons who live in the parish of Collingham or who have a parent or parents living there.

Types of grants: One-off and recurrent grants and loans to school children, undergraduates and vocational students.

Annual grant total: In 2006 the foundation had an income of £1,400 and a total expenditure of £2,000.

Applications: In writing to the correspondent.

Correspondent: David Marshall, 2 Keats Drive, Hucknall, Nottingham, NG15 6TE (0115 963 5428)

The Mylne Trust

Eligibility: Members of the Protestant faith who have been engaged in evangelistic work, including missionaries and retired missionaries, and Christian workers whose finances are inadequate. Married ordinands with children are also supported when all other sources of funding have failed to cover their needs.

Types of grants: Grants are given towards educational training at theological colleges, for the cost of books and living expenses to undergraduates and overseas students.

Annual grant total: Previously grants were made totalling £47,000. Unfortunately, more up-to-date financial information was unavailable.

Applications: On a form available from the correspondent or to download from the trust's website. Applications should be returned to: The Mylne Trust, PO Box 530, Farnham, GU9 1BP. The trustees meet quarterly to consider applications.

Correspondent: Graeme Aston, Hadfields Butt & Bowyer, 104 West street, Farnham, Surrey GU9 7ET (email: admin@ mylnetrust.org.uk; website: www. mylnetrust.org.uk)

Religion – Quaker

The Friends Educational Foundation

Eligibility: Members of Britain Yearly Meeting of the Religious Society of Friends (Quakers) or those closely associated with the society (for example, regular attenders).

Types of grants: Two types of award exist: (i) bursaries for children attending Quaker schools; and (ii) grants for Quakers pursuing courses of further or higher education.

Exclusions: Retrospective applications or applications for more than a year ahead cannot normally be considered.

Annual grant total: Around £100,000 per year.

Applications: For bursaries for children attending Quaker schools – via the Quaker schools upon entry; and for grants for Quakers pursuing courses of further or higher education – to the correspondent in the year before the course begins.

The closing dates for applications each year is 30 April. Initial enquiries by telephone, email or letter.

Correspondent: Debbie Taylor, Friends House, 173 Euston Road, London NW1 2BJ (020 7663 1000; email: debbiet@ quaker.org.uk)

Religion – Roman Catholic

The Duchess of Leeds Foundation for Boys and Girls

Eligibility: Orphaned or fatherless Catholic children aged between 11 and 18 who attend fee-paying Catholic schools and are in need. Children must live in England, Wales or the Channel Islands. Help is concentrated on secondary education; children in primary and secondary school are helped only in exceptional circumstances.

Types of grants: Grants to help with the cost of school fees only. Grants may continue until the end of an A level course.

Annual grant total: In 2006 the foundation had an income of £57,000. There were 43 grants made totalling £36,000.

Applications: On a form available form the correspondent to be submitted directly by the individual or a parent/guardian. The deadline for applications in 31 January.

Correspondent: B L Cawley, Clerk, 15 High Oaks, Enfield, EN2 8JJ (020 8367 1077; Fax: 020 8367 1077)

Religion – United Reformed Church

Milton Mount Foundation

Eligibility: The children of ministers of the United Reformed Church, the Congregational Federation, the Evangelical Fellowship of Congregational Churches and the Unaffiliated Congregational Churches; also daughters of members of these churches.

Types of grants: The foundation gives bursaries towards school fees for children aged 11 to 18, both at United Reformed Church and Congregational schools, and at other independent boarding or day schools approved by the trustees. Grants may also be given towards the cost of school uniform for eligible boys or girls on entry to secondary school at both independent and maintained schools. Women taking up further/higher education at a later stage can also receive grants towards books and fees. Up to one third only of the income may be spent on boys as the funds arise from the sale of a girls' school, thereby limiting the number of bursaries available to the sons of ministers.

Annual grant total: In 2006/07 the trust had assets of £3.3 million, generating an income of £102,000. Grants were made to individuals totalling £81,000

Applications: On a form available from the correspondent, with information about total family income. Applications are considered in May and June.

Correspondent: Revd Erna Stevenson, 11 Copse Close, Cippenham, Slough, Berkshire SL1 5DT (01753 748713)

Sport

The Francis Drake Fellowship

Eligibility: Dependants of members of the fellowship who have died.

Types of grants: Allowances of £52 per month per child is given to children in full-time education, up to the end of their A levels.

Annual grant total: Previously the fellowship made grants totalling £14,000.

Applications: In writing to the correspondent, requesting an application form. Applications should be submitted through the bowling club's Francis Drake Fellowship delegate. Applications are accepted two years after the date of the member's death.

Correspondent: Joan Jupp, 24 Haldane Close, London N10 2PB (020 8883 8725)

The Rugby Football Union Charitable Fund

Eligibility: Individuals injured while participating in any sport and any dependant of any person who was killed while participating in any sport.

Types of grants: One-off grants of up to £500 towards, for instance, hospital visits, personal and domestic expenses and educational expenses.

Annual grant total: In 2007 four grants were made to individuals totalling £1,500.

Applications: On a form available from the correspondent.

Correspondent: Tim Bonnet, Executive Officer, 41 Station Road, North Harrow, Middlesex HA2 7SX (020 8863 0220; email: postmaster@rfuspiretrust.co.uk; website: www.rfuspiretrust.co.uk/index. html)

Other information: Grants are also made to organisations.

Vegetarian

The Vegetarian Charity

Eligibility: People under the age of 26 who are vegetarian or vegan and are sick or in need.

Types of grants: One-off and recurrent grants of £250 to £1,000 for general educational purposes.

Annual grant total: In 2006/07 the charity had assets of £1.1 million and an income of £49,000. Grants totalled £29,000 of which £26,000 went to individuals.

Applications: On a form available from the correspondent, including details of any other grants received, a CV, a letter of recommendation from a tutor, school reports, covering letter and three references. Applications are considered throughout the year.

Correspondent: Susan Lenihan, 56 Parliament Street, Chippenham, Wiltshire, SN14 0DE

Other information: Grants are also made to organisations which promote vegetarianism among young people and to vegetarian children's homes.

Volunteers

The Roger & Sarah Bancroft Clark Charitable Trust see entry on page 82

The Alec Dickson Trust

Eligibility: Young people under 30 years of age and living in the UK, involved in volunteering or community service.

Types of grants: 'The trust's mission is to support young people who are able to demonstrate that through volunteering or community service projects they can enhance the lives of others, particularly those most marginalised by society. The trust particularly welcomes applications from innovative projects in the spirit of Alec Dickson – projects which young people themselves have devised and which are unlikely to be funded by other charitable trusts. As a result, it is unlikely that applications from young people embarking on organised 'gap year' projects overseas or requesting a grant for college/university course fees will match with the trust's funding criteria.' Grants are generally between £100 and £250.

Annual grant total: Around £3,000 each year.

Applications: Directly by the individual on a form available from the correspondent.

Applications are considered in April and October.

Correspondent: Miss Angela Lazenbury, Flat 11, Barbrook House, Chatham Place, London E9 6PE (020 7643 1338)

The Duveen Trust

Eligibility: Individuals aged up to 25 who wish to get involved with projects which require initiative and which give something back to the community, and who are in need of support because self-help has proved to be insufficient.

Types of grants: One-off grants of £100 to £500.

Annual grant total: In 2006/07 the trust had an income of £18,000 and a total expenditure of £13,000. The trust gives can give up to £20,000 a year in grants to individuals.

Applications: Application forms and guidelines are available from the correspondent or on the website. The deadlines for applications are just before the trustees' meetings, three times a year.

Correspondent: The Trustees, 26 Beechwood Avenue, London N3 3AX (Fax: 020 8349 9649; website: www.theduveentrust.org.uk)

The Emmaus Charitable Trust

Eligibility: Christians involved in voluntary projects. Grants are given internationally but in practice there is a preference for Greater London.

Types of grants: One-off and recurrent grants according to need.

Annual grant total: In 2007/08 the trust had an income of £6,000 and a total expenditure of £8,000.

Applications: In writing to the correspondent.

Correspondent: R J Silman, Trustee, 4 Church Avenue, Lancaster LA1 4SP (01524 368824)

Women

The Altrusa Careers Trust

Eligibility: Women in the UK and Eire who wish to further their career prospects or to retrain after bringing up a family, and who are in extreme need or facing an emergency.

Types of grants: A loan of up to £500 is available. All loans are interest free and should be repaid within two years of completion of course

Exclusions: Loans are not available to those still at school and there is probably a restriction on those going on to do a second degree.

Annual grant total: In 2007 the trust had an income of £18,000

Applications: On a form available from the correspondent. Applications are reviewed after 31 March each year. A shortlist is drawn up and references taken up. Applicants are requested to keep in touch with the trustees once a year so that their progress can be noted.

Correspondent: Raye Lennie, P O Box 6160, Orkney, KW16 3WY

The Golden Jubilee Fellowship

Eligibility: Women who live 'permanently' within the boundaries of Soroptimist International of Great Britain and Ireland, who need not be Soroptimists. The countries are: Anguilla, Antigua and Barbuda, Bangladesh, Barbados, Cameroon, Gambia, Grenada, Guernsey, India, Isle of Man, Jamaica, Jersey, Republic of Ireland, Malawi, Malta, Mauritius, Mozambique, Nigeria, Pakistan, Seychelles, Sierra Leone, South Africa, Sri Lanka, St Vincent and the Grenadines, Trinidad & Tobago, Turks & Caicos Islands, Uganda, UK and Zimbabwe.

Types of grants: Preference is given to women seeking to improve their skills or gain new ones to seek employment after years in the home, or to enter a field where prospects of employment and advancement are greater. One-off grants of £100 to £500 are awarded each year. About 30 awards, usually in the range of £100 to £500 are made each year.

Annual grant total: In 2006/07 the trust had an annual income of £8,000 and a total expenditure of £19,000.

Applications: On an application form, to be requested by writing to the correspondent, enclosing an sae. Completed forms should be returned by 15 April each year for the academic year beginning the following autumn. The committee meets to consider applications in May/June and successful applicants are informed by the end of July. Please enclose an sae/international reply coupon.

Correspondent: The Chair, Soroptimist International Great Britain and Ireland, 127 Wellington Road South, Stockport SK1 3TS (0161 480 7686; Fax: 0161 477 6152; email: hq@soroptimistgbi.prestel.co.uk; website: www.soroptimist-gbi.org)

The Hilda Martindale Educational Trust

Eligibility: 'Women of the British Isles whose intention it is to fit themselves for some profession or career likely to be of use or value to the community, and for which vocational training is required.'

Types of grants: One-off grants are of between £200 and £1,000. Grants can be used for books, equipment, fees, living expenses or childcare.

Exclusions: Applicants under 21 are not considered. Grants are not available to women doing wholly academic courses, academic research, short courses, access courses, courses outside the UK, elective studies, intercalated BSc years during a medical, dental, veterinary or nursing course, special projects in the UK or abroad, or Masters' courses immediately after a first degree. Students eligible for grants from research councils, British Academy or other public sources are also ineligible. Candidates eligible for career development loans are expected to have tried this option before applying.

Annual grant total: Previously grants were awarded to 36 individuals totalling £30,000.

Applications: On a form available from the correspondent. Applications must be returned by 1 March for the following academic year, with the results of application announced in mid-June. Applications should be submitted directly by the individual including a reference.

Correspondent: The Secretary to the Trustees, Royal Holloway University of London, Egham, Surrey TW20 0EX

Other information: Due to a large number of applicants, in general only 10% of applications are funded. People who do not exactly suit the eligibility criteria are asked not to apply.

President's Fund

Eligibility: Women in their final year of study for a degree (postgraduate or undergraduate) at a British university who face unexpected financial hardship.

Types of grants: One-off grants between £150 and £500. Applicants receive only one award which is for current study. Grants are intended to help with costs of books, equipment and maintenance/living expenses.

Exclusions: Grants are not given towards access courses, diplomas, certificates, study or work outside the UK, childcare, any year of study other than final year, one year undergraduate and one year postgraduate degrees.

Annual grant total: The trust has an annual income of about £15,000.

Applications: On a form only available by writing to the correspondent. Requests for application forms must be submitted directly by the applicant (not third parties). The trustees meet to consider applications in February, April/May, October and November.

Correspondent: The Secretary, Flat 5, 5 Victoria Circus, Glasgow, G12 9LB

Other information: The trust stated that 'applications which disregard the exclusions listed above will not be acknowledged'.

The Womens Careers Foundation (Girls of The Realm Guild)

Eligibility: Women only, who are UK citizens. Applicants should be seeking assistance to begin or continue studies for a career and should be 21 or over, except for music or dancing when the minimum age is 16.

Types of grants: One-off grants and loans to help with any costs relating to further education relevant to a career.

Exclusions: Grants are not given for PhD study or postgraduate studies if the subject indicates a complete change of direction.

Annual grant total: In 2006 the foundation had an income of £11,000 and a total expenditure of £14,000.

Applications: In writing to the correspondent. Applications should be submitted between the 1 September and 31 January for the following academic year. An sae is essential. The correspondent has stated that timing is crucial: 'so many people write for immediate help which we cannot give'. Applications must be submitted well in advance.

Correspondent: Mrs B Hayward, Secretary, 2 Watchoak, Blackham, Tunbridge Wells, Kent TN3 9TP (01892 740602)

Yorkshire Ladies' Council of Education (Incorporated)

Eligibility: British women who are aged 21 or over 'who can present a case of special need in funding their further or higher education at a British institution'. Applicants must not qualify for Local Authority support. A separate fund has been set up in association with the Sir James Knott Trust, to enable grants to be offered exclusively to applicants from the North East of England (defined as Tyne and Wear, Northumberland, County Durham inclusive of Hartlepool but exclusive of Darlington, Stockton-on-Tees, Middlesborough, Redcar and Cleveland).

Types of grants: Grants in the range of £200 and £300 a year are made towards fees.

Exclusions: YLCE members and their dependants are not eligible for support.

Annual grant total: In 2006/07 the trust had assets of £521,000, an income of £37,000 and a total expenditure of £28,000. Educational awards totalled £16,000.

Applications: Applications forms can be requested from the correspondent, or are available to download from the charity's website. Completed forms should be submitted directly by the individual by the first of January, March, June or September for consideration later in the month. Applicants for grants from the Sir James Knott Trust (who may be asked for proof of residency) should label their form 'SPECIAL FUND

Correspondent: The Secretary, Forest Hill, 11 Park Crescent, Leeds LS8 1DH (0113 269 1471; website: www.ylce.org.uk)

Work/study overseas

Lady Allen of Hurtwood Memorial Trust

Eligibility: Individuals wishing to carry out a specific travel project that will help them gain specific additional knowledge and experience which will enhance the quality and the nature of their work with young children (particularly children with disabilities or children from disadvantaged backgrounds) and their families.

Types of grants: Travel awards, ranging from £500 to £1,000.

Annual grant total: In 2006/07 the trust had an income of £1,400 and a total expenditure of £400.

Applications: On a form available, with guidelines for applicants, from the correspondent. Applicants must have a specific project in mind and offer positive evidence of how the award will help them, and how the knowledge gained will be shared with others. Short listing is in February and the awards are made in March.

Correspondent: Mrs Caroline Richards, Hon. Secretary, 89 Thurleigh Road, London, SW12 8TY

Captain F G Boot Scholarships

Eligibility: Young people aged 17 to 25.

Types of grants: These scholarships enable school leavers to spend at least six months abroad to learn a foreign language or a certain foreign culture prior to further education. Each scholarship may be for an amount up to £1,000. Grants are not given to Project Trust applicants.

Annual grant total: Previously £5,000, typically around 5 grants a year are awarded.

Applications: Application forms can be downloaded from the Worshipful Company of Cutlers website.

Correspondent: The Clerk, The Worshipful Company of Cutlers, Cutlers' Hall, Warwick Lane, London EC4M 7BR (website: www.cutlerslondon.co.uk)

The British & Foreign School Society – International Award Scheme

Eligibility: Individuals from the UK who wish to engage in educational activities in developing countries, and vice versa.

Types of grants: Grants of up to £2,000 per individual. Other grants have been given to support or sponsor individuals engaging in educational activities overseas, engaging in projects that will benefit the local communities. About £25,000 is available each year for grants to individuals.

Most UK awards are made to young people who volunteer to teach abroad for an academic year and most awards in developing countries are made to individuals of any age who want to visit the UK for an academic year, to acquire specific skills and knowledge.

All awards are channelled through existing links and organisations to ensure volunteers are fully briefed and supported.

In previous years, volunteers from the UK have travelled to Tanzania, Uganda, Sri Lanka, India, Namibia, Ecuador, Chile, China and Cambodia. grants were also given to 4 individuals from Tanzania and Kazakhstan coming to study in the UK.

Annual grant total: In 2006 the trust had assets of £11 million and an income of £464,000. Grants made to 21 individuals totalled £38,000.

Applications: Guidelines for applications are available from the correspondent.

Correspondent: Charles Crawford, Director, Maybrook House, Godstone Road, Caterham, Surrey CR3 6RE (01883 331177; Fax: 01883 344429; email: britforeign@aol.com; website: www.bfss.org.uk)

The Winston Churchill Memorial Trust

Eligibility: Men and women from all walks of life who wish to travel overseas and learn about the life, work and people of other countries. Each year the trust selects a group of different categories from which candidates for that year will be chosen.

Types of grants: 'Travelling Fellowships are awarded for originality, quality of character, enterprise and a sense of responsibility. The primary consideration is whether the contribution which candidates can make to their trade, industry, profession, business, community or calling will be increased by personal travel overseas. The awards are open to any man or woman who is a UK citizen and resident in the UK, regardless of age. Everyone has an equal chance. Those who are selected travel to all corners of the world as representatives of this country, in the name of Sir Winston Churchill.'

Categories supported change each year.

Exclusions: The trust cannot award grants for attending courses or academic studies, nor for student grants; this includes electives, degree placements and post-graduate studies unless it is clear that the proposed fellowship would meet the principles set out under 'types of grants' above. Applications under the guise of a 'gap' year will not normally be considered.

Annual grant total: In 2006/07 the trust had assets of £27.5 million and an income of just over £1 million. Grants were made to 98 individuals totalling £985,000.

Applications: The categories for the following year are published in June of the preceding year and applications should be received by the end of October.

Correspondent: Alexandra Sibun, 15 Queen's Gate Terrace, London SW7 5PR (020 7584 9315; Fax: 020 7581 0410; email: office@wcmt.org.uk; website: www.wcmt.org.uk)

The Gilchrist Educational Trust
see entry on page 20

Correspondent: The Secretary, 13 Brookfield Avenue, Larkfield, Aylesford, ME20 6RU (01903 746723; email: gilchrist.et@blueyonder.co.uk; website: www.gilchristgrants.org.uk)

The Rotary Foundation Scholarships

Eligibility: Scholarships overseas to further international understanding, for vocational study, graduates, undergraduates who have completed two years of university study, teachers of people with disabilities or professional journalists.

Types of grants: The purpose of the scholarships is to further international understanding and friendly relations among peoples of different countries, rather than to enable beneficiaries to achieve any particular qualification.

Annual grant total: Previously about £1 million.

Applications: Applications can only be made through a rotary club in the district where the applicant lives, studies or works.

Correspondent: The Secretary, Rotary International in Great Britain & Ireland, Kinwarton Road, Alcester, Warwickshire, B49 6PB (01789 765411; Fax: 01789 756570; website: www.rotary.org)

The Tropical Agricultural Association Award Fund

Eligibility: UK graduates, people with a diploma or senior students up to the age of 30 wishing to spend at least six months working on a rural development project in a developing country. Usually grant recipients have had a training in agriculture, forestry, agroforestry, environmental science or geography.

Types of grants: Grants of up to a maximum of £2,000 to help with airfares or living costs arising from their proposed projects (paid or unpaid).

Annual grant total: In 2006/07 the association had an income of £45,000 and a total expenditure of £46,000. Grants expenses totalled about £19,000.

Applications: Application forms are available from the association's website. Applications are considered every two months.

Correspondent: The Secretary, 144 Mostyn Road, London, SW19 3LR (020 8543 7563; email: general_secretary@taa.org.uk; website: www.taa.org.uk)

The WR Foundation

Eligibility: Undergraduates and people undertaking educational trips overseas.

Types of grants: One-off grants averaging £1,000 each.

Annual grant total: About £10,000.

Applications: In writing to the correspondent.

Correspondent: J Malthouse, Trustee, Malthouse & Co, America House, Rumford Court, Rumford Place, Liverpool L3 9DD (0151 284 2000)

Other information: The trust makes grants to organisations and individuals.

Work/study overseas – Antarctic

The Trans-Antarctic Association

Eligibility: Citizens of the UK, Australia, South Africa and New Zealand seeking to further knowledge or exploration of the Antarctic.

Types of grants: Cash grants of up to £1,500.

Exclusions: No grants for Arctic work or for people who are not nationals of the countries named above.

Annual grant total: In 2007 the association had an income of £13,000 and a total expenditure of £9,000.

Applications: Applications should be made by 31 January each year on a form available as a download from the association's website.

Correspondent: Dr Mike Curtis, c/o British Antarctic Survey, High Cross, Madingley Road, Cambridge, CB3 0ET (01223 221429; Fax: 01223 362616; email: taagrants@bas.ac.uk; website: www.transantarctic.org.uk)

Work/study overseas – Europe

Erasmus Mobility Grants

Eligibility: Students from the EU who wish to study and work abroad. (Support is also available to professors and business staff who want to teach abroad and for university staff who want to be trained abroad.)

Types of grants: Grants for students carrying out study or work placements, based on the duration of the period abroad. Grant amounts are subject to change each year subject to the anticipated number of participants from UK higher education institutions.

Annual grant total: The annual budget is in excess of €400 million, more than 3,100 higher education institutions in 31 countries participate. (This budget relates to all of the participating countries not just the UK.)

Applications: Students should enquire about the programme at their home university department or International/ European office.

Correspondent: The Erasmus Team, 28 Park Place, Cardiff, CF10 3QE (029 2039 7405; email: erasmus@ britishcouncil.org; website: www. britishcouncil.org/erasmus)

Other information: 'The European Commission has integrated its various educational and training initiatives under a single umbrella, the Lifelong Learning Programme. With a significant budget of nearly €7 billion for 2007 to 2013, the new programme replaces previous education, vocational training and e-Learning programmes, which ended in 2006.'

The Peter Kirk Memorial Fund

Eligibility: Citizens of any European country aged between 18 and 26 years.

Types of grants: One-off grants of £1,500 to help young people increase their understanding of Europe by undertaking a project on any aspect of modern European life. This must involve active research in at least one other European country for two to three months.

Annual grant total: In 2006/07 scholarships totalling approximately £20,000 were awarded to 13 individuals.

Applications: On a form available from the correspondent, by email or on receipt of an sae. Application forms can also be downloaded from the website. Projects must be submitted by 16 Feb, with selection/interviews normally being completed by the end of April. Interviews take place in London at the applicant's expense. The fund would prefer applications to be submitted by email if possible.

Correspondent: Mrs Angela Pearson, Secretary, 11 Luttrell Avenue, Putney, London, SW15 6PA (01943 839210; Fax: 01943 839210; email: mail@kirkfund. org.uk; website: www.kirkfund.org.uk)

The Trades Union Congress Educational Trust

Eligibility: Members of TUC affiliated trade unions who are attending a course and are not in receipt of other grants.

Types of grants: The European study bursary offers two bursaries of £800 each to allow members to visit an EU country to study an aspect of trade unionism, industrial relations, training or employment or to write a report for the TUC educational service.

Annual grant total: In 2007 the trust had a total income of about £567,000 and a total expenditure of £8,000. Bursaries totalled £4,000.

Applications: Applications should be made through the participating colleges.

Correspondent: The Trustees, Congress House, 23-28 Great Russell Street, London WC1B 3LQ

Work/study overseas – New Zealand

The Link Foundation

Eligibility: People wishing to participate in a vocational exchange between the UK and New Zealand, through specific joint schemes such as Equine Fertility, Hospitality Awards and Social Sciences Awards. The schemes are advertised through the governing bodies and specialist press belonging to these areas.

Types of grants: Grants of between £200 and £10,000 towards educational and cultural exchange linked to a vocation, including for research.

Exclusions: Grants are not made to individuals seeking funds for one-off trips such as medical residencies or to applicants wishing to visit countries other than Britain or New Zealand. Grants are not usually made for study.

Annual grant total: About £80,000.

Applications: In writing to the correspondent or to the organisation with which the foundation is jointly offering the award. Applications can be submitted directly by the individual or through the school/college or educational welfare agency.

Correspondent: Francis King, Executive Officer, New Zealand Link Foundation, New Zealand House, Haymarket, London SW1Y 4TQ (020 7839 3423; email: linkuknz@dircon.co.uk)

Work/study overseas – Scandinavia

CoScan Trust Fund

Eligibility: British people aged between 15 and 25 who are undertaking a project of an educational nature involving travel between the UK and Scandinavia and within Scandinavia. Only short visits will be considered.

Types of grants: One-off grants of between £75 and £150.

Annual grant total: In previous years approximately 15 grants have been awarded annually.

Applications: On a form available from the correspondent, accompanied by a personal letter. Applications are considered once a year and should be submitted by March for consideration in April/May.

Correspondent: Dr Brita Green, 103 Long Ridge Lane, Nether Poppleton, York YO26 6LW (01904 794438; email: PSGBEG@aol.com)

Work/study overseas – Sweden

Anglo-Swedish Literary Foundation

Eligibility: Individuals wishing to participate in study visits connected to research on Swedish literature. The foundation aims to encourage cultural exchange between Sweden and the British Isles by promoting and diffusing knowledge and the appreciation of Swedish art and literature in the UK.

Types of grants: Grants may be spent on study visits connected with research on Swedish literature. Grants may also be used for translations and publishing subsidies and so on.

Annual grant total: In 2006/07 the trust had an income of £11,000 and a total expenditure of £18,000.

Applications: In writing, outlining your project or activity and stating required funding and any other sources of funding.

Correspondent: c/o Swedish Embassy, Swedish Embassy, 11 Montagu Place, London W1H 2AL (020 7917 6400)

Airline Pilots

The British Airline Pilots' Association Benevolent Fund (BALPA)

Eligibility: Dependants of retired or deceased commercial pilots and flight engineers, who are or have been members of BALPA.

Types of grants: Limited grants are made towards the cost of books, uniforms and associated educational expenses.

Exclusions: Grants are not given for school fees.

Annual grant total: In 2006/07 the trust had assets of £928,000 and an income of £30,000. The trust made grants totalling £4,100 and gave £28,000 in interest-free loans.

Applications: In writing to the correspondent requesting an application form. Applications are considered quarterly.

Correspondent: Gillian Pole, BALPA House, 5 Heathrow Boulevard, 278 Bath Road, West Drayton, UB7 0DQ (020 8476 4000; Fax: 020 8476 4077; email: balpa@balpa.org)

Artists

The Artists' Orphan Fund

Eligibility: The fund offers grants to help with maintenance expenses and educational costs for children of a professional artist (for example painter, sculptor, illustrator or designer), where either one or both parents have died. Applicants must be in full-time education and under the age of 25.

Types of grants: Recurrent grants according to need. Individuals can be supported throughout their education but they must reapply each year.

Exclusions: Funding is rarely provided for private or boarding education, but will be considered when a child has a scholarship, considerable bursary or the family circumstances present a genuine need for the child to be living outside of the family unit.

Annual grant total: In 2006/07 the trust had an income of £57,000 and a total expenditure of £63,000. Grants paid to applicants totalled £415,000, including associated costs

Applications: In writing to the correspondent, including career details of qualifying parent and the present financial position of the family. Appropriate applicants will receive a form which they will need to complete, and are considered upon receipt.

Correspondent: Miss April Connett-Dance, Secretary, Burlington House, Piccadilly, London W1J 0BB (020 7734 1193; Fax: 020 7734 9966)

Other information: The fund also invites grant applications from professional artists such as painters, sculptors, designers (and their widows) who through accident, old age or illness are unable to continue working. Grants are awarded for one year at a time and applicants are welcome to submit a second application, through which funding will be continued for a further year if necessary, at the discretion of the Council.

Equity Trust Fund

Eligibility: Professional performers (under Equity or ITC contracts) with a minimum of 10 years experience as an adult (work performed below the age of 16 is not counted).

Types of grants: Grants to enable people to pursue a new career. They can be used towards books, equipment, instruments, fees, living expenses or childcare.

Exclusions: No grants to amateur performers, musicians or drama students.

Annual grant total: In 2006/07 the fund had assets of £9.7 million and an income of £400,000. Grants to individuals totalled £157,000 and were divided as follows:

- education – £91,000
- welfare and benevolence – £62,000
- John Fernald award – £5,000.

Applications: On a form available from the correspondent. There are normally three meetings each year, with the first one taking place normally around about the middle of May.

Correspondent: Keith Carter, Secretary, 222 Africa House, 64 Kingsway, London WC2B 6BD (020 7404 6041; Fax: 020 7831 4953; email: keith@ equitytrustfund.org.uk; website: www. equitytrustfund.org.uk)

Other information: Grants are also made to organisations.

Kraszna-Krausz Foundation

Eligibility: Writers, film-makers and researchers involved in the fields of photography or the moving image. Projects must be based in the UK.

Types of grants: One-off grants in the range of £1,000 and £3,000, with a maximum of £5,000, to encourage a higher standard of research, publishing and other projects. Grants are not made for courses but for living expenses and study or travel overseas for research purposes.

Annual grant total: About £14,000.

Applications: Application forms are available from the correspondent. They are considered twice a year – applications for consideration in July should reach the foundation by 1 May and those for consideration in December by 1 October.

Correspondent: Angela English, Administrator, 3 Downscourt Road, Purley, Surrey, CR8 1BE (0208 668 3375; email: grants@k-k.org.uk.; website: www.k-k.org.uk)

Peggy Ramsay Foundation

Eligibility: Writers for the stage who have been produced publicly, are 'of promise' and are in need of time to write which they cannot afford, or are in need of other assistance. Applicants must live in the British Isles (including Republic of Ireland and the Channel Islands).

Types of grants: One-off grants. Individual awards rarely exceed £5,000 for writing time or £1,000 for word processors.

Exclusions: No grants towards production costs or to writers who have not been produced. Drama students or other artists learning their trade are not supported, just experienced writers who could not otherwise follow their career. No grants are made for writing not intended for the theatre.

Annual grant total: In 2007 the foundation had assets of £5.4 million and an income of £268,000. There were 90 grants made to individuals totalling £223,000.

Applications: Apply by writing a short letter to the correspondent, submitted with a CV directly by the individual. Scripts and publicity material must not be included. Applications, which are always acknowledged, are considered four or five times a year.

Correspondent: G Laurence Harbottle, Trustee, Hanover House, 14 Hanover Square, London W1S 1HP (020 7667 5000; Fax: 020 7667 5100; email: laurence. harbottle@harbottle.com; website: www. peggyramsayfoundation.org)

Other information: Grants to organisations totalled £77,000.

TACT Education Fund

Eligibility: Dependants of members of the theatrical profession who are over the age of 18 and who wish to pursue higher education in the arts.

Types of grants: Grants of up to £1,200 to students in further and higher education, including mature students and postgraduates.

Exclusions: Grants are not available for drama school fees or study abroad.

Annual grant total: In 2007/08 the fund had an income of £24,000 and a total expenditure of £34,000.

Applications: On a form available from the correspondent. Applications are to be submitted directly by the individual for consideration at any time, and should include details of the theatrical parent's cv.

Correspondent: Robert Ashby, The Actors Charitable Trust, 58 Bloomsbury Street, London, WC1B 3QT (020 7636 7868; email: robert@tactactors.org; website: www.tactactors.org)

Bankers

The Bankers Benevolent Fund

Eligibility: Children of bank employees who have died or are not able to work because of ill health.

Types of grants: Help towards the education and maintenance of children who are at school or are studying for a first degree or similar qualification. Most children helped are being educated within the state system, with help towards all normal schooling expenses including fares,

lunches, sports equipment, school trips and extra-curricular activities together with regular clothing allowances and, to those on low incomes, additional maintenance allowances. Grants are given towards school fees only in certain limited circumstances. Help is also given to students in higher/further education to supplement loans. Grants are usually reviewed annually.

Exclusions: The fund does not provide assistance for debt repayment, business ventures, private medical treatment or situations where statutory or other sources of funding are available.

Annual grant total: In 2006/07 the trust had assets of £45 million and an income of £2.9 million. The fund gave £548,000 in grants for educational purposes, including scholarships and grants for arts, sports and musical education projects.

Applications: Application forms are available from the fund; they can also be downloaded from its website. Once the form has been received it will be reviewed by staff. Additional contact may be required to obtain further information or clarification. The trustees meet quarterly to consider new cases.

Correspondent: The Clerk, Pinners Hall, 105–108 Old Broad Street, London EC2N 1EX (020 7216 8981; email: infor@ bbfund.org.uk; website: www.bbfund.org. uk)

Other information: The fund also gives to older people for welfare purposes (£532,000)

The Alfred Foster Settlement

Eligibility: Employees and former employees of banks and their dependants who are in need. Applicants must be students aged under 28 years.

Types of grants: One-off grants, for example, to help with university fees, books, travel costs and living expenses while in further education.

Annual grant total: In 2006/07 the trust had an income of £26,000 and a total expenditure of £22,000. Charitable expenditure came to £15,000.

Applications: In writing to the correspondent. Applications can be submitted directly by the individual or through the school/college or educational welfare agency.

Correspondent: Russell Jones, Barclays Bank Trust Co. Ltd, Executorship & Trustee Service, Osborne Court, Gadbrook Park, Rudheath, Northwich, CW9 7UE

Barristers

The Barristers' Benevolent Association

Eligibility: The dependants of past or present practising members of the Bar in England and Wales, who are in need.

Types of grants: Educational grants for dependants are only given in the most exceptional circumstances, for example where the death or disability of a barrister leaves his or her children stranded in mid-education. Grants or loans are given to schoolchildren towards fees, books, educational outings, maintenance or school uniforms or clothing; students in further/higher education for help with books, fees and living expenses; mature students for books, travel, fees or childcare; and people starting work for books, equipment, clothing and travel.

Annual grant total: In 2006 the trust had an income of £758,000 and a total expenditure of £584,000. A total of £278,000 was given in welfare and educational grants. No recent information was available.

Applications: In writing to the correspondent. Applications are considered throughout the year and should include the name and address of the chambers where they last practised as a barrister.

Correspondent: Janet South, Director, 14 Gray's Inn Square, London WC1R 5JP (020 7242 4764 / 0207 242 4761; email: enquiries@the-baa.com; website: www.the-bba.com)

Book retail

The Book Trade Benevolent Society

Eligibility: People in need who have worked in the book trade in the UK for at least one year (normally publishing/ distribution/book-selling), and their dependants.

Types of grants: One-off and recurrent grants of up to £1,500 are given to help retrain people from the book trade who have been made redundant. These grants are given to mature students where a welfare need is evident. The society is a relief-in-need charity, with retraining of such people as part of their work. Therefore, general educational grants are generally not made.

Annual grant total: In 2006/07 the society had assets of £1.9 million and an income of £684,000. Grants were made to 81

individuals totalling £92,000, and were broken down as follows:

- Welfare and financial support, £82,000
- Medical costs, £6,700
- Training, retraining and education, £3,500.

Applications: On a form available from the correspondent. Applications can be submitted by the individual or through a recognised referral agency (social worker, Citizens Advice, doctor and so on) and are considered quarterly.

Correspondent: David Hicks, Chief Executive, The Foyle Centre, The Retreat, Abbots Road, Kings Langley, Hertfordshire WD4 8LT (01923 263128; Fax: 01923 270732; email: btbs@ booktradecharity.demon.co.uk; website: www.booktradecharity.demon.co.uk)

Coalminers

The Miners' Welfare National Educational Fund

Eligibility: People who are at least 17 years old and (i) employed in the coalmining industry of Great Britain (including any activity conducted by British Coal) or who have ceased to be so employed by reason of age or disability or who, having ceased to be so employed for any other reason, have not subsequently changed their occupation; or (ii) the dependant sons and daughters (and other dependants) of those described above.

Types of grants: Grants of not more than £500 a year to help with the costs of taking educational courses at degree or equivalent level. For applicants in category (i) above, all full-time courses and Open University courses are eligible. Otherwise the course must be one for which local education authority grants are mandatory. Grants are only considered for those taking postgraduate courses directly after and related to a first degree where it is essential for entry into a profession.

Annual grant total: About £50,000.

Applications: Application forms are available from the correspondent to be submitted by the individual's school/college for considered at any time from August through to March. Confirmation of A-level results and confirmation of award of student support must be included.

Correspondent: V O S Jones, Secretary, The Old Rectory, Rectory Drive, Whiston, Rotherham, South Yorkshire S60 4JG (01709 728115; website: www.ciswo.org.uk)

Other information: Grants awarded are not recurrent. Applicants must reapply in each academic year of an eligible course.

Commerce

The George Drexler Foundation

Eligibility: People who have a direct link with commerce, i.e. who have owned and run their own commercial business. Applicants whose parents or grandparents have this link can also be supported. This does not include professional people such as doctors, lawyers, dentists, architects or accountants. No exceptions can be made. Preference is given to schoolchildren with serious family difficulties so that the child has to be educated away from home, and to people with special educational needs.

Types of grants: One-off and recurrent grants of £500 to £6,000. Schoolchildren, further and higher education students, including mature students, and postgraduates can receive support for books, fees and study or travel abroad. Grants can also be made to; schoolchildren for uniforms or other school clothing and educational outings in the UK; further and higher education students for maintenance/living expenses and equipment/instruments; and mature students and postgraduates for maintenance/living expenses.

Annual grant total: In 2006/07 the trust had assets of £6.6 million and an income of £246,000. Grants awarded totalled £220,000, of which £56,000 was allocated for welfare purposes and £114,000 was given in educational grants to individuals

Applications: On a form available from the correspondent, submitted directly by the individual, enclosing an sae. Applications should be submitted in May for consideration in June/July.

Correspondent: The Trustee, 35–43 Lincolns Inn Fields, London, WC2A 3PE (020 7869 6080; email: ljary@rcseng.ac.uk)

The Ruby & Will George Trust

Eligibility: The dependants of people in need who have been or who are employed in commerce. Preference is given to people who live in the north of England.

Types of grants: One-off and recurrent grants of up to £2,000 towards maintenance and fees. Grants relating to fees are usually paid directly to the educational establishment. Occasionally assistance with maintenance, books and basic travel expenses will be awarded.

Exclusions: Expeditions, study visits and student exchanges are not funded.

Annual grant total: In 2006/07 the trust had assets of £3.4 million, an income of £115,000 and a total expenditure of £144,000. Grants totalling £91,000 were made to 83 individuals.

Applications: In writing to the correspondent. Submission of applications are to be made at least 2 weeks in advance of quarterly meetings, these are to be held usually in January, April, July & October. Specific deadline dates can be obtained from the Administrator.

Correspondent: David John Simpson, Administrator, 18 Ghyll Edge, Lancaster Park, Morpeth, Northumberland NE61 3QZ (01670 516657; email: davejsimpson@btopenworld.com)

Other information: Grants are also given to institutions (£2,200 in 2006/07).

Farming

The Dairy Crest and NFU Fund

Eligibility: Children of farmers, ex-farmers, smallholders and ex-smallholders, 16 years old or over, living in Cornwall, Devon, Dorset and Somerset. The applicant must be studying a dairy-related topic in further education, which will contribute to the future industry.

Types of grants: This fund aims to promote and encourage 'practical and scientific education in dairying and dairy farming'. Grants usually range from £200 up to £2,000 a year and can be for books, fees, equipment and maintenance/living expenses.

Annual grant total: In 2006/07 the trust had an income of £21,000 and a total expenditure of £24,000. The trust usually distributes the majority of its income in grants to individuals.

Applications: On a form available from the correspondent; two references will be required. Applications should be submitted by the individual by August each year; for consideration in September.

Correspondent: Mrs C Booth, Higher Moorlake Cottage, Crediton, Devon, EX17 5EL (01363 776623)

Fire service

The Fire Services National Benevolent Fund

Eligibility: Orphans who have lost a parent who was a member, or in certain circumstances was a retired member, of the Fire Service, or widows/widowers whose spouse was a member, or in certain circumstances was a retired member, of the Fire Service.

Types of grants: Grants of £550 to £850 to help with items such as books for students in higher or further education. Grants may be paid directly to the student, but do take into account parental/guardian's financial status.

Exclusions: Grants are not made to clear debts.

Annual grant total: In 2006/07 the fund gave £416,000 in grants to individuals, of which £6,000 was given for educational purposes.

Applications: In writing to the benevolent fund officer at the local county fire brigade headquarters, or to the address below. Applicants should contact the fund before they apply.

Correspondent: Grants and Services, The Fire Fighters Charity, Copenhagen Court, 32 New Street, Basingstoke, RG21 7DT (0800 389 8820; email: cdonohue@ firefighterscharity.org.uk; website: www. firefighterscharity.org.uk)

Other information: This fund was founded in 1943 to help all types of fire-fighters and their widows or widowers and young dependants. It also provides short-term convalescence, rehabilitation, therapy and sheltered housing, but does not have residential or nursing homes.

Forestry/timber

Confederation of Forest Industries

Eligibility: Members of the Forestry and Timber Association (or ConFor) and their dependants who are in need. Members must have been involved with the association for at least one year.

Types of grants: One-off grants are made towards educational, training or professional development purposes in the field of forestry.

Annual grant total: This fund has an average income of around £4,500 per year. Grant giving has recently decreased to around £200 a year for both educational and welfare grants. This is not due to a lack of funding but declining applications.

Applications: Application forms are available from the correspondent.

Correspondent: Ms J Karthaus, Woodland Place, Belford, Northumberland NE70 7QA (01668 213937; Fax: 01668 213555; email: jane@apfs. demon.co.uk; website: www.confor.org.uk)

Other information: Anyone can join ConFor who has an interest in trees, woodlands or timber.

Furnishing trade

Furnishing Trades Benevolent Association

Eligibility: Children whose parent (or guardian) are, or have been, employed in the UK furnishing industry for a minimum of two years, and is permanently or temporarily unable to maintain them.

Types of grants: One-off grants averaging £250 are given for uniforms, books, instruments, equipment and maintenance and living expenses. Preference is given to children with special needs.

Annual grant total: In 2006 the association had assets of £5.6 million and an income of £358,000. Grants were made to 280 individuals totalling £116,000.

Applications: To request an application pack write, email or telephone the association giving a brief summary of your employment history and the reasons why you are applying for financial or medical assistance. Applications should be submitted through a third party such as a social worker, teacher, citizen's advice bureau or school.

Correspondent: Welfare Officer, Furniture Maker's Hall, 12 Austin Friars, London, EC2N 2HE (020 7256 5954; Fax: 020 7256 6035; email: welfare@ftba.co. uk; website: www.ftba.co.uk)

Other information: The trust states that grants are mainly for the relief of need; education grants are of secondary importance.

Gardeners

The Royal Fund for Gardeners' Children

Eligibility: Children in need, particularly orphans, whose parents are or have been employed full-time in horticulture. The associated Constance Spry Fund can assist such children who go on to full-time further education. Assistance is also given to children of horticulturalists who are living with a mental or physical disability. Applicants should be under 25.

Types of grants: Quarterly allowances to orphaned children who are still in full-time education. Grants can be given towards school uniforms, books, educational outings, maintenance fees, travel expenses, school fees and study and travel overseas. Each case is assessed individually by the executive committee.

Annual grant total: In 2007 the fund had assets of £970,000 and an income of £120,000. Grants were made to 79 individuals for educational and welfare needs totalling £63,000. Of this, £58,000 was given to orphaned children, while £5,000 was awarded to children with special needs.

Applications: Ideally, applicants should obtain an application form to be submitted at least two weeks before one of the committee meetings, which take place in March, September and November each year. Applications can be submitted directly by the individual or through the individual's school/college or educational welfare agency, with details of parents' and/or applicant's income and expenditure.

Correspondent: Kate Wallis, 10 Deards Wood, Knebworth, Hertfordshire, SG3 6PG (01438 813939; Fax: 01438 813939; email: rfgc@btinternet. com; website: www.rfgc.org.uk)

Other information: This charity was formerly known as the 'Royal Gardeners' Orphan Fund'.

The Constance Spry Fund

Eligibility: See the entry for the The Royal Fund for Gardeners' Children.

Horse-racing and breeding

National Trainers' Federation Charitable Trust

Eligibility: People in need who work or have worked in the thoroughbred horse-racing and breeding industry, and their dependants.

Types of grants: Mainly ongoing grants towards course fees for retraining.

Annual grant total: About £3,000.

Applications: In writing to the correspondent, with details of the course you wish to pursue, proof you have approached your local authority for a grant and been unsuccessful, and two referees who are authorities connected with the industry.

Correspondent: The Trustees, 20b Park Lane, Newmarket, Suffolk CB8 8QD (01638 560763; email: info@racingwelfare. co.uk; website: www.racingwelfare.co.uk)

Insurance

The Insurance Charities – The Orphans' Fund

Eligibility: University students whose parents have been in the insurance industry for at least five years.

Types of grants: Help may be given to first degree students towards day-to-day expenses.

Annual grant total: In 2006/07 the charities had assets of £26 million and an income of £1.2 million. Grants were made totalling £965,000.

Applications: An initial form can be completed online, or can be downloaded from the trust's website.

Correspondent: Mrs A J Thornicroft, 20 Aldermanbury, London EC2V 7HY (020 7606 3763; Fax: 020 7600 1170; email: info@theinsurancecharities.org.uk; website: www.theinsurancecharities.org.uk)

Meat Trade

The Worshipful Company of Butchers' Educational Charity

Eligibility: People involved in the meat trade who are studying courses related to the trade.

Types of grants: One-off grants towards further and higher education fees.

Annual grant total: In 2006/07 the trust had assets of £339,000 and an income of £64,000. The trust gave £550 in grants to individuals.

Applications: In writing to the correspondent. Applications should be submitted directly by the individual for consideration monthly.

Correspondent: The Clerk, Butchers' Hall, 87 Bartholomew Close, London EC1A 7EB (020 7600 4106; Fax: 020 7606 4108; email: clerk@butchershall.com; website: www.butchershall.com)

Other information: The trust also gives to organisations (£3,700).

Media

The Chartered Institute of Journalists Orphan Fund

Eligibility: Orphaned children of institute members who are in need, aged between 5 and 22 and in full-time education.

Types of grants: Grants are given for schoolchildren towards the cost of school clothing, books, educational outings and school fees. Grants are also given to students in further or higher education towards the cost of books, help with fees/living expenses and study or travel abroad. Grants are also given for birthdays, Christmas and summer holidays.

Annual grant total: Previously grants to individuals totalled around £32,000.

Applications: Applications should be submitted by the child's surviving parent or other third party. Applications are considered quarterly.

Correspondent: Norman Barlett, The Honorary Treasurer, 2 Dock Offices, Surrey Quays Road, London SE16 2XU (020 7252 1187; email: memberservices@cioj.co.uk; website: www.cioj.co.uk)

Other information: This fund also gives grants for relief-in-need purposes.

The Grace Wyndham Goldie (BBC) Trust Fund

Eligibility: Employees and ex-employees engaged in radio or television broadcasting or an associated activity, and their dependants.

Types of grants: One-off grants to help with educational costs such as school or college fees, travelling expenses, school uniforms, books and equipment, living expenses or to supplement existing educational awards.

Exclusions: Recurrent grants are not made.

Annual grant total: In 2006 the trust had assets of £1.3 million and an income of £40,000. The trust awarded 16 grants totalling £35,000, of which £34,000 went in 15 grants for educational purposes.

Applications: On a form available from the correspondent. The deadline for applications is 31 July; they are considered in September. As the income of the fund is limited, and to ensure help can be given where it is most needed, applicants must be prepared to give full information about their circumstances.

Correspondent: Christine Geen, BBC Pension and Benefits Centre, Broadcasting House, Cardiff CF5 2YQ (029 2032 3772; Fax: 029 2032 2408; website: www.bbc.co.uk/charityappeals/grant/gwg.shtml)

The Journalists' Charity

Eligibility: The dependants of journalists in need.

Types of grants: This fund mainly supports welfare, not educational causes, although there is often some crossover.

Exclusions: Vocational support will only be made if the parent of the child is/was a journalist and there is evidence of need.

Annual grant total: In 2007 the charity had assets of £15 million and an income of approximately £1 million. Grants were made to 158 individuals totalling £335,000.

Applications: On a form available from the correspondent, to be submitted directly by the individual or a family member. Applications should include details of the career in journalism and are considered monthly.

Correspondent: David Ilott, Director and Secretary, Dickens House, 35 Wathen Road, Dorking, Surrey RH4 1JY (01306 887511; Fax: 01306 888212; email: enquiries@journalistscharity.org.uk; website: www.journalistscharity.org.uk)

Other information: The fund also runs residential homes in Dorking.

Medicine

The Chartered Society of Physiotherapy Members' Benevolent Fund

Eligibility: Members and past members of the society, including full and assistant members and students.

Types of grants: Grants towards retraining costs.

Exclusions: No grants towards payment of debts or when statutory help is available.

Annual grant total: In 2006 the society had assets of £1.3 million and an income of £93,000. Grants were made to 40 beneficiaries totalling £52,000.

Applications: On a form available from the correspondent. Applications should be submitted directly by the individual or by a third party such as a carer or partner. Applications are considered in January, April, July and October.

Correspondent: Christine Cox, 14 Bedford Row, London WC1R 4ED (020 7306 6642; Fax: 020 7306 6643; email: coxc@csp.org.uk; website: www.csp.org.uk)

The Dain Fund

Eligibility: Children of doctors or deceased doctors (not nurses or physiotherapists and so on) who are at a critical stage of their education and are in need.

Types of grants: The principal objective and activity of the fund is to assist with the educational expenses of doctors' children when a family crisis threatens the continuity of that education.

The fund gives one-off and recurrent grants to;

- Children who are in private education already and approaching public examinations
- Children in state school towards the costs of school uniforms and field trips
- Originally the fund was intended only to help schoolchildren but, now that statutory grants have been withdrawn for students in higher education, a small number of awards are being made to support undergraduates. If students have been supported by the fund throughout their degree course, they may receive an interest-free loan for the final year instead of a grant.

Normally support will be given to only one child in a family.

Annual grant total: In 2006 the fund had assets of £1.3 million and an income of £77,000, with grants to individuals totalling £11,000.

Applications: On a form available from the correspondent, to be submitted directly by the individual or a parent/guardian or through a social worker, Citizens Advice or other welfare agency

Correspondent: J M Frostick, BMA Charities, BMA House, Tavistock Square, London WC1H 9JP (020 7383 6142; Fax: 020 7554 6334; email: info. bmacharities@bma.org.uk; website: www. bma.org.uk)

Other information: This fund is designed to help families in an emergency and is not a scholarship trust.

The Hume Kendall Educational Trust

Eligibility: Children of doctors or dentists whose fathers have died or are unable to work.

Types of grants: Contributions towards the cost of the education of beneficiaries up to and including first degree level.

Annual grant total: In 2006/07 the trust had an income of £4,600 and a total expenditure of £6,700. Grants totalled about £700.

Applications: In writing to the correspondent. Applications can be made at any time.

Correspondent: H M Green, Hon. Secretary, c/o Finance Department, King's College London, Room G37, James Clerk Maxwell Building, 57 Waterloo Road, London SE1 8WA

The Royal Medical Benevolent Fund

Eligibility: Registered medical practitioners, their wives, husbands, widows, widowers and dependant children who are in need and are resident in Great Britain. The registered medical practitioner's name must appear in a General Medical Council (GMC) register. Preference is given to schoolchildren with serious family difficulties resulting in them being educated away from home and children with special educational needs.

There is also a medical student bursary scheme which helps medical students in their second or third year of study.

Types of grants: Schoolchildren may receive help towards school uniform and clothing, books and travel to school. People starting work can be awarded grants for books, equipment/instruments and clothing. In exceptional cases, the fund may assist with fees and expenses.

Bursaries of £2,000 each are awarded for three academic terms. Beneficiaries are expected to attend an initial induction event, an end-of-year review, promote the fund to other medical students and undertake research into medical student debt.

Exclusions: Children of working parents cannot be considered for help, nor can children who are not (or whose parents are not) already beneficiaries of the fund. No assistance is given with any of the following: second degree/postgraduate courses; fees/living expenses; travel abroad; and PLAB (Professional & Linguistic Assessment Board) and associated fees/ living expenses for doctors not on the GMC register.

Annual grant total: In 2007/08 the fund had assets of £24 million and an income of £4.6 million. Grants were made to individuals totalling £899,000.

Applications: For general educational grants: On a form available from the correspondent, which can be submitted either directly by the individual or through a medical colleague or other medical and general charities. Applications are considered almost every month. Two references are taken up (at least one of which should be from a medical practitioner). All applicants are visited before a report is submitted to the case committee. Income/capital and expenditure are fully investigated, with similar rules applying as for those receiving Income Support.

For bursaries: on a form available from the correspondent, to be returned by early February each year. Applicants are interviewed before a bursary is awarded (reasonable travel expenses paid).

Correspondent: The Senior Case Manager, 24 King's Road, Wimbledon, London SW19 8QN (020 8540 9194; Fax: 020 8542 0494; email: info@rmbf.org; website: www.rmbf.org)

Other information: Voluntary visitors liaise between beneficiaries and the office.

The Royal Medical Foundation

Eligibility: Dependants, aged up to 18, of medical practitioners who are in need.

Types of grants: Grants of between £500 and £15,000 are given to schoolchildren and college students towards fees. Preference is given to pupils with family difficulties so that they have to be educated away from home, pupils with special educational needs and medical students.

Annual grant total: In 2006/07 the foundation gave grants to individuals totalling £268,000, which were broken down as follows:

- Foundation Scholars at Epsom College (two awards) £34,000
- Educational and Maintenance awards (40 awards) £195,000
- Medical Charitable Gifts (24 awards) £40,000

Applications: On a form available from the correspondent, for consideration throughout the year. Applications can be submitted either by the individual or a family member, through a third party such as a social worker or teacher, or through an organisation such as Citizens Advice or a school. The trust advises applicants to be honest about their needs. All applicants are means tested.

Correspondent: John Higgs and Nickie Colville, College Road, Epsom, Surrey KT17 4JQ (01372 821010; Fax: 01372 821013; email: caseworker@ royalmedicalfoundation.org; website: www.royalmedicalfoundation.org)

Metal trades

The Institution of Materials, Minerals & Mining

Eligibility: Members of the institution and former members and their dependants.

Types of grants: One-off grants, recurrent grants and one-off grants in kind towards educational needs. Grants are made to schoolchildren for fees and to college students for fees, books and equipment/ instruments.

Annual grant total: In 2007 the charity had assets of £10 million and an income of £5.9 million. Direct charitable expenditure totalled £985,000.

Applications: On a form available from the correspondent for consideration at any time.

Correspondent: R Milbank, c/o The Institution of Materials, Minerals & Mining, 1 Carlton House Terrace, London, SW1Y 5DB (website: www.iom3.org)

Mining

Mining Institute of Scotland Trust

Eligibility: Members or former members of the Mining Institute of Scotland who are taking a university course with a mining element in it. The trust has a preference for supporting people from Fife in the first instance, and secondly, those who are of Scottish origin, although other people can be considered. Applicants who are not already members of the institute will be invited to join. Members of the Mining Institute of Scotland, and their dependants, can also receive 'hardship grants'.

Types of grants: Educational grants are one-off or recurrent, normally of £1,500 a year. A recent grant was made, for example, towards an engineering course that had a mining element to it. Grants can be for the student's general upkeep, or for course fees, and so on.

Hardship grants are one-off or recurrent of up to £1,000 a year. A recent grant was made, for example, to the son of a member for travel to university.

Annual grant total: The trust has about £25,000 available to give in grants each year for both education and hardship.

Applications: In writing to the correspondent in the first instance, to request an application form.

Correspondent: The Secretary, 2 Ashfield Gardens, Kelty, Fife, KY4 0JY

Other information: Schools are also supported.

Patent Agents

The Chartered Institute of Patent Agents' Incorporated Benevolent Association

Eligibility: British members and former members of the institute, and their dependants.

Types of grants: One-off and recurrent grants or loans according to need.

Annual grant total: In 2007 the association had assets of £976,000 and an income of £53,000. Educational grants totalled £37,000.

Applications: In writing to the correspondent, marked 'Private and Confidential'. Applications can be submitted at any time.

Correspondent: D R Chandler, Secretary of The Chartered Institute of Patent Agents' Incorporated Benevolent Association, c/o Chartered Institute of Patent Agents, 95 Chancery Lane, London WC2A 1DT

Other information: Grants are also made for welfare purposes.

Police

The Gurney Fund for Police Orphans

Eligibility: Children under 18 of deceased or incapacitated police officers from 22 subscribing forces in southern and south midland areas of England and South and Mid-Wales, excluding the Metropolitan and City of London Police Forces.

Types of grants: Grants are available for students up to 18 years old; applications from older students will be considered in certain circumstances at the discretion of the trustees. Grants can be for books, uniforms, equipment, educational travel, school trips, music lessons, sport and other extra-curricular activities. Grants can be both one-off cash grants for amounts of up to £1,800 each, or recurrent, ranging from between £10 and £60 per week.

Exclusions: No grants for school fees or skiing holidays, but in the case of school fees exceptions can be made for children with special educational needs. The fund does not make grants to beneficiaries who go on to higher education. It may, however, consider assisting with the payment of annual tuition fees and, or, a grant towards the cost of books and ancillary equipment.

Annual grant total: In 2007/08 the fund had assets of £5.9 million and an income of £545,000. A total of £28,000 was distributed in grants to 54 individuals.

Applications: Applications can be made at any time and are considered in February, May, August and November. They must include a copy of the child's birth certificate and successful applicants will be asked to complete an income and expenditure form and provide receipts when assistance with specific expenditure is requested. A force welfare officer or local representative then assesses the application for a later decision by the trustees.

Correspondent: Miss C McNicol, The Director, 9 Bath Road, Worthing, West Sussex, BN11 3NU (01903 237256)

The National Police Fund

Eligibility: Children of serving, retired or deceased members of police forces in England, Wales and Scotland who are aged over 18 years.

Types of grants: One-off and recurrent grants for general assistance to students in further or higher education, up to a maximum of £800. Grants are sometimes, though rarely, given to mature students and younger children.

Annual grant total: £90,000 in 2006.

Applications: Application forms can be obtained from the welfare officer of the police force where the officer is serving or has served. Applications must be returned by the individual in November for consideration in December. A reference from the student's college or university must be included.

Correspondent: Hannah Muella, National Police Fund, 3 Mount Mews, High Street, Hampton TW12 2SH (020 8941 7661; Fax: 020 8979 4323; website: www. nationalpolicefund.org.uk/)

Police Dependants' Trust

Eligibility: (i.) Dependants of current police officers or former police officers who have died from injuries received in the execution of duty.

(ii.) Police officers or former police officers incapacitated as a result of injury received in the execution of duty, or their dependants.

Types of grants: One-off grants ranging from £120 to £100,000, averaging about £1,400 each. Grants are available for retraining and to the children of police officers who are at school or university. Under the Children's grant scheme funding is given for the purchase of sports and computer equipment, musical instruments and other educational facilities. However, it is important to note that this is primarily a relief-in-need charity, so most of the grants are given for welfare rather than educational purposes.

Annual grant total: In 2006/07 the trust had assets of £28 million and an income of £1.5 million. Grants totalled £2.3 million and were distributed as follows:

Type	No.
Maintenance Grants	311
Children's grants	292
Special Purpose Grants	348
Holiday Grants	689
Funeral Grants	2

Applications: On a form available from the correspondent, to be submitted through one of the force's welfare officers. Applications are generally considered every two months although urgent cases can be addressed between meetings.

Correspondent: David French, Chief Executive, 3 Mount Mews, High Street, Hampton, Middlesex TW12 2SH (020 8941 6907; Fax: 020 8979 4323; email: office@policedependantstrust.org. uk; website: www.policedependantstrust. org.uk)

Precious metals

The Johnson Matthey Educational Trust

Eligibility: People over the age of 16 with a parent or grandparent employed by Johnson Matthey or currently connected with the precious metals industry, and who are studying a scientific or technical subject.

Types of grants: Grants to college students and undergraduates for fees, books, equipment and maintenance/living expenses. Grants are usually for between £400 and £500.

Exclusions: Grants are not made to students studying second degrees or mature students.

Annual grant total: In 2006/07 the trust had an income of £24,000 and a total expenditure of £45,000.

Applications: On a form available from the correspondent. Applications should be submitted by the relevant parent or grandparent, if possible, on behalf of the individual in October for consideration in December. Advertisements appear in the relevant trade journals.

Correspondent: R Hewitt, Mr Roger Hewitt, Johnson Matthey Ltd, 4th Floor, 6-7 Cross Street, London, EC1N 8UA (020 7269 8124; email: hewittr@matthey. com)

Railway workers

Railway Benevolent Institution

Eligibility: Active and retired members of the British Railway Board, its subsidiaries and related organisations, and their spouses and children.

Types of grants: One-off grants ranging from £100 to £1,650 to schoolchildren, college students, people starting work and those with special educational needs towards uniforms, clothing, books and equipment and maintenance/living expenses.

Annual grant total: In 2007 the institution had assets of £4 million and an income of £390,000. Grants were made to over 700 individuals totalling £510,000, of which about £7,000 was awarded for educational purposes.

Applications: On a form available from the correspondent. Applications can be submitted either directly by the individual or family member, or through a third party such as a social worker, teacher or citizen's advice bureau. Applicants must be able to provide verification of railway service.

Correspondent: Keith Alldread, Electra Way, Crewe, Cheshire CW1 6HS (01270 251316; email: director@ railwaybenefitfund.org.uk; website: www. railwaybenefitfund.org.uk)

Other information: This is primarily a welfare charity, and these educational grants are part of its wider welfare work.

Religious workers

Children of the Clergy Trust

Eligibility: Children of deceased ministers of the Church of Scotland.

Types of grants: One-off or recurrent grants according to need. Previously grants have ranged from £500 to £1,000 for any educational need.

Annual grant total: Grants totalled around £2,000.

Applications: In writing to the correspondent. Applications should be submitted directly by the individual and should include information about the applicant's ministerial parent, general family circumstances and other relevant information.

Correspondent: Revd Iain U Thomson, The Manse, Manse Road, Kirkton of Skene, Westhill, Aberdeenshire AB32 6LX (01224 743277)

The Corporation of the Sons of the Clergy

Eligibility: Dependant children (under 25 years of age) of Anglican clergy of the dioceses of the UK and Ireland and of the diocese in Europe or of the widows/ widowers and separated or divorced spouses of such clergy. Grants are made only to the parent, not the child.

Types of grants: The corporation runs three different grant schemes; miscellaneous education grants, school fee grants for children attending independent schools and grants for children continuing in education after leaving school.

Miscellaneous education grant scheme:

The corporation is able to consider help in the following areas associated with the education of children over the age of 11 attending independent schools;

- school uniforms
- travel costs
- school trips
- language exchanges
- music lessons and musical instruments
- arts and sports activities.

School fee grants for children attending independent schools:

- Grants towards school fees can be considered where independent education is necessary for a clergy child.
- Grants are paid in instalments three times a year just before the beginning of the school terms and can be considered towards both tuition fees and boarding fees.
- The level of any grant is based upon the amount of fees the parents have to find after help from other sources, e.g. clergy bursary or scholarship, or other financial support. The normal grant is for a proportion of the net fees the applicant has to pay, up to a maximum limit which will be advised to applicants when the initial enquiry is made.
- Grants are awarded up to GCSE level and will only be considered under special circumstances after this age.
- Help is provided only where there is a demonstrable need for a child to be educated at the independent school in question, parental preference is not accepted.

Grants for children continuing in education after leaving school:

- The corporation is able to help with special outfits or equipment (but not books) required by a child who has left school and is undertaking vocational training.
- Maintenance grants can be considered for children of the clergy who are undergraduates, but not post-graduates, at university.

Exclusions: Grants are not awarded retrospectively and are generally based on one year's costs for any particular category.

Grants towards school fees are not normally available for those serving outside Great Britain and Ireland.

Children under 11 can only be considered for help towards the costs of school uniforms, school trips, and in some cases, if the child is a chorister (or has a probationary place) at a choir school for school fees.

Annual grant total: In 2006 the corporation had assets of £37 million and an income of £2 million. Grants awarded totalled £1 million, of which £516,000 was given for educational purposes

Applications: Before any grants are made, the corporation's educational advisor will usually contact the parents to discuss the application and needs of the child. Applicants will also be required to provide evidence of the need for independent education in support of their education, as parental preference is not accepted.

A certificate from the principal of the school is also needed before the grant is awarded. This should state that the pupil is, or will be, in attendance and not under notice of withdrawal, and that his or her progress is satisfactory. A copy of the relevant certificate will be issued with the application form.

Applications may be made during the year in which the child becomes 11 years of age and should ideally be submitted at least two clear terms before the grant is required. Initial enquiries may be made up to one year in advance of the proposed start date. When parents know they are likely to require help with school fees, they should approach the corporation before committing their child to a particular school. Failure to do so could result in disappointment, for both parents and child, if a grant is not awarded.

Grants are made for the school stated in the application only and are not transferable to any other school. Applicants are noted to advise the corporation at the earliest opportunity when a change of school is considered necessary.

Applications will need to be made each year for the renewal of any school fee grant

Correspondent: Robert Welsford, Registrar, 1 Dean Trench Street, Westminster, London SW1P 3HB (020 7799 3696; Fax: 020 7222 3468; email: registrar@sonsoftheclergy.org.uk; website: www.clergycharities.org.uk)

Other information: This charity incorporates The Clergy Orphan Corporation.

The EAC Educational Trust

Eligibility: Children of Church of England clergymen and of single parent families, aged 8 to 16. Preference is often given to the sons of clergymen.

Types of grants: Grants are almost exclusively for school fees including boarding. The trust has a close link with one particular school which specialises in educating the families of clergy. However, it accepts applications from other sources especially for the education of children in choir schools or other establishments with musical or dramatic emphasis. Individual grants almost never exceed one-third of the pupil's annual fees.

Annual grant total: In 2006/07 the trust had an income of £35,000 and gave £33,000 in grants to 31 individuals.

Applications: In writing to the correspondent. Applications are considered in the spring.

Correspondent: Julian Bewick, Garvards Cottage, Fullers Lane, Woolton Hill, Newbury, Berkshire, RG20 9TY (email: julian@bewick.org)

The Friends of the Clergy Corporation

Eligibility: The children of Anglican clergy who are under 25 years old and in need.

Types of grants: One off grants for school uniforms and undergraduate maintenance costs.

Annual grant total: In 2006/07 the trust had assets of £32 million and an income of £1.3 million. Grants totalling £642,000 were made to 686 individuals, including £111,000 for university maintenance and £35,000 for school clothing.

Applications: Applicants should first write to the correspondent (post or email) providing a brief summary of their circumstances and requesting an applications form. Forms should be completed as fully as possible and returned with all necessary supporting information.

Correspondent: Robert Welsford, Registrar, 1 Dean Trench Street, Westminster, London SW1P 3HB (020 7799 3696; Fax: 020 7222 3468; email: registrar@sonsoftheclergy.org.uk; website: www.clergycharities.org.uk)

Other information: This trust works very closely with The Corporation of the Sons of the Clergy, which gives for a wider range of educational needs. (See the entry in this section).

The Silcock Trust

Eligibility: Children of clergy with learning and/or other difficulties.

Types of grants: Help with maintenance and fees for schoolchildren. Preference will be given to children with serious family difficulties and special educational needs. Grants range from £250 to £2,000.

Annual grant total: In 2007 the trust had an income of £9,800 and a total expenditure of £6,200.

Applications: In writing to the correspondent.

Correspondent: A R T Hancock, Trustee, 4 Church Street, Old Isleworth, Middlesex TW7 6BH

Wells Clerical Charity

Eligibility: People in need who are under 25 years old who are children of members of clergy of the Church of England who are serving (or who have retired or died and last served) in the former archdeaconry of Wells as constituted in 1738.

Types of grants: Grants are made to support eligible individuals in preparing for entering any profession or employment by paying travel fees, the costs of clothing/uniform or maintenance costs.

Annual grant total: About £500.

Applications: In writing to the correspondent.

Correspondent: Revd Peter Thomas, The Rectory, Cat Street, Chiselborough, Stoke-Sub-Hamdon, Somerset, TA14 6TT

Women's Continuing Ministerial Education Trust (formerly The Deaconess Trust Funds)

Eligibility: Any woman, ordained or not, who is licensed into a nationally recognised ministry in the Church of England or the Scottish Episcopal Church (with the exception of Readers). Religious Sisters and retired clergy who are involved in active ministry may also apply

Types of grants: Grants usually help with continuing education expenses including part-time degree course fees, conferences, sabbaticals and workshops, and also some welfare needs. Grants are intended to supplement funds available from the applicant's diocese.

Annual grant total: About £50,000.

Applications: On a form available either as a download from the Church of England website, or via email on request. Applications must be endorsed by the Diocesan CME Officer or Dean of the Women's Ministry. Applications will normally be considered in March, June, September and December.

Correspondent: The Director of Ministry, Ministry Division, Church House, Great Smith Street, London SW1P 3AZ (020 7898 1410 or 1396; email: grants@c-of-e.org.uk; website: www.cofe.anglican.org)

Sales representatives

The Royal Pinner School Foundation

Eligibility: Children, preferably under 25, of travelling sales representatives and manufacturer's agents, where the family has experienced adversity or hardship.

Types of grants: Help is given in the following ways:

(i) Education: maintenance allowances or grants tenable at any school, college, university or other place of learning approved by the trustees. Most beneficiaries attend local state schools, or special schools in the case of disabled children, with parents awarded grants per term to cover books, equipment, travel and so on.

(ii) Careers: financial assistance, outfits, clothing, tools, instruments or books to help beneficiaries on leaving school, university or other educational establishment to prepare for or to assist their entry into a profession, trade or calling.

(iii) Travel: awards to assist beneficiaries to travel, whether in this country or abroad, in order to further their education and to participate in school-sponsored visits and field courses.

(iv) The arts: financial assistance to enable beneficiaries to study music or other arts.

(v) Continued education: in otherwise promoting the education (including social and physical training) of beneficiaries.

Exclusions: No loans or help for part-time education is given.

Annual grant total: In 2006/07 the foundation had net assets of £6.1 million and an income of £207,000. Total expenditure was £449,000, of which £362,000 was given in grants to individuals.

Applications: Application forms may be obtained from the correspondent, and should be submitted directly by the individual throughout the year. Note that no applications can be considered except those applying for the sons and daughters of travelling sales representatives or manufacturer's agents.

Correspondent: David Crawford, Secretary, 110 Old Brompton Road, South Kensington, London SW7 3RB (020 7373 6168)

Other information: The Royal Pinner School, which was formerly the Royal Commercial Travellers' Schools, was closed in 1967. The foundation was endowed with the proceeds of the closure.

Science

Royal Society of Chemistry Benevolent Fund

Eligibility: People who have been members of the society for the last three years, or ex-members who were in the society for at least 10 years, and their dependants, who are in need.

Types of grants: This fund is essentially a relief-in-need charity which also makes grants for education. It offers regular allowances, one-off grants and loans towards needs such as school uniforms and educational trips.

Exclusions: Anything which should be provided by the government or local authority is ineligible for funding.

Annual grant total: In 2007 the fund had an income of £39 million. Direct charitable expenditure totalled £181,000.

Applications: In writing or by telephone in the first instance, to the correspondent. Applicants will be requested to provide a financial statement (forms supplied by the secretary) and include a covering letter describing their application as fully as possible. Applications can be made either

directly by the individual, or through a third party such as a social worker or citizen's advice bureau. They are considered every other month, although urgent appeals can be considered at any time.

Correspondent: Jennifer Tunbridge, 290-292 Science Park, Milton Road, Cambridge, CB4 0WF (01223 432237; website: www.rsc.org)

Other information: The fund acts as an advisory service, as well as a grant provider.

Seafarers

Royal Liverpool Seamen's Orphan Institution

Eligibility: Children of deceased British merchant seafarers, who are of pre-school age or in full-time education (including further education). Help can also be given to seafarers who are at home caring for their family alone.

Types of grants: Monthly maintenance and annual clothing grants. Help may also be given for school fees.

Annual grant total: In 2007 the trust had assets of £3.5 million and an income of £270,000. Grants were made to 109 individuals totalling £275,000, of which £261,000 was given in maintenance grants and £13,000 was awarded in clothing grants. No grants were given for specifically for education in 2007 but this was due to a lack of suitable applications rather than a decision by the trust to discontinue its educational grants.

Applications: On a form available from the correspondent, to be considered at any time. Applications can be submitted either directly by the individual, or by the parent or guardian. They need to include confirmation of the seafarer's death, the child's birth certificate and proof of their educational status.

Correspondent: Linda Gidman, C/O Mrs Linda Gidman Room 19, 2nd Floor, Tower Building, 22 Water Street, Liverpool L3 1BA (0151 227 3417; Fax: 0151 227 3417; email: enquiries@rlsoi-uk.org; website: www.rlsoi-uk.org)

The Royal Merchant Navy School Foundation

Eligibility: Children in need who have a parent who has served or is serving as a seaman of any grade in the British merchant service for not less than six years. The child's parents are expected to contribute towards the educational costs of their children according to their means. All beneficiaries must have British nationality.

Full eligibility requirements are available from the correspondent.

Types of grants: One-off and recurrent grants are made. Grants are tailored to meet the needs of each individual and are usually paid directly to schools and colleges. Schoolchildren are awarded grants for general educational needs. College and vocational students may receive support for uniform and other school clothing, fees, books and equipment/instruments. Vocational students can also be awarded grants for maintenance/living expenses. Higher education students can receive help for fees, study or travel abroad, books, equipment and maintenance/living expenses.

Annual grant total: In 2006 the foundation had assets of £17.2 million and made grants totalling £230,000.

Applications: On a form available from the correspondent. Applications can be submitted at any time, either by the individual or their parent/guardian. Information about the parents' employment and financial situation is required. The application procedure normally includes a visit by the correspondent to the applicant's home.

Correspondent: The Secretary to the Trustees, Winnersh, Wokingham, Berkshire, RG41 5BG (0118 974 8380; email: sec@merchantnavy.org.uk; website: www.merchantnavy.org.uk)

The Sailors' Families' Society

Eligibility: People under 22 who are the dependants of UK seafarers who are in one-parent families with children aged below 16 years. Grants can also be given if the seafarer is in a two-parent family, but is permanently disabled. Usually, the only source of income for the family is Income Support or Incapacity Benefit.

Types of grants: (i) Discretionary clothing grants payable per child twice a year – £75 in August and £40 in January – to help children to start off the new school year and to buy a new winter coat. (ii) Educational holiday grants of up to £250 per child for holidays 'with a difference' (Outward Bound Courses, Sail Training Association trips) where the experience can be character building. (iii) Special equipment grants of up to £250 to help with non-academic abilities such as musical instruments and sports equipment, or for training in special skills which may benefit them in securing employment.

Annual grant total: In 2006/07 the society had assets of £2.8 million and an income of £498,000. The sum of £248,000 went to seafarers families.

Applications: On a form available from the correspondent, with details about children, income and expenditure, home environment and with copies of relevant certificates, for example, birth certificates and proof of seafaring service. Applications can be submitted directly by the individual or through a social worker, Citizens Advice, other welfare agency, or through seafaring organisations. Applications are considered every other month, beginning in February.

Correspondent: Ian Scott, Welfare Manager, Newland, Cottingham Road, Hull HU6 7RJ (01482 342331; Fax: 01482 447868; email: info@sailors-families.org.uk; website: www.sailors-families.org.uk)

Other information: This trust is essentially set up to give relief-in-need to seafarers, but some of their grants are of an educational nature.

Service/ex-service

The Army Benevolent Fund

Eligibility: Members and ex-members of the British Army and their dependants who are in need.

Types of grants: Mature student education/training grants for ex-soldiers who are unemployed and receiving training or education to enhance their prospect of gaining long-term employment. Such assistance is also available to soldiers who became disabled whilst with the army or after service and need to change their vocation.

Bursaries are also available in exceptional circumstances for the private education of dependants. Preference is given to orphans or children with only one parent, especially if the parent was killed in service. Other priorities include those where a parent is severely disabled or where the child has special needs, which may include where the home environment is such that the child has to be educated away from home.

Annual grant total: In 2006/07 the fund had assets of £41 million, an income of £7.6 million and a total expenditure of £8 million. Grants to individuals totalled £2 million.

Applications: Applications are considered as need arises, but all are reviewed annually in July. The fund does not deal directly with individual cases which should be referred initially to the appropriate corps or regimental association. Enquiries may be made directly to the fund to determine the appropriate corps or regimental association.

Correspondent: The Director of Grants and Welfare, Mountbarrow House, 6-20 Elizabeth Street, London, SW1W 9RB (0845 241 4820; email: enquiries@armybenfund.org; website: www.armybenfund.org)

Other information: The trust also gives grants to individuals for relief-in-need purposes and to organisations.

The Association of Royal Navy Officers (ARNO)

Eligibility: Officers and retired officers of the Royal Navy, Royal Marines, WRNS, QARNNS and their Reserves, who have joined and are members of the association, and their dependants.

Types of grants: One-off grants for educational purposes.

Annual grant total: In 2007 the trust had assets of £4.8 million, an income of £195,000 and a total expenditure of £228,000. Grants were made to 238 individuals totalling £133,000, of which £12,000 went towards paying the school fees of 11 individuals, and £4,000 was given towards scholarships. The remaining £117,000 was given in welfare grants.

Applications: In writing to the correspondent.

Correspondent: Cmdr Ridley, 70 Porchester Terrace, Bayswater, London W2 3TP (020 7402 5231; email: arno@eurosurf.com, rnbso@arno.org.uk; website: www.arno.org.uk)

Greenwich Hospital

Eligibility: Dependants, aged between 7 and 18 years old, of members and former members of the Royal Navy and Royal Marines.

Types of grants: Grants are given in the following categories:

(i) Grants to children of officers. Grants are available to help with the education and maintenance of the sons and daughters of deceased or distressed commissioned officers of the Royal Navy or Royal Marines.

(ii) Grants for children of ratings. Grants are available in aid of the education and maintenance of children of non-commissioned officers, petty-officers and men, the children of such people if they are deceased or distressed, and children of members of the Naval or Marine reserve forces killed in service.

Grants are up to a maximum of £1,500 a year for help with school or college fees. Preference is given to schoolchildren with serious family difficulties so the child has to be educated away from home.

Annual grant total: About £15,000.

Applications: On a form available from the correspondent.

Correspondent: John Gamp, Charity Director, Greenwich Hospital, 40 Queen Anne's Gate, London SW1H 9AP

Other information: Greenwich Hospital is a charity responsible to the Admiralty Board. Its main functions are supporting the Royal Hospital School near Ipswich (an independent boarding school for the children and grandchildren of seafarers) through meeting the cost of fees, building sheltered housing for elderly naval families, and granting pensions and bursaries to those in need.

Lloyd's Patriotic Fund

Eligibility: Children of ex-servicemen and women. Preference is given to school children with serious family difficulties so that the child has to be educated away from home, and people with special educational needs.

Types of grants: Bursaries ranging from £800 to £1,500 per year for school fees at nominated schools.

Annual grant total: In 2006/07 the fund had assets of £2.2 million and an income of £86,000. Grants for welfare purposes were made to 107 individuals totalling £53,000. A further £15,000 was distributed in 14 educational grants and £18,000 was given in 39 annuity payments.

Applications: Grants are awarded through the school and institutions listed below and all applications should be made through them.

- The Royal School, Haslemere
- The Royal Navy and Royal Marines Children's Fund
- The Royal Navy Scholarship Fund

Correspondent: The Secretary, Lloyd's, One Lime Street, London EC3M 7HA (020 7327 5921; email: communityaffairs@lloyds.com; website: www.lloyds.com)

Other information: The fund makes an annual grant to The Gurkha Welfare Trust.

The Officers' Association

Eligibility: The dependants of ex-officers who have held a commission in HM Forces.

Types of grants: Limited assistance for education and training needs will be given in only in exceptional circumstances. Help towards school fees will not normally be given unless the father has died, or become unemployed, at a stage in the children's education when it would seriously prejudice their future for them to be moved to non-fee-paying schools. In such cases, the applicant will be expected to apply first to the county education officer for a grant and to the school for reduced fees. Advice can be given about other charities specialising in educational assistance.

Exclusions: The association does not assist with the cost of further education.

Annual grant total: In 2006/07 the association had assets of £13.5 million and both an income and expenditure of £3.1 million. Grants were made to 842 individuals totalling £1.2 million and were given mainly for relief-in-need purposes.

Applications: On a form available from the Benevolence Secretary. Applications can be submitted either directly by the individual or via a third party. The association has a network of honorary representatives throughout the UK who will normally visit the applicant to discuss their problems and offer advice.

Correspondent: General Secretary, 1st Floor, Mountbarrow House, 6-20 Elizabeth Street, London SW1W 9RB (020 7808 4175 / 0845 873 7150; email: postmaster@oaed.org.uk; website: www.officersassociation.org.uk)

Other information: For applicants in Scotland: See entry for the Officers' Association Scotland.

Royal Air Force Benevolent Fund

Eligibility: The children (aged 8 to 18) of officers and airmen who have died or were severely disabled while serving in the Royal Air Force. Additionally, help may be considered in those circumstances where the parent dies or becomes severely disabled after leaving the Royal Air Force.

Types of grants: Grants to enable the education plans commenced or envisaged by the child's parents to be fulfilled. Help with the costs of boarding school fees may be given from the age of 8 years up to the end of secondary phase only (i.e. up to A-level examinations). Educational assistance from the fund is subject to a parental contribution which is reviewed annually. Grants range from £250 to over £20,000. Where, at the time of the parent's death or disablement, the child has already commenced a 'critical stage' of education at a fee-paying school, education assistance may be provided to the end of the GCSE or A-level course; where the child is not at a 'critical stage', appropriate assistance may be provided only to the end of the current academic year. A 'critical stage' is the two-year course leading to GCSE examinations or A-level examinations. Those children eligible for help with education costs will also be eligible for a modest scholarship to assist with their studies towards a first degree or equivalent. Children are given priority at the Duke of Kent School in Surrey.

Exclusions: No grants for private medical costs or for legal fees.

Annual grant total: In 2007 the fund had assets of £172 million and an income of £19 million. Grants totalled £18.3 million, of which £557,000 was given for educational purposes.

Applications: On a form available directly from the correspondent or on their website. Applications can be submitted by the individual or through an ex-service welfare agency such as RAFA or SSAFA. The fund runs a free helpline which potential applicants are welcome to call for advice and support on the application process. Applications are considered on a continual basis.

Correspondent: The Welfare Director, 67 Portland Place, London W1B 1AR (0800 169 2942; email: info@rafbf.org.uk; website: www.raf-benfund.org.uk)

Other information: The fund maintains a short-term care home in Sussex and a further three homes in Northumberland, Avon and Lancashire which are operated jointly with the RAFA.

The fund also makes grants to organisations (£2.7 million in 2006).

Royal Artillery Charitable Fund

Eligibility: Dependants of members of the Royal Regiment of Artillery who are unable to work due to illness or death.

Types of grants: This is a relief-in-need charity, which as part of its welfare work supports the children of its members who have started private education before the family's 'breadwinner' became unable to earn – and therefore unable to help them continue their education. It also supports specialist clothing and fees for mature students and people starting work.

Exclusions: No grants towards loans, credit card debts or telephone bills.

Annual grant total: In 2007 the fund had assets of £14 million and an income of £1.4 million. Welfare grants were made to around 2,170 individuals totalling £741,000. No educational grants were made in the year.

Applications: In writing to SSAFA Forces Help (details of local branches can be found in telephone directories or from Citizens Advice). Applications can also be made to the Royal British Legion in England and Wales or to Earl Haig Fund in Scotland (see Scotland section of this guide). Applications can be considered at any time.

Correspondent: The Welfare Secretary, Artillery House, Artillery Centre, Larkhill, Salisbury, SP4 8QT (01980 634309; Fax: 01980 634020)

Royal British Legion Women's Section President's Award Scheme

Eligibility: Ex-servicewomen and their dependents who are in need.

Types of grants: One-off and recurrent educational grants and scholarships for young people aged under 25. Help is given for first degrees, re-training programmes, equipment, travel costs and so on.

Annual grant total: Previously £25,000, though this figure varies from year to year.

Applications: Initial enquiries by telephone or in writing requesting a visit by a welfare visitor who will submit an application form, which includes a financial statement. Applications are considered on a regular basis.

Correspondent: Welfare Advisor, 199 Borough High Street, London, SE1 1AA (020 3207 2100; email: woman@britishlegion.org.uk; website: www.britishlegion.org.uk)

Other information: Grants are made through the Women's Section which is an autonomous organisation within the Royal British Legion, concentrating on the needs of widows and ex-servicewomen and dependant children of ex-service personnel. It works in close association with the Legion but has its own funds and its own local welfare visitors.

Royal Naval Benevolent Trust

Eligibility: Serving and ex-serving men and women of the Royal Navy and Royal Marines (not officers) and their dependants.

Types of grants: Educational grants are available to schoolchildren and people wishing to change their careers. This is a welfare charity which makes these educational grants as part of its wider work.

Annual grant total: In 2006/07 the trust had assets of £34 million and an income of £3.9 million. Grants were made to 4,510 individuals totalling £1.8 million. The sum of £16,000 was given in 37 educational grants.

Applications: On a form available from the correspondent, to be submitted through a social worker, welfare agency, SSAFA Forces Help, Royal British Legion or any Royal Naval Association branch. Applications are considered twice a week.

Correspondent: The Grants Administrator, Castaway House, 311 Twyford Avenue, Portsmouth PO2 8NR (023 9269 0112; Fax: 023 9266 0852; email: rnbt@rnbt.org.uk; website: www.rnbt.org.uk)

Other information: The trust advises that: 'The very wide discretionary powers of the Grants Committee are such that there are but few cases of genuine distress to which the committee is unable to bring prompt relief. Once a need is known to exist and the applicant is deemed to be eligible to benefit and deserving of help, the trust's aim is to provide assistance at a sufficiently high level to enable the beneficiary to make a fresh start with a reasonable prospect of avoiding a further set-back often, however, no such satisfactory solution is possible. [Many] face the prospect of long-term unemployment or low living standards and there is little that can be done to improve their lot. Occasional grants can be made to meet exceptional circumstances but frequently recurring applications have to be discouraged because the trust's resources cannot be stretched to permit a regular supplementation of income.'

The Royal Naval Reserve (V) Benevolent Fund

Eligibility: The children of members or former members of the Royal Naval Volunteer Reserve, Women's Royal Naval Volunteer Reserve, Royal Naval Reserve and the Women's Royal Naval Reserve who are serving or who have served as non-commissioned rates.

Types of grants: One-off grants mainly for schoolchildren who, because of the poverty of their families, need help with clothes, books, equipment or necessary educational visits, and, secondly, for eligible children with aptitudes or disabilities which need special provision. Grants are normally limited to a maximum of £200 for any applicant.

Annual grant total: About £2,000.

Applications: In writing to the correspondent.

Correspondent: Commander J M D Curteis, Hon. Secretary and Treasurer, The Cottage, St Hilary, Cowbridge, Vale of Glamorgan CF71 7DP (01446 771108)

The Royal Navy & Royal Marines Children's Fund

Eligibility: Young people under 25 who are in need and are the dependant of somebody who has served, or is serving, in the Royal Navy or Royal Marines.

Types of grants: One-off and recurrent grants are made to schoolchildren, college students, undergraduates and vocational students where there is a special need. Grants given include those towards schools fees, uniforms, clothing, books, equipment, instruments, maintenance, living expenses and childcare.

Annual grant total: In 2006/07 the fund had assets of £10 million, an income of £910,000 and a total expenditure of £1.2 million. The sum of £380,000 was distributed in children's miscellaneous grants with a further £670,000 distributed in school fees.

Applications: On a form available from the correspondent or to download from the website. Applications can be submitted directly by the individual or through the individual's school/college, an educational welfare agency, SSAFA or any other third party. They are considered on a monthly basis, though urgent cases can be dealt with between meetings.

Correspondent: Monique Bateman, 311 Twyford Avenue, Stamshaw, Portsmouth PO2 8RN (023 9263 9534; Fax: 023 9267 7574; email: rnchildren@btconnect.com; website: www.rnrmchildrensfund.org)

The WRNS Benevolent Trust

Eligibility: Ex-Wrens and female serving members of the Royal Navy (officers and ratings) who joined the service between 3 September 1939 and 1 November 1993 who are in need. People who deserted from the service are not eligible.

Types of grants: This charity is essentially a relief-in-need charity which offers grants for educational purposes. These are usually given to schoolchildren for uniforms and other clothing and to students in further or higher education, including mature students, towards books, equipment, instruments, fees and maintenance.

Annual grant total: In 2007 the trust had assets of £3.2 million and an income of £330,000. Grants, mainly for welfare purposes, totalled £407,000. Grants for educational purposes totalled £6,300.

Applications: Applications can be made direct to the correspondent, or through SSAFA.

Correspondent: Sarah Ayton, General Secretary, Castaway House, 311 Twyford Avenue, Portsmouth, Hampshire PO2 8RN (023 9265 5301; Fax: 023 9267 9040 (mark "for the attention of WRNS BT"); email: admin@wrnsbt.org.uk; website: www.wrnsbt.org.uk/)

Shipping

The Bonno Krull Fund

Eligibility: Individuals connected to the shipping industry.

Types of grants: One-off according to need.

Annual grant total: In 2006/07 the fund had an income of £18,000 and a total expenditure of £17,000.

Applications: In writing to the correspondent.

Correspondent: The Secretary, The Baltic Exchange, St Mary Axe, London EC3A 8BH

Social work

The Social Workers' Educational Trust

Eligibility: Registered social workers, with at least two years' post-qualifying experience, involved with improving social work practice.

Types of grants: One-off and recurrent grants from £100 to £300 for fees, travel costs, childcare and books. Up to £1,500 is available for scholarships.

Exclusions: The trust cannot assist those undertaking initial social work training or qualifications.

Annual grant total: In 2006/07 grants totalled £13,000.

Applications: On a form available from the correspondent. Applications are considered in February, June and October.

Correspondent: The Hon. Secretary, BASW, 16 Kent Street, Birmingham, B5 6RD (website: www.socialworkerseducationaltrust.org/)

Other information: The trust also makes awards from specific bequests (one or two a year) following a competition; details are available in the Professional Social Worker journal and from the Hon. Secretary.

Solicitors

The Solicitors' Benevolent Association

Eligibility: Solicitors on the Roll for England and Wales, and their dependants, who are in need.

Types of grants: One-off and recurrent grants, and interest-free loans where applicable, towards welfare needs, which may be used towards educational needs if appropriate.

Exclusions: Solicitors who have been considered to have brought the profession into disrepute are not eligible.

Annual grant total: Previously grants to individuals have totalled £1.3 million, including £221,000 for educational support. Further monies were distributed in the form of loans.

Applications: By application form available on request from the correspondent.

Correspondent: Adrian Rees, 1 Jaggard Way, Wandsworth Common, London SW12 8SG (020 8675 6440; email: sec@sba.org.uk; website: www.sba.org.uk)

Stationers

The Stationers & Newspaper Makers Educational Charity

Eligibility: UK residents under the age of 25 who are in need of financial assistance with their education. Preference is given to: children of the Stationers and Newspaper Makers Company's liverymen; and students intending to enter the stationery, printing, newspaper or any allied industries.

Types of grants: All applications from eligible individuals are considered, provided that they are not otherwise eligible for state grants. The company can also make two annual travel scholarships for young men and women in the printing, publishing or paper industries.

Annual grant total: In 2006/07 the charity had net assets of £3 million and an income of £94,000. Grants totalled £92,000, of which £25,000 went to individuals.

Applications: On a form available from the correspondent, they are considered quarterly.

Correspondent: J P Thornton, Secretary, The Old Dairy, Adstockfields, Adstock, Buckingham MK18 2JE (01296 714886)

Tailoring

The Merchant Taylors' Company

Eligibility: 'Owing to the enormous demands for grants, the company limits its support to members of the company; the tailoring trade; and the schools with which the company has an association or interest.'

Types of grants: Loans and grants to cover direct educational costs.

Annual grant total: About £25,000. There are two charitable trusts: (i) The Marler Trust and (ii) Merchant Taylors' Consolidated Loans Charities.

Applications: Applications may be made to the correspondent at any time. Only one application is required for consideration by both charities.

Correspondent: The Clerk, Merchant Taylors' Hall, 30 Threadneedle Street, London EC2R 8AY (020 7450 4440)

Other information: The company owns two schools – Merchant Taylors' School, Sandy Lodge and St John's Preparatory School, Pinner. It is associated with six other schools by foundation – Merchant Taylors' School, Crosby; Merchant Taylors' School for Girls, Crosby; Wolverhampton Grammar School; Foyle and Londonderry College, Wallingford School and King's School, Macclesfield.

Tallow chandlers

Tallow Chandlers Benevolent Fund

Eligibility: People in need who have a connection with the company in the City of London and adjoining boroughs.

Types of grants: Bursaries and scholarships.

Annual grant total: In 2007/08 the fund had assets of £3.8 million, an income of £437,000 and made grants totalling £170,000, all to organisations. The trust mostly makes grants to schools and charities for educational purposes and only rarely supports individuals.

Applications: In writing to the correspondent.

Correspondent: The Clerk, Tallow Chandlers Hall, 4 Dowgate Hill, London EC4R 2SH (020 7248 4726; email: clerk@ tallowchandlers.org; website: www. tallowchandlers.org/)

Textile workers

Textile Industry Children's Trust

Eligibility: Children and young people under 20 whose parents work or have worked for in the retail or manufacturing sectors, principally selling clothing or household textiles (not footwear).

Types of grants: The trust concentrates its grant giving on 'the essential costs of education'; in practice this means particularly, but not exclusively, the payment of school fees. There is a preference for those with serious family difficulties so the child has to be educated away from home or at schools which offer vital pastoral care. The trust will also fund places at specialist schools for children with learning difficulties or for those who would benefit from attending a school that focuses on music or sport. Help is given with existing school fees where there has been a 'dramatic' change in family circumstances. Hardship grants are also available for clothing, books, computers, travel costs to attend school and educational trips. Grants usually range from £250 to £1,500 a term.

Exclusions: No grants are given towards study/travel abroad; overseas students studying in Britain; student exchange; or people starting work. No grants are available for those in higher education.

Annual grant total: In 2006/07 the trust had assets of £8 million and an income of £400,000. Grants for educational and welfare purposes were made to 136 individuals totalling £285,000.

Applications: On a form available from the correspondent. Applications can be submitted at anytime either directly by the individual or through a third party such as a social worker, teacher or citizen's advice bureau.

Correspondent: G Sullivan, Director, Lynnhaven House, Columbine Way, Gislingham, Eye, Suffolk IP23 8HL (01379 788644; Fax: 01379 788644; email: info@tict.org.uk; website: www.tict.org.uk/)

Actuary

Company of Actuaries Charitable Trust Fund

Eligibility: Further and higher education students progressing towards actuarial qualifications.

Types of grants: One-off grants of around £600 each to help students with course/exam fees so that they can complete their training for the profession.

Annual grant total: In 2006/07 the trust had assets of £330,000 and an income of £87,000. Grants for individuals for educational purposes totalled £15,000. A further £77,000 went to organisations.

Applications: In writing to the correspondent supported by a tutor's report. Applications are mainly considered in October, but also in January, April and July.

Correspondent: Mr Lyndon Jones, Second Floor, 55 Station Road, Beaconsfield, Buckinghamshire, HP9 1QL (07831865513; email: clerk@ actuariescompany.co.uk; website: www. actuariescompany.co.uk)

The Institute of Actuaries Research and Education Fund

Eligibility: Overseas students who are studying or researching in actuarial science or related fields in the UK.

Types of grants: Small travel grants.

Annual grant total: In 2006/07 the trust had an income of £6,700 and a total expenditure of £34,000.

Applications: Applicants should normally be nominated by an actuarial authority abroad.

Correspondent: Miss P A Hargreaves, Institute of Actuaries, Staple Inn Hall, 1–3 Staple Inn, London WC1V 7QJ (email: pauline.hargraves@actuaries.org. uk; website: www.actuaries.org.uk)

Other information: An annual research grants programme also supports actuarial research in universities at postdoctoral and PhD level. Applications for this programme should be made via the relevant university department.

Agriculture & related rural issues

The Dick Harrison Trust

Eligibility: Further and higher education, mature and postgraduate students who are in need and are training in livestock auctioneering and/or rural estate management and who were born in Cumbria, Northumberland or Scotland, or who are (or whose parents or guardians are) at the time of the award living in any of these places.

Types of grants: One-off grants towards fees, books, equipment/instruments, maintenance/living expenses and study or travel abroad.

Annual grant total: About £1,000

Applications: On a form available from the correspondent, or from the trust's website. Applications should be submitted directly by the individual and are considered at any time.

Correspondent: R Addison, Secretary, Harrison and Hetherington Ltd, Borderway Mart, Rosehill, Carlisle CA1 2RS (01228 590490; Fax: 01228 640901; website: www. dickharrisontrust.org.uk)

The Institute of Chartered Foresters Educational & Scientific Trust

Eligibility: Students of forestry and related disciplines.

Types of grants: Grants are available for students and others at an early stage in their career in forestry. The trust offers three types of grant:

- EST travel bursary: one award of £500 made to one applicant for travel to benefit professional development
- EST professional development awards: a discretionary award of any amount made to one applicant
- EST Events awards: several awards of £100 made for attending the ICF National Conference or Study Tour.

Annual grant total: The amount given in grants varies from year to year. Recent grants have totalled about £1,500.

Applications: On a form available from the correspondent.

Applications for the Events Bursary and the Professional Development Awards are considered four times a year and should be received at the latest by March 31st, June 30th, September 30th, December 31st for consideration by Trustees. Applications for the Annual Travel Bursary should be received by the 31st March.

Correspondent: The Secretary, 59 George Street, Edinburgh, EH2 2JG (0131 240 1425; Fax: 0131 240 1424; email: icf@charteredforesters.org; website: www.charteredforesters.org)

Nuffield Farming Scholarships Trust

Eligibility: UK residents aged 25 to 40 who are working in farming, growing, forestry, fish farming, and countryside management businesses and fields ancillary to these, and people in positions to influence them.

Types of grants: Grants are given to study topics of interest to rural industry, which can be worldwide. The grants cover a period of eight weeks, and are for travel and subsistence costs.

Exclusions: Full-time education and research projects will not be funded.

Annual grant total: In 2006/07 the trust had an income of £243,000 and a total expenditure of £236,000. Scholarships awarded to individuals totalled £76,000.

Applications: Awards are advertised in October each year.

Correspondent: John G Stones, Blaston Lodge, Blaston, Market Harborough, Leicestershire LE16 8DB (01858 555544; email: nuffielddirector@aol.com; website: www.nuffieldscholar.org)

The John Oldacre Foundation

Eligibility: Undergraduates and postgraduates who are carrying out research in the agricultural sciences which is meaningful to the UK agricultural industry. The research must be published.

Types of grants: One-off and recurrent grants according to need towards structured research in the UK and overseas.

Annual grant total: In 2006/07 the trust's assets totalled £6.7 million and it had an income of £121,000. Grants totalled £135,000 including one grant to an individual totalling £2,500.

Applications: In writing to the correspondent through the individual's college/university. Applications are usually considered twice a year, in the autumn and spring.

Correspondent: Henry Bonner Shouler, Hazleton House, Hazleton, Cheltenham, Gloucester GL5 4EB

The Royal Bath & West of England Society

Eligibility: People studying any aspect of agriculture, horticulture, forestry, conservation or any form of food production or marketing.

Types of grants: Scholarships.

Annual grant total: In 2007 the fund had an income of £3.6 million and a total expenditure of £4.1 million. A total of £21,000 was designated for education.

Applications: On a form available from the correspondent.

Correspondent: Jane Guise, The Showground, Shepton Mallett, Somerset BA4 6QN (website: www.bathandwest. com)

The Studley College Trust

Eligibility: Those who are training for a career in agriculture, horticulture, forestry and allied land-based industries whose progress is barred by insufficient financial resources. Applicants should be British nationals aged 17 to 30, with priority being given to those seeking their initial technical qualification (postgraduate and veterinary studies are only awarded grants in special cases). Pre-course practical experience is regarded as essential and students on industrial placements are not assisted as they are expected to be worth a wage and therefore self-supporting. The trust annually sponsors a number of scholarships. It also has an emergency fund to help eligible students for whom changed circumstances and a financial crisis threatens their continued studies.

Types of grants: One-off and recurrent grants towards fees, books, travel and maintenance for students in the above subjects. Grants can be for up to £2,000 according to circumstances. Applicants must be studying in public sector institutions within the UK and must be providing a contribution to the cost of their proposal.

Annual grant total: About £50,000 a year.

Applications: The trustees consider applications in May, July and September submitted by the 1st of the previous month. Two referees will be required and applicants will be interviewed by the administrator. Application forms are available from the administrator.

Correspondent: D J Brazier, Hill View, Chapel Lane, Ratley, Banbury OX15 6DS (01295 670397; email: z4b10r@btinternet. com; website: www.studleytrust.co.uk)

Jack Wright Memorial Trust

Eligibility: Young people wishing to travel overseas to study aspects of water management in agriculture, including irrigation.

Types of grants: One or more scholarships awarded annually, with a maximum value of £1,750.

Annual grant total: About £2,000.

Applications: Further details can be obtained by writing to the correspondent. The successful applicants will have prepared a 'well thought out and costed proposal, which highlights how they, and the wider community, will benefit from the award.' Short-listed candidates will be asked to defend their proposal at interview.

Correspondent: John Gowing, Secretary, c/o Centre for Water Resources, Food and Rural Development, University of Newcastle NE1 7RU (website: www. jackwright.org.uk/)

Archaeology/ antiquarian studies

Society of Antiquaries of London

Eligibility: People in higher education, including postgraduates, with an interest in archaeological and antiquarian subjects.

Types of grants: A limited range of awards are available for a variety of study levels in archaeological and antiquarian subjects.

Annual grant total: In 2006/07 the society had assets of £15 million, an income of £2.3 million and a total expenditure of £1.8 million. Grants were made to individuals totalling £49,000.

Applications: On a form available from the correspondent or via website. Applications should be submitted directly by the individual in December for consideration in March.

Correspondent: The General Secretary, Burlington House, Piccadilly, London W1J 0BE (020 7479 7080; email: admin@ sal.org.uk; website: www.sal.org.uk)

Arts

The Artistic Endeavours Trust

Eligibility: Students undertaking education in the arts or entering artistic professions.

Types of grants: Grants to graduates and undergraduates for fees, clothing equipment, books, travel and general subsistence.

Annual grant total: In 2006 the trust had an income of £3,800 and a total expenditure of £5,400.

Applications: In writing to the correspondent.

Correspondent: R J Midgley, Macintyre Hudson, 30-34 New Bridge Street, London, EC4V 6BJ

The William Barry Trust

Eligibility: People engaged, or about to engage in technical, craft and artistic occupations.

Types of grants: One-off cash grants in the range of £600 and £1,000, including those for fees and maintenance/living expenses.

Annual grant total: In 2006/07 the trust had assets of £1.3 million and an income of £50,000. Grants were made totalling £21,000.

Applications: In writing to the correspondent. Applications should be submitted directly by the individual or a family member.

Correspondent: W S Barry, 56 Avenue Close, London NW8 6DA (020 7722 3974)

The Canada House Arts Trust

Eligibility: Individuals and groups involved in projects in the visual and performing arts, music, literature, film, TV and media which have a Canadian focus or theme. Projects must take place in the UK.

Types of grants: The average grant is between £1,000 and £2,000.

Exclusions: The trust does not support travel and accommodation expenses or costs for work in development.

Annual grant total: About £20,000.

Applications: In writing to the correspondent describing the nature of the project and the aspects, with costings, for which the application is being made. The trustees meet quarterly to decide allocation of funds.

Correspondent: The Administrator, PO Box 63120, London, W14 4AS (website: www.canadahouseartstrust.org/)

Henry Dixon's Foundation for Apprenticing

Eligibility: Apprentices or students under 25 studying in the fields of music, technical textiles and art.

Types of grants: One-off grants ranging from £100 to £2,000. Grants are made to four London music colleges and one London art college.

Annual grant total: In 2006/07 the trust had assets of £2.1 million and an income of £58,000. Grants awarded came to £45,000.

Applications: The trust makes block grants to educational institutions, who then administer the grants. Therefore grant recipients must apply to their educational institutions rather than the trust.

Correspondent: Charities Administrator, Drapers' Company, Drapers' Hall, London EC2N 2DQ (020 7588 5001; Fax: 020 7628 1988; website: www.thedrapers.co.uk)

Other information: This trust was formerly called Drapers' Educational Foundation.

The Ann Driver Trust

Eligibility: Young people from the EU wishing to pursue an education in the arts, particularly music.

Types of grants: The trust makes awards to institutions on a rota basis which changes annually.

Annual grant total: £20,000 to £25,000 per year.

Applications: Application forms should be requested by the principle or head of department at place of study

Correspondent: Kay Tyler, Administrator, PO Box 2761, London, W1A 5HD

Other information: The trust selects different institutes for support in May of each year. A copy of the list of institutes can be obtained from the administrator by sending an sae.

The Exuberant Trust

Eligibility: Young people up to the age of 30, who are interested in developing their interest in the arts.

Types of grants: One-off grants up to a maximum of £500 for a specific project or activity.

Annual grant total: In 2006 the trust had an income of £7,500 and a total expenditure of £4,000.

Applications: Full guidelines are available from the trust's website, or by contacting the correspondent in writing.

Correspondent: M Hofman, 11 St Margaret's Road, Oxford, OX2 6RU

(email: exuberant.trust@ntlworld.com; website: www.exuberant-trust.org.uk)

Other information: Successful applicants are encouraged to take part in concerts and other activities in support of the trust.

The Fenton Arts Trust

Eligibility: People who are making, or who aspire to make, a worthwhile contribution to the artistic and cultural life of the UK. Grants are made towards the creative arts, principally painting and drama. Students should have British nationality and be aged under 35.

Types of grants: Scholarships/bursaries are awarded for a one-year period to final year or postgraduate students undertaking arts courses. Grants are also made for individual works, activities, performances, exhibitions or prizes.

Annual grant total: In 2006/07 the trust had assets of £3.1 million and an income of £121,000. Grants to individuals totalled £1,200. Grants are mainly awarded to organisations, totalling around £50,000 a year.

Applications: Applications for The Fenton Arts Trust Scholarships/Bursaries may come from any institution which provides appropriate study opportunities and wishes to offer its students the scholarships/bursaries. (Individuals should only apply via their institution.)

Applications for other grants can be made in writing directly by the individual to the administrator at the address below. Requests should include a fully budgeted proposal with the amount requested and information regarding other sponsors to the project.

Applications should preferably be sent nine months to a year in advance.

The trustees meet to discuss applications four times a year.

Correspondent: Shelley Baxter, PO Box 135, Leatherhead, Surrey KT24 9AB (website: www.fentonartstrust.org.uk/)

The Gordon Foundation

Eligibility: Young people up to the age of 30. 'To support their education in the fine or performing arts, particularly music, drama or design, or to allow them to engage in educational travel which involves physical challenge and endeavour.'

Types of grants: One-off and recurrent grants according to need.

Annual grant total: In 2006/07 the foundation had assets of £809,000 and an income of £38,000. Grants to organisations and individuals totalled £196,000.

Applications: Application forms are available by email or post. They can also be downloaded from the foundation's website.

Correspondent: Gillian Hoyle, Administrator, PO Box 214, Cobham,

Surrey, KT11 2WG (01483 456347; email: gordon.foundation@btinternet.com; website: www.gordon.foundation.btinternet.co.uk)

Other information: The foundation also owns and maintains two long wheelbase Land Rovers which it loans without charge to groups of young people for expeditions or field trips.

The Haworth Charitable Trust

Eligibility: Young musicians and painters in their final year of full-time study or the first year of their professional career. Preference is given to applicants from the north west of England, Herefordshire, Shropshire, The Wrekin and London.

Types of grants: Grants of £1,000 to £2,000 for one year only, paid in instalments over the year. Grants are for any purposes to further the establishment of a career in music, painting and the fine arts. Grants are not made for general welfare purposes.

Exclusions: Loans are not made and mature students cannot be funded.

Annual grant total: In 2006/07 the trust had an income of £9,400 and a total expenditure of £4,600. The trust usually gives about £3,000 a year in grants to individuals.

Applications: Applications should be made by letter, with a cv, to the correspondent, and must be supported by a recommendation of a tutor of a full-time course.

Correspondent: Rooks Rider Solicitors, Rooks Rider Solicitors, Challoner House, London EC1R 0AA

The Martin Smith Foundation

Eligibility: People undertaking further, higher or postgraduate training in ecology, environment and natural resources, music or performing arts.

Types of grants: One-off grants, of up to £2,500, towards books, equipment, fees, bursaries or fellowships.

Exclusions: Travel expenses are not funded.

Annual grant total: In 2006/07 the foundation had an income of £322,000, mainly from donations and legacies and made grants totalling £221,000. Grants are mainly made to organisations. Previously around £4,000 a year has been given to individuals.

Applications: The trustees state that they do their own research and do not consider unsolicited applications.

Correspondent: The Trustees, 4 Essex Villas, London, W8 7BN

The Society for Theatre Research

Eligibility: People involved with research into the history, historiography, art and practice of the British theatre, including music-hall, opera, dance, and other associated performing arts. Applicants should be aged 18 or over. There are no restrictions on status, nationality, or the location of the research.

Applications are not restricted to those engaged in formal academic work and academic staff, postgraduate students, theatre professionals and private researchers are all equally eligible.

Types of grants: Annual theatre research awards ranging between £100 and £1,000. Grants can go towards research costs, study or travel overseas and foreign students studying in the UK.

Exclusions: Exclusively literary topics are not eligible, nor are applications for course fees unless for specific professional training in research techniques. No grants for course fees or purely for subsistence

Annual grant total: In 2008 grants totalled £6,600.

Applications: Application forms can be downloaded from the society's website. Completed forms should be returned by 1 February, with a detailed breakdown of costing and the names of two referees. Applications received later than this date, for whatever reason, will not be admitted.

Correspondent: Eileen Cottis, Hon. Secretary, c/o The Theatre Museum, 1e Tavistock Street, London WC2E 7PR (website: www.str.org.uk)

The South Square Trust

Eligibility: Students aged 18 years and over studying full-time practical degree courses in the fine and applied arts, especially those related to gold, silver and metalwork, but also music, drama and dance. The trustees prefer to help people commencing their academic studies at undergraduate level. Assistance is given to postgraduates but they do not support individuals undertaking research degrees at PhD level. Courses have to be within the UK. Preference is given to UK nationals.

Types of grants: One-off and recurrent grants for assistance with fees or living expenses. Grants to individuals range from £500 to £2,000. No assistance will be given to individuals where a bursary has been set up with a school. No grants are made for expeditions, travel bursaries, courses outside the UK or short courses.

Exclusions: No grants for: people under 18; part-time or short courses; expeditions, travel or shoes; courses outside the UK; or courses not concerned with fine or applied arts.

Annual grant total: In 2006/07 the trust had assets of almost £4 million and an income of £188,000. Grants were made to

21 individuals totalling £17,000, with a further £111,000 given to schools and colleges for their bursary/scholarship funds. Grants to organisations totalled £54,000.

Applications: On a form available from the correspondent, for submission from January to April for consideration in May for courses starting in September. Initial enquiries by telephone are welcomed. Two references and a photograph are required for submission with the application form (along with photographs of work if on an arts-related course).

Correspondent: Mrs Nicola Chrimes, Clerk to the Trustees, PO Box 169, Lewes, East Sussex, BN7 9FB

Other information: Various bursaries have been set up with schools connected with the fine and applied arts. These are as follows: Byam Shaw School of Art; West Dean College (Metalwork); The Slade School of Fine Art; The Royal Academy Schools; London Metropolitan University (Silversmithing and Metalwork); Royal College of Music; Bristol Old Vic Theatre School; GSA Conservatoire; Royal Academy of Dramatic Art (RADA); School of Jewellery, Birmingham Institute of Art & Design; Guildhall School of Music & Drama; Royal Academy of Music; Royal College of Art; Textile Conservation Centre; and Royal Northern College of Music.

The Talbot House Trust

Eligibility: Individuals undertaking courses in the performing arts, such as drama, dance and music. Only UK residents will be awarded grants, for study in the UK.

Types of grants: One-off grants to students in further/higher education to help with the cost of fees. In exceptional circumstances a contribution towards equipment and instruments or maintenance and living costs will be considered.

Exclusions: No grants to postgraduates.

Annual grant total: In 2006/07 the trust had an income of £8,500 and a total expenditure of £9,300.

Applications: On a form available from the correspondent. All completed application forms must be received by March for consideration in May. The applicant should provide any detail of financial or other hardship, and any reason why special consideration should be given to their application.

Correspondent: Mrs Jayne Day, Pothecary Witham Weld, 25c North Street, Bishop's Stortford, Hertfordshire, CM23 2LD (01279 506421; email: charities@pwwsolicitors.co.uk)

The Wall Trust

Eligibility: Students, including students from overseas who are studying in the UK, who are aged 16 and over and are nominated by an organisation with which the trust has a scholarship scheme (see Applications section). Individuals may be undertaking further, higher or postgraduate education or vocational training in the performing arts and be studying music, drama or dance.

Types of grants: Normally grants are paid for each year of a scholar's course – on average for three years. Grants normally range between £1,000 and £3,000 a year and are limited to training or tuition fees.

Annual grant total: In 2006/07 the trust had an income of £34,000. Expenditure on scholarships, grants and bursaries totalled £33,000.

Applications: Applications should only be made via an organisation with which the trust has a scholarship scheme. These are the Royal Ballet School, London Studio Centre, RADA, Royal College of Music, Royal Academy of Music, Royal Northern College of Music and the Purcell School. The trust has previously stated that all its funds were allocated.

Correspondent: Charles Wall, 19 Waterside Point, 2 Anhalt Road, London SW11 4PD (020 7978 5838; email: charles@thewalltrust.org)

S D Whitehead's Charitable Trust

Eligibility: Children under 16 with special artistic talents, especially in music, dance or ballet.

Types of grants: Grants are available to help pay school fees or to help fund one-off purchases (for example musical instruments) for talented children, and range from £500 to £2,500.

Annual grant total: About £20,000.

Applications: On a form available from the correspondent, to be submitted directly by the individual for consideration in June.

Correspondent: Andy Mullett, Moore Stephens, Chartered Accountants, 30 Gay Street, Bath, BA1 2PA

Arts – Crafts

The Queen Elizabeth Scholarship Trust

Eligibility: People involved in modern or traditional crafts who are reasonably well-established in the field, rather than those who are starting off. Applicants must be permanently resident in the UK.

Types of grants: One-off and staged grants, over a maximum of four years, of up to £10,000 each for further education, such as work experience and training and can include related travel and research costs.

Exclusions: Grants are not made for tools, leasing studios/workshops, materials, staging exhibitions or for general educational courses.

Annual grant total: In 2006 the trust had assets of £3 million, an income of £132,000 and a total expenditure of £113,000. Grants totalling £81,000 were made to 13 individuals.

Applications: On an application form available on written request with an A4 sae from the correspondent, and from the website. Applications are considered in March/April and June/July and should be submitted by mid-January and mid-June respectively.

Correspondent: The Secretary, 1 Buckingham Place, London SW1E 6HR (020 7828 2268; email: qest@rwha.co.uk; website: www.qest.org.uk)

Arts – Dance

The Lionel Bart Foundation

Eligibility: Drama students (undergraduate and postgraduate).

Types of grants: One-off grants towards fees are given in the range of £200 to £5,000. About 12 grants are made each year.

Annual grant total: In 2006/07 the foundation had an income of £400 and a total expenditure of £3,200. Grant expenditure is dependant on the foundation's income, which can fluctuate from year to year.

Applications: In writing to the correspondent to be received by May 15 each year. Applications are considered in late May.

Correspondent: John Michael Roth Cohen, 55 Drury Lane, London WC2B 5SQ (02073796080; email: jc@clintons.co.uk)

The Adaline Calder Memorial Trust

Eligibility: People aged 16 to 19 who are resident in Scotland and are taking or about to undertake a three year, full time training course in dance.

Types of grants: The trust awards a single scholarship of £700 each year to a nominated 'winner' after holding auditions in June. The purpose of the scholarship is to enable the successful candidate to receive assistance for one year. It can be used towards the purchase of dancewear, books, training, return home travel fares and any other item necessary to pursue a career in dance. Any remaining income, which is generated by the audition fees, is given to the runner–up candidate.

Annual grant total: The winner of the scholarship receives £700. A second grant is dependent on income.

Applications: In writing to the correspondent, requesting an audition in June.

Correspondent: The Trustees, c/o 5 Rutland Square, Edinburgh, EH1 2AX

The Lisa Ullmann Travelling Scholarship Fund

Eligibility: Individuals working in all areas of movement and dance who wish to travel abroad or in the UK.

Types of grants: Scholarships are awarded to fund the travel of individuals abroad or in the UK to attend conferences, to pursue a research project, or undertake a short course of study in the field of movement or dance.

Exclusions: The following are not supported: fees for courses or conferences are not paid; fees or travel for 'long' courses, e.g. courses extending over one, two or three years; these include, for example, most diploma, certificate, degree and postgraduate courses; individuals under the age of 18; projects which directly support the work of companies, institutions or organisations; set up costs of projects or festivals; those not resident in the UK for a minimum of two years continuously prior to the application; previous recipients of LUTSF scholarships are considered for a second award only after at least five years have passed and/or in exceptional circumstances.

Annual grant total: In 2006/07 the fund had an income of £4,100 and a total expenditure of £7,000.

Applications: On a form available from 1 September from the fund's website. Four signed copies of the form must be sent by post to arrive no later than 25 January. Forms not received by this date cannot be considered. Forms sent by email or fax are not acceptable. Applicants are informed of the outcome of their application by the end of March, and scholarships winners may travel from April onward.

Correspondent: The Secretary, Breach, Kilmington, Axminster, Devon EX13 7ST (website: www.lutsf.org.uk)

The Jeremy & Kim White Foundation

Eligibility: Young people in the performing arts with a special emphasis on jazz and classical ballet.

Types of grants: One-off scholarships according to need.

Annual grant total: About £2,000.

Applications: In writing to the correspondent.

Correspondent: c/o C L White, 102 Alwoodley Lane, Leeds LS17 7PP (website: www.whitefoundation.com)

Arts – Music

The Tom Acton Memorial Trust

Eligibility: People up to the age of thirty involved in music.

Types of grants: Grants and loans according to need.

Annual grant total: In 2006/07 the trust had an income of £2,000 and total expenditures of £3,000.

Applications: In writing to the correspondent.

Correspondent: A T Gage, Hamilton House, Cobblers Green, Felsted, Dunmow, Essex, CM6 3LX (01371 820382; Fax: 01371 821100)

The Alper Charitable Trust

Eligibility: Young musicians in full-time education.

Types of grants: The trust usually gives an interest-free loan (generally £200 to £500) to help buy a musical instrument.

Exclusions: People on postgraduate courses are ineligible for help.

Annual grant total: According to previously submitted accounts, the trust had an income of £12,000 and a total expenditure of £11,000. Accounts were last returned in 2004.

Applications: Write to the correspondent for an application form (enclosing an sae). Applications can be submitted directly by the individual at any time. Two references are essential.

Correspondent: Simon Alper, Chilford Hall, Linton, Cambridge CB1 6LE (01223 892641; Fax: 01223 895605; email: simonalper@chilfordhall.co.uk)

The Australian Music Foundation in London

Eligibility: Australian singers and instrumentalists under 30 years of age for study in Europe. Students should either be resident in Australia or the UK.

Types of grants: In 2007, grants were given to 7 individuals for the purchase of instruments and other costs.

Exclusions: Composers are not considered for grants.

Annual grant total: In 2007 the trust had assets of £628,000, an income of £53,000

and a total expenditure of 31,000. Grants to individuals totalled £27,000.

Applications: In writing to the correspondent. Applications should be submitted by the end of January each year.

Correspondent: Guy Parsons, Blackfriars, 17 Lewes Road, Haywards Heath, West Sussex, RH17 7SP (01444 454773; Fax: 01444 456192; website: www.amf-uk.com/)

Other information: There is a separate award jointly funded by the Australian Music Foundation and Sir Charles Mackerras, which is specifically for Australian conductors of merit. Potential applicants should request further information from The Australian Musical Foundation.

The Josephine Baker Trust

Eligibility: People studying vocal music in the UK.

Types of grants: Help to establish singers in their careers.

Annual grant total: In 2007/08 the trust had an income of £26,000 and a total expenditure of £22,000. Grants to individuals totalled £21,000

Applications: In writing to the correspondent. The trust has established links with the Royal Academy of Music and the Royal College of Music.

Correspondent: David Monro, Grange Cottage, Frensham, Farnham, Surrey, GU10 3DS

The BBC Performing Arts Fund

Eligibility: 'Aspiring music-makers and performers looking for a way to get ahead.'

Types of grants: Bursaries worth up to £20,000 each to people aged 16 to 30. Grants towards instrument and equipment awards are also available, worth up to £1,200 each, for applicants aged 11 to 15.

Annual grant total: In 2006/07 the trust had assets of £1.7 million, an income of £469,000 and made grants totalling £515,000.

Applications: Full guidelines can found on the BBC website.

Correspondent: Gilly Hall, Room 6080, BBC Television Centre, Wood Lane, London, W12 7RJ (email: gilly.hall@bbc.co.uk; website: www.bbc.co.uk/performingartsfund/)

The Busenhart Morgan-Evans Foundation

Eligibility: Young musicians at the start of their professional career.

Types of grants: One-off and recurrent grants towards equipment, instrument and fees.

Annual grant total: Previously about £25,000.

Applications: Through the individual's college, to be submitted to the Worshipful Company of Musicians, 6th Floor, 2 London Wall Buildings, London EC2M 5PP (020 7496 8980).

Correspondent: John F Bedford, Trustee, Brambletye, 455 Woodham Lane, Woodham, Surrey KT15 3QG (01932 344806; Fax: 01932 343908; email: johnbedford@compuserve.com)

The Choir Schools' Association Bursary Trust Fund

Eligibility: Pupils or proposed pupils, aged 7 to 13, at a member school.

Types of grants: Grants are available to pay the fees of choristers attending CSA schools. Applications are means tested. Grants range from £300 to £2,400.

Annual grant total: In 2006/07 the trust had assets of £276,000 and an income of £279,000. Grants to individuals totalled £209,000 and were awarded for scholarships and bursaries.

Applications: On an application form to the headmaster of the choir school concerned. Applications should be submitted by 15 March, 31 August and 15 December for consideration in May, October and February.

Correspondent: Mrs W A Jackson, Administrator, The Minster School, Deangate, York YO1 7JA (01904 624900; Fax: 01904 557232; email: info@choirschools.org.uk; website: www.choirschools.org.uk)

The Else & Leonard Cross Charitable Trust

Eligibility: Students of music who have considerable potential as pianists and are in financial need.

Types of grants: The trust makes scholarships to musical institutes which are in turn passed on to individuals.

Annual grant total: In 2006/07 the trust had an income of £9,900 and a total expenditure of £37,000.

Applications: Applications must be made through the college the student is with, not directly to the trust.

Correspondent: Mrs H Gillingwater, Trustee, The Wall House, 2 Lichfield Road, Richmond, Surrey TW9 3JR (020 8948 4950; email: helengillingwater@hotmail.com)

The EMI Music Sound Foundation

Eligibility: Young people in the UK who are undertaking music education.

Types of grants: Grants are given up to £2,500 for the purchase of musical instruments for children in full-time education and for funding music teachers

to advance training and attend relevant courses.

The foundation also operates a bursary scheme of £5,000 for students at seven musical colleges and institutes; Irish World Music Centre, Birmingham Conservatoire, Liverpool Institute of Popular Music, Tech Music Schools, Royal Academy of Music, Royal Welsh College of Music and Drama.

Exclusions: No grants are given to applications from outside the UK, or that relate to community projects or music therapy.

Annual grant total: In 2006/07 the foundation had assets of £7.9 million and an income of £384,000. Grants expenditure totalled £134,000.

Applications: On a form available from the correspondent, which can be downloaded from the website. Completed forms can be submitted either directly by the individual or through the individual's school. The trustees meet every six months, in March and September, and applications need to be received three weeks before the relevant meeting, with references and supplier's quotes. Applications for bursaries are considered by the colleges themselves.

Correspondent: Ms Janie Orr, Administrator, 27 Wrights Lane, London W8 5SW (020 7795 7000; Fax: 020 7795 7296; email: orrj@emigroup.com; website: www.emimusicsoundfoundation.com)

Other information: The foundation also gives grants to non-specialist schools to fund music education.

The Gerald Finzi Charitable Trust

Eligibility: Students of music aged between 25 and 70. Formal training or qualifications are not necessary.

Types of grants: The trust offers grants for the purchase of musical instruments and music scholarships for projects in the UK and overseas, lasting ideally between 3 to 8 weeks. If a project involves travel then the trust can meet expenses along with the costs of accommodation, subsistence and equipment for the period involved.

Scholarships can be made for a variety of projects, such as gaining practical experience in performance, attending summer schools or education and research projects. Scholarships awarded in recent years have covered studies in Estonia, Finland, France, Germany, India, Ireland, Italy, South America, Sweden, the UK and the USA.

Grants in 2006/07 ranged between £125 to £4,000.

Exclusions: No grants are made for attendance at courses, for the support of academic degree courses, or for fees or living expenses. Applications from students of other art forms will not be supported and group applications are not considered.

Annual grant total: In 2006/07 the trust had an income of £62,000 and awarded £19,000 in grants to 16 individuals.

Applications: Applications can be made on a form available by post from the trust or as a download from the trust's website. Applicants must include an outline of their proposal and an estimate of the cost. Applications are considered throughout the year.

Correspondent: Elizabeth Pooley, The Finzi Trust, PO Box 137, Shaftesbury, SP7 0WX (0845 241 0369; email: admin@ geraldfinzi.org; website: www.geraldfinzi. org)

Other information: Grants are also made to organisations (2006/07 £15,000).

The Simon Fletcher Charitable Trust

Eligibility: People studying music, usually singers under 30, studying at a recognised music academy. Grants are made in the UK and Australia.

Types of grants: One-off grants of up to £1,000. Grants are made to schoolchildren for books and equipment/instruments and to college students, undergraduates, vocational students, mature students and overseas students for fees, study/travel abroad and maintenance/living expenses.

Annual grant total: In 2007 the trust made awards to four individuals totalling approximately £4,000.

Applications: On a form available from the correspondent. Applications can be submitted directly by the individual, including an sae.

The trust also administers the Simon Fletcher Award, an annual award given to one individual, usually of £1,000. This is awarded after a process of application, audition and interview, usually in June.

Correspondent: Miss V Fletcher, 74 Hamstead Road, London NW1 2NT (020 7330 0982; email: info@ simonfletcher.org.uk; website: www. simonfletcher.org.uk)

Other information: Grants are also made to schools for the purchase of instruments, music and so on.

The Jean Ginsburg Memorial Foundation

Eligibility: People who wish to pursue a career in medicine or to train as a classical pianist.

Types of grants: Awards and scholarships.

Annual grant total: In 2006/07 the trust had an income of £11,000 and a total expenditure of £56,000. The trust gives most of its awards out of the proceeds of a memorial concert held in 2004.

Applications: Initial contact can be made via email.

Correspondent: Ian Henry, The Garden Gouse, 9 Ardwick Road, London, NW2 2BX (email: info@janginsburgh.com; website: www.jeanginsburg.com/)

Other information: The trust also supports scholarships at The Royal Free Medical School, The Royal Academy of Music in London and Somerville College, Oxford University.

The Michael James Music Trust

Eligibility: Individuals engaged in any musical education, particularly in a Christian context.

Types of grants: One-off and recurrent grants are given towards tuition fees and expenses.

Annual grant total: In 2006/07 the trust had an income of £17,000 and a total expenditure of £13,000. Grants totalled about £10,000.

Applications: On an application form available from the correspondent. Applications should be received by 30 April each year.

Correspondent: Edward Monds, 4 Onslow Gardens, Wimborne, Dorset, BH21 2QG (01202 842103)

The Kathleen Trust

Eligibility: Young musicians of outstanding ability who are in need.

Types of grants: Loans in the form of musical instruments and sometimes bursaries to attend music courses, ranging between £500 and £2,500.

Annual grant total: In 2007 the trust had assets of £1.2 million and an income of £30,000. Grants to individuals totalled £33,000.

Applications: In writing to the correspondent.

Correspondent: Edward Perks, Secretary, Currey & Co, 21 Buckingham Gate, London SW1 6LS (020 7828 4091; Fax: 020 7828 5049)

The Macfarlane Walker Trust

Eligibility: Music students who are in need with a preference for those who live in Gloucestershire.

Types of grants: One-off grants ranging from £500 to £2,000, for the purchase of musical instruments for music students.

Annual grant total: In 2006/07 grants given mostly to organisations totalled £25,000.

Applications: In writing to the correspondent, directly by the individual, giving the reason for the application and an outline of the project with a financial forecast. An sae and references from an academic referee must accompany the initial application.

Correspondent: Mrs Sara Walker, Secretary, 50 Courthope Road, London NW3 2LD

The Music Libraries Trust

Eligibility: Music librarians involved in education or training, or people carrying out research into music librarianship and music bibliography.

Types of grants: 'The trust has a regular programme of allocating grants in support of projects, research and course attendance with a preference for supporting those who have been unable to receive financial support from elsewhere. Awards of between £100 and £1000 have been given for initial funding, with second grants being considered in exceptional cases.'

Annual grant total: About £1,000.

Applications: In writing to the correspondent. Applications can be submitted directly by the individual or through the school/college or educational welfare agency.

Correspondent: Claire Kidwell, Secretary, Trinty College of Music, King Charles Court, Old Royal Naval College, King William Walk, London SE10 9JF (020 8305 4425; Fax: 020 8305 9425; email: ckidwell@tcm.ac.uk; website: www. musiclibrariestrust.org)

The Ouseley Trust

Eligibility: Children aged 9 to 16 who are choristers in recognised choral foundations in the Church of England, Church of Ireland or Church in Wales.

Types of grants: Grants towards choir school fees for up to three years. Grants usually range from £1,000 to £5,000.

Exclusions: No grants for music lessons. Help is unlikely to be available for chorists at Rochester, Ely or St Albans where the trust has donated funds to be used for scholarships. It does not usually award further grants to successful applicants within a two-year period.

Annual grant total: In 2007 the trust had assets of almost £4 million, an income of £145,000 and a total expenditure of £129,000. Grants towards fees totalled £43,000.

Applications: On a form available from the correspondent by the school or choral foundation concerned, not by the chorister or his/her parents. A statement of financial resources by the child's parents or guardian will be required. Applications should be submitted by the end of January or June for consideration in April or October. The trust states that applicants are strongly advised to obtain and study the guidelines for applications.

Correspondent: Martin Williams, 127 Coleherne Court, London SW5 0EB (020 7373 1950; Fax: 020 7341 0043; website: www.ouseleytrust.org.uk)

Other information: Grants are also made towards projects that promote the use of the choral liturgy, for example, for organ repairs and purchase of music.

The Geoffrey Parsons Memorial Trust

Eligibility: Concert pianists and people with the ability to become concert pianists, who have a particular interest in the accompaniment of song or in chamber music. There is a preference for people under 35.

Types of grants: One-off and recurrent grants, usually of sums up to £2,000, towards piano lessons with pre-eminent teachers and the purchase of music (i.e. sheet music and scores).

Annual grant total: In 2006/07 the trust had an income of £2,500 and a total expenditure of £1,200.

Applications: Unsolicited applications will not be considered.

Correspondent: B P Griffin, 50 Broadway, Westminster, London SW1H 0BL (020 7227 7000)

The Pratt Green Trust

Eligibility: Hymn writers, church musicians and others involved in education, research, composition and performance in the area of church music and hymnody.

Types of grants: Scholarships, bursaries, prizes, research expenses and other grants.

Annual grant total: In 2007/08 the trust had an income of £33,000 and a total expenditure of £37,000. Grants totalled £5,800 and included one grant of £300 to an individual.

Applications: In writing to correspondent. All applications must be accompanied by a detailed budget covering the project/ purpose for which the grant is requested, together with full details of any other grants or sponsorship applied for. Applications should be supported by a suitable second signatory, for example, college principal or other person with a connection to the purpose and by two references.

Correspondent: Revd Brian Hoare, 5 Flaxdale Close, Knaresborough, North Yorkshire, HG5 0NZ (01423 860750; email: brianhoare@ntlworld.com; website: www.prattgreentrust.org.uk/)

Other information: Grants are also made to organisations.

The Royal College of Organists

Eligibility: Students of organ playing who are members of the Royal College of Organists.

Types of grants: There are various scholarships and awards available, please consult the Royal College of Organists' website for further details.

Annual grant total: In 2006/07 the trust had assets of £1.2 million and an income of £512,000. From a direct charitable expenditure of £290,000, grants totalled £12,000.

Applications: On a form which can be downloaded from the charity's website.

Correspondent: The Registrar, PO Box 56357, London, SE16 7XL (website: www. rco.org.uk)

The Rushworth Trust

Eligibility: People who are studying music who live within a 60-mile radius of Liverpool. Grants are awarded to composers, young conductors, young performers, student singers and instrumentalists, and choirs and choir singers, for assistance with publication, copying, training, promotion, equipment, instruments, music tours, apprenticeships, concerts and maintenance.

Types of grants: One-off grants of up to £300 to help with the cost of the study of music and to stimulate and encourage beneficiaries in their musical pursuits. Only single payments are made and can only be given if the individual is not eligible for grants from any other sources. Awards are not usually repeated.

Exclusions: No grants for course fees or maintenance costs of higher education.

Annual grant total: In 2006/07 the trust had an income of £4,100 and a total expenditure of £5,600.

Applications: By the individual on a form available from the correspondent, including all relevant information and documentary evidence. Applications are considered in March, June, September and December, and applications should be received before the start of the month. Applicants are advised of the outcome by the last day of the same month.

Correspondent: The Grants Team, Liverpool Charity and Voluntary Services, 151 Dale Street, Liverpool, L2 2AH

Other information: The trust has been formed by the merging of The William Rushworth Trust, The Thew Bequest and The A K Holland Memorial Award.

The Schools Music Association of Great Britain

Eligibility: Musicians in full-time education up to the age of 18 who are in financial need.

Types of grants: Help towards buying musical instruments, summer schools, short courses and so on. Grants are one-off and usually range from £50 to £150.

Exclusions: Ongoing courses cannot be funded.

Annual grant total: In 2006/07 the trust had an income of £60,000 and a total expenditure of £58,000.

Applications: On a form available from the correspondent. Applications must be supported in writing by a headteacher, principal, music teacher or music adviser/ inspector, and by a member of the Schools Music Association.

Grants can be made upon receipt of written evidence of the expenditure having been made during the 12 months following the date of application, for example, a receipt for an instrument bought, or a summer school certificate of attendance. Grants are not normally made for expenditure before the date of application.

Correspondent: The Hon Secretary, Educamus, 71 Margaret Road, New Barnet, Hertfordshire EN4 9NT (020 8440 6919; website: www.schoolsmusic.org.uk)

The Raphael Sommer Music Scholarship Trust

Eligibility: Music students, in practice locally in London.

Types of grants: One-off and recurrent grants according to need.

Annual grant total: In 2006/07 the trust had an income of £7,300 and a total expenditure of £7,400.

Applications: In writing to the correspondent.

Correspondent: Genevieve Sommer, 55 Quickswood, London, NW3 3SA

The Stringwise Trust

Eligibility: People who play stringed instruments.

Types of grants: Grants towards attendance at any training or experiential event.

Annual grant total: About £2,000.

Applications: In writing to the correspondent.

Correspondent: Gilbert Holbourn, Lion House, Red Lion Street, London, WC1R 4FP

Other information: Grants are also made to organisations.

John Wates Charitable Trust

Eligibility: Further and higher education students, including mature students and postgraduates, who are studying music and singing and live in London or the south east of England.

Types of grants: One-off grants ranging from £500 to £1,000 for fees and maintenance/living expenses.

Exclusions: No grants are made for expeditions or travel.

Annual grant total: About £20,000 to students.

Applications: In writing to the correspondent. Applications should be submitted directly by the individual for consideration on a rolling basis.

Correspondent: The Trustees, c/o Slater Maidment, 7 St James's Square, London, SW1Y 4JU

Other information: Grants are also made to organisations.

The Society for Wessex Young Musicians Trust

Eligibility: Young musicians who live in Dorset and Hampshire.

Types of grants: Grants towards equipment and facilities.

Annual grant total: About £2,000 a year.

Applications: In writing to the correspondent.

Correspondent: Lyn Bain, 126 Parkstone Avenue, Poole, Dorset, BH14 9LS

Arts – Performing arts

The Elizabeth Evans Trust

Eligibility: Young people between 16 and 26 who wish to pursue a professional career in the performing arts – as an actor, singer, instrumentalist or within stage management. Priority will be given to applicants who can demonstrate a close association, or connection with Carmarthenshire.

Types of grants: Funding may be applied for either a college or university course at both undergraduate and postgraduate level, or alternately for a short-term project such as a summer course or private study.

Annual grant total: Around £5,000

Applications: Application forms can be downloaded from the trust's website. Nearly all the trust's correspondence is done via email.

Applicants will not be means tested, but an applicant's personal circumstances may be a factor determining the amount and extent of any award.

Applications received by email or exceptionally by post will be considered between the 1 January and 30 April in any year. Consideration of applications received at other times will be deferred until the 1 January following receipt of the application, unless sufficient reason can be established for expediting the application.

Correspondent: The Trust Secretary, c/o Ungoed Thomas and King, Gwynne House, 6 Quay Street, Carmarthen, SA31 3AD (email: hazelthorogood@theelizabethevanstrust.co.uk;

website: www.theelizabethevanstrust.co.uk)

The Rebecca McNie Foundation
see entry on page 229

Correspondent: Mrs Melanie McNie, Trustee, Mowll & Mowll, Trafalgar House, Gordon Road, Whitfield, Dover, CT16 3PN

Arts – Theatre

The Actors' Charitable Trust (TACT)

Eligibility: Children (aged under 21) of people in the theatrical profession who are in financial need.

Types of grants: One-off and recurrent grants of up to £1,200 towards educational 'extras', for example music lessons, uniforms and so on. Grants are also made in the form of gift vouchers and payments to service providers.

Exclusions: No grants are made towards private school fees.

Annual grant total: In 2006/07 the trust had assets of £6.4 million and an income of £542,000. Grants to 100 families with 180 children between them totalled £195,000.

Applications: On a form available from the trust. Applications can be considered at any time, and can be submitted either by the individual or a parent. Forms are also available on the trust's website.

Correspondent: Robert Ashby, The Actors Charitable Trust, 58 Bloomsbury Street, London, WC1B 3QT (020 7636 7868; email: robert@tactactors.org; website: www.tactactors.org)

Other information: The Actors' Charitable Trust also offers residential, nursing, dementia and palliative care for those over 70 from the acting profession in Denville Hall, which they have run since 1965.

The Costume Society

Eligibility: Students in history and theory of design (fashion and textiles) and theatre wardrobe and costume design. Support is given to students engaged in part-time study on further, higher and post-graduate courses.

Types of grants: Annual grants available: the Museum Placement Award – supports a placement offered jointly with a museum clothing/fashion/dress/costume collection (£1,000); the Patterns of Fashion Award – open to students in theatre wardrobe and costume design (£500); the Yarwood Award – restricted to students on a designated MA course (£500); the Student Bursary – offers full attendance and

accommodation at the society's annual conference, *The Symposium* (about £400).

Annual grant total: In 2006 the society had assets of £102,000, an income of £53,000 and gave £2,000 in student grants.

Applications: Information is available on the society's website and is published in *Costume*, the annual journal of the society. Information can also be obtained by writing to the individual awards co-ordinators c/o the Costume Society.

Correspondent: Jill Salen, 39 Palace Road, Llandaff, Cardiff, CF5 2AG (02920 566912; email: jill.salen@rwcmd.ac.uk; website: www.costumesociety.org.uk)

The John Thaw Foundation

Eligibility: People wishing to pursue a career in the theatre.

Types of grants: Funding for arts-based training courses.

Annual grant total: In 2006/07 the foundation had an income of £285,000 and made had a direct charitable expenditure of £188,000. The charity works with a number of partner organisations to help achieve its objectives. Grants are also made to organisations and individuals.

Applications: In writing to the correspondent.

Correspondent: The Trustees, PO Box 38848, London, W12 9XH

Aviation

The Guild of Air Pilots Benevolent Fund

Eligibility: Young people who want to become pilots or wish to gain further qualifications in the aviation industry.

Types of grants: Scholarships and bursaries for young people who want to become pilots or to further their qualifications as pilots.

Annual grant total: In 2006/07 the guild had assets of £843,000 and an income of £33,000. Scholarships totalling approximately £57,000 were made to 10 individuals and a further £10,000 was also given in welfare grants.

Applications: On a form available from the website. Details of individual criteria and dates relating to each scholarship are included in the application forms available from the guild's website. The fund works closely with the other aviation trusts for individuals (both military and civilian). If an applicant has approached another such trust, they should say so in their application to this fund.

Correspondent: Paul J Tacon, Clerk, Cobham House, 9 Warwick Court, Gray's Inn, London WC1R 5DJ (020 7404 4032;

Fax: 020 7404 4035; email: gapan@gapan. org; website: www.gapan.org)

Other information: The guild also gives grants for welfare purposes to members of the guild and those who have been engaged professionally as air pilots or air navigators in commercial aviation and their dependants.

Built environment

Alan Baxter Foundation

Eligibility: People involved with the study of the built and natural environment.

Types of grants: Grants given according to need.

Annual grant total: In 2006/07 the foundation had an income of £31,000 and a total expenditure of £24,000.

Applications: In writing to the correspondent.

Correspondent: Nigel Bamping, Cowcross Court, 75 Cowcross Street, London, EC1M 6EL

Other information: Grants are also made to organisations and for research.

Carpentry & construction

The Carpenters Company Charitable Trust

Eligibility: The trust is set up to 'support the craft' i.e. people wishing to set up in or to study carpentry.

Types of grants: Educational grants are awarded up to £2,400 to help with fees, maintenance, equipment and other necessities.

Annual grant total: In 2006/07 the trust had assets of £20 million and an income of £1 million. About 250 grants are made each year, 'totalling around £50,000'.

Applications: On a form available from the correspondent. Applications are considered in November, February and June.

Correspondent: Miss Mead, Charities Administrator, Carpenters Hall, 1 Throgmorton Avenue, London EC2N 2JJ (020 7588 7001; email: info@carpentersco. com; website: www.carpentersco.com/ pages/charities/ carpenters_company_charitable_trust1)

Other information: Grants are also made to organisations.

Norton Folgate Trust

Eligibility: People who engaged in or studying the craft of carpentry or any branch of the building industry.

Types of grants: Grants, to a usual maximum of about £100, (a) for school pupils to help with the cost of books, equipment, clothing or travel and (b) to help with school, college or university fees or to supplement existing grants.

Annual grant total: In 2006/07 the trust had assets of £4.1 million, an income of £173,000 and a total expenditure of £168,000. There were 38 craft education grants made to individuals totalling £82,000.

Applications: On a form available from the correspondent.

Correspondent: The Charities Administrator, Carpenter's Company, Carpenter's Hall, 1 Throgmorton Avenue, London EC2N 2JJ (020 7588 7001; website: www.carpentersco.com)

Other information: Grants are also made to organisations and individuals for welfare purposes.

Clockmaking

Clockmakers Museum and Educational Trust

Eligibility: Intending clockmakers from 18 to 22 years of age. Applicants must be British, be intending to work in the horological industry in the UK, and expect to have a reasonable working life at the end of three years' training.

Types of grants: One-off grants of between £400 and £1,200 are available to horology students in further/higher education for help with fees and living expenses.

Annual grant total: In 2006 the trust had assets of £1.3 million and received an income of £75,000. Grants to individuals are made each year usually totalling about £2,000.

Applications: In writing to the correspondent. Applications can be submitted at any time by the individual and will be considered within three months; meetings are organised when there are sufficient applications to justify one.

Correspondent: J W H Buxton, Salter's Hall, Fore Street, London EC2Y 5DE (020 7638 5500; email: clockmakersco@aol. com; website: www.clockmakers.org)

Commerce

The Gustav Adolph & Ernest Koettgen Memorial Fund

Eligibility: 'British-born subjects who wish to educate themselves or to obtain tuition for a higher commercial career but whose means are insufficient for them to obtain such education or tuition at their own expense.'

Types of grants: Students and mature students of British nationality who are studying in this country and are in higher education can apply for financial help towards the costs of books, fees, living expenses and childcare. Applicants are only considered if they are in the final year of a course and if they have managed to raise almost the whole amount needed, or if they encounter unexpected difficulty, as these grants are only intended to be supplementary.

Exclusions: Grants cannot be given for postgraduate study.

Annual grant total: In 2006/07 the fund had an income of £8,700 and a total expenditure of £6,900.

Applications: On a form available from the correspondent, submitted directly by the individual and supported by an academic reference. Trustees meet monthly.

Correspondent: Ms Fiona Macgillivray, Family Welfare Association, 501– 505 Kingsland Road, Dalston, London E8 4AU (020 7254 6251; Fax: 020 7249 5443; email: grants.enquiry@ fwa.org.uk; website: www.fwa.org.uk)

Other information: Preference is given to employees of John Batt and Company (London) Limited or members of their families.

The Worshipful Company of Chartered Secretaries and Administrators General Charitable Trust Fund

Eligibility: Chartered secretaries and administrators who are undertaking studies connected with commerce.

Types of grants: Scholarships of £1,000 and prizes of between £50 and £500 for commercial education at various universities.

Annual grant total: In 2007 the trust had assets of £1.1 million and an income of £864,000. Grants were awarded totalling £25,000, of which £2,000 went to individuals for educational purposes.

Applications: In writing to the correspondent. Grants are considered every three months, usually January, April, July and October.

Correspondent: Donald Kirkham, 2 Chaundrye Close, London, SE9 5QB (020 8859 4295; email: clerk@wccsa.org. uk)

The London Chamber of Commerce & Industry Commercial Education Trust

Eligibility: People who wish to further their career with an LCCI vocational qualification, or enter into higher education in the business/commercial field at a recognised UK university

Types of grants: The Charles R E Bell Scholarship is open to UK Higher Education students and provides financial support towards course fees and candidate support materials.

The Standard LCCI Scholarship is open to any candidate who already has an LCCI certificate and is looking to study for a further LCCI qualification at a higher level.

Annual grant total: About £25,000.

Applications: Application forms for both scholarships are available from the London Chamber of Commerce and Industry website.

Correspondent: The Secretary, 33 Queen Street, London, EC4R 1AP (website: www. lccieb.com/)

Engineering

The Douglas Bomford Trust

Eligibility: EU citizens who are or will be professional engineers or scientists applying their skills to mainly rural engineering problems.

Types of grants: Mainly grants for travel, language training and conference attendance. Some discretionary awards in cases of hardship or for special projects, and some research projects.

Annual grant total: In 2006/07 the trust had assets of £2.1 million, an income of £778,000, of which £681,000 was generated through a donation. Grants to individuals totalled £51,000.

Applications: In writing to the correspondent. Full application details are available from the trust's website.

Correspondent: The Secretary, Barton Road, Silsoe, Bedford, MK45 4FH (email: enquiries@dbt.org.uk; website: www.dbt.org.uk)

The Bernard Butler Trust Fund

Eligibility: Students in the field of engineering.

Types of grants: One-off and recurrent grants in the range of £700 and £2,000. About 12 grants are made each year.

Grants are given to college students, undergraduates, vocational students and mature students for fees, study/travel abroad, books, equipment/instruments and maintenance/living expenses.

Annual grant total: In 2006/07 the trust had an income of £18,000 and a total expenditure of £39,000.

Applications: Application forms are available from the correspondent, alternatively they can be downloaded from the fund's website, or completed online. They should be submitted directly by the individual or a family member and are considered in May and November.

Correspondent: The Secretary, 37 Oasthouse Drive, Fleet, Hampshire GU51 2UL (01252-793276; email: info@ bernardbutlertrust.org; website: www. bernardbutlertrust.org)

Other information: Grants are also made to organisations.

The Coachmakers and Coach Harness Makers Charitable Trust 1977

Eligibility: People studying/working in the aerospace, automotive, carriage building and associated trades.

Types of grants: Bursaries of £2,500 each for college students and undergraduates for study/travel overseas and maintenance/ living expenses and to mature students for awards for excellence.

Annual grant total: In 2006/07 the trust had assets of £527,000 and an income of £93,000. Grants to two individuals totalled £5,000, with a further £6,000 to organisations.

Applications: In writing to the correspondent. Application deadlines are in December for consideration in January and October for consideration in November.

Correspondent: Grp Capt. Gerry Bunn, Clerk, Elmtree Cottage, Bottom House Farm Lane, Chalfont St. Giles, Buckinghamshire, HP8 4EE (07971 017255; website: www. coachmakers.co.uk)

The Worshipful Company of Engineers Charitable Trust Fund

Eligibility: Final year undergraduates and postgraduate students who are in need and taking courses related to the science and technology of engineering; principally those who are in the UK.

Types of grants: One-off grants up to £1,000. Grants are given for one year only or as a top-up to people nearing the end of their course, towards fees, maintenance/ living costs or awards for excellence.

Annual grant total: In 2007 the trust had assets of £525,000 and an income of

£84,000. The trust gave approximately £16,000 in grants to individuals for educational purposes, which was broken down into the following categories:

- £5,000 in one award to an post-graduate to attend international technology conferences
- £9,500 in miscellaneous education awards
- £1,000 in hardship awards to three students of engineering to help with living expenses.

Applications: In writing to the correspondent at any time providing as much detail about your circumstances as possible. For hardship on completing a course, support from the Dean of Engineering is required. Applications are considered throughout the year and information on grant schemes and the range of awards are available on the company's website.

Correspondent: Air Vice-Marshal G Skinner, The Worshipful Company of Engineers, Wax Chandlers Hall, 6 Gresham Street, London EC2V 7AD (020 7726 4830; Fax: 020 7726 4820; email: clerk@ engineerscompany.org.uk; website: www. engineerscompany.org.uk)

Other information: Grants are also made to charities with educational roles and to individuals in need.

The Caroline Haslett Memorial Trust

Eligibility: Women undertaking a full-time course in electronic, electrical and mechanical or allied engineering subjects leading to a HND or Incorporated Engineer-level degree. People on sandwich courses, involving periods in industry, are also eligible, but the award is available only for the academic parts of the course.

Types of grants: Scholarships of £1,000 a year.

Annual grant total: Around £10,000 a year is given in grants to individuals.

Applications: On a form available from the correspondent, to be returned by 16 October. Applicants may be required to attend an interview in London (reasonable travel costs will be met) and applicants are required to submit a report on their progress at the end of each academic year.

Correspondent: A F Wilson, The Institution of Engineering and Technology, Savoy Place, London WC2R 0BL (0207 344 5415; email: afwilson@theiet. org; website: www.theiet.org)

The Institution of Engineering and Technology (IET)

Eligibility: The following regulations apply as a general rule to all scholarships and prizes, however candidates should refer to the website for individual criteria:

(i) Students must be studying or about to study (in the next academic session) on an IEE-accredited degree course at a UK university.

(ii) Each candidate must be nominated by the head of the educational or training establishment, the course tutor, the university head of department or by a chartered member of the IEE.

(iii) A candidate who is shortlisted for an award may be required to attend an interview at the IEE.

(iv) During the tenure of an award, the professor or other person under whom the grant holder is studying will be asked to certify that the holder is making satisfactory progress.

(vi) The scholarship will be paid in instalments, as determined by the IEE. It will be withdrawn and any unpaid instalments withheld if the holder leaves the course.

(vii) Successful candidates must not hold any other IEE scholarships or grants at the same time.

(viii) Candidates must start their studies within one month of the planned start date unless they have approval otherwise from the IEE.

(ix) The application must be made on a form and must be returned by the closing date (see below).

Types of grants: The IET offers a range of scholarships, prizes and travel awards ranging from £350 to £3,000.

Annual grant total: During 2007 the institution distributed £346,000 in undergraduate and postgraduate scholarships and travel awards and prizes.

Applications: Further details and application forms are available from the website. Applications are usually made by IEE members or people applying for membership.

Correspondent: Andrew Wilson, The Institution of Engineering and Technology, 2 Savoy Place, London, WC2R 0BL (020 7344 5415; email: governance@theiet.org; website: www.theiet.org)

Other information: The IEE also administers the following:

(a) The Princess Royal Scholarship

One grant of £1,000, to help an IEE member to use his or her professional knowledge and experience to provide a benefit to an underprivileged community, or similar, in a developing country. The closing date for this award is 30 April.

(b) J R Beard Travelling Fund

Six grants of £500 are available, preferably to younger members, to assist them to travel overseas to further the objects of the IEE and to broaden their horizons, especially in manufacturing techniques. This could be achieved, for example, by a study tour, by working in industry or by participation in an international conference or seminar.

(c) Hudswell Bequest Travelling Fellowship

Four fellowships of £500 to fund travel overseas in furtherance of research being undertaken. Applicants should have financial security in respect of maintenance and research fees and demonstrate a genuine need for the award. Applications can only be considered if submitted through the applicant's head of department.

(d) Postgraduate scholarships

Several scholarships; further details available from the IEE. Value of awards varies from £1,250 to £10,000.

Full details can be found on the IEE website.

Institution of Mechanical Engineers (IMechE)

Eligibility: Members of IMechE who are studying or who are about to study mechanical engineering at degree level (see below).

Types of grants: Awards for undergraduates:

Student Hardship Awards

Grants of up to £1,000 to affiliated members of an IMechE accredited degree programme who are experiencing financial hardship. Students must be making good progress. Applicants must be recommended by a professor or head of department, and must show that their difficulty lies outside the scope of other sources of financial aid. Applicants are required to submit detailed information about their budget. Applicants should normally be resident in the UK. There are normally 10 awards made each year.

IMechE Undergraduate Scholarship

IMechE offers scholarships valued at £4,000 each, usually paid at £1,000 per year for four years, for exceptional students who have achieved excellent A-level (or equivalent) results, and wish to pursue an IMechE accredited degree. Students must be living in the UK.

Whitworth Scholarship

Scholarships for engineering apprentices studying for an MEng or MSc degree in any engineering discipline

Overseas Study Award

Grants of up to £750 for students studying or carrying out work placements overseas as part of their IMechE accredited degree programmes. Applicants must be affiliate members of the Institution, studying an IMechE accredited degree programme and must have a working knowledge of the language of the country they will be visiting.

Group Project Award

Awards for IMechE Affiliate members undertaking group projects. Grants are available of up to £500 per individual, with a limit of eight members per group, to cover the expenses of attending international conferences and travel abroad for participation in engineering, science and technology-based projects overseas.

Overseas/Third World Engineering Projects Award

Grants of up to £1,000 towards overseas voluntary or project work to assist the developing world. Applicants must be student members of the institution and hold or be studying for a degree accredited by the institution.

Annual grant total: Around £600,000 is given in grants annually.

Applications: Applicants should request the appropriate form from the correspondent. Three months are needed to process applications; this should be three months prior to when a decision is required, not necessarily the date of the activity. Closing dates are determined by the approximate dates of the committee meetings, which are held in March, June and September. Applicants requiring an interview will be notified.

Correspondent: Prizes and Awards Department, 1 Birdcage Walk, Westminster, London, SW1H 9JJ (020 7222 7899; email: prizesandawards@imeche.org.uk; website: www.imeche.org.uk)

Other information: The institution makes a number of other awards to postgraduates and for research purposes and for travel and attending conferences, including the Overseas Study Awards and Flatman Grants towards travel overseas for undergraduate mechanical engineers.

The Benevolent Fund of the Institution of Mechanical Engineers

Eligibility: Students studying Mechanical Engineering on an IMechE accredited course at a UK university who are living with a disability or are financially disadvantaged. Applicants should be IMechE members and have started their university studies.

Types of grants: One-off grants of up to £1,000 are available for course materials and equipment, living costs, travel and accommodation.

Exclusions: Grants are not given to individuals who have mismanaged their finances and just run out of money.

Annual grant total: In 2007 the fund had assets of £16 million and an income of £1.3 million. Grants to 305 individuals totalled £500,000.

Applications: Applications should be made directly through the university's student service department. Grants are available from September and repeat applications may be made each year.

Correspondent: R I Money, 3 Birdcage Walk, London SW1H 9JJ (020 7304 6812;

Fax: 020 7973 1262; email: info@bfime.org; website: www.bfime.org)

Other information: The fund also operates a free confidential helpline which offers advice on a range of issues from childcare to bereavement (call 0800 243 458 or minicom 01895 813845). It can also help those in search of a new job through its links with the HR firm, Chiumento.

Mott MacDonald Charitable Trust

Eligibility: People undertaking higher education in the fields of civil, structural, mechanical, electrical and allied engineering.

Types of grants: Grants, bursaries and scholarships. Generally bursaries are committed on an annual basis. Scholarships are usually committed for longer periods but are reviewed annually.

Annual grant total: In 2006 the trust had an income of £184,000 and made grants totalling £199,000.

Applications: In writing to the correspondent.

Correspondent: Steve Wise, St Anne House, 20-26 Wellesley Road, Croydon, CR9 2UL

The Worshipful Company of Scientific Instrument Makers

Eligibility: Undergraduates and postgraduates with outstanding ability in science and mathematics and a creative and practical interest in branches of engineering connected with instrumentation and measurement. Students must attend one of the following universities: Brunel, Cambridge, City, Glasgow Caledonian, Imperial, Oxford, Teesside, UCL, UMIST, Warwick.

Types of grants: The company awards prizes to encourage third year undergraduates taking courses which will equip them to work in the instrumentation and measurement industry. These are worth £500.

Additionally the company awards bursaries for postgraduate students taking MSc courses in metrology. These bursaries are worth £1,000 for one year. Students reading for a PhD are eligible for these scholarships.

Annual grant total: In 2006/07 the trust had an income of £83,000 and a total expenditure of £50,000. Grants totalled £25,000.

Applications: All applications must be made through the applicants' university and not directly to the company.

Correspondent: The Clerk, Glaziers Hall, 9 Montague Close, London SE1 9DD (020 7407 4832; email: theclerk@wcsim.co.uk; website: www.wcsim.co.uk)

Other information: The company stated: 'no individual applications are accepted

without following the procedure outlined above'. Furthermore 'there is no additional funding for any applicants outside the above universities.'

Environmental studies

Alan Baxter Foundation *see entry on page 74*

Correspondent: Nigel Bamping, Cowcross Court, 75 Cowcross Street, London, EC1M 6EL

The Alice McCosh Trust

Eligibility: People of any age undertaking work or study related to natural history and/or the environment. Preference will be given to individuals from Scotland, England and Turkey.

Types of grants: One-off grants in the range of £500 to £1,000, for example, to cover the cost of a school field trip or project, an expedition as part of a research project or the development of new teaching materials for schools or institutes of higher education.

Exclusions: Projects involving joining an existing commercial organisation on a pre-paid tour will not be considered.

Annual grant total: Up to £1,000 a year.

Applications: In writing to the correspondent to be received by 30 November each year. Applications should be concise (no more than four typed pages). Full guidelines can be downloaded from the trust's website.

Correspondent: The Trust Secretary, 2 Friars' Mews, Pinwell Road, Lewes, Sussex, BN7 2LW (email: info@thealicemccoshtrust.org.uk; website: www.thealicemccoshtrust.org.uk)

The Martin Smith Foundation *see entry on page 67*

Correspondent: The Trustees, 4 Essex Villas, London, W8 7BN

The Water Conservation Trust

Eligibility: People who are working or intending to work in the water and environment industry.

Types of grants: One-off grants for approved projects and courses of study.

Exclusions: Unsolicited applications are not accepted.

Annual grant total: In 2006/07 the trust had an income of £24,000 and a total expenditure of £13,000.

Applications: When funds are available the trustees invite applications for scholarships through the water and environmental press.

Correspondent: The Secretary, Waterman's Hall, 16 St Mary at Hill, London, EC3R 8EF

Other information: Grants are also made towards research and to organisations.

Esperanto

Norwich Jubilee Esperanto Foundation

Eligibility: Students under 26 who are in need of financial help, who have a high level of Esperanto and are prepared to use it for travel abroad. Preference among non-Britons is normally given to those whose native language is not English, since contact with such is more useful to British students of Esperanto.

Types of grants: One-off grants are given to British students for travel to approved venues including insurance, conference fees and accommodation; and to overseas students for travel in the UK and simple accommodation where this is not provided by host groups. Grants to overseas students are only given towards the costs of travel to and from the UK in exceptional circumstances.

Research grants are given to teachers of Esperanto of any age on similar conditions.

Annual grant total: About £4,000.

Applications: Letters of applications should be in Esperanto, including if possible some details of travel plans, and preferably letters of support from one or two referees. Applications showing no knowledge of or interest in Esperanto are not normally acknowledged.

Correspondent: David Kelso, 5 Craigenhill Road, Carluke, ML8 4QT (website: www.esperanto-gb.org/nojef/)

Other information: All grants are conditional on the recipient sending a written report in Esperanto on the visit. A proportion of the grant may be withheld until the report is received.

Fire-fighting, fire engineering, fire protection or fire research

Institution of Fire Engineers

Eligibility: People living and working within the UK who are studying fire-fighting, fire engineering, fire protection or fire research.

Types of grants: One-off grants according to need.

Annual grant total: The income for the trust is donated by another charity, and varies greatly. In 2006/07 grants were made totalling around £45,000.

Applications: In writing to the correspondent. Applications are considered four times a year.

Correspondent: Professional Development Officer, London Road, Moreton-in-Marsh, Gloucestershire GL56 0RH

Furniture

The Worshipful Company of Furniture Makers Company

Eligibility: Young people working or studying to work in the furniture industry.

Types of grants: There are awards for each branch of the industry, for example, design, manufacturing and retail. Students intending to enter the industry are eligible and there are awards for postgraduate studies. Grants can be made towards fees, study/travel abroad, equipment and instruments and range between £500 and £1,000 each. It also gives awards for excellence.

Exclusions: No grants are given for childcare.

Annual grant total: In 2006/07 the company had assets of £1.5 million and an income of £319,000. Grants, bursaries and general donations totalled £50,000, of which £1,200 was given in directly to one individual.

Applications: On a form available from the correspondent to be submitted directly by an individual or a parent/guardian. Applications are considered throughout the year.

Correspondent: The Clerk, Furniture Maker' Hall, 12 Austin Friars, London, EC2N 2HE (020 7256 5558; Fax: 020 7256 5155; email: clerk@

furnituremkrs.co.uk; website: www. furnituremakers.co.uk)

Other information: Grants are also made for group college projects.

Gas engineering

The Institution of Gas Engineers Benevolent Fund

Eligibility: UK and overseas students wishing to study gas engineering.

Types of grants: A range of awards are on offer.

Annual grant total: In 2007 the trust had an income of £11,000 and a total expenditure of £15,000.

Applications: In writing to the correspondent.

Correspondent: John N Williams, Charnwood Wing, Holywell Park, Ashby Road, Loughborough, Leicestershire LE11 3GH (01509 282728; email: lesley@ igem.org.uk; website: www.igem.org.uk)

Geography

Royal Geographical Society (with the Institute of British Geographers)

Eligibility: Scientists, including non-academics, who are over 19 and are carrying out geographical research in the UK and overseas. Travel awards are also available.

Types of grants: Grants are normally one-off, but can be recurrent. Some grants are restricted to teams or to fellows of the society. Grants range from £500 to £15,000.

Annual grant total: In 2007 the society had an income of £4.3 million and a total expenditure of £4.4 million. Grants to individuals total about £100,000 a year.

Applications: All grant details, guidelines and forms can be obtained from the society's website.

Correspondent: D J Riviere, 1 Kensington Gore, London SW7 2AR (020 7591 3000; email: enquiries@rgs.org; website: www. rgs.org)

Other information: The society is a primary source of funding for geographical research projects in the UK and overseas.

Grants include Ralph Brown Expedition Award, Neville Shulman Challenge Award, Gilchrist Fieldwork Award and Innovative Geography Teaching Grants and a number of small travel awards and bursaries.

Greece

The Hellenic Foundation

Eligibility: Students studying the culture, tradition and heritage of Greece.

Types of grants: One-off and recurrent grants for projects involving education, research, music and dance, books and library facilities and university symposia. Grants for individuals rarely exceed £5,000 each.

Annual grant total: In 2006 the foundation had assets of £463,000 and income of £32,000. Grants to individuals totalled £2,700, of which £700 was given for the production of publications in Hellenic studies and £2,000 was given towards Hellenic arts.

Applications: In writing to the correspondent.

Correspondent: G D Lemos, Hon. Secretary, St Paul's House, Warwick Lane, London EC4P 4BN

Other information: Grants are also made to organisations (£20,000 in 2006).

Historic conservation

Zibby Garnett Travelling Fellowship

Eligibility: People working in one of the following conservation subjects: historic buildings, gardens and landscape; the traditional building trades; artefacts; historic and decorative crafts. Applicants can be at university or college, or within the formative years of their careers, trade apprentices, trainee architects or landscape architects.

Types of grants: Grants for short study trips abroad. The awards are not restricted to British nationals, but overseas students should plan projects outside their country of origin.

Exclusions: Generally grants are given for practical work in preference to pure study or research.

Annual grant total: In 2006/07 the fellowship had an income of £5,000 and an expenditure of £3,000.

Applications: On a form available from the trustees to be submitted directly by the individual. The deadline for applications is 1 March for consideration that month.

Correspondent: The Trustees, The Grange, Norwell, Newark, Nottinghamshire NG23 6JN (01636 636288; Fax: 01636 636760; email: mail@ davidgarnett.fsnet.co.uk)

Home economics

The British & Foreign School Society – Berridge Bursary Fund

Eligibility: Students of home economics, food and nutrition or dietetics.

Types of grants: One-off grants according to need.

Annual grant total: In 2006 the trust had an income of £1,300. Grants were made to two individuals totalling £1,750

Applications: In writing to the correspondent directly by the individual. The application should be submitted with an sae and the names and addresses of two referees.

Correspondent: Charles Crawford, Director, Maybrook House, Godstone Road, Caterham, Surrey CR3 6RE (01883 331177; website: www.bfss.org.uk)

Horticulture/ botany

The Merlin Trust

Eligibility: UK and Irish nationals, aged between 20 and 35, who are horticulturists or botanists and wish to extend their knowledge of plants, gardens and gardening by travelling. Other nationalities are only eligible if they are studying full time at a UK horticultural establishment.

Types of grants: Grants towards visiting gardens in different parts of the country or abroad, or travelling to see wild plants in their native habitats. Previous support has been awarded for an expedition to southern Chile to observe the range of plants, a trip to New York's community gardens and a visit to Peru in search of orchids.

Exclusions: Grants are not given towards postgraduate study or to fund highly technical laboratory-based research.

Annual grant total: In 2006/07 the trust had assets of £604,000 and an income of £29,000. Grants to 16 individuals totalled £8,400.

Applications: Application forms are available from the correspondent.

Correspondent: Fiona Crumley, 55 Deodar Road, London, SW15 2NU (020 8874 7636; Fax: 020 8874 7636; website: www.merlin-trust.org.uk)

The Royal Horticultural Society

Eligibility: Priority is given to professional horticulturists and student gardeners, but applications are also considered from serious amateur gardeners, botanists and other related professions and institutions. Eligible proposals must be closely identified with horticulture.

Types of grants: Grants for horticultural projects including study visits or working placements in gardens, plant exploration and study, taxonomy and research, attendance at conferences and distinct projects of educational or historical value. More recently there has been the introduction of specific bursaries for exhibiting botanical art and botanical photography.

'The Royal Horticultural Society administers a number of bursary funds, established and maintained through generous bequests and donations, to assist horticulturists and gardeners in financing specific horticultural projects, including overseas travel.'

Exclusions: Grants are not made for salary costs, tuition fees, exam fees or living costs for educational courses.

Annual grant total: In 2008 grants totalled £91,000

Applications: Full guidelines can be downloaded from the Royal Horticultural Society website.

Correspondent: The Secretary, RHS Bursaries Committee, Education Department, The RHS Garden, Wisley, Woking, Surrey GU23 6QB (01483 212380; Fax: 01483 212382; email: bursaries@rhs.org.uk; website: www.rhs.org.uk/Learning/Education/bursaries.htm)

Hospitality trades

The Savoy Educational Trust

Eligibility: People entering or working in the hospitality industry throughout the UK. People starting work, further and higher education students, mature students and postgraduates can be supported.

Types of grants: Individuals can receive up to £500 for uniforms or other school clothing, books, equipment, instruments, fees, educational outings in the UK and study or travel abroad. In addition, two or three Reeves-Smith scholarships of £5,500 each are given to young men and women to help with their training for the industry.

Exclusions: Funding is not offered to students undertaking a non-hospitality related course.

Annual grant total: In 2007/08 the trust had assets of £42.5 million, an income of £1.5 million and made grants totalling £630,000. Grants to individuals totalled about £8,000.

Applications: On a form available from the correspondent. A college application must always accompany the application. Meetings of the trustees are held in March, July, September and December, and applications can be submitted directly by the individual or through a third party such as the individual's school, college or educational welfare agency throughout the year.

Correspondent: Margaret Georgiou, Queens House, 55-56 Lincoln's Inn Fields, London WC2A 3BH (020 7269 9692; email: info@savoyeducationaltrust.org.uk; website: www.savoyeducationaltrust.org.uk)

Other information: Regular grants are made to educational institutions and associations connected with the hospitality industry.

Information technology

Misys Charitable Foundation

Eligibility: People in need who are studying or wish to study IT, both in the UK and internationally. Mainly undergraduates are supported. Beneficiaries have high academic ability and financial need. Grants are only made to people attending certain universities, colleges and schools that are partners of this foundation. This includes certain colleges of Oxford and Cambridge universities.

Types of grants: Grants are given to fund IT scholarships and to fund university courses for people who would otherwise be unable to afford them.

Annual grant total: About £200,000

Applications: Applications should not be made directly to the foundation in any circumstance. Grants are only made via the institutions that work in partnership with the foundation, who recommend beneficiaries to the foundation.

Correspondent: The Director, 125 Kensington High Street, London, W8 5SF

Other information: The foundation only makes awards on the recommendation of partner institutions.

International affairs

Gilbert Murray Trust: International Studies Committee

Eligibility: People who are studying, or have studied, international relations (or international law) at an institution of higher education in the UK. Applicants should be 25 years or younger on 1 April of the year they are applying, although other people can receive grants if they are able to put forward special reasons for their delayed education.

Types of grants: Awards are 'given to support a specific project (such as a research visit to the headquarters of an international organisation, to a particular country or a short course at an institution abroad) which will assist the applicant in his or her study of international affairs in relation to the purposes and work of the United Nations'.

Exclusions: No grants to assist with fees or maintenance costs for people studying international affairs.

Annual grant total: Around £3,000 a year.

Applications: In writing to the correspondent by 1 April. The letter should be supported by a short cv, a statement of career intentions and a description of the project for which the award is sought, with an estimate of its total cost and the sources of additional funding if required. (Preference will be given to applications where the award will cover all or the greater part of the project.) An assessment by a person in a position to judge the applicant in his or her suitability for the award is also necessary. All of this information should be submitted with four other copies, in typed form, only using one side of the paper.

Correspondent: The Secretary, 99 Blacketts Wood Drive, Chorleywood, Rickmansworth, Hertfordshire WD3 5PS

Italian culture

Il Circolo Italian Cultural Association Limited

Eligibility: Students attending a British higher education institution, either at undergraduate or postgraduate level, pursuing studies, training or research relating to Italian culture (humanities, arts and crafts, sciences and performing arts).

Types of grants: Scholarships.

Annual grant total: In 2008 grants totalling £12,000 were made to 12 students. The amount given varies each year.

Applications: See the Il Circolo website for full guidelines. Selected candidates will be interviewed.

Correspondent: John Cullis, Secretary, Il Circolo, Pini Bingham & Partners, 30 St John's Lane, London, EC1M 4NB (email: info@ilcircolo.org.uk; website: www.ilcircolo.org.uk)

Other information: Grants are also made to organisations.

Languages

John Speak Trust

Eligibility: People who are over 18 and who have a sound basic knowledge (at least GCSE) of the foreign language they wish to study. Applicants must be British born.

Types of grants: Grants to help with the cost of studying a foreign language abroad, normally for a continuous period of six months. They are aimed at people who are intending to follow a career connected with the export trade of the UK, so applicants should usually be (or should stand a reasonable chance of becoming) a representative who will travel abroad to secure business for the UK. The applicant is expected to obtain a post as an unpaid volunteer with a respectable firm or to attend a school, college, university or be on another suitable training course. The value of the ten-month scholarship is approximately £1,800 (to cover living and travel expenses).

Annual grant total: In 2007/08 the trust had an income of £14,000, and a total expenditure of £9,900.

Applications: The scholarships are advertised in February, May and October each year. Applicants will be expected to read, translate and converse in their chosen language (at least to GCSE level) in their interview.

Correspondent: Mrs S Needham, Bradford Chamber of Commerce, Devere House, Vicar Lane, Bradford, West Yorkshire, BD1 5AH (01274 230090; email: sandy.needham@bradfordchamber.co.uk)

Leadership

The London Youth Trust (W H Smith Memorial) *see entry on page 250*

Correspondent: Bhavnita Bhorkatria, Administrator, PO Box 49749, ASGBI, London, WC21 3WY (020 7304 4780; email: info@londonyouthtrust.org.uk; website: www.londonyouthtrust.org.uk)

Leather industry

Dr Dorothy Jordan Lloyd Memorial Trust

Eligibility: People employed in the production of leather or research directly relevant to this sector. Non-UK students must be fluent in English and intend to return to their home country to work in the leather industry. The fellowship may not be offered to an applicant resident in, or a citizen of, a country which restricts free trade in hides, skins or leather. Applicants must be aged 20 to 40.

Types of grants: Grants ranging from £100 to £1,500 each are made towards travel and international exchange among young people involved in the leather industry. It does not aim to support students in following standard courses of education.

Annual grant total: Grants are made totalling about £4,000 each year to around 10 individuals.

Applications: In writing to the correspondent, to be submitted by the individual for consideration at any time.

Correspondent: Paul Pearson, Leather Trade House, Kings Park Road, Moulton Park, Northampton NN3 6JD

Levant

Council for British Research in the Levant

Eligibility: British citizens or those ordinarily resident in the UK, Isle of Man or the Channel Islands carrying out arts, humanities and social sciences research in connection with the countries of the Levant (Cyprus, Israel, Jordan, Lebanon, Palestine and Syria). Students registered on a full-time undergraduate or postgraduate degree in a UK university are eligible to apply for travel grants.

Types of grants: Research awards are open to individuals seeking support for advanced research at postdoctoral or equivalent level. Travel grants are open to individuals undertaking study or research at undergraduate, postgraduate or postdoctoral level.

Exclusions: No grants towards maintenance, fees, conferences, language courses, field schools/group tours, books or equipment.

Annual grant total: In 2006/07 the trust had assets of £213,000 and an income of £555,000. A total of £113,000 was given in grants to individuals, mostly in research awards, but also for pump-priming awards, travel grants, scholarships and direct costs of beneficiaries.

Applications: On a form available from the correspondent or available to download from the website. Research award forms to be submitted by 1 December; travel grant forms to be submitted by 31 January.

Correspondent: The UK Secretary, The British Academy, 10 Carlton House Terrace, London SW1Y 5AH (020 7969 5296; Fax: 020 7969 5401; email: cbrl@britac.ac.uk; website: www. cbrl.org.uk)

Other information: For further details or advice, please contact the UK secretary (cbrl@britac.ac.uk) or the Director (b.finlayson@cbrl.org.uk).

Littoral

The British Institute of Archaeology at Ankara

Eligibility: British undergraduates and postgraduates studying the Turkish and Black Sea littoral in all academic disciplines within the arts, humanities and social sciences. Scholars from Turkey and the countries surrounding the Black Sea who are studying in the UK can also be supported. Applicants for travel and conference grants must be based at a UK university or academic institution.

Types of grants: The trust gives grants for the following purposes:

- Travel grants – up to £500 to students in the fields of arts, humanities and social sciences for travel to and around Turkey and the region of the Black Sea littoral.

- Study grants – comprising of an airfare (£300) and funding for basic subsistence and accommodation (£500 per month) for individuals carrying at doctoral or postdoctoral research in the arts, humanities and social sciences relating to Turkey and the Black Sea littoral

- Fieldwork grants – up to £400 to enable an undergraduate or postgraduate fieldwork project that relates to Hellenic studies in its widest sense

- Conference grants – up to £500 to support conferences, day-schools, workshops and seminars in the fields of the arts, humanities and social sciences relating to Turkey and the Black Sea littoral. Grants are mainly intended to be used to pay the travel expenses of speakers.

The trust offers funding for an annual post-doctoral research fellowship and a research scholarship based at the Institute in Ankara, and also provides scholarships to enable students from Turkey and the Black Sea region to travel to the UK.

Annual grant total: In 2006/07 the institute had assets of £430,000 and an income of £504,000. Grants made to individuals totalled £71,000.

Applications: Application forms are available from the correspondent.

Correspondent: Gina Coulthard, 10 Carlton House Terrace, London SW1Y 5AH (020 7969 5204; Fax: 020 7969 5401; email: biaa@britac.ac. uk; website: www.biaa.ac.uk)

Other information: The institute also runs a number of schemes solely for postgraduates as well as overseeing a number of other funds. Please see the institute's website for further details.

Marxism, socialism & working class history

The Barry Amiel & Norman Melburn Trust

Eligibility: Groups and individuals working to advance public education in the philosophy of Marxism, the history of socialism, and the working class movement.

Types of grants: Grants to individuals and organisations range from £200 to £7,000, and are paid for a range of archiving, research, printing, publishing and conference costs.

Previously funded projects have included the organisation of lectures, discussions, seminars and workshops; the carrying out of research, written work and publications; and the maintenance of libraries and archive material.

Exclusions: The trust does not award funds to subsidise the continuation or running of university/college courses, or subsidise fees/maintenance for undergraduate/postgraduate students.

Annual grant total: In 2006/07 the trust had assets of £1.7 million and an income of £43,000. Grants were made totalling £70,000 and were distributed as follows:

- conferences and seminars – £27,000
- website project – £22,000
- publications and pamphlets – £11,000
- research and archiving – £10,000.

Applications: On a form available from the correspondent. The trustees meet twice a year to consider applications, usually in January and June.

Correspondent: Willow Grylls, 8 Wilton Way, London, E8 3EE (020 7254 1561; Fax: 020 7254 1561; email: williow.grylls@ companypictures.co.uk, or to apply for funding, apply@amielandmelburn.org.uk; website: www.amielandmelburn.org.uk)

Media

Frank Copplestone Trust

Eligibility: People involved with media projects related to Cornish culture.

Types of grants: Grants and bursaries.

Annual grant total: In 2006/07 the trust had an income of £600 and a total expenditure of £3,900. Grants to individuals usually total about £3,000 a year.

Applications: In writing to the correspondent.

Correspondent: Karen Winn, Finance Office, University College Falmouth, 25 Woodlane, Falmouth, Cornwall, TR11 4RH

Other information: Grants are also made to organisations.

George Viner Memorial Fund

Eligibility: British black and asian students wishing to gain employment in radio, print and photo journalism.

Types of grants: Grants for course fees, books or travel payments.

Annual grant total: In 2006/07 the fund had an income of £10,000 and a total expenditure of £23,000.

Applications: On a form available form the fund.

Correspondent: The General Secretary, Headland House, 308–312 Grays Inn Road, London WC1X 8DP (020 7278 7916; email: georgeviner@nuj.org.uk; website: www.georgeviner.org.uk)

Other information: The trust also provides mentoring, course and careers guidance.

The Welsh Broadcasting Trust

Eligibility: People who wish to expand their knowledge of the media. Applicants must have been fully resident in Wales for at least two years prior to making the application, have been born in Wales, or be Welsh speakers.

Types of grants: Participation in appropriate training or career development courses, full or part-time, for example writing workshops/specialist technical skills/business development; attendance of educational courses at higher degree level; travel grants to accredited festivals/ markets; projects which enrich the cultural experience through the medium of television, film, radio and new media.

Exclusions: The trust does not fund undergraduate entry to courses.

Annual grant total: About £12,000.

Applications: Application forms are available from trust's website, or contact the trust for a printed application form.

The trustees meet twice a year, usually at the end of March and beginning of September to assess applications.

Correspondent: The Secretary, Islwyn, Lôn Terfyn, Morfa Nefyn, Pwllheli, Gwynedd, LL53 6AP (01758 720 132 (after 6pm); email: info@wbt.org.uk; website: www.ydg. org.uk)

Other information: Grants are also made to training bodies or companies which offer specific training/educational programmes.

Medicine, including medical research, nursing & veterinary studies

The Ted Adams Trust Limited

Eligibility: Students of nursing/midwifery, whether pre or post registration, undergoing courses in the Guildford area.

Types of grants: Funding for course fees or other costs, to enable nurses and midwives to further their professional education and development. The trust is particularly keen to fund individuals where the outcomes of their course/study will enhance patient care in the local area.

Exclusions: The trust cannot help with debts or living expenses.

Annual grant total: In 2006/07 the trust had an income of £126,000 and out of a total expenditure of £109,000, made grants totalling £15,000.

Applications: An application form can be downloaded from the trust's website, or is available by email.

Correspondent: The Trustees, Ashcombe Court, Woolsack Way, Godalming, Surrey, GU7 1LQ (email: tedadamstrust@live.co. uk; website: www.tedadamstrust.org.uk)

Other information: The trust also maintains Ted Adams House for the use of

pre-registration students of nursing and midwifery.

The Worshipful Society of Apothecaries General Charity Limited

Eligibility: Penultimate and final year medical and pharmaceutical students who are in need.

Types of grants: One-off and recurrent grants of about £1,000 a year.

Annual grant total: In 2006/07 the trust had assets of £1.1 million, an income of £68,000 and a total expenditure of £78,000. Grants given to 32 individuals totalled around £38,000.

Applications: Every year the trustees write to the dean of every medical school in the country requesting nominations of eligible students, to be submitted by 30 June. The committee considers the recommendations in July, and the grants are disbursed in August.

Correspondent: Andrew Wallington Smith, Apothecaries Hall, Black Friars Lane, London EC4V 6EJ (020 7236 1189; email: clerk@apothecaries.org)

Other information: Organisations are also supported.

British Society for Antimicrobial Chemotherapy

Eligibility: Postgraduate and undergraduate students involved in research and training in antimicrobial chemotherapy.

Types of grants: The trust offers the following grants, which details of how to apply for each individual award on the society's website,

- Project Grants – up to £10,000 for projects of up to one year duration
- Research Grants – up to £45,000 for projects of up to one year duration
- Overseas Scholarships – up to £1,000 per calendar month, to enable workers from other countries the opportunity to work in UK departments for up to six months
- Vacation Grants – £180 per week for up to ten weeks, designed to give undergraduate experience in research, candidates should be on a full-time first degree course in the sciences, medicine, veterinary medicine or dentistry. Grants not available for students on MA courses.
- Travel Grants – up to £1500, restricted to BSAC members, to enable individuals to attend the annual meetings of ECCMID and ICAAC

Annual grant total: In 2006 the society had assets of £5 million and an income of £1.8 million. £19,000 was given in grants to individuals, with a further £126,000 given through institutions, namely universities.

Applications: On a form available from the correspondent, or on-line. Apart from travel grants, all grants have to be made via the institution attended by the student. The closing dates for submission of applications for travel grants are 31 August and 31 January each year; applicants will be informed of the result of their application in January and May of each year respectively.

Correspondent: Tracey Guest, 11 The Wharf, 16 Bridge Street, Birmingham B1 2JS (0121 633 0410; Fax: 0121 643 9497; email: tguest@bsac.org.uk; website: www. bsac.org.uk)

The Roger & Sarah Bancroft Clark Charitable Trust

Eligibility: People studying in the UK, including overseas students. Grants are mainly for medical and dental electives, and for overseas voluntary aid work.

Types of grants: Grants are given according to need.

Exclusions: Grants are not made for overseas outward bound activities and expeditions.

Annual grant total: In 2006 the trust had net assets of £4.8 million, an income of around £187,000 and a total expenditure of £225,000. Grants were given to 219 individuals totalling £59,000.

Applications: In writing to the correspondent, enclosing an sae. Applications are considered about three or four times a year. Applicants cannot receive more than one grant a year.

Correspondent: Lynette Cooper, KPMG, 100 Temple Street, Bristol, BS1 6AG (0117 9054694; Fax: 0117 9054065; email: lynette.cooper@clarks.com)

The Jean Ginsburg Memorial Foundation *see entry on page 71*

Correspondent: Ian Henry, The Garden Gouse, 9 Ardwick Road, London, NW2 2BX (email: info@janginsburgh.com; website: www.jeanginsburg.com/)

The Dr Robert Malcolm Trust

Eligibility: Students studying for a medicine degree. Grants are only given for first degrees. Applicants do not have to be in Scotland.

Types of grants: Grants towards the cost of medical education.

Annual grant total: The trustees state that this is a 'small family trust with limited assets'.

Applications: In writing to the correspondent. Recently the trustees have found it more successful to directly target potential applicants through referral from school headteachers. The headteachers must give details of the students' potential ability and their funding needs.

Correspondent: Ian Brash, Trustee, Fa'side Castle, Tranent, East Lothian EH33 2LE

The Nightingale Fund

Eligibility: Nurses and hospital attendants seeking further training.

Types of grants: One-off and recurrent grants in the range of £300 to £3,000.

Annual grant total: About £25,000.

Applications: On a form available form the Honorary Secretary to be submitted directly by the individual in January, May or September. Two references are required.

Correspondent: Mrs J Chambers, Honorary Secretary, 55 Recreation Road, Shortlands, Bromley, Kent, BR2 0DY

The Nurses Association of Jamaica (NAJ) (UK)

Eligibility: Primarily people from black and ethnic minority groups, especially African-Caribbean groups, who are aged 18 or over. The trust will consider any studies to promote the practice of nursing, midwifery and health visiting. This may range from students undertaking studies in health education, nursing courses at degree, diploma, certificate and attendance levels, sociology, psychology, nursing and other health and health science related programmes, in particular where the course of study will impact positively on the health and health care of ethnic minority groups. The trust also considers the following funding priorities: business schools and pre-school education; IT training; special needs education; and training for community development. Preference is given to people living in Birmingham, London, Nottingham and internationally.

Types of grants: One-off grants ranging between £50 and £300 towards books, fees, educational outings in the UK, study or travel abroad, student exchanges and people who are black or part of an ethnic minority group studying in the UK.

Priority is given to part-funding for one year or less, although a period of up to two years may be considered.

Annual grant total: Previously grants have totalled about £15,000.

Applications: Application forms are available from the association. Application forms can be submitted directly by the individual, through a school/college or educational welfare agency, or through another third party. All applications should be supported with a reference. The completed form can be returned in February or August, with supporting statements to justify the purpose of the application, costings and how the money will be used, and specific details about the study/projects supported. They are considered in September and March.

Correspondent: NAJ (UK), PO Box 1270, Croydon, Surrey CR9 3DA (email: info@ najuk.org; website: www.najuk.org)

The May Price SRN Award *see entry on page 109*

Correspondent: Roger Jones, The Old School, Llansteffan Road, Johnstown, Carmarthen, Dyfed, SA31 3LZ

Sandra Charitable Trust

Eligibility: People pursuing a career in nursing.

Types of grants: One-off and recurrent grants according to need.

Annual grant total: In 2006/07 the trust had assets of £15.9 million, an income of £350,000 and a total expenditure £367,000. There were 134 grants to individuals made totalling £70,000. Grants to organisations totalled £293,000.

Applications: In writing to the correspondent, although the trust's funds are largely committed. The trustees meet on a frequent basis to consider applications.

Correspondent: Keith Lawrence, Moore Stephens, St Paul's House, Warwick Lane, London EC4M 7BP (020 7334 9191)

The Society for Relief of Widows & Orphans of Medical Men

Eligibility: Medical students who have at least one parent who is a doctor, and whose family is in financial need.

Types of grants: One-off and recurrent grants of £500 to £3,000 to college students, undergraduates, vocational and mature students for fees, books, maintenance/living expenses, instruments/ equipment and clothing (not to mature students), and to schoolchildren and people starting work for maintenance/ living expenses.

Exclusions: Grants are not normally given for second degrees.

Annual grant total: In 2007 a total of 68 grants were made to widows and orphans totalling £39,000.

Applications: On a form available from the correspondent. Applications should be submitted directly by the individual and are considered in February, May, August and November.

Correspondent: The Secretary, Medical Society of London, Lettsom House, 11 Chandos Street, Cavendish Square, London W1G 9EB

Sir John Sumner's Trust

Eligibility: People studying nursing or medicine, including veterinary studies, who are in need and living in the UK, although there is a strong preference for the Midlands.

Types of grants: Grants towards equipment, instruments, fees or living expenses.

Exclusions: No grants towards religious or political causes.

Annual grant total: In 2006/07 the trust had assets of £953,000 and an income of £45,000. Grants totalled £28,000.

Applications: In writing to the correspondent, through the individual's college or a welfare agency. Two referees should be provided, one of whom must be from the relevant educational establishment. Applications can be considered at any time.

Correspondent: The Secretary to the Trustees, No. 1 Colmore Square, Birmingham, B4 6AA

Metal work & metal jewellery

The Goldsmiths Arts Trust Fund

Eligibility: Apprentices and students studying silversmithing and precious metal jewellery at art colleges.

Types of grants: Bursaries for specific projects of £100 to £500. Previous donations have been made for financing exhibitions, assistance with educating apprentices, bursaries, masterclasses and courses.

Exclusions: Grants are not normally made for fees or subsistence on standard courses at further or higher education institutions. Grants are not made to overseas students studying in the UK.

Annual grant total: In 2006 the trust had assets of £75,000 and an income of £888,000. Bursaries were awarded to 106 individuals totalling £29,000. A further £72,000 was given in grants to organisations.

Applications: In writing to the correspondent, through an organisation such as a college or university. Applications are considered quarterly.

Correspondent: The Clerk, The Goldsmiths' Company, Goldsmiths' Hall, Foster Lane, London EC2V 6BN (020 7606 7010; Fax: 020 7606 1511; email: the.clerk@thegoldsmiths.co.uk; website: www.thegoldsmiths.co.uk)

The South Square Trust *see entry on page 68*

Correspondent: Mrs Nicola Chrimes, Clerk to the Trustees, PO Box 169, Lewes, East Sussex, BN7 9FB

Nautical or maritime courses

Reardon Smith Nautical Trust

Eligibility: Residents of Wales up to the age of 25 studying recognised nautical or maritime courses. These should relate to shipping, maritime law and commerce, navigation, sailing, oceanography and marine related environmental issues, in particular those which give the individual first hand practical experience of being at sea.

Types of grants: Grants, scholarships, exhibitions and bursaries.

Annual grant total: In 2007/08 the trust had assets of £2.9 million and an income of £184,000. Awards totalled £156,000.

Applications: Applications should be made via a relevant educational establishment.

Correspondent: John Cory, Cob Cottage, Garth Hill, Pentyrch, Cardiff, CF15 9NS

Polish history, literature or art

The Broncel Trust

Eligibility: People working in the fields of Polish history, literature or art.

Types of grants: Scholarships, research and grants for publishing Polish works of literature.

Annual grant total: In 2006/07 the trust had an income of £16,000 and a total expenditure of £14,000. In previous years, around £4,800 was given in grants to individuals.

Applications: In writing to the correspondent.

Correspondent: Ms A Marianska, Secretary, 294 Acton High Street, London, W3 9BJ

Other information: Grants are made to organisations with occasional financial support for libraries, museums and exhibitions.

Postal history

The Stuart Rossiter Trust Fund

Eligibility: Anyone of any nationality undertaking original research into postal history with a view to publication. English language is preferred in published or electronic form to promote accessibility.

Types of grants: Grants towards: translations; cost of hire of researchers; publication costs; and costs of research. Part or the entire grant may be recovered from sales of the publication.

Exclusions: The trust only gives grants for research into postal history with a view to publication.

Annual grant total: In 2007 the trust had assets of £347,000 and an income of £23,000. Grants totalled £1,400.

Applications: Application forms are available from the correspondent, or from the trust's website.

Correspondent: R Pizer, 6 Drews Court, Churchdown, Gloucestershire, GL3 2LD (website: www.rossitertrust.com)

Religion/ministry

The Andrew Anderson Trust

Eligibility: People studying theology.

Types of grants: One-off and recurrent grants according to need.

Annual grant total: In 2006/07 the trust had assets of £10 million and an income of £255,000. Grants to organisations and individuals totalled £247,000.

Applications: The trust states that it rarely gives to people who are not known to the trustees or who have been personally recommended by people known to the trustees. Unsolicited applications are therefore unlikely to be successful.

Correspondent: The Trustees, 84 Uphill Road, Mill Hill, London NW7 4QE (020 8959 2145)

Other information: Grants are also made to organisations.

The Aria (Portsmouth) Trust

Eligibility: Men under 25 in Great Britain who intend to enter the Anglo-Jewish ministry and attend a recognised educational establishment.

Types of grants: One-off grants according to need.

Annual grant total: In 2006/07 the trust had an income of £5,500 and a total expenditure of £10,500.

Applications: In writing to the correspondent, directly by the individual.

Correspondent: Mrs Joanna Benarroch, Office of the Chief Rabbi, Adler House, 735 High Road, London N12 0US (020 8343 6301; Fax: 020 8343 6310; email: info@chiefrabbi.org; website: www.chiefrabbi.org)

The Barnabas Trust

Eligibility: People embarking on Christian mission activities, and people on religious education courses.

Types of grants: One-off grants according to need.

Annual grant total: In 2006/07 the trust had assets of £3.2 million, an income of £136,000 and a total expenditure of £347,000. Grants totalling £31,000 were given to 26 individuals, covering areas of education and Christian missionary work both overseas and in the UK.

Applications: In writing to the correspondent. Applications should be submitted by the end of February. Trustees meet quarterly.

Correspondent: Mrs Doris Edwards, 63 Wolsey Drive, Walton-on-Thames, Surrey KT12 3BB (01932 220622)

The CPAS Ministers in Training Fund

Eligibility: Evangelical Anglican ordinands who are in financial need during their training.

Types of grants: Recurrent grants, one per academic year, to help with maintenance and personal expenses. They range between £50 and £500.

Annual grant total: In 2006/07 the fund had an income of £1.9 million, of which £16,000 was distributed to individuals through the Ministers in Training Fund.

Applications: Application forms are available from the correspondent. Applications should be submitted in October or January. Applicants are asked for two referees and a completed budget form to detail income and expenditure. Time should be allowed for references to be taken up.

Correspondent: Mrs Pauline Walden, CPAS, Athena Drive, Tachbrook Park, Warwick CV34 6NG (01926 458480; Fax: 01926 458459; email: pwalden@cpas.org.uk; website: www.cpas.org.uk)

Other information: The fund gives a large proportion of its income to other ecumenical causes such as parish support, publications, training events and children and youth projects.

The Elland Society

Eligibility: Men and women in training for the ordained ministry of the Church of England who are evangelical in conviction and outlook. Priority for grants is given to ordinands from dioceses in the province of York or who will serve their title in that province.

Types of grants: Grants are given to those who have already started training at theological college, be it residential or non-residential, and who have financial needs outside their anticipated agreed budget relating to actual items of expenditure. Recent grants given were towards, for example, family educational expenses, postgraduate study, car expenses where it was needed for training or a spouse's job, replacement of fridge and dental treatment. Grants to individuals seldom exceed £500 per person.

Annual grant total: In 2006/07 the trust had an income of £6,200 and a total expenditure of £5,000.

Applications: In writing to the correspondent.

Correspondent: Revd C I Judd, Secretary, 57 Grosvenor Road, Shipley, West Yorkshire BD18 4RB (01274 584775; email: www.thejudds@saltsvillage. wanadoo.co.uk)

The Lady Hewley Trust

Eligibility: Young men or women preparing for Baptist or United Reformed Church ministries. Preference will be given to students who were born in the north of England.

Types of grants: Exhibitions are given to students who are approved by the relevant church authorities and attend one of the following colleges: Northern Baptist College, Manchester; Northern College, Manchester; Mansfield College, Oxford; Westminster College, Cambridge; or The Queen's Foundation, Birmingham. The size of grants given is related to other income, although the usual maximum is £300 to £400.

Exclusions: No grants will be given when local authority funds are available.

Annual grant total: In 2006/07 the trust had assets of £5.1 million and an income of £180,000. Grants to individuals totalled £65,000, of which £15,000 was given in student grants.

Applications: Should be made on a form available from the college concerned. Applications should be submitted via the college by 15 July for the meeting of the trustees in November.

Correspondent: D R Wharrie, Clerk, Woodside House, Ashton, Chester CH3 8AE (01829 751544)

Lady Peel Legacy Trust

Eligibility: Individuals training to be priests in the Anglo-Catholic tradition.

Types of grants: One-off or recurrent grants according to need.

Annual grant total: About £4,000 a year for educational and welfare purposes.

Applications: In writing to the correspondent. The closing dates for applications are 1 April and 1 November each year. Telephone contact is not invited.

Correspondent: Revd Preb James Trevelyan, Bridge End, Barbon, Carnforth LA6 2LT

Powis Exhibition Fund

Eligibility: People who are training as ordinands in the Church in Wales. Applicants must: have an adequate knowledge of the Welsh language; and have been born, or be resident, in Wales.

Types of grants: Grants of up to £700 annually, for no longer than the period of study.

Annual grant total: About £1,500.

Applications: Application forms are available form the correspondent or from individual dioceses.

Correspondent: John Richfield, 37–39 Cathedral Road, Cardiff CF11 9XF (029 2034 8200; Fax: 029 2038 7835; email: johnrichfield@churchinwales.org. uk)

St Christopher's College Educational Trust

Eligibility: People studying religious education connected with promoting the objects of the Church of England/Wales.

Types of grants: One-off and recurrent grants in the range of £250 and £2,000.

Exclusions: No grants to students studying overseas.

Annual grant total: In 2006 grants totalled £15,000 and included a grant of £400 to an individual towards the cost of an MA.

Applications: In writing to the correspondent.

Correspondent: The Trustees, c/o The National Society, Church House, Great Smith Street, Westminster, London SW1P 3NZ

The Foundation of St Matthias

Eligibility: Further and higher education students, including mature students and occasionally postgraduates, who are studying in accordance with the doctrine of the Church of England. Preference is given to people studying teaching or religious education who are living in the dioceses of Bristol, Bath & Wells and Gloucester. In practice funding is absorbed by people who meet these preferences.

Types of grants: One-off grants usually ranging from £100 to £750. Grants can be for books, fees, maintenance/living expenses, childcare and for some study or travel abroad. Foreign students studying in the UK may also be supported (but not at postgraduate level).

Annual grant total: In 2007 the foundation had net assets of £6.4 million and an income of £212,000. The foundation gave grants to individuals totalling £12,000.

Applications: Applicants should telephone in the first instance to discuss the nature of study and so on. Applications must be made on a form available from the foundation's website. They should be submitted directly by the individual by 1 January, 1 June and 1 September for consideration in February, July and October, respectively.

Correspondent: Lynette Cox, Church House, 23 Great George Street, Bristol BS1 5QZ (0117 906 0100; email: lynette. cox@bristoldiocese.org; website: www. stmatthiastrust.org.uk/)

Other information: Grants can also be given to educational organisations and schools with a Christian focus.

The Thornton Fund

Eligibility: Students at Unitarian colleges or training for Unitarian ministry.

Types of grants: Grants between £250 and £1,500 to help with books, equipment, instruments, living expenses, study exchange and study or travel abroad.

Annual grant total: Grants usually total around £15,000 per year.

Applications: In writing to the correspondent through a third party such as a minister, including the total and annual estimated costs of study. They are considered on an ongoing basis.

Correspondent: Dr Jane Williams, 93 Fitzjohn Avenue, Barnet, Hertfordshire EN5 2HR (020 8440 2211)

Torchbearer Trust Fund

Eligibility: People engaged in full-time Christian instruction or training. Preference is given to students and former students of Torchbearer Bible schools.

Types of grants: One-off grants and bursaries according to need.

Annual grant total: In 2006/07 the trust had assets of £156,000 and an income of £42,000. Grants totalled £49,000.

Applications: In writing to the correspondent.

Correspondent: The Secretary, Capernwray Hall, Carnforth, Lancashire LA6 1AG (01524 733908; Fax: 01524 736681; email: info@ capernwray.org.uk; website: www. capernwray.org.uk)

Other information: Grants are also available for missionary work.

Seafaring

The Corporation of Trinity House, London

Eligibility: Candidates must be between 16 and $18\frac{1}{2}$ years old with five GCSE at grade C or better and must also have passed the Department of Transport medical examination. Applicants must also be British and permanently resident in the British Isles. Applicants must be applying to become an officer in the Merchant Navy.

Types of grants: The Trinity House Merchant Navy Scholarship Scheme provides financial support for young people seeking careers as officers in the Merchant Navy.

Cadets undertake a three or four year programme split between nautical college and time at sea in a variety of British-managed vessels. Cadets can train as either Deck or Engineer Officers or pursue a Marine Cadetship encompassing both disciplines. Full scholarships are available for this programme of £7,000, under the Trinity House Cadet Training Scheme.

Annual grant total: In 2006/07, the corporation had net assets of £96 million, an income of £4.6 million, and a total expenditure of £4.3 million. Scholarships were awarded to 14 individuals totalling £98,000. Most of the corporation's funds are reserved for welfare purposes, namely almshouse accommodation.

Applications: Details of the scholarship scheme are available upon application in writing to the correspondent.

Correspondent: Peter Galloway, Trinity House, Tower Hill, London, EC3N 4DH (020 7481 6900; email: peter.galloway@ thls.org; website: www.trinityhouse.co.uk)

The Honourable Company of Master Mariners

Eligibility: People who are serving or intending to serve in the Merchant Navy.

Types of grants: Grants to encourage the education, instruction and training of applicants.

Annual grant total: Previously about £14,000 per year.

Applications: On a form available from the correspondent. Applications can be submitted directly by the individual, through a social worker, Citizens Advice, or other welfare agency, or by a friend or relative. They are considered throughout the year.

Correspondent: The Clerk, HQS Wellington, Temple Stairs, Victoria Embankment, London, WC2R 2PN (website: www.hcmm.org.uk)

The Marine Society and Sea Cadets

Eligibility: Professional seafarers, active or retired. Those who, while not professional seafarers, would prepare themselves to join sea services in time of emergency.

Types of grants: 'It is the society's policy to help where financial hardship is evident. If the applicant is likely to be employed or re-employed then interest-free loans may be given rather than grants. The award of a loan or grant is usually made to an applicant who is attempting to improve his career prospects, or who has to change his career due to unforeseen circumstances.' In addition, the society offers a scholarship scheme for seafarers or prospective seafarers.

Exclusions: Recurrent grants are not made.

Annual grant total: In 2006/07 the trust had assets of £14.5 million and an income of £11.3 million. Grants to individuals totalled £1.7 million, although the trust states that 'individual grants given are small and not material within the overall total.'

Applications: On a form obtainable from the correspondent. Applications are considered as they arrive.

Correspondent: Miss Claire E Barnett, 202 Lambeth Road, London SE1 7JW (020 7654 7011; Fax: 020 7928 8914; email: info@ms-sc.org; website: www.ms-sc.org)

Other information: Grants are also made to sea cadet units.

Shipbuilding

The Worshipful Company of Shipwrights' Educational Trust

Eligibility: UK citizens, preferably under 25, who are involved in any craft or discipline connected with ship and boatbuilding, design or research.

Types of grants: Grants range from assistance given to apprentices in the boatbuilding trade to postgraduate research costs. Many grants are to individuals to develop their skills rather than for help with professional education for which local education authority grants are usually available.

Exclusions: No grants to non-UK citizens.

Annual grant total: In 2006/07 the trust had assets of £1.1 million, an income of £64,000 and made grants totalling £43,000 to organisations and individuals.

Applications: Application forms can be downloaded from the trust's website.

Correspondent: The Clerk, Worshipful Company of Shipwrights, Ironmongers' Hall, Shaftesbury Place, Barbican, London EC2Y 8AA (020 7606 2376; email: clerk@ shipwrights.co.uk; website: www. shipwrights.co.uk/)

Sport

Athletics for the Young

Eligibility: Young people under the age of 25 who are in school, college or university.

Types of grants: One-off educational grants towards athletic pursuits.

Annual grant total: In 2006/07 the charity had an income of £27,000 and made grants totalling £2,500.

Applications: In writing to the correspondent.

Correspondent: Alan Barlow, 12 Redcar Close, Hazel Grove, Stockport, SK7 4SQ (0161 483 9330)

Other information: The charity has also made grants to athletics clubs in previous years.

The Dickie Bird Foundation

Eligibility: Disadvantaged young people under the age of 18 who are participating in sport.

Types of grants: One-off grants usually ranging from £100 to £1,000, according to need. Grants are usually given for items of clothing such as shirts, shorts and footwear, and for equipment and travel within the UK.

Exclusions: Grants cannot be given for:

- Professional fees of any kind, including club membership, or club fees
- Travel outside the UK
- Scholarships, summer/winter/training camps
- Equipment that is available for use elsewhere.

Annual grant total: In 2006/07 the foundation had both an income and total expenditure of approximately £50,000 and made grants totalling around £5,000.

Applications: Application forms can be downloaded from the foundation's website. Applicants need to show that they are unable to raise the finance necessary through any other means. Applications also need to be supported by two independent referees.

Correspondent: The Grants Officer, 47 Ripon Road, Earlsheaton, Dewsbury, West Yorkshire, WF12 7LG (email: info@ thedickiebirdfoundation.org, dbfgrants@ btinternet.com; website: www. thedickiebirdfoundation.org)

The Monica Elwes Shipway Sporting Foundation

Eligibility: Schoolchildren engaged in sporting activities who live in England and Wales and have limited resources.

Types of grants: One-off grants ranging from £100 to £250 to schoolchildren towards school clothing, equipment and fees.

Annual grant total: In 2006/07 the trust had an income of £3,300 and a total expenditure of £2,400.

Applications: In writing to the correspondent, for consideration throughout the year.

Correspondent: S Goldring, 23 Tufton Road, Gillingham, Kent ME8 7SH (01634 260012; Fax: 01634 263575)

The John Taylor Foundation for Young Athletes

Eligibility: Young amateur athletes based within the UK.

Types of grants: Grants given include those towards equipment and travel costs.

Annual grant total: In 2006/07 the trust had an income of £1,800 and a total expenditure of £610.

Applications: On a form which can be downloaded from the trust's website.

Correspondent: Kirstin Bailey, 1 Smithy Fold, Rushton Spencer, Macclesfield, Cheshire, SK11 0SD (email: enquiries@ johntaylorfoundation.org.uk; website: www.johntaylorfoundation.org. uk)

Other information: John Taylor was a young international athlete who died from a heart condition known as cardiomyopathy. One of the aims of the foundation is to provide awareness of this condition.

Stationery

The Stationers & Newspaper Makers Educational Charity *see entry on page 63*

Correspondent: J P Thornton, Secretary, The Old Dairy, Adstockfields, Adstock, Buckingham MK18 2JE (01296 714886)

Surveying

Company of Chartered Surveyors 1991 Trust

Eligibility: Further and higher education students of the surveying profession who live in the UK.

Types of grants: One-off grants ranging from £100 to £500 for books, fees and maintenance/living expenses.

Annual grant total: In 2006 the trust had assets of £1 million and an income of £93,000. Around £1,000 a year is given in grants to individuals.

Applications: In writing to the correspondent. Applications can be submitted at any time in the year directly by the individual or through the individual's college, university or educational establishment. Letters of support from the individual's tutor or head of department must be provided. Applications are considered quarterly, in January, March, June and September.

Correspondent: Mrs A Jackson, 75 Meadway Drive, Horsell, Woking, Surrey GU21 4TF (01483 727113; Fax: 01483 720098; email: wccsurveyors@ btopenworld.com; website: www. surveyorslivery.org.uk)

Other information: This trust also gives grants to universities to be given to students as prizes.

Teaching

All Saints Educational Trust

Eligibility: People aged 18 or over who are training to be teachers, or are connected with education, in home economics or related subjects, and in religious subjects including multi-cultural and inter-faith matters. Applicants must be UK or EU citizens at UK institutions. Serving teachers who are seeking further relevant qualifications are also supported.

Types of grants: One-off and recurrent grants are given to help with fees, maintenance, books and travel costs. The trust only gives partial funding. Students on part-time or one-year courses take preference over people on longer courses. Grants usually range from £300 to £10,000.

Exclusions: No grants are made people who are: classified as an overseas student (grants to overseas students who are Commonwealth citizens, engaged in one-year courses at postgraduate level, enrolled in a UK higher education institution, will be received with effect from September 2007); under 18 years of age; hoping to have a career in business/management, engineering, law, medicine, nursery nursing, social or welfare care; intending to train for ordination; requesting a Sabbatical period; or eligible for government assistance, such as an NHS bursary.

Annual grant total: In 2006/07 the trust had assets of £11.6 million. The trust had an income of £481,000 of which £81,000 went to individual grants. A further £143,000 went to organisations.

Applications: On an initial form available from the website, or by sending an A4 sae to the correspondent. Once it has been verified that the candidate is eligible, a full application form will be sent. The closing date for this completed form is 31 March. Applicants are advised to complete the initial form as early as possible as extensions to the final deadline are only made at the clerk's discretion.

Correspondent: The Clerk, St Katharine Cree Church, 86 Leadenhall Street, London EC3A 3DH (020 7283 4485; Fax: 020 7261 9758; email: aset@aset.org. uk; website: www.aset.org.uk)

Other information: The trust was formed following the closure and sale of the College of All Saints in 1978. The college itself had been formed in 1964 from St Katharine's College, Tottenham (founded by the Society for Promoting Christian Knowledge) and Berridge House (founded by the National Society For Promoting Religious Education).

The Bell Educational Trust Ltd

Eligibility: Funds are used for providing opportunities for the English language learning and teacher training to students and teachers from overseas who would not otherwise have the chance to benefit from this educational opportunity. Providing scholarships is only a small part of the trust's activities.

Types of grants: Attendance at a relevant Bell course.

Annual grant total: In 2006 the trust had assets of £10 million and an income of £16 million. Previously a small number of grants have been made to individuals.

Applications: In writing to the correspondent or via the ESU or British Council.

Correspondent: Chief Executive, Hillscross, Red Cross Lane, Cambridge CB2 3QX (01223 212333; email: ynda. connon@bell-centres.com; website: www. bell-centres.com)

The Hockerill Educational Foundation *see entry on page 23*

Correspondent: Colin Broomfield, 16 Hagsdell Road, Hertford SG13 8AG (01992 303053; Fax: 01992 425950; email: hockerill.trust@ntlworld.com)

Textiles

The British Cotton Growing Association: Work People's Collection Fund

Eligibility: Anyone, including postgraduates, undertaking approved study and/or research of a medical, nursing or social nature beneficial to workers in the UK textile industry.

Types of grants: Research grants, of up to £30,000 per year, for approved study or research of a medical, nursing or social nature which will benefit the industry, including PhD studentships. The association also considers fees, maintenance costs and foreign students living and studying in the UK.

Annual grant total: In 2006/07 the trust had assets of £1.4 million and an income of £39,000. Grants made to individuals to support research totalled £64,000.

Applications: In writing to the correspondent. Applications (1 to 2 pages) should include full details of the proposed research, background, relevant publications, costings and the names of two referees. Applications should be submitted by mid-April for consideration in May.

Correspondent: Steven Delderfield, Research & Graduate Support Unit, Christie Building, University of Manchester, Oxford Road, Manchester M13 9PL (email: steven.delderfield@ manchester.ac.uk; website: www.campus. manchester.ac.uk/researchoffice/finding/ cotton/)

Coats Foundation Trust

Eligibility: University students living in the UK who are studying textile and thread-related subjects.

Types of grants: One-off grants according to need. Grants are made to college students, undergraduates and mature students for fees, books and equipment/ instruments. Schoolchildren may also receive grants for books and equipment/ instruments.

Annual grant total: In 2006/07 the trust had assets of £2.2 million and an income of £192,000. Grants to individuals for educational purposes totalled £38,000

Applications: In writing to the correspondent enclosing a cv, an sae, details of circumstances (e.g. student status, name of college), the nature and amount of funding required and referee names and addresses. There is no formal application form. Only applicants enclosing an sae will receive a reply. Applications are considered four times a year.

Correspondent: Jenny Mcfarlane, Coats plc, Pension Office, Pacific House, 70 Wellington Street, Glasgow G2 6UB (0141 207 6821; Fax: 0141 207 6856; email: gwen.mckerrell@coats.com)

Other information: Grants are also made to organisations (£97,000 2006/07).

Henry Dixon's Foundation for Apprenticing *see entry on page 67*

Correspondent: Charities Administrator, Drapers' Company, Drapers' Hall, London EC2N 2DQ (020 7588 5001; Fax: 020 7628 1988; website: www. thedrapers.co.uk)

The Weavers' Company Textile Education Fund

Eligibility: Students of weaving technology or design attending six specified centres of excellence: Central St Martins College of Art and Design, Chelsea College of Art and Design, Glasgow School of Art, Loughborough University, Royal College of Art and University of Manchester.

Types of grants: Scholarships.

Annual grant total: In the academic year 2008/09 the sum of £30,000 was allocated for scholarships.

Applications: Students must apply via their course tutor. The company will not accept direct applications

Correspondent: The Clerk, The Worshipful Company of Weavers, Saddlers' House, Gutter Lane, London, EC2V 6BR, The Worshipful Company of Weavers, Saddlers' House, Gutter Lane, London, EC2V 6BR (website: www. weavers.org.uk)

Other information: Grants are also made to educational establishments in the UK to encourage the quality of textile teaching.

Wine making

The Wine Guild Charitable Trust

Eligibility: Individuals wishing to further their studies in the wine making industry.

Types of grants: Grants, loans or bursaries.

Annual grant total: About £1,000.

Applications: In writing to the correspondent.

Correspondent: Mrs Jane Grey-Edwards, Council Secretary, Christmas Cottage, North Street, Petworth, West Sussex, GU28 0DF (email: jgrey-edwards@tiscali. co.uk)

Work/study overseas

The English Speaking Union of the Commonwealth

Eligibility: People involved in teaching the English language overseas and other education-related or cross-cultural projects.

Types of grants: The union administers a number of small funds that give grants to young people, often in the form of travel scholarships. For details of individual funds, applicants are advised to approach the union.

Annual grant total: In 2007 the trust had assets of £20 million and an income of £334,000. Scholarships were awarded totalling £317,000.

Applications: In writing to the correspondent, with a supporting letter if possible. Applications should be submitted in March and are considered in April.

Correspondent: The Clerk, Dartmouth House, 37 Charles Street, London W1J 5ED (020 7529 1550; email: esu@esu. org)

Other information: Applicants will be interviewed.

LOCAL CHARITIES

This section lists local charities that give grants to individuals for educational purposes. The information in the entry applies only to educational grants and concentrates on what the charity actually does rather than on what its trust deed allows it to do. It does not give a complete picture of the charity's work.

All the charities listed have a grant-making potential of £500 a year for individuals; most are spending considerably more than this.

Regional classification

We have divided the UK into nine geographical areas, as numbered on the map on page 91. Scotland, Wales and England have been separated into areas or counties in a similar way to previous editions of this guide. On page 90, we have included a list under each area or county of the unitary and local authorities they include.

The Northern Ireland section has not been subdivided into smaller areas. Within the other sections, the trusts are ordered as follows.

Scotland:

- Firstly, the charities which apply to the whole of Scotland, or at least two areas in Scotland.

- Secondly, Scotland is sub-divided into five areas. The entries which apply to the whole area, or to at least two unitary authorities within, appear first.

- The rest of the charities in the area are listed in alphabetical order of unitary authority.

Wales:

- Firstly, the charities which apply to the whole of Wales, or at least two areas in Wales.

- Secondly, Wales is sub-divided into three areas. The entries which apply to the whole area, or to at least two unitary authorities within, appear first.

- The rest of the charities in the area are listed in alphabetical order of unitary authority.

England:

- Firstly, the charities which apply to the whole area, or at least two counties in the area.

- Secondly, each area is sub-divided into counties. The entries which apply to the whole county, or to at least two towns within it, appear first.

- The rest of the charities in the county are listed in alphabetical order of city, town or parish.

Please note, in the North East section, we have included a section called Teesside incorporating Hartlepool and Stockton-on-Tees and Middlesbrough and Redcar & Cleveland.

London:

- Firstly, the charities which apply to the whole of Greater London, or to at least two boroughs.

- Secondly, London is sub-divided into the boroughs. The entries are listed in alphabetical order within each borough.

In summary, within each county or area section, the trusts in Scotland and Wales are arranged alphabetically by the unitary or local authority which they benefit, while in England they are listed by the city, town or parish and in London by borough.

To be sure of identifying every relevant local charity, look first at the entries under the heading for your:

- unitary authority for people in Scotland and Wales

- city, town or parish under the relevant regional chapter heading for people living in England

- borough for people living in London.

People in London should then go straight to the start of the London chapter, where trusts which give to individuals in more than one borough in London are listed.

Other individuals should look at the sections for trusts which give to more than one unitary authority or town before finally considering those trusts at the start of the chapter that make grants across different areas or counties in your country or region.

For example, if you live in Liverpool, first establish which region Merseyside is in by looking at the map on page 91. Then having established that Merseyside is in region 5, look at the Geographical areas list on page 90 and see on which page the entries for Merseyside start. Then look under the heading for Liverpool to see if there are any relevant charities. Next check the charities which apply to Merseyside generally. Finally, check under the heading for the North West generally.

Having found the trusts covering your area, please read carefully any other eligibility requirements. While some trusts can and do give for any need for people in their area of benefit, most have other criteria which potential applicants must meet.

Geographical areas

1. NORTHERN IRELAND

Aisling Bursaries

Eligibility: Students over 18 in West Belfast going into full-time or part-time further or higher education or vocational training courses. Bursaries are not available for people repeating all or part of a course unless it is due to medical or personal reasons.

Types of grants: One-off and recurrent grants of up to £1,000 each. The trust also administers bursaries sponsored by local businesses.

Annual grant total: Previously grants were made totalling £42,000. The amount given each year depends on the number of sponsors.

Applications: In writing to the correspondent. Deadlines are advertised in the Andersonstown News, usually in March for consideration in June/July. Grants are only awarded once per individual, although previous applicants not supported may reapply.

Correspondent: The Clerk, West Belfast Partnership Board, 218-226 Falls Road, Belfast BT12 6FB (028 9080 9202; email: info@wbpb.org; website: www.westbelfast-partnership.com)

Bank of Ireland Millennium Scholars Trust

Eligibility: People aged 16 or over who have been resident in Ireland or Northern Ireland for at least one year prior to the date of their application, or who can demonstrate a real and substantial connection with the region, and who, because of economic circumstances or other barriers such as disability, are prevented or held back from reaching their full potential.

Applicants should be: students in their final year of secondary education, mature students or other candidates preparing to enter higher education; students in higher education who would be unlikely to continue their courses without financial support; or people with exceptional ability in the creative/performing arts who face obstacles to fulfilling their potential through advanced study or training.

Types of grants: Scholarships of up to €6,300 a year towards living expenses.

Total scholarships to one individual over a number of years can not exceed €38,000.

Annual grant total: 100 scholarships are given each year.

Applications: Applications must be made through one of the trust's nominating bodies, which are Irish organisations and groups approved by the trust to support potential applicants. A full list of these nominating bodies are available on the trust's website. Applications should then be made on a form available with guidelines from the correspondent, to be returned with an appropriate reference. Suitable applicants will be interviewed.

Correspondent: Bank of Ireland Millennium Scholars Trust Office, National College of Ireland, Mayor Street, Dublin 1 (00 3531 449 8500; Fax: 00 3531 497 2200; email: boischolars@ncirl.ie; website: www.boi.ie)

Other information: This trust was established to award 60 scholarships annually for the first 10 years of the 21st century.

The Belfast Association for the Blind

Eligibility: People who are registered blind in Northern Ireland. Consideration may also be given to those registered as partially sighted.

Types of grants: One-off grants for educational needs such as computers, course fees and so on. Grants are also given for welfare purposes.

Annual grant total: In 2007 grants were made totalling £74,000, of which £16,000 was given in grants to individuals.

Applications: In writing to the correspondent through a social worker. Applications are considered throughout the year.

Correspondent: R Gillespie, Hon. Secretary, 30 Glenwell Crescent, Newtownabbey, County Antrim BT36 7TF (028 9083 6407)

Other information: Grants are also made to organisations.

Educational Trust

Eligibility: Ex-prisoners, ex-offenders and their immediate relatives from Ireland who are seeking access to education and/or training and for whom no other sources of funding are available.

Types of grants: The Educational Trust is a North/South charitable Trust which helps ex-offenders and ex-prisoners in Ireland to access education and training. The trust helps ex-offenders to complete academic qualifications and vocational training upon leaving prison. One-off and recurrent grants are offered towards degrees, postgraduate qualifications, NVQs and HGV driving licences. The client group has also been extended to include all offenders and ex-prisoners and their families, and the coverage includes the whole of Ireland.

Exclusions: No grants are made towards computer hardware, capital equipment or setting-up costs of small business initiatives.

Annual grant total: About £1,000 is given in grants each year.

Applications: On a form available from the correspondent. They are considered every four to six weeks.

Correspondent: Heather Reid, c/o NIACRO, 4 Amelia Street, Belfast BT2 7GS (028 9032 0157; email: heather@niacro.co.uk; website: www.niacro.co.uk)

EMMS International

Eligibility: Medical, nursing, dental and therapy (i.e. physiotherapy, occupational therapy) students at universities in Scotland, Northern Ireland or the third world who are undertaking a placement abroad for their elective period, usually in mission hospitals in developing countries. Applicants should normally be in the later stages of the course of study so that the benefits are maximised.

It is preferred that applicants have an active Christian Testimony, but this is not essential. If a grant is awarded however, it is on condition that the applicant spends their elective at an overseas mission hospital.

The trust states that 'Grants are not awarded solely on the basis of academic merit, but rather on your desire to experience healthcare in a 'mission' context. Each application is assessed on its merits'.

Types of grants: Bursaries usually range from £200 to £300, however more may be awarded to applicants working in one of the trusts partnership hospitals in India, Israel, Malawi or Nepal.

Exclusions: Students studying at universities in England and Wales are not eligible.

Annual grant total: In 2007 the trust had an income of £880,000. Previously grants to 26 students totalled approximately £5,100.

Applications: Applications can be submitted at any time of the year and are normally considered within a period of six to eight weeks. Successful applicants will receive their bursaries four weeks prior to an elective starting.

References are required from two referees, with one preferably as a contact from the local church such as a minister or an elder.

Correspondent: Robin G K Arnott, Chief Executive, 7 Washington Lane, Edinburgh EH11 2HA (0131 313 3828; Fax: 0131 313 4662; email: info@emms.org; website: www.emms.org)

The Presbyterian Orphan and Children's Society

Eligibility: Children aged 23 or under who are in full or part-time education, living in Northern Ireland and Republic of Ireland, usually in single parent families. One parent must be a Presbyterian.

Types of grants: Regular grants paid each quarter. Depending on financial resources, a summer grant and Christmas grant is paid to each family.

Annual grant total: Between £400,000 to £500,000 per year.

Applications: Applications are made by Presbyterian clergy; forms are available from the correspondent. They are considered in April and October. As recurrent grants are means tested, applications should be submitted with details of the applicant's income and expenditure.

Correspondent: Dr Paul Gray, Glengall Exchange, 3 Glengall Street, Belfast, BT12 5AB (028 9032 3737; email: paul-gray@ presbyterianorphanandchildrenssociety. org; website: www. presbyterianorphanandchildrenssociety. org)

The Royal Ulster Constabulary Benevolent Fund

Eligibility: Members and ex-members of the Royal Ulster Constabulary and their dependants who are in need.

Types of grants: Support is given to schoolchildren, college students, undergraduates, mature students, people with special educational needs and overseas students towards uniforms, fees, study/travel overseas, books and equipment.

Annual grant total: About £800,000.

Applications: In writing to the correspondent at any time. Applications must be submitted via a regional representative. Grants below £500 are considered throughout the year, while larger donations up to £10,000 are assessed monthly.

Correspondent: The Secretary, Police Federation for Northern Ireland, 77–79 Garnerville Road, Belfast BT4 2NX (44 28 9076 4215; email: info@ rucbenevolentfund.org; website: www. rucbenevolentfund.org)

The Society for the Orphans and Children of Ministers & Missionaries of the Presbyterian Church in Ireland

Eligibility: Children and young people aged under 26 who are orphaned and whose parents were ministers, missionaries or deaconesses of the Presbyterian Church in Ireland.

Types of grants: One-off grants of £300 to £2,000 for general educational purposes.

Annual grant total: Grants to individuals for educational and welfare purposes total about £30,000.

Applications: On a form available from the correspondent. Applications should be submitted directly by the individual in March for consideration in April.

Correspondent: Paul Gray, Glengall Exchange, 3 Glengall Street, Belfast, BT12 5AB (028 9032 3737)

Other information: The trust also gives welfare grants to the children of deceased ministers, missionaries and deaconesses.

The Sydney Stewart Memorial Trust *see entry on page 28*

Correspondent: Grants Officer, Voluntary Service Bureau, 34 Shaftesbury Square, Belfast BT2 7DB (028 9020 0850; Fax: 028 9020 0860; email: info@vsb.org. uk; website: www.vsb.org.uk/)

2. SCOTLAND

The Arrol Trust *see entry on page 25*

Correspondent: C S Kennedy, Lindsays, Caledonian Exchange, 19a Canning Street, Edinburgh, EH3 8HE (0131 229 1212)

The June Baker Trust

Eligibility: Individuals working in the conservation of historic and artistic artefacts in Scotland, or those training to do so.

Types of grants: Awards of £200 to £500 each will be available for travel, training, fees, purchase of equipment, short courses and other suitable projects to students, mature and vocational students and people starting work.

Exclusions: Fees for long, full-time courses are not given.

Annual grant total: The trust has an annual income of £1,000, all of which is usually given in four educational grants.

Applications: On a form available from the correspondent. Applicants may have to attend an interview. A cv and two referees should also be provided. Applications are considered in June, and should be submitted directly by the individual.

Correspondent: Mrs Priscilla Ramsey, Goose Croft House, Kintore, Aberdeenshire AB51 0US (01467 632337; email: ramseyph@tiscali.co.uk)

The Black Watch Association

Eligibility: Serving and retired Black Watch soldiers, their wives, widows and children.

Types of grants: One-off grants in the range of £250 and £500. Grants can be made to schoolchildren, people starting work and students in further/higher education for equipment/instruments, fees, books and maintenance/living expenses.

Exclusions: No grants towards council tax arrears, loans or large debts.

Annual grant total: In 2007 the trust had an income of £130,000.

Applications: On an application form to be completed by a caseworker from SSAFA Forces Help (19 Queen Elizabeth Street, London SE1 2LP. Tel: 020 7403 8783;

Fax: 020 7403 8815; website: www.ssafa.org.uk). Applications are considered on a monthly basis.

Correspondent: Maj. A R McKinnell, Balhousie Castle, Hay Street, Perth PH1 5HR (01738 623214; Fax: 01738 643245)

The Buchanan Society

Eligibility: People with any of the following surnames: Buchanan, McAuslan (any spelling), McWattie or Risk.

Types of grants: Bursaries for students in severe financial difficulties of about £1,000. One-off grants can also be given for general educational purposes.

Annual grant total: About 70 people are supported each year. In 2006/07 the trust had an income of £58,000.

Applications: On a form available from the correspondent, to be submitted either directly by the individual or a family member, or through a third party such as a social worker or teacher. Applications are considered throughout the year.

Correspondent: Mrs Fiona Risk, Secretary, 18 Iddesleigh Avenue, Milngavie, Glasgow G62 8NT (0141 956 1939; Fax: 0141 956 1939)

Other information: The Buchanan Society is the oldest Clan Society in Scotland having been founded in 1725. Grantmaking is its sole function.

The Carnegie Trust for the Universities of Scotland

Eligibility: For fee assistance: undergraduates taking a first degree at, a Scottish university who were born in Scotland, or had a parent born in Scotland, or have had at least two years of secondary education in Scotland.

For university expeditions: the expedition must have a coherent programme of research and must not comprise a number of unrelated individual research projects. To qualify for a grant, an expedition must be sponsored by, and given the name of, the appropriate Scottish university or combination of Universities, and must receive some material support in money or equipment. The trust will give preference

to expeditions that are multi-disciplinary; but this is not a requirement.

Scholarships: graduates of a Scottish university holding a degree with first-class honours in any subject and intending to pursue three years of postgraduate research for a PhD degree.

Small research grants: members of staff or, on a discretionary basis, retired members of staff of a Scottish university for personal research, personally conducted.

Types of grants: Fee assistance: help with tuition fees for a first degree course at a Scottish university.

University expeditions: expeditions which are approved and supported by a Scottish University.

Scholarships: the value of the scholarship for the 2007/08 academic year was £14,000; this figure is expected to rise in future academic years in line with awards funded by the Research Councils.

Small research grants: up to £2,500 can be awarded for travel and accommodation, for up to three months, incurred while undertaking the project. Assistance can also be given with the publication of scholarly books.

Exclusions: See full guidelines, available from the trust's website, for details.

Annual grant total: In 2006/07 the trust had assets of £68.8 million generating an income of £2.3 million. Grants were made through all schemes totalling £2.1 million.

Applications: Directly by the individual, on a form available from the correspondent or the website. A preliminary telephone call may be helpful.

Applications are considered as follows:

Fee assistance: applications are considered from 1 April to 1 October for assistance with fees for the following academic year.

University expeditions: applications must be received by 15 January.

Scholarships: applications must be received by 15 March.

Small research grants: the closing dates for applications are 15 January, 15 May and 15 October.

Correspondent: The Secretary, Andrew Carnegie House, Pittencrief Street, Dunfermline, Fife KY12 8AW (01383 724990; Fax: 01383 749799;

email: jgray@carnegie-trust.org; website: www.carnegie-trust.org)

Other information: Large grants are also given to Scottish universities as a whole.

Churchill University Scholarships Trust for Scotland
see entry on page 25

Correspondent: Kenneth MacRae, McLeish Carswell, 29 St Vincent Place, Glasgow G1 2DT (0141 248 4134)

The James Clark Bequest Fund

Eligibility: Members (including student members) of the Educational Institute of Scotland.

Types of grants: One-off cash grants up to a maximum of £500 each. Between one and four grants are made a year.

Annual grant total: Several grants of £500 are usually awarded each year.

Applications: On a form available from the correspondent to be submitted directly by the individual or a family member. Applications are considered five times a year.

Correspondent: The General Secretary, Educational Institute of Scotland, 46 Moray Place, Edinburgh EH3 6BH (0131 225 6244; Fax: 0131 220 3151; email: sharris@eis.org.uk; website: www. eis.org.uk)

The Cross Trust

Eligibility: Young people aged 16 to 35 who are of Scottish birth or parentage.

Types of grants: Grants of £150 to £1,500 for university or college costs (some courses are subject to restrictions), grants for travel and study abroad in respect of approved projects, and support for vacation projects and study visits. The trustees will consider proposals from university students for study at an overseas institution. Attendance at conferences, symposia and extra-curricular courses can be considered. Voluntary work performed through a recognised charity, such as gap year activities, can also be funded.

Annual grant total: In 2006/07 the trust had assets of £5.1 million and an income of £197,000. Grants were made to 184 individuals totalling approximately £175,000.

Applications: On a form available from the correspondent with guidelines.

Correspondent: Mrs Dorothy Shaw, Assistant Secretary, 25 South Methven Street, Perth PH1 5ES (01738 620451; Fax: 01738 631155; email: Crosstrust@ mccash.co.uk; website: www.thecrosstrust. org.uk/)

Allan Currie Memorial Trust

Eligibility: Young business people with a preference for those living in Glasgow, although people living in other parts of Scotland will be considered.

Types of grants: One-off and recurrent grants for business training.

Annual grant total: The trust has an income of around £1,500, with grants totalling about £1,000.

Applications: In writing to the correspondent.

Correspondent: W Cairns, Messrs Cairns Brown Solicitors, 112 Main Street, Alexandria, Glasgow G83 0NZ (01389 756979; Fax: 01389 754281; email: b.cairns@cairnsbrown.co.uk)

EMMS International *see entry on page 93*

Correspondent: Robin G K Arnott, Chief Executive, 7 Washington Lane, Edinburgh EH11 2HA (0131 313 3828; Fax: 0131 313 4662; email: info@emms.org; website: www.emms.org)

The Esdaile Trust

Eligibility: Ministers of the Church of Scotland or Deaconesses of the Church of Scotland who are widows and missionaries appointed or nominated by the Overseas Council of the Church of Scotland with daughters at secondary school and university.

Daughters should normally be between 12 and 25 years of age and preference is given to families with a low income.

Types of grants: Annual grants towards the cost of education, ranging between £100 and £500.

Annual grant total: In 2006/07 the trust had an income of £37,000. Approximately 75 grants are made annually totalling around £23,000 each year.

Applications: Application forms can be obtained from the website and should be completed and returned to the Clerk and Treasurer. Applications should be submitted by no later than 31 May each year and grants are distributed by early September.

Correspondent: R Graeme Thom, 17 Melville Street, Edinburgh EH3 7PH (email: graeme.thom@scott-moncrieff. com; website: www.scott-moncrieff.com/ charitable_trusts/page2.html)

The Ferguson Bequest

Eligibility: Ministers, or people intending to become ministers, who live in south west Scotland.

Types of grants: Scholarships are given.

Annual grant total: In 2006 the trust had an income of £183,000. Previously only a

small proportion of grants have been given to individuals.

Applications: On a form available by writing to the correspondent, to be considered at any time.

Correspondent: Ronald D Oakes, Secretary, 182 Bath Street, Glasgow G2 4HG

The Caroline Fitzmaurice Trust

Eligibility: Young women under the age of 23 who live in the diocese of St Andrews, Dunkeld and Dunblane. Broadly speaking, the diocese covers the whole of Perthshire and Fife, part of Stirlingshire and a small part of Angus, including Forfar and the towns to the west of Forfar, but excluding Dundee.

The trust states that applicants must show both financial need and a good academic background.

Types of grants: Grants of between £200 and £5,000 are given if there is a specific need. The trust aims 'to assist applicants who show promise of future excellence in their educational, cultural or social fields; applicants are expected to show the intention, in their turn, to contribute to the community wherever they may settle; and are endeavouring to raise funds through their own personal efforts'.

Annual grant total: In 2007/08 the trust had an income of £16,000. Previously grants have totalled around £2,300.

Applications: On a form available from the correspondent. Written references and details of parents' financial situation are required. The trustees meet once a year. The closing date for full, complete applications (including referees' reports and reports on parents' means) is 30 April.

Correspondent: The Secretaries, Pagan Osborne Solicitors, 12 St Catherine Street, Cupar, Fife KY15 4HN (01334 653777; Fax: 01334 655063; email: enquiries@ pagan.co.uk)

James Gillan's Trust

Eligibility: People training for the ordained ministry in the Church of Scotland who have lived in, or whose parents have lived in, Moray or Nairn for at least three years. There is a preference for those native to the parishes of Forres and Dyke, Kinloss, Rafford, Edinkillie and Dallas.

Types of grants: Grants of up to £1,000.

Annual grant total: In 2006/07 the trust had an income of £7,700. The trust normally gives approximately £2,000 in grants to individuals each year.

Applications: In writing to the correspondent.

Correspondent: Stewart Michael Murray, Solicitor, c/o R & R Urquhart, 121 High Street, Forres IV36 0AB (01309 672216)

The Glasgow Highland Society

Eligibility: Students who have a connection with the Highlands (for example, lived or went to school there) and who are now studying in Glasgow. Grants are normally given for first degrees only, unless postgraduate studies are a natural progression of the degree.

Types of grants: Grants of around £100 to help with fees for people at college or university or who are in vocational training (including mature students). Grants may also be given for Gaelic research projects and apprenticeships.

Annual grant total: In 2006 the trust had an income of £7,700.

Applications: On a form available from the correspondent or downloadable from the website. Applications should be submitted directly by the individual by 30 November and are considered in December.

Correspondent: The Secretaries, Alexander Sloan & Co, 144 West George Street, Glasgow G2 2HG (0141 354 0354; Fax: 0141 354 0355; email: kt@ alexandersloan.co.uk; website: www. alexandersloan.co.uk/ghs)

The Glasgow Society of the Sons of Ministers of the Church of Scotland

Eligibility: Children of ministers of the Church of Scotland who are in need, particularly students and the children of deceased ministers.

Types of grants: One-off and recurrent grants according to need.

Annual grant total: About £55,000 a year is given in educational and welfare grants to individuals.

Applications: On a form available from the correspondent. Applications from students are considered in August.

Correspondent: Fiona Watson, Secretary and Treasurer, Scott-Moncrieff, 17 Melville Street, Edinburgh EH3 7PH (0131 473 3500; Fax: 0131 473 3535; email: fiona.watson@scott-moncrieff.com)

The Grand Lodge of Antient, Free & Accepted Masons of Scotland

Eligibility: Children of members and deceased members.

Types of grants: Grants for people entering further education.

Annual grant total: In 2006/07 the trust had an income of £1.7 million. About £155,000 is given in welfare grants each year and £25,000 in educational grants.

Applications: On a form available from the correspondent, or by direct approach to the local lodge. They are considered three times a year, although urgent requests can be dealt with between meetings.

Correspondent: D M Begg, Grand Secretary, Freemasons Hall, 96 George Street, Edinburgh EH2 3DH (0131 225 5304)

Other information: The trust also runs care homes for older people.

The Highlands & Islands Educational Trust

Eligibility: Students living in the counties of Argyll, Bute, Caithness, Inverness, Orkney, Ross and Cromarty, Sutherland or Shetland and be of the protestant faith. Applicants should be in the fifth or sixth form at school and about to leave to go on to university or other institution of further education. Preference is given to Gaelic speakers.

Types of grants: Grants of £120 to £160 a year are given to students about to study for a first degree at college/university, towards their university/college books and maintenance. Bursaries are awarded at the discretion of the governors on merit, based on the results of the 'Higher' grade examinations. In determining the award, parental means are taken into account.

Annual grant total: In 2006/07 the trust had an income of £21,000. About £7,000 is given annually in grants to individuals.

Applications: In writing to the correspondent. Applications should be submitted through the individual's school between March and June inclusive and include: confirmation that the applicant is of the protestant faith; details of the occupation and gross income of parent/ guardian; ability at Gaelic, if any; university/college course to be undertaken; and intended career of the applicant. Decisions are made in September.

Correspondent: The Trustees, c/o Tods Murray LLP, Edinburgh Quay, 133 Fountainbridge, Edinburgh, EH3 9AG

Jewish Care Scotland

Eligibility: Schoolchildren, people starting work and students in further or higher education, including mature students, who are Jewish and live in Scotland.

Types of grants: One-off grants are given towards uniforms, other school clothing, equipment, instruments, fees, maintenance and living expenses. There is a preference for schoolchildren with serious family difficulties so that the child has to be educated away from home.

Exclusions: No grants are given to postgraduates.

Annual grant total: Educational grants to individuals usually total around £18,000.

Applications: The charity has previously stated that it was not accepting applications for the 'foreseeable future'.

Correspondent: Ethne Woldman, The Walton Community Care Centre, May Terrace, Giffnock, Glasgow G46 6LD (0141 620 1800; email: admin@jcarescot. org.uk; website: www.jcarescot.org.uk)

Other information: The board also helps with friendship clubs, housing requirements, clothing, meals-on-wheels, counselling and so on.

The Lethendy Trust

Eligibility: Young people in need who live in Scotland, with a preference for Tayside.

Types of grants: One-off and recurrent grants of £50 to £350 towards educational and development activities.

Annual grant total: In 2006/07 the trust had an income of £56,000. Grants are made to organisations and individuals.

Applications: In writing to the correspondent. The trustees usually meet to consider grants in July.

Correspondent: George Hay, Henderson Loggie, Chartered Accountants, Royal Exchange, Panmure Street, Dundee DD1 1DZ (01382 200055; email: ghay@ hendersonloggie.co.uk)

The Dr Thomas Lyon Bequest

Eligibility: Scottish orphans, aged 5 to 18, of members of Her Majesty's Forces and those of the Mercantile Marine, who are in need.

Types of grants: Grants are given towards primary and secondary education for school uniforms, other school clothing, books, educational outings and school fees. They range from £500 to £1,000.

Annual grant total: In 2006/07 the charity had an income of £11,000.

Applications: In writing to the correspondent. Applicants must state their total income, the regiment/service of their parent and the cause and date of their death.

Correspondent: The Secretary, The Merchant Company, The Merchants' Hall, 22 Hanover Street, Edinburgh EH2 2EP

The Catherine Mackichan Trust

Eligibility: People who are researching various aspects of Scottish history, including archaeology, genealogy and language studies.

Types of grants: Grants of up to £500 are given to: schoolchildren for books and educational outings; and students in further or higher education, including mature and overseas students, towards books, living expenses and study or travel overseas.

Exclusions: No grants are given to people whose education or research should be funded by statutory sources.

Annual grant total: About £1,500.

Applications: On a form available from: I Fraser, Vice-Chairman, School of Scottish Studies, 27 George Square, Edinburgh EH8 9LD.

Correspondent: The Administrator, 2 Hutton Avenue, Houston, Renfrewshire PA6 7JS

Other information: Grants are also given to schools and local history societies for local history and archaeological purposes

The Mathew Trust

Eligibility: Adults in need who live in the local government areas of the City of Dundee, Angus, Perth and Kinross and Fife.

Types of grants: One-off grants for study/travel abroad are given to college students, undergraduates, vocational students, mature students, people starting work, overseas students and people with special educational needs.

Annual grant total: About £10,000 to individuals.

Applications: In writing to the correspondent. Applications can be submitted directly by the individual for consideration every two months.

Correspondent: The Secretary, Henderson Loggie, Chartered Accountants, Royal Exchange, Panmure Street, Dundee DD1 1DZ

Other information: Grants are also made to organisations.

The McGlashan Charitable Trust

Eligibility: Students of music, other arts studies, medicine, veterinary science, architecture, law, together with science and technology, aged 16 to 30 who were born in, or are studying or working in, Scotland.

Types of grants: One-off and recurrent grants in the range of £250 and £1,000 are given to people in further or higher education, including mature, vocational and overseas students and undergraduates, towards fees, books, equipment, instruments and living expenses.

Exclusions: No grants are given towards sports.

Annual grant total: Previously around £36,000 to individuals.

Applications: Initially, in writing to the correspondent directly by the individual. Initial applications must be comprehensive enough for trustees to decide on issuing a formal application form or not. Applications are considered at irregular times during the year.

Correspondent: The Administrator, Brodies LLP, 2 Blythswood Square, Glasgow G2 4AD

Other information: Grants are also made to organisations.

The Muirhead Trust

Eligibility: Female students in Scotland.

Types of grants: Grants for those studying to become doctors or dentists. Grants are primarily given to students who are studying medicine after obtaining a first degree in another subject. These grants are for two years, after which the student is eligible for a statutory grant for the further three years.

Annual grant total: The trust has an annual income of around £7,000.

Applications: On a form available from the correspondent. Applications should arrive in September for consideration in October.

Correspondent: Clerk to the Trust, 24 St Enoch Square, Glasgow G1 4DB

North of Scotland Quaker Trust

Eligibility: Children of people who are associated with the Religious Society of Friends in the North of Scotland Monthly Meeting area.

Types of grants: Grants are given to schoolchildren and to people studying in further or higher education for books, equipment, instruments and educational outings.

Exclusions: No grants are given to people studying above first degree level.

Annual grant total: Previously about £10,000 for educational and welfare purposes.

Applications: Please note that due to maintenance and building costs the trust has been unable to make any substantial grants in recent years.

Correspondent: The Clerk, 2 Thornton Place, Watson Street, Banchory, Aberdeenshire, AB31 5UU

Other information: This trust was previously known as The Aberdeen Two Months' Meeting Trust.

The Royal Scottish Corporation (also known as The Scottish Hospital of the Foundation of King Charles II)

Eligibility: Scottish people, their children and widows, who are in need and live within a 35-mile radius of Charing Cross.

Types of grants: This welfare charity gives training grants to enable people to secure qualifications with a view to gaining employment. Support is also given to students on low incomes or from deprived backgrounds.

Annual grant total: In 2006/07 the trust had assets of £41 million and an income of £1.8 million. Education and training grants amounted to £29,000.

Applications: On a form available from the trust; upon receiving the completed form, which should include copies of the birth/wedding certificates, the corporation decides whether to submit the application for consideration at the trustees' monthly meeting. They may also decide to visit or ask the applicant to visit the corporation's office to discuss their case.

Correspondent: Willie Docherty, Chief Executive, 37 King Street, Covent Garden, London WC2E 8JS (020 7240 3718 (UK helpline 0800 652 2989); Fax: 020 7497 0184; email: info@scotscare. com; website: www.scotscare.com)

Scottish Arts Council – Professional Development Fund

Eligibility: People working at professional level in the arts in Scotland.

Types of grants: 'We offer support to individual artists for research and development, training, production and presentation/promotion of work. This may take the form of grants, awards, bursaries, artists' residencies or support to artist-led projects.'

Annual grant total: About £300,000 is available each year.

Applications: On a form available from the correspondent, or available from its website.

Correspondent: The Grants Administration Department, Scottish Arts Council, 12 Manor Place, Edinburgh EH3 7DD (0845 603 6000/0131 226 6051; email: help.desk@scottisharts.org.uk; website: www.scottisharts.org.uk)

The Scottish Chartered Accountants' Benevolent Association

Eligibility: The dependents of members of the Institute of Chartered Accountants of Scotland who are in financial need.

Types of grants: One-off grants for a variety of needs. Recent grants have been given for school fees, maintenance expenses and retraining.

Annual grant total: Grants usually total about £120,000 each year.

Applications: An initial letter or telephone call should be made to the correspondent. A member of the fund will then make contact and arrange a visit if appropriate. Following this, an application, report and recommendation will be made to the fund's council for approval.

Correspondent: Robert Linton, Secretary, Robert Linton & Co, 53 Bothwell Street, Glasgow, G2 6TS (0141 572 8465; Fax: 0141 248 7456; email: mail@ robertlinton.co.uk)

Other information: Grants are also made for welfare purposes.

The Society for the Benefit of Sons & Daughters of the Clergy of the Church of Scotland

Eligibility: Ministers of the Church of Scotland with children at secondary school and university.

Types of grants: Annual grant towards the cost of education, typically in the range of £100 and £1,000.

Annual grant total: About £20,000.

Applications: An application form can be downloaded from the Scott-Moncrieff website. Applications should be sent in no later than 31 May each year and grants are distributed by early September.

Correspondent: The Secretary, Scott-Moncrieff, 17 Melville Street, Edinburgh EH3 7PH (website: www.scott-moncrieff.com/charitable_trusts/index.html)

John Suttie Memorial Fund

Eligibility: People who live in Moray and Nairn, with preference for people under 30 who are starting on an agricultural or veterinary career.

Types of grants: Grants towards further or higher education.

Annual grant total: About £500.

Applications: Information regarding awards is circulated annually to schools and through agricultural and veterinary organisations. Applications should be made in writing to the correspondent.

Correspondent: W Cowie, Solicitor, R and R Urquhart Solicitors, 117–121 High Street, Forres, Moray IV36 1AB (01309 672216)

John Watson Foundation Trust

Eligibility: One parent families in Scotland with children in secondary education.

Types of grants: One-off and recurrent grants, mainly towards school fees for three to four schoolchildren a year.

Annual grant total: About £6,000 a year.

Applications: Funds are fully committed; the trust does not accept unsolicited applications.

Correspondent: The Trustees, c/o Pollock & Co, 14 Newington Road, Edinburgh, EH9 1QS

John Watson's Trust

Eligibility: Children or young people under the age of 21 who have a physical or learning disability or are socially disadvantaged and who live in Scotland. There is a preference for people who live in or are connected with the Lothian region.

Types of grants: Help in connection with special tuition, educational trips, computers for people with special educational needs, books, tools or expenses for further training and education, and equipment, travel and other activities contributing to education and advancement in life. Grants range from £30 to £2,000.

The trust also gives grants towards the cost of a boarding education for children normally resident in Scotland who are experiencing serious family difficulties and who would benefit from an education away from home.

Grants are one-off and range from £50 to £2,000, apart from boarding school grants which range from £300 to £1,000 a year and may be recurrent.

Exclusions: No grants for day school fees.

Annual grant total: The grants committee an annual budget of approximately £150,000 to disburse in grants.

Applications: On a form available from the correspondent or from the trust's website. Applications can be submitted directly by the individual, or through a social worker, Citizens Advice, other welfare agency or through another third party on behalf of an individual. Applications must include full details and dates and locations of any trips being undertaken. The grants committee meets approximately six times a year.

Correspondent: Ms I Wilson, Signet Library, Parliament Square, Edinburgh EH1 1RF (0131 220 1640; email: johnwatson@onetel.com; website: www.johnwatsons.com)

Other information: Grants are also made to organisations and groups.

Aberdeen & Perthshire

The Aberdeen Endowments Trust

Eligibility: Secondary schoolchildren who live in the former Grampian region, and adult students in Aberdeen.

Types of grants: Grants of up to £200 are available to children in secondary school in the former Grampian region according to need and academic performance, with most of the support given to pupils at Robert Gordon's College. Grants are also given towards adult education.

Annual grant total: In 2006 the trust had an income of £868,000, most of which is given in grants. The majority of financial assistance is given to pupils attending Robert Gordon's College, Aberdeen, and in previous years this has represented around 90% to 95% of the trust's expenditure.

Applications: On a form available from the correspondent. Applications are considered nine or ten times a year.

Correspondent: William Russell, Clerk, 19 Albert Street, Aberdeen AB25 1QF (01224 640194; Fax: 01224 643918)

Other information: Grants are also occasionally made to organisations.

Dr John Calder's Fund

Eligibility: People in need who live in the parish of Machar, or within the city of Aberdeen, including people only resident for their education and people from the area studying elsewhere.

Types of grants: Grants for educational needs.

Annual grant total: Around £2,000 is available for individuals. A further £8,000 is given in grants towards educational projects or organisations.

Applications: The trust stated in January 2006 that funds were fully committed and that this situation was likely to remain so for the medium to long term.

Correspondent: Clive Phillips, Paull & Williamsons, New Investment House, 214 Union Row, Aberdeen AB10 1QY

The Cyril and Margaret Gates Charitable Trust

Eligibility: Journalists under 30, born or working in Aberdeen, the north east and north of Scotland (the area north of Stonehaven), who may need assistance for the furthering of his/her education by way of travel or instruction. Support is also given to their dependants.

Types of grants: Usually one-off payments according to need. Maximum grant is normally in the region of £1,000.

Annual grant total: In 2007 the trust had an income of £14,000. Approximately £1,000 is distributed annually in grants to individuals, mostly for welfare purposes.

Applications: In writing to the correspondent.

Correspondent: Alan J Innes, 100 Union Street, Aberdeen AB10 1QR (01224 428000)

The Anne Herd Educational Trust

Eligibility: Pupils at Merchiston Castle School, Harrogate College, High School of Dundee or other independent schools.

Types of grants: Payment of school fees when parents would not have otherwise been able to afford the full tuition fees.

Annual grant total: In 2006/07 the trust received an income of £119,000. Approximately £10,000 a year is given in grants to individuals.

Applications: Applicants should contact the schools named in 'eligibility', but more information can be obtained from the correspondent.

Correspondent: The Trustees, Messrs Bowman, 27 Bank Street, Dundee DD1 1RP

The Anne Herd Memorial Trust

Eligibility: People who are blind or partially sighted who live in Broughty Ferry (applicants from the city of Dundee, region of Tayside or those who have connections with these areas and reside in Scotland will also be considered).

Types of grants: Grants are given for educational equipment such as computers and books. Grants are usually at least £50.

Annual grant total: In 2006/07 the trust had an income of £151,000. The trust gives approximately £25,000 a year in grants.

Applications: In writing to the correspondent, to be submitted directly by the individual in March/April for consideration in June.

Correspondent: The Trustees, Bowman Solicitors, 27 Bank Street, Dundee DD1 1RP (01382 322267; Fax: 01382 225000)

The Morgan Trust

Eligibility: Children of people who: (i) were born or educated in the former royal burghs of Dundee, Forfar, Arbroath and Montrose; or (ii) have been resident in one or more these burghs for five years immediately before applying for an award or immediately before his/her death.

Types of grants: One-off and recurrent grants of up to £200, usually for maintenance/living expenses. Grants are reviewed each year.

Exclusions: Grants are not given to people with an income of more than £10,000, unless there are exceptional circumstances.

Annual grant total: About £10,000.

Applications: On a form available from the correspondent, for completion on behalf of the applicant with full details of their financial situation. Applications are usually considered at May and November meetings.

Correspondent: The Clerk, Miller Hendry, 13 Ward Road, Dundee DD1 1LU

The Gertrude Muriel Pattullo Advancement Award Scheme

Eligibility: Young people aged 16 to 25 who are physically disabled and live in the city of Dundee or the county of Angus.

Types of grants: One-off and recurrent grants of £100 to £500 to schoolchildren and students in further or higher education towards books, equipment, instruments, fees and educational outings in the UK.

Exclusions: No grants are given towards the repayment of debts.

Annual grant total: The trust has an income of around £4,000 per year. Grants are made to organisations and individuals.

Applications: On a form available from the correspondent at any time. Applications can be submitted directly by the individual or through any third party.

Correspondent: The Clerk, Blackadders Solicitors, 30–34 Reform Street, Dundee DD1 1RJ

Aberdeen & Aberdeenshire

Aberdeenshire Educational Trust

Eligibility: Residents of, or schoolchildren or students whose parents reside in, the former county of Aberdeen.

Types of grants: Grants of between £10 and £200 are given as: postgraduate scholarships for research work or advanced study; supplementary bursaries to students at university, central institution or a college of education in cases of need; grants towards travel, fees, books or equipment for apprentices; grants to student apprentices at university or central institution; travel grants for educational purposes (including educational outings for primary school pupils); further education grants for courses not usually recognised by LEAs or further educational bursaries; special grants to people over 21 applying for university places; grants promoting education in arts, music and drama; and grants to help individuals to undertake educational experiments and research which will be for the educational benefit of people in the county.

Annual grant total: In 2006/07 the trust had an income of £91,000.

Applications: On a form available from the correspondent, to be considered throughout the year.

Correspondent: The Clerk, St Leonards, Sandyhill Road, Banff, AB45 1BH

Other information: Grants are also made to clubs, schools and other educational establishments.

Huntly Educational Trust 1997

Eligibility: People living in the district of Huntly.

Types of grants: Grants are given for the education and training of individuals and average £200.

Annual grant total: In 2006/07 the trust had an income of approximately £2,000. Grant total varies from year to year dependant on income.

Applications: In writing to the correspondent for consideration at a monthly meeting.

Correspondent: A B Mitchell, Stuart Wilson Dickson & Co, Huntly Business Centre, Huntly AB54 8ES (01466 792101)

Kincardineshire Educational Trust

Eligibility: People who live in Kincardine County, and schoolchildren and young people who either attend schools or further educational centres there or whose parents live there.

Types of grants: Grants of up to £200 are given to: schoolchildren towards books, equipment, instruments and educational outings; and people in further or higher education, including mature students and postgraduates, towards books, equipment instruments, fees, living expenses, student exchanges and educational outings and trips in the UK and overseas.

Annual grant total: In 2006/07 the trust had an income of £4,500. Grants to individuals have previously totalled about £1,400.

Applications: On a form available from the correspondent, to be received by 30 November for consideration in March.

Correspondent: Amanda Watson, Aberdeenshire Finance, Trust Section, St Leonard's, Sandyhill Road, Banff, AB45 1BH

Other information: Grants are also made to clubs, schools and other educational establishments.

Angus

Angus Educational Trust

Eligibility: Residents of the Angus Council area who have been offered a place on, or are attending, any full-time or part-time courses at University. Any student entitled to apply for a loan under the Student Loads Scheme must have taken up this option before an application to this trust will be considered.

Types of grants: The trust provides financial assistance in the following areas,

- Travel for those studying higher educational courses outside of Scotland
- Residents of the Angus Council area for undergraduate university courses
- Young people travelling abroad for educational purposes
- Clubs and groups working to improve educational opportunities and learning in the Angus Council area
- Rural primary schools, for excursions of an educational nature.

Grants are given to supplement existing grants. Household income is taken into account in determining whether or not a grant is awarded.

Annual grant total: In 2006/07 the trust had an income of £27,000.

Applications: On a form available from the correspondent. The governors meet twice a year in March and September to consider applications.

Correspondent: The Clerk, Education Offices, County Buildings, Forfar, Angus DD8 3WE (01307 473212)

Other information: Grants for gap-years prior to university are also considered, and are provided specifically for the purpose of improving educational outcomes either for the individual or for the group that they are visiting. Individuals applying for such a grant must state the specific outcomes from their visit and a predetermined length of stay, and should contact the Trust outlining the costs and support that are envisaged.

The David Barnet Christie Trust

Eligibility: Men or women aged up to 40, preferably living in or originating from the Arbroath area (or failing this Angus), who are about to enter into an engineering apprenticeship, have already taken up such or similar training, or wish to progress by taking further engineering qualifications.

Types of grants: One-off grants of up to £500 to people starting work or students in further or higher education, including mature students and postgraduates, towards books, study or travel abroad, equipment, instruments, maintenance and living expenses.

Exclusions: Students from any other area in the UK, EU or overseas are not eligible for funding.

Annual grant total: In 2006 the trust had an income of £2,500. No further information was available.

Applications: On a form available from the correspondent. Applications should be submitted directly by the individual by the end of September each year.

Correspondent: Graham McNicol, Thorntons WS, Brothockbank House, Arbroath DD11 1NJ (01241 872683; Fax: 01241 871541)

The Duncan Trust

Eligibility: Candidates for the Ministry of the Church of Scotland, especially those who have a connection with the former Presbytery of Arbroath.

Types of grants: Cash grants to student applicants studying for their first degree.

Exclusions: Postgraduate studies.

Annual grant total: In 2006/07 the trust had an income of £21,000. The trust typically gives around £5,000 a year in grants.

Applications: In writing to the correspondent to request an application form, to be returned by 31 October each year.

Correspondent: G J M Dunlop, Solicitor, Thorntons Solicitors, Brothockbank House, Arbroath, Angus DD11 1NE (01241 872683)

Dundee Masonic Temple Trust

Eligibility: Children of Freemasons who are, or who were immediately prior to death, members of Lodges in Angus.

Types of grants: Recurrent grants of £200 to £500 to students in further or higher education, including mature students, for living expenses.

Annual grant total: In 2006/07 the trust had an income of £2,400.

Applications: On a form available from the correspondent. Forms should be returned directly by the individual in October for consideration in November/December.

Correspondent: The Trustees, 2 India Buildings, 86 Bell Street, Dundee DD1 1JQ

Dundee

City of Dundee Educational Trust

Eligibility: Students in further or higher education who have a strong connection with Dundee. Priority is given to students who do not receive a mandatory award.

Types of grants: Grants of around £300 each.

Annual grant total: In 2006 the trust had an income of £18,000, with approximately £12,000 given in grants to individuals annually.

Applications: On a form available from the correspondent, to be accompanied by a full cv. Applications should be submitted at least two weeks before the quarterly meetings in March, June, September and December.

Correspondent: J Hope, Miller Hendry, 13 Ward Road, Dundee DD1 1LU (01382 200000)

The Polack Travelling Scholarship Fund

Eligibility: People over 17 attending an educational institution within Dundee or the surrounding area.

Types of grants: To enable attendance on courses or conferences abroad to study foreign languages, international law, management studies or aspects of company and commercial education. Grants are one-off and range from £250 to £400.

Annual grant total: About £1,500.

Applications: In writing to the correspondent directly by the individual. Applications are to be submitted by 30 April for consideration in May.

Correspondent: The Clerk, Henderson Loggie, Royal Exchange, Panmure Street, Dundee DD1 1DZ (01382 200055)

Moray

The Banffshire Educational Trust

Eligibility: Residents of the former county of Banffshire, people who attend schools or further education centres in the former county, and school pupils whose parents live in the former county of Banffshire. Grants are means tested to those earning £25,000 a year or less.

Types of grants: One-off grants of between £15 and £200 are given towards postgraduate scholarships, higher education bursaries, mature students, apprentices and trainees, travel scholarships for people studying outside Scotland, and travel and educational excursions for schoolchildren and people in adult education.

Annual grant total: Grants totalling around £10,000 are made annually, usually to around 50 individuals.

Applications: On a form available from the correspondent which should be submitted by 30 September for consideration in November/December.

Correspondent: Jean-Anne Goodbrand, Administrative Officer, Educational Services, Moray Council Headquarters, High Street, Elgin, Moray IV30 1LL (01343 563151; Fax: 01343 563478; email: jeananne.goodbrand@moray.gov.uk; website: www.moray.gov.uk)

Moray and Nairn Educational Trust

Eligibility: People who have lived in the former counties of Moray and Nairn for at least five years. No grants are given to people whose household earnings are over £20,000 a year, less £800 for each dependent child.

Types of grants: One-off grants, ranging from £50 to £200, are available to schoolchildren for educational outings in the UK and study or travel abroad and to students in further or higher education, including mature students and postgraduates, for any purpose.

Annual grant total: About £6,000 to individuals.

Applications: On a form available from the correspondent and should be submitted by 30 September each year for consideration in November/December.

Correspondent: Administrative Officer, Educational Services, Moray Council Headquarters, High Street, Elgin, Moray IV30 1LL (01343 563151; Fax: 01343 563478; email: educationalservices@moray.gov.uk; website: www.moray.gov.uk)

Other information: Grants are also made to organisations.

Ian Wilson Ski Fund

Eligibility: Young people aged under 21 who are in full time education in a school run by Moray council. Preference is given to families with a restricted income.

Types of grants: One-off grants are given to advance education by promoting outdoor activities, including sport and related studies.

Annual grant total: About £1,500.

Applications: On a form available from the correspondent. Applicants are encouraged to apply in plenty of time, by the end of the school holidays in October for consideration by the trustees later that month, as there are a limited number of grants available. Applications can be submitted either directly by the individual or through his or her school, college, educational welfare agency, or another third party.

Correspondent: Ian Hamilton, Hon. Secretary and Treasurer, Slack Villa, King Edwards Terrace, Portknockie, Moray AB56 4NX

Perth & Kinross

The Guildry Incorporation of Perth

Eligibility: Young people aged 17 to 25 who are in need, living in Perth or Guilldtown and following a course of further or higher education in the UK. The guild also supports young people taking part in Raleigh International, Link Overseas Exchange Projects and similar activities.

Types of grants: Grants up to £800.

Annual grant total: In 2006/07 the guild had an income of £200,000. Previously grants to individuals have totalled around £80,000, with approximately £20,000 given for educational purposes.

Applications: Application forms can be requested from the correspondent. They are considered at the trustees' meetings on the last Tuesday of every month. Applicants are required to write a short covering letter of around 250 words explaining why they require funding and how the grant they receive could help their local community.

Correspondent: Lorna Peacock, Secretary, 42 George Street, Perth PH1 5JL (01738 623195)

Miss Isabella MacDougall's Trust

Eligibility: Students who were born within the former county of Perth and are studying first degree courses in the faculty of arts at the following universities: Edinburgh, Glasgow, St Andrews, Aberdeen, Dundee, Sterling and Strathclyde.

Types of grants: A maximum bursary of £200 per year for a period not exceeding three years.

Exclusions: No grants are made to postgraduates.

Annual grant total: Previously about £800 in bursaries.

Applications: In writing to the correspondent.

Correspondent: A G Dorward, Messrs Miller Hendry, 10 Blackfriars Street, Perth PH1 5NS

Other information: Bursaries will be awarded on the basis of academic achievement within the state education system plus a further examination or interview by the trustees.

Perth & Kinross Educational Trust

Eligibility: Students in further or higher education, including mature students and postgraduates, who were born or attended school in Perth and Kinross.

Types of grants: Grants of up to £150 towards books, fees, living expenses and study or travel abroad.

Annual grant total: Previously about £8,000.

Applications: On a form available from the correspondent. Applications should be received by mid-May for consideration in June. The exact closing date can be found on the application form. Late applications cannot be considered.

Correspondent: The Trust Administrator, Finance Section, Education & Children's Services, Perth & Kinross Council, Pullar House, 35 Kinnoull Street, Perth PH1 5GD (01738 476767; Fax: 01738 476210)

Central Scotland

Clackmannanshire

Clackmannanshire Educational Trust

Eligibility: People who live in the county of Clackmannanshire.

Types of grants: Grants of up to £100 towards education travel (in the UK or overseas) and adult education.

Annual grant total: In 2006/07 the trust had an income of £1,400. Grants usually total about £500 each year.

Applications: Directly by the individual on a form available from the facilities, schools & welfare team at the address above. Applications are considered on the first Thursday of January, April, July and October.

Correspondent: Facilities, Schools and Welfare Team, Services to People, Clackmannanshire Council, Lime Tree House, Alloa FK10 1EX (01259 452363; Fax: 01259 452440)

Paton Educational Trust

Eligibility: People (usually aged 16 to 26) who live in the burgh of Alloa or Clackmannanshire or whose parent was employed by Patons & Baldwins Ltd – Alloa or who are members or adherents of West Church of Scotland – Alloa or Moncrieff U F Church – Alloa.

Types of grants: Supplementary grants of £50 to £100 per year for students in further and higher education. Grants can go towards books and fees/living expenses. Grants can also sometimes be given for study or travel abroad or for student exchanges.

Annual grant total: About £400.

Applications: On a form available from the correspondent. Applications are usually considered in September/October.

Correspondent: William Jarvis, Solicitor, 27 Mar Street, Alloa FK10 1HX (01259 723408)

Fife

Fife Educational Trust

Eligibility: People who have a permanent address within the Fife council area and who attended a secondary or primary school there.

Types of grants: Support for individuals below postgraduate level is usually restricted to travel grants where this is an integral part of the course of study, but can also be given for music, drama and visual arts. Grants range from £50 to about £75.

Annual grant total: In 2006/07 the trust had an income of £68,000. Grants to individuals usually total about £1,200 a year.

Applications: In writing to the correspondent. Applicants must give their permanent address, details of schools they attended within Fife with dates of attendance, and details of other money available. Applications are considered in March.

Correspondent: Education Services, Fife Council, Rothesay House, Rothesay Place, Glenrothes KY7 5PQ

New St Andrews Japan Golf Trust

Eligibility: Children and young people in need living in the county of Fife who are undertaking sports and recreational activities.

Types of grants: One-off and recurrent grants ranging from £200 to £1,500, for sports equipment, travel, accommodation and coaching assistance to individuals, and university fees for sports scholarships.

Annual grant total: In 2006/07 the trust had an income of £10,000. Grants are made to organisations and individuals.

Applications: In writing to the correspondent, providing the contact details of two referees.

Correspondent: The Secretary, 18 Buchanan Gardens, St Andrews, Fife KY16 9LU

Stirling

The Stirlingshire Educational Trust

Eligibility: People who were born in, or have lived for five years in, Stirlingshire and are in need.

Types of grants: Grants are made to schoolchildren for study/travel abroad and excursions and to college students, undergraduates, vocational students and mature students, including those for clothing/uniforms, fees, study/travel abroad, books, equipment/instruments and excursions.

Grants range from £150 to £500.

Annual grant total: About £85,000.

Applications: On a form available from the correspondent. Applications must be received by February, May, August and November for consideration on the first Wednesday of the following month.

Correspondent: The Clerk/Treasurer, 68 Port Street, Stirling FK8 2LJ

Edinburgh, the Lothians & Scottish Borders

The Avenel Trust

Eligibility: Children in need under 18 and students of nursery nursing living in the Lothians.

Types of grants: One-off grants of £10 to £500 are given for safety items such as fireguards and safety gates, shoes, clothing, bedding, cots and pushchairs. Recent awards have included money for bus passes, recreational activities for young carers and washing machines for families where children have a medical condition which makes one essential.

Exclusions: Grants are not given for holidays, toys or household furnishings.

Annual grant total: In 2007 the trust had an income of £20,000.

Applications: Applications are considered every two months and should be submitted through a tutor or third party such as a social worker, health visitor or teacher. Applicants are encouraged to provide as much information about their family or individual circumstances and needs as possible in their applications.

Correspondent: Alison Kennedy, 75 Comiston Drive, Edinburgh EH10 5QT (0131 447 2250)

City of Edinburgh

The Colin O'Riordan Trust

Eligibility: Children and young people under the age of 20 who are involved in music and live in Edinburgh (EH postcode).

Types of grants: Grants given according need.

Exclusions: No grants are made outside the EH postcode area.

Annual grant total: About £4,000 a year.

Applications: In writing to the correspondent before the annual closing date of 31 May each year.

Correspondent: Rory O'Riordan, Chair, 23 Glencairn Crescent, Edinburgh, EH12 5BT (website: www.thecolinoriordantrust.org.uk)

Other information: The trust also supports groups of young musicians studying all forms of music including classical orchestral, solo performers, jazz, and folk and wind bands.

The James Scott Law Charitable Fund

Eligibility: Young people, aged between 5 and 18 years who attend primary or secondary Edinburgh Merchant Company Schools.

Types of grants: Grants are given for school fees, clothing, books and allowances. The maximum award is about £2,000.

Annual grant total: In 2006/07 the fund had an income of £5,700.

Applications: On a form available from the correspondent for consideration in August, a bursar at their school usually interviews applicants.

Correspondent: Alistair Beattie, Merchants' Hall, 22 Hanover Street, Edinburgh EH2 2EP (0131 225 7202)

East Lothian

East Lothian Educational Trust

Eligibility: People in education who live in the former county of East Lothian and are in need.

Types of grants: One-off grants in the range of £100 and £700 are given to: schoolchildren, college students, undergraduates, vocational students, mature students and people with special educational needs, including those towards uniforms/clothing, fees, study/travel abroad, books, equipment/instruments, maintenance/living expenses, accommodation and excursions.

Annual grant total: In 2006/07 the trust had an income of £51,000.

Applications: On a form available from the correspondent. Applications can be submitted directly by the individual or a parent/guardian, through a third party such as a teacher, or through an organisation such as a school or an educational welfare agency. Applications should be submitted between August and October for consideration between September and November.

Correspondent: K Brand, Clerk, John Muir House, Council Buildings, Haddington, East Lothian EH41 3HA (01620 827436; email: eleducationaltrust@eastlothian.gov.uk; website: www.eastlothian.gov.uk)

Other information: Grants are also available to clubs and organisations for a variety of educational purposes, such as equipment, travel costs or specific trips and projects.

The Red House Home Trust

Eligibility: Young people under the age of 22 who are in need and live in East Lothian.

Types of grants: Grants in the range of £250 to £1,000.

Annual grant total: About £10,000 is available for distribution each year to individuals and groups.

Applications: On a form available from the trust's website, or from the correspondent. The trustees normally meet three times a year to review applications and to agree grants.

Correspondent: Graeme Thom, Clerk or Mrs Janice Couper, Scott-Moncrieff, 17 Melville Street, Edinburgh EH3 7PH (0131 473 3500; Fax: 0131 473 3500; email: graeme.thom@scott-moncrieff.com)

Scottish Borders

The Elizabeth Hume Trust

Eligibility: People in need who live in the parish of Chirnside.

Types of grants: Grants are made to schoolchildren for uniforms/clothing and equipment/instruments and to undergraduates for fees and books.

Annual grant total: This trust generally has an income of around £19,000. No further information was available.

Applications: Applications can be made either directly by an individual or family member, through a third party such as a social worker or teacher, through an organisation such as Citizens Advice or a school or through a church elder.

Correspondent: The Minister, The Manse, The Glebe, Chirnside, Duns, Berwickshire TD11 3XL

Charities Administered by Scottish Borders Council

Eligibility: Within the Scottish Borders there are four educational trusts corresponding to the four former counties of Berwickshire, Peeblesshire, Roxburghshire and Selkirkshire. Grants may be awarded for a variety of educational purposes to people who are ordinarily living in the above areas.

Types of grants: One-off and recurrent grants are made under the following headings: (i) educational excursions; (ii) special grants; (iii) travel grants; (iv) adult education; and (v) drama, visual arts and music.

Annual grant total: The annual grants budget is about £10,000.

Applications: On a form available from the correspondent. Applications are considered all year round.

Correspondent: The Clerk, Education and Lifelong Learning, Newtown St Boswells, Melrose, Roxburghshire TD6 0SA

Other information: Grants are also given to schools.

West Lothian

The West Lothian Educational Trust

Eligibility: People who live in the former county of West Lothian.

Types of grants: Grants are given towards books and equipment, fees, maintenance, travel abroad and travel to/from college for students in further and higher education. Grants are also given to mature students, part-time students and for short course attendance.

Annual grant total: In 2006/07 the trust had an income of £18,000. Grants are made to both organisations and individuals.

Applications: Application forms are available from the correspondent. Applications must be received by 1 February, 1 May and 1 September each year.

Correspondent: The Secretary, Scott-Moncrieff, 17 Melville Street, Edinburgh EH3 7PH (0131 473 3500)

Glasgow & West of Scotland

The Ayrshire Educational Trust

Eligibility: People who live in the former county of Ayrshire.

Types of grants: Grants are given to students in further/higher education for travel in either the UK or abroad for educational purposes, and are given to schoolchildren for educational outings or for Scottish Youth Theatre or Scottish Youth Choir. Grants can also be made to buy special equipment for mentally or physically disabled students. Equipment for pilot projects or of an experimental nature will be considered.

Exclusions: Assistance cannot be given towards personal equipment or to help with student's course fees when following full-time or part-time courses of education.

Annual grant total: In 2007 the trust had an income of £28,000.

Applications: On a form available from the correspondent. Applications are usually considered four times a year. They should be submitted directly by the individual.

Correspondent: Mrs Catherine Martin, Principal Administration Officer, Community Learning and Development, East Ayrshire Council, Rennie Street Office, Rennie Street, Kilmarnock KA1 3AR (01563 578106; Fax: 01563 576269; email: catherine.martin@east-ayrshire.gov.uk)

Other information: Grants are also given to support the formation, maintenance and encouragement of clubs, societies and organisations that provide educational benefit to young people and children in Ayshire.

Dunbartonshire Educational Trust

Eligibility: People who live in the old county area of Dumbarton district aged 16 and over. There is a preference for people from deprived areas and a policy of positive discrimination (for instance, people with disabilities or children of single parents).

Types of grants: Grants towards fees, maintenance, travel and equipment for students in further or higher education and to obtain practical experience of trades, for example the cost of books during an apprenticeship. Generally grants range from £25 to £50; the maximum given is £100 in exceptional circumstances.

Annual grant total: About £2,000 is available each year.

Applications: On a form available from the correspondent. Applications can be considered at any time, but students usually apply before the start of the course.

Correspondent: The Trustees, West Dunbartonshire Council, Council Offices, Garshake Road, Dumbarton G82 3PU

The Glasgow Society for the Education of the Deaf & Dumb

Eligibility: Children over school age who are deaf and/or speech impaired and live in the west of Scotland.

Types of grants: Grants to help with the cost of providing tutors to support deaf people, courses (for example, sign language, lip reading), holidays, radio aids, computers and so on.

Annual grant total: In 2006/07 the trust had an income of £41,000. In previous years grants have totalled around £33,000

Applications: On a form available form the correspondent, or from the society's website. Applications can be submitted at any time directly by the individual or through a social worker. Applications usually take between 3 and 8 weeks to be processed, giving time for the possible need for additional information.

Correspondent: Nancy Ward, Administrator, Alexander Sloan Chartered Accountants, 144 West George Street, Glasgow G2 2HG (0141 354 0354; Fax: 0141 354 0355; email: nancy.ward@alexandersloan.co.uk; website: www.gsedd.org.uk)

Other information: The society also gives grants to organisations and schools.

The Logan & Johnstone School Scheme

Eligibility: Students in further/higher education, including mature students, people starting work and postgraduates, who live in the former Strathclyde region.

Types of grants: One-off grants for books, equipment, instruments and fees.

Exclusions: Grants are not made towards living or travel expenses.

Annual grant total: About £5,000.

Applications: On a form available from the correspondent. Applications should be submitted directly by the individual between April and June for consideration in August.

Correspondent: Deputy Director of Education, Education Services, Wheatley House, 25 Cochrane Street, Merchant City, Glasgow G1 1HL

Colonel MacLean Trust Scheme

Eligibility: Students in further/higher education, including mature students and postgraduates, who live in the former Strathclyde region.

Types of grants: One-off grants for books, equipment, instruments and fees.

Annual grant total: About £5,000.

Applications: On a form available from Marianne Hosie, Principal Officer (Finance) also based at Education Services, Wheatley House. Applications should be submitted directly by the individual between April and June for consideration in August.

Correspondent: Deputy Director of Education, Education Services, Wheatley House, 25 Cochrane Street, Merchant City, Glasgow G1 1HL

Renfrewshire Educational Trust

Eligibility: People who have lived within either the Renfrewshire, East Renfrewshire or Inverclyde areas for the last three years or have come from one of the aforementioned areas but currently live elsewhere in order to undertake their course of studies. Student's family income must not exceed £30,000 per annum. For children's excursions the minimum criteria is receiving free school meals.

Types of grants: Scholarships and grants towards fees and maintenance for students in further and higher education, including mature students and travel grants for study in the UK or overseas, such as medical electives. Schoolchildren can receive help with the costs of educational outings. Grants usually range from £400 to £750, but larger grants can be considered.

Exclusions: No grants for individuals whose household income is £30,000 or over.

Annual grant total: About £10,000 a year in educational grants to individuals, with the remainder being given in grants for music, drama and sport.

Applications: On a form available from the correspondent. (Separate application forms are available for general grants and travel grants.) Details of household income are requested. Applications can be submitted either directly by the individual or via their school. Applications are considered every six weeks.

Correspondent: Sarah White, Renfrewshire Council, Cotton Street, Paisley PA1 1JB

The Spiers Trust

Eligibility: People in need who live in the parishes of Beith, Dalry, Dunlop, Kilbirnie, Lochwinnoch and Neilston. Preference is given to students from families with restricted income.

Types of grants: Awards known as Spier Grants to help secondary school pupils and students in further/higher education to meet the cost of attending a course or obtaining special tuition in any academic, artistic, scientific or technological subject or subjects, in or outside of Scotland. Grants may also be given to help with travelling costs.

Annual grant total: Previously about £2,000.

Applications: Applications can be submitted directly by the individual on an application form available by phoning the correspondent. Evidence of need will have to be shown. Each year applications are considered regularly until all the funds have been spent.

Correspondent: The Head of Service, North Ayrshire Council, Educational Services, Resources Section (Finance), Cunninghame House, Irvine KA12 8EE (01294 324428)

Argyll & Bute

Charles & Barbara Tyre Trust

Eligibility: People aged 18 to 25 who live in the former county of Argyll and are of the protestant faith.

Types of grants: Grants of up to £1,500 are made for a wide variety of purposes to college students, undergraduates, vocational students and people with special educational needs.

Annual grant total: In 2006/07 the trust had an income of £37,000. Grants are distributed for educational and welfare purposes.

Applications: In writing to the correspondent including references, by 31 May for consideration in August/September. Proof of continued attendance of the course must be produced at the start of each term.

Correspondent: The Clerk, c/o Wylie & Bisset, 168 Bath Street, Argyll, G2 4TP

City of Glasgow

Glasgow Educational & Marshall Trust

Eligibility: People over 18 years old who are in need and who have lived in the city of Glasgow (as at the re-organisation in 1975) for a minimum of five years (excluding time spent studying in the city with a home address elsewhere).

Types of grants: Grants range from £100 to £1,000, although in exceptional cases higher awards have been made. They are given towards: educational outings for schoolchildren; books, course fees/living expenses, study/travel abroad for people in further/higher education; and course fees, travel, books, equipment/instruments for people wishing to undertake vocational training. Mature students can also qualify for assistance with childcare costs, books, travel and fees.

Grants can be one-off or recurrent and are normally given for courses where a Scottish Education Department grant is not available, or where such grants do not cover the total costs.

Exclusions: No grants are given retrospectively or for courses run by privately owned institutions.

Annual grant total: In 2006/07 the trust had an income of £96,000. Grants to individuals have previously totalled around £36,000.

Applications: Directly by the individual on a form available from the trust, together with two written references.

The main meetings of governors are held on the first Wednesday of March, June, September and December. Interim meetings may be held if required as a result of the number of applications received.

Correspondent: Mrs Avril Sloane, Secretary & Treasurer, 21 Beaton Road, Glasgow, G41 4NW (0141 423 2169; Fax: 0141 424 1731; email: enquiries@gemt.org.uk; website: www.gemt.org.uk/)

The JTH Charitable Trust

Eligibility: People in need who live in Glasgow and are undertaking education which enhances the cultural and social fabric of society with a view to meeting unmet local needs which are not municipal, governmental or religious.

Types of grants: One-off grants ranging from £100 to £1,000 to schoolchildren for study/travel overseas, books, equipment/instruments and maintenance/living expenses, to college students, undergraduates, vocational students and mature students for fees, study/travel overseas, books, equipment/instruments, maintenance/living expenses and childcare, to overseas students for fees, books, equipment/instruments and maintenance/living expenses and to individuals with special educational needs for excursions.

Exclusions: Grants are unlikely to be made to people at Glasgow or Strathclyde Universities or Royal Scottish Academy of Music and Dance as the trust makes block payments to the hardship funds of these institutions. Grants are also not normally awarded towards medical electives, second or further qualifications, payments of school fees or costs incurred at tertiary educational establishments.

Annual grant total: In 2007/08 the trust had an income of £208,000. Previously grants to individuals totalled £11,000, with the majority of grant-giving focused towards organisations.

Applications: An application form to be submitted together with a summary in the applicant's own words, extending to no more than a single A4 sheet, of the purpose and need of the grant. The possible costs and financial need should also be broken down.

The trustees meet four times a year normally in March, June, September and December, but this can vary. All applications should be submitted one month prior to the meeting.

It is a condition that with any grant given, a report should be made as to how the funds have been used. Grants not used for the purposes stated must be returned. Applicants receiving help one year may expect to be refused in the next.

Correspondent: Lynne Faulkner, Biggart Baillie, Dalmore House, 310 St Vincent Street, Glasgow G2 5QR (0141 228 8000; email: jlane@biggartbaillie.co.uk)

The Trades House of Glasgow

Eligibility: People in need who live in Glasgow.

Types of grants: Grants to encourage promising young people in university or colleges.

Annual grant total: About £15,000 in educational grants to individuals.

Applications: In writing to the correspondent.

Correspondent: The Clerk, Administration Centre, North Gallery – Trades Hall, 85 Glassford Street, Glasgow, G1 1UH (0141 553 1605; website: www.tradeshouse.org.uk/)

Other information: Grants are also made to organisations.

Dumfries & Galloway

The Dumfriesshire Educational Trust

Eligibility: People normally living in Dumfriesshire who have had at least five years of education in Dumfriesshire.

Types of grants: Grants of up to £60, usually recurrent, are given to: schoolchildren towards educational outings; students in further/higher education for books, fees/living expenses, study/travel abroad and student exchanges; and mature students towards books and travel.

Exclusions: Grants are not available for childcare for mature students or foreign students studying in the UK.

Annual grant total: In 2006 the trust had an income of £43,000. About £18,000 a year is given to individuals and organisations.

Applications: On a form available from the correspondent, for consideration in March, June, September or December. Applications should be submitted in the preceding month directly by the individual or through the relevant school/college/

educational welfare agency or through another third party and signed by the applicant.

For recurrent grants, applicants must reapply each academic year.

Correspondent: Alex Heswell, Dumfries and Galloway Council, Municipal Chambers, Buccleuch Street, Dumfries DG1 2AD (01387 260000; Fax: 01387 245961)

The Holywood Trust

Eligibility: Young people aged 15 to 25 living in the Dumfries and Galloway region, with a preference for people who are mentally, physically or socially disadvantaged.

Types of grants: One-off and recurrent grants of £50 to £500 to schoolchildren, people in further or higher education, vocational students, people with special educational needs and people starting work for books, equipment, instruments, fees, living expenses, childcare, educational outings and study or travel overseas. Applications which contribute to their personal development are more likely to receive support. This could include financial or material assistance to participate in education or training, access employment, establish a home or involve themselves in a project or activity which will help them or their community.

Exclusions: No grants are given towards carpets or accommodation deposits.

Annual grant total: Grants to individuals totalled around £150,000.

Applications: On a form available from the correspondent, or which can be downloaded from the trust's website. Applications are considered at least four times a year. The trust encourages applicants to provide additional information about any disadvantage which affects them where their application form has not given them an opportunity to do so. It also welcomes any supporting information from third party workers.

Correspondent: Richard Lye, Trust Administrator, Mount St Michael, Craigs Road, Dumfries DG1 4UT (01387 269176; Fax: 01387 269175; email: funds@holywood-trust.org.uk; website: www.holywood-trust.org.uk)

Other information: The trust also supports groups and project applications which benefit young people.

The John Primrose Trust

Eligibility: Young people in need with a connection to Dumfries and Maxwelltown by parentage or by living there.

Types of grants: Grants to students to help with educational needs or help for people starting work.

Annual grant total: About £10,000, half of which is given to individuals for relief-in-need and educational purposes.

Applications: On an application form available from the correspondent, to be considered in June and December.

Correspondent: The Trustees, 92 Irish Street, Dumfries DG1 2PF

The Stewartry Educational Trust

Eligibility: Persons belonging to the Stewartry of Kirkcudbright (i.e. the area of the Stewartry of Kirkcudbright prior to local government re-organisation in 1975).

Types of grants: One-off grants are given to schoolchildren for educational outings in Scotland and for general study costs to people starting work and students in further or higher education, including mature students and postgraduates.

Annual grant total: In 2006/07 the trust had a total income of £4,900.

Applications: On a form available from the correspondent with details of any grants available from other sources. Applications can be submitted directly by the individual or through a parent/guardian, social worker, Citizen's Advice, other welfare agency or other third party. They should be submitted in February, May or August for consideration in the following month.

Correspondent: The Clerk, Corselet College, Buittle, Castle Douglas, DG7 1NJ

The John Wallace Trust Scheme

Eligibility: Young people who live in the following areas: the electoral wards of Kirkland, Kello, Crichton, Douglas, Cairn, Morton and that part of Dalswinton Ward lying outside the parish of Dumfries and all in the local government area of Nithsdale District.

Types of grants: Bursaries for educational costs and travel grants for visits of an educational nature.

Annual grant total: About £4,000.

Applications: Application forms are available from the correspondent. The closing date is 31 December each year.

Correspondent: The Department for Finance And Corporate Services, Dumfries And Galloway Council, Carruthers House, English Street, Dumfries, DG1 2HP

Wigtownshire Educational Trust

Eligibility: People who live in the former county of Wigtownshire who can demonstrate personal hardship and that no other source of funding is available.

Types of grants: Grants ranging from £50 to £300 to schoolchildren, college students, undergraduates, vocational students, mature students and people with special educational needs. Grants given include those towards, clothing/uniforms, fees, study/travel abroad, books, equipment/instruments and excursions. Assistance is also given towards gaining practical experience of trades and promoting education in the visual arts, music and drama.

Annual grant total: About £1,500.

Applications: On a form available from the above address. Applications are considered throughout the year. If the applicant is a child/young person, details of parental income are required.

Correspondent: Council Secretariat, Dumfries and Galloway Council, Department Of Corporate Finance, Carruthers House, English Street, Dumfries DG1 2HP

East, North & South Ayrshire

The John Longwill Education Trust

Eligibility: Scholars or students who are attending Higher grade school or university in Scotland and who are native to Dalry and of Scottish descent.

Types of grants: Payments of about £100 each.

Annual grant total: Annual income of around £750.

Applications: In writing to the correspondent at any time.

Correspondent: James McCosh, J & J McCosh Solicitors, Clydesdale Bank Chambers, Dalry, Ayrshire KA24 5AB

The C K Marr Educational Trust

Eligibility: People who currently live in Troon or the Troon electoral wards.

Types of grants: Mainly bursaries, scholarships and educational travel grants for those at college or university.

Annual grant total: Over £200,000 a year.

Applications: On a form available from the correspondent to be submitted either directly by the individual, or through an organisation such as a school or an educational welfare agency.

Correspondent: Alan A Stewart, Clerk, 1 Howard Street, Kilmarnock KA1 2BW

North & South Lanarkshire

Loaningdale School Company

Eligibility: Children and young people aged 12 to 20 who are in need and live within the Clydesdale local area of South Lanarkshire.

Types of grants: One-off grants ranging from £100 to £1,000 towards furthering the individual's education or employment

prospects. Priority is given to creative or outdoor pursuits for young people, young unemployed people and post-school education and training of young people.

Annual grant total: The trust has an annual income of around £10,000. Grants total around £6,000, about £1,500 of which is given to individuals

Applications: On a form available from the correspondent, with guidelines for applicants. Applications are considered in March, June, September and December, and should be submitted in the previous month.

Correspondent: Fiona Watson, Scott-Moncrieff, 17 Melville Street, Edinburgh EH3 7PH (0131 473 3500)

Other information: Grants are also made to organisations.

Highlands & Islands

The Fresson Trust

Eligibility: People wishing to further their career in aviation who are living in, or visiting, the Highlands and Islands.

Types of grants: Grants in the past have been given to assist in the payment of flying lessons and in the form of a scholarship bursary. One-off grants can be given to help people starting work to buy books, equipment and clothing and help with their travel expenses. Students in further or higher education may be provided with money for books, fees or living expenses. Mature students can receive grants for books, travel, fees and childcare.

Annual grant total: About £500.

Applications: In writing to the correspondent at any time. Applicants should state how they can assist in the development of aviation in the Highlands and Islands.

Correspondent: The Secretary, 24 Drumsmittar Road, North Kessock, Inverness IV1 3JU (email: info@fressontrust.org.uk; website: www.fressontrust.org.uk)

Highland

The Highland Children's Trust

Eligibility: Children and young people in need who are under 25 and live in the Highlands.

Types of grants: One-off grants of £50 to £500 are available for the following purposes:

● student hardship funding

● school or educational trips
● family holidays
● educational items for children with special educational needs.

Exclusions: Grants are not given for postgraduate study, to pay off debts, nor to purchase clothing, footwear, food, furniture or cars and so on.

Annual grant total: In 2006/07 the trust had an income of £48,000. Previously grants to individuals have totalled around £20,000

Applications: On a form available from the correspondent. They can be submitted at any time either directly by the individual or through a social worker, Citizens Advice or other welfare agency. Applications must include details of income and savings and are considered at board meetings held on a regular basis.

Correspondent: Mrs Alison Harbinson, 105 Castle Street, Inverness IV2 3EA (01463 243872; Fax: 01463 243872; email: info@hctrust.co.uk; website: www.hctrust.co.uk)

Other information: No funding is given to organisations.

The Morar Trust

Eligibility: People who live in the community of Morar.

Types of grants: Funds are used to support educational, social and charitable occasions in the local community. The trust has in the past assisted with payments for educational equipment, trips and festivities, along with supporting the hospital, ambulance and welfare purposes. Grants are given as one-off payments.

Annual grant total: £1,000 for educational and welfare purposes.

Applications: In writing to the council via the correspondent or through a social or medical worker.

Correspondent: The Secretary, Mallaig and Morar Community Centre, West Bay, Mallaig, PH41 4PX

Isle of Lewis

Ross & Cromarty Educational Trust

Eligibility: People who live on the Isle of Lewis.

Types of grants: Grants range from £50 to £200 for: (a) books, fees and living expenses and study or travel abroad for students in further and higher education; (b) books, equipment, instruments and clothing for people starting work; (c) books, travel and fees for mature students; and (d) books and educational outings for schoolchildren. Grants are sometimes considered for various social, cultural and recreational purposes for individuals.

Annual grant total: The trust has an income of about £10,000 each year, all of which is available in grants to individuals and organisations.

Applications: On a form available from the Comhairle nan Eilean Siar website.

Correspondent: The Director of Education, Comhairle nan Eilean, Sandwick Road, Stornoway, Isle of Lewis, HS1 2BW (01851 709546; website: www. cne-siar.gov.uk/education/)

Orkney Islands

Orkney Educational Trust Scheme 1961

Eligibility: People on postgraduate courses, in further education or on apprenticeships who live in the former county of Orkney.

Types of grants: Subsidiary grants of £8 to £50 to help with travel, material costs and fees/living expenses for further education students. Grants are also made to people starting work to help with books, equipment/instruments, clothing and travel costs, and to schoolchildren to help with books and educational outings. Grants may also be given for the promotion of education in the community.

Annual grant total: Grants totalling about £2,500 are made to around 50 individuals each year.

Applications: In writing to the correspondent. Applications are considered in October.

Correspondent: The Director of Education, Orkney Islands Council, Education Department, Council Offices, School Place, Kirkwall, Orkney KW15 1NY

3. WALES

The Cambrian Educational Foundation for Deaf Children

Eligibility: Deaf and partially hearing children aged between 3 and 25 who live or whose parents live in Wales. Beneficiaries can be in special classes (units) in ordinary and special schools in Wales; students in further education; and people entering employment.

Types of grants: One-off and occasionally annual grants of £100 to £500. Grants have been provided to schoolchildren for school uniforms, occasionally for educational outings in the UK and for study or travel abroad, to people starting work and to further and higher education students for books.

Exclusions: Grants are not given for leisure trips.

Annual grant total: In 2006/07 the trust had an income of £22,000 and a total expenditure of £24,000.

Applications: Applications, on a form available from the correspondent, can be submitted directly by the individual, or through their school/college/educational welfare agency or other third party. They are considered throughout the year.

Correspondent: Mrs Pamela Brown, Montreux, 30 Lon Cedwyn, Sketty, Swansea SA2 0TH (01792 207628; email: pamela@brown.fsworld.co.uk)

The Cambrian Educational Trust Fund

Eligibility: People under the age of 21 who are blind or partially-sighted and were born in, or live in, Wales.

Types of grants: One-off grants to promote education, such as towards care and maintenance costs.

Annual grant total: In 2007/08 the trust had an income of £1,600 and a total expenditure of £2,000. Grants previously totalled around £2,000.

Applications: On a form available from the correspondent. Applications are considered quarterly. The trust welcomes telephone enquiries from potential applications to discuss suitability and how to apply.

Correspondent: Owen Williams, Wales Council for the Blind, 3rd Floor, Shand House, 20 Newport Road, Cardiff CF24 0DB (029 2047 3954; Fax: 029 2043 3920; email: owen@wcb-ccd.org.uk; website: www.wcb-ccd.org.uk/)

The James Pantyfedwen Foundation

Eligibility: Candidates for Christian ministry from Wales and Welsh postgraduate students.

Types of grants: One-off and recurrent grants according to need.

Annual grant total: In 2006/07 the foundation had assets of £11.3 million, which generated an income of £462,000. Grants totalled £327,000, of which grants to students totalled £83,000.

Applications: On a form available from the correspondent. The closing date is 30 June preceding the academic year for which the application is being made. Applications are considered in July.

Correspondent: Richard H Morgan, Executive Secretary, Pantyfedwen, 9 Market Street, Aberystwyth SY23 1DL (01970 612806; email: pantyfedwen@btinternet.com)

Other information: This trust mostly supports organisations.

The May Price SRN Award

Eligibility: People who have lived in Cardiganshire, Carmarthenshire or Pembrokeshire for at least two years and who are pursuing a course in medical or medically-related studies.

Types of grants: Grants to help with the cost of books or equipment or to supplement existing grants.

Annual grant total: In 2006/07 the trust had an income of £1,600 and an expenditure of £250.

Applications: On a form available from the correspondent, to be returned by 31 October each year.

Correspondent: Roger Jones, The Old School, Llansteffan Road, Johnstown, Carmarthen, Dyfed, SA31 3LZ

Reardon Smith Nautical Trust
see entry on page 84

Correspondent: John Cory, Cob Cottage, Garth Hill, Pentyrch, Cardiff, CF15 9NS

The Michael Sobell Welsh People's Charitable Trust

Eligibility: People in need who live in Wales.

Types of grants: One-off and recurrent grants ranging from £40 to £500.

Annual grant total: Previously grants have totalled around £16,000. The trust makes grants to both individuals and organisations.

Applications: In writing to the correspondent.

Correspondent: Mrs S E Davies, Dolenog, Old Hall, Llanidloeas, Powys SY18 6PP

The Welsh Broadcasting Trust
see entry on page 81

Correspondent: The Secretary, Islwyn, Lôn Terfyn, Morfa Nefyn, Pwllheli, Gwynedd, LL53 6AP (01758 720 132 (after 6pm); email: info@wbt.org.uk; website: www.ydg.org.uk)

Ymddiriedolaeth Bryntaf (the Bryn-Taf Trust)

Eligibility: Children of school age (2 to 16) who have some special educational need and are either Welsh speaking or are receiving Welsh medium education or the parents desire such provision for their child.

Types of grants: Educational expenses for children in special schools or hospitals. This includes the cost of equipment and travel costs for parents to visit children, the cost of school clothing, books, educational outings and school fees.

Annual grant total: In recent years no grants have been made by the trust. Previously assets have stood at £18,000.

Applications: On a form available from the correspondent. Applications can be submitted either through the individual's school/college/educational welfare agency on behalf of the child or parent, directly by the individual or by another third party on their behalf.

Correspondent: Dafydd Hampson-Jones, 11 Greenwood Road, Llandaff, Cardiff, CF5 2QD

Other information: Grants are also given towards conferences and research on Welsh language issues in special education.

Mid-Wales

Ceredigion

The Cardiganshire Intermediate & Technical Educational Fund

Eligibility: Individuals over the age of 25 who have, at any time, been in attendance for at least two years at a maintained secondary school in the Ceredigion area (the former county of Cardiganshire).

Types of grants: Grants of £100 to £150 a year, to help with college or university fees or to supplement existing grants.

Annual grant total: In 2007/08 the trust had an income of £15,000 and a total expenditure of £16,000.

Applications: Application forms are available from the correspondent from August, to be submitted by 30 November.

Correspondent: Gerwyn Richards, The Students Awards Section, Education Department, County Offices, Ceredigion County Council, Marine Terrace, Aberystwyth SY23 2DE (email: gerwynr@ceredigion.gov.uk)

Visual Impairment Breconshire

Eligibility: Blind and partially-sighted people living in Brecknock.

Types of grants: One-off grants at Christmas and for special equipment/special needs, for example, cookers, talking books and college fees.

Annual grant total: In 2006/07 the trust had an income of £5,500 and a total expenditure of £4,000.

Applications: In writing to the correspondent, to be considered when received.

Correspondent: E J Vince, Ken Dy Gwair, Aber, Talybont-on-Usk, Brecon, LD3 7YS (01874 676202)

Powys

The Thomas John Jones Memorial Fund for Scholarships and Exhibitions

Eligibility: People under the age of 26 whom, for a period of at least two years, have both lived and attended a secondary school in the former county of Brecknockshire.

Types of grants: Preference is given to applicants undertaking courses of study or training in civil engineering at universities or colleges.

Annual grant total: Previously the fund has had an income of around £40,000. No further information was available.

Applications: In writing to the correspondent.

Correspondent: D Meredith, Clerk to the Trustees, Cilmery, The Avenue, Brecon, Powys LD3 9BG

Edmund Jones' Charity

Eligibility: People under the age of 25 who live or work within the town of Brecon.

Types of grants: Help towards the cost of education, training, apprenticeship or equipment for those starting work and grants tenable at any Brecon town secondary school, training college for teachers, university or other institution of further education approved by the trustees. Grants range from £50 to £300.

Annual grant total: In 2006 the trust had assets of £380,000 and an income of £33,000. Grant to individuals totalled £16,000.

Applications: On a form available from the correspondent giving details of the college/course/apprenticeship and the anticipated cost, together with details of any other grants received or applied for. Applications may be submitted by the individual, parent or college. They are considered at any time, but mainly in October.

Correspondent: Mrs Gail Elizabeth Rofe, Secretary, The Guildhall, Lion Street, Brecon, Powys LD3 7AL (01874 622884; email: brecon.guildhall@btinternet.com)

The Llanidloes Relief-in-Need Charity

Eligibility: Students who live in the communities of Llanidloes and Llanidloes Without. No support to students not living within three miles of the town, or to foreign students studying in the area.

Types of grants: Grants to help with the cost of books, living expenses and other essential items for those at college or university.

Annual grant total: About £1,000.

Applications: In writing to the correspondent.

Correspondent: Mrs S J Jarman, Clerk, Llwynderw, Old Hall, Llanidloes, Powys SY18 6PW (01686 412636)

The Powys Welsh Church Acts Fund

Eligibility: People less than 25 years living in Powys.

Types of grants: Grants, ranging from £50 to £250 for those wishing to follow a course of study at college or university for uniforms/clothing, fees, study/travel aboard, equipment/instruments and books. Help may also be available for those preparing for, or entering a trade, profession or calling.

Annual grant total: About £700 to individuals.

Applications: On a form available from the correspondent to be submitted directly by the individual.

Correspondent: The Clerk, Powys County Council, County Hall, Llandrindod Wells, Powys LD1 5LG

Other information: Grants are also made to organisations.

North Wales

Doctor William Lewis' Charity

Eligibility: Students under the age of 25 who live in the former counties of Anglesey, Caernarvon, Merioneth, Montgomery, Flint and Denbigh.

Types of grants: A portion of the income of the foundation is used to make awards for students at Oxford, Cambridge or the University of Wales and St David's University College, Lampeter. Grants are also given to applicants who are in training for a profession or trade.

Annual grant total: About £1,500.

Applications: On a form available from the correspondent, to be submitted directly by the individual by the beginning of October.

Correspondent: The Secretary, The Diocesan Centre, Cathedral Close, Bangor, Gwynedd LL57 IRL

The Wrexham (Parochial) Educational Foundation

Eligibility: People under 25 who live in the county borough of Wrexham and who attended for at least two years one of the following: Minera and Brymbo Aided Primary School or St Giles Voluntary Controlled Infant and/or Junior Schools, Wrexham.

Types of grants: Grants to help students in secondary and further education, and those starting an apprenticeship or training. Grants have included supporting a student with disabilities who was living at home and unable to receive a statutory grant.

Annual grant total: About £10,000.

Applications: In writing to the correspondent. Applications must be submitted directly by the individual.

Correspondent: P J Blore, 49 Norfolk Road, Wrexham LL12 7RT (01978 356901)

Anglesey

The Owen Lloyd Educational Foundation

Eligibility: People between 16 and 25 who live in the parishes of Penrhoslligwy, Moelfre or the neighbouring civil or ecclesiastical parishes. Preference is given (larger grants) to residents of Penrhoslligwy, as this was the original area covered by the trust's deed.

Types of grants: Grants are given to help with: books, fees/living expenses, travel costs (but not for study/travel abroad) and tools and equipment for students in further/higher education; and apprenticeship costs such as books, equipment, clothing and travel.

Annual grant total: About £5,000.

Applications: On a form available from the correspondent, including details of income and expenditure. Applications are considered in October. Grants are given in June.

Correspondent: Emlyn Evans, Nant Bychan Farm, Moelfre, Gwynedd LL72 8HF

The Ynys Mon Trust Fund

Eligibility: People under the age of 25 who are in need, have lived in Anglesey for not less than two years and have received at least two years of their secondary education in Anglesey.

Types of grants: Grants to help with school, college or university fees or to supplement existing grants.

Annual grant total: Previously about £30,000.

Applications: In writing to the correspondent. Applications are considered at meetings of the committee, and meetings are arranged in accordance with the number of applications. It is advisable to submit applications through the college/tutor/head of department.

Correspondent: David Elis-Williams, Corporate Director, Anglesey Further Education Trust Fund, Isle of Anglesey County Council, County Offices,

Llangefni, Ynys Mon, LL77 7TW (01248 752 600; Fax: 01248 752 696)

Conwy

The Sir John Henry Morris-Jones Trust Fund

Eligibility: People living in the former municipal borough of Colwyn Bay, as existing on 31 March 1974 (that is, prior to the reorganisation of local government in 1974). Applicants must be under the age of 19 on the 31 March.

Types of grants: Applicants have to satisfy the trustees, at a personal interview, of their degree of excellence in one of the following activities: arts and crafts; sport; academic and research; science and technology; industry and commerce; and any other field of activity that applicants may feel would meet the requirements of the trustees. Grants are one-off.

Annual grant total: In 2007/08 the trust had an income of £1,800 and £2,500.

Applications: On a form available from the correspondent. Applications are considered in April/May.

Correspondent: J M Roberts, Clerk to the Trustees, Town Hall, 7 Rhiw Road, Colwyn Bay LL29 7TG (01492 532248)

Richard Owen Scholarships

Eligibility: People aged under 25 who live in Llandudno. Preference is given to undergraduates at University of Bangor, but not exclusively so.

Types of grants: Grants, ranging from £70 to £100 are given towards clothing, tools, instruments or books for people leaving education and preparing for work. Student bursaries are also available as are grants towards educational travel abroad.

Annual grant total: About £500.

Applications: On a form available from the correspondent, to be submitted in September for consideration in August.

Correspondent: The Clerk, Llandudno Town Council, Town Hall, Lloyd Street, Llandudno, Gwynedd LL30 2UP

Denbighshire

The Freeman Evans St David's Day Denbigh Charity

Eligibility: People in need who live in Denbigh and Henllan.

Types of grants: One-off grants towards the cost of volunteer programmes overseas, educational equipment and so on.

Annual grant total: In 2006/07 the charity had assets of £50,000 and an income of £70,000. Grants were made totalling £44,000 and were given to both individuals

and organisations. Of this, about £3,000 was given in individual grants for educational purposes.

Applications: In writing to the correspondent. Applications can be made either directly by the individual or through a third party such as a social worker, Citizens Advice or other welfare agency. The trustees meet regularly throughout the year to consider applications.

Correspondent: Medwyn Jones, Denbigh Town Council, Town Hall, Crown Square, Denbigh, Clwyd LL16 3TB (01745 815 984; email: townclerk@denbightowncouncil. gov.uk)

Other information: Grants are also given for welfare purposes.

The Robert David Hughes Scholarship Foundation

Eligibility: University students who were either born in the community of Denbigh, or had a parent or parents resident in the area at the time of his or her birth, or at the date of the award have a parent or parents resident in the area who have lived there for at least ten years. Full documentary evidence is required.

Types of grants: Grants are made according to need to university students.

Exclusions: Individuals attending colleges of further education do not qualify for a grant.

Annual grant total: In 2006/07 the foundation had an income of £21,000 and a total expenditure of £19,000. Previously the foundation has spent the majority of its income on grants to individuals.

Applications: On a form available from the correspondent, to be submitted not later than 30 September. Applications are considered in November each year. Grants are made each term on receipt of completed certificates of attendance, signed by the principal or registrar of the university. After the first year, applicants are automatically sent forms for subsequent years.

Correspondent: E Emrys Williams, Clerk, Highfield, 2 Llewellyn's Estate, Denbigh LL16 3NR (01745 812724)

The Llanynys Educational Foundation

Eligibility: People under 25 who live in the community of Llanynys Rural, and that part of the community of Ruthin which was formerly the parish of Llanynys Urban.

Types of grants: One-off and recurrent grants up to £100 for students in further and higher education to assist with books, fees/living expenses, and study/travel abroad.

Annual grant total: About £600 is available each year.

Applications: The charity places advertisements in the local press shortly after A level results are published. Applications are considered in September. If a large number of requests are received in relation to the funds available, preference is given to first time applicants.

Applicants should include details of their: age; place of residence; course to be followed; qualification pursued; institution attended; and the purpose to which the grant will be put.

Correspondent: Robert Ian Kinnier, Rhewl Post Office, Ruthin, Denbighshire LL15 1TH (01824 702730)

John Matthews Educational Charity

Eligibility: People under 25 who live in the district of Glyndwr and the borough of Wrexham Maelor, both in the county of Denbighshire and the borough of Oswestry in the county of Shropshire.

Types of grants: 'Usually to enable a desirable or necessary course of education to be followed which would otherwise be financially impossible, with the emphasis on development of exceptional talents.' Grants range from £150 to £2,000.

The charity favours postgraduate or second degree students who are not getting other financial support, although undergraduates can be supported.

Annual grant total: About £5,000.

Applications: In writing to the correspondent. Applicants must provide information about their parents' financial circumstances once their eligibility has been established.

Correspondent: The Bursar, Ruthin School, Mold Road, Ruthin, Denbighshire LL15 1EE (01824 702543; email: secretary@ruthinschool.co.uk)

Flintshire

The Owen Jones Charity

Eligibility: College and university students and apprentices from Northop who are in need.

Types of grants: One-off and recurrent grants according to need. Recent grants have been given to students with inadequate grants to allow them to buy basic food and to apprentices entering a trade for tools and equipment.

Annual grant total: In 2006/07 the charity had assets of £410,000 and an income of £42,000. Grants were made totalling £3,000. The charity states that it has struggled to identify people eligible for support and hopes that in future years more of its expenditure can go to individuals in need.

Applications: In writing to the correspondent. An application form for students to use is currently being drafted and should be used when available.

Correspondent: Jack Wolstenholme, Secretary, 18 St Peter's Park, Northop, Mold, Clwyd CH7 6DP (01352 840739)

Other information: The charity also makes grants to local schools.

Gwynedd

The Morgan Scholarship Fund

Eligibility: People born or living in the civil parish of Llanengan who are under the age of 25. When funds permit, the area of benefit may be extended to include other parishes in the rural district of Lleyn.

Types of grants: Preference is given to undergraduates of the University College of North Wales. However, grants are also given for the following purposes: for those at college or university; for those going abroad to pursue their education; financial assistance, clothing, tools, instruments or books to help those leaving school, college or university to prepare for, or enter, a profession, trade or calling.

Annual grant total: About £1,000.

Applications: On a form available from the correspondent. Applications are considered in September.

Correspondent: The Clerk, Gwynedd Council, Shirehall Street, Caernarfon, Gwynedd LL55 ISH

The R H Owen Memorial Fund (Gronfa Goffa R H Owen)

Eligibility: People aged between 12 and 25 who were born in, or whose parents have lived for at least five years in, the parish of Llanberis and Brynrefail Comprehensive School catchment area.

Types of grants: Recurrent grants are given to schoolchildren, undergraduates, vocational students and people starting work for any academic or vocational need.

Annual grant total: Grants total around £500 a each year.

Applications: On a form available from the correspondent which should be submitted directly by the individual. The closing date for applications is 31 August.

Correspondent: J H Hughes, Tan-y-Clogwyn, Llanberis, Caernarfon, Gwynedd LL55 4LF (01286 871562)

The Peter Saunders Trust

Eligibility: People who live within Tywyn and the surrounding villages. 'The trust favours projects which show endeavour, a measure of self reliance and spirit of enterprise.'

Types of grants: Grants towards providing opportunities and learning experiences.

Annual grant total: In 2007/08 the trust had income of £130,000 and made grants, mostly to organisations, totalling £41,000.

Applications: In writing to the correspondent. Full guidelines are available from the trust's website.

Correspondent: The Trustees, PO Box 67, Tywyn, LL36 6AH (01654 713939; email: enquiries@petersaunderstrust.co.uk; website: www.petersaunderstrust.co.uk)

Dr Daniel William's Educational Fund

Eligibility: People under 25 attending college or university, particularly schoolchildren with serious family difficulties and people with special educational needs. Preference for (i) former pupils or close relatives of former pupils of Dr William's School, Dolgellau and (ii) people who live, or who have a parent who lives, in the district of Meirionnydd. This preference is strictly applied in view of the demands on the trust's income.

Types of grants: Recurrent grants towards the cost of books, equipment, fees/living expenses and study or travel abroad for students who are part of or linked to an educational course. Awards are usually of a maximum of £500.

Annual grant total: Over 150 grants awarded each year totalling around £30,000 to £40,000.

Applications: In writing, directly by the individual to the correspondent, requesting an application form.

Correspondent: T Meirion Wynne, Clogwyn Hal, Betws-y-coed, Gwynedd LL24 0BL (01690 710264)

Wrexham

Dame Dorothy Jeffreys Educational Foundation

Eligibility: People in need aged between 16 and 25 who live in the former borough of Wrexham or the communities of Abenbury, Bersham, Broughton, Bieston, Brymbo, Esclusham Above, Esculsham Below, Gresford, Gwersyllt and Minera.

Types of grants: Grants of £50 minimum. Grants for general education purposes are given to schoolchildren, further/higher education students, people starting work and vocational students. Mature students up to the age of 25 can also receive grants.

Annual grant total: In 2006 the trust had an income of £3,500 and a total expenditure of £4,800. Grants usually total around £3,500.

Applications: On a form available from the correspondent to be submitted directly by the individual. Applications are considered in November/December and should be submitted by 1 October.

Correspondent: P J Blore, 49 Norfolk Road, Wrexham LL12 7RT (01978 356901)

The Ruabon & District Relief-in-Need Charity

Eligibility: People in need who live in the county borough of Wrexham, which covers the community council districts of Cefn Mawr, Penycae, Rhosllanerchrugog (including Johnstown) and Ruabon.

Types of grants: One-off and occasionally recurrent grants of up to £200. Grants are given to schoolchildren towards uniforms/clothing, equipment/instruments and educational visits/excursions.

Exclusions: Loans are not given, nor are grants given to investigate bankruptcy proceedings.

Annual grant total: About £1,400 in educational and relief-in-need grants.

Applications: In writing to the correspondent either directly by the individual or a family member, through a third party such as a social worker or teacher, or through an organisation such as Citizens Advice or a school. Applications are considered on an ongoing basis.

Correspondent: J R Fenner, Secretary, Cyncoed, 65 Albert Grove, Ruabon, Wrexham LL14 6AF (01978 820102; email: jamesrfenner@tiscali.co.uk)

South Wales

The David Davies Memorial Trusts

Eligibility: South Wales mineworkers or their (unemployed) dependants, or redundant or retired mineworkers who have not taken up employment since leaving the coalmining industry.

Types of grants: Grants ranging from £200 to £500, to enable people to pursue educational courses or other approved studies at university which they otherwise could not afford.

Annual grant total: In 2006 the trust had both an income and expenditure of around £10,000.

Applications: On a form available from the correspondent. Applications can be made directly by the individual and are considered throughout the year.

Correspondent: Andrew Morse, Coal Industry Social Welfare Organisation, Woodland Terrace, Maesycoed, Pontypridd, Mid-Glamorgan CF37 1DZ (01443 485233; Fax: 01443 486226; email: andrew.morse@ciswo.org.uk)

The Gane Charitable Trust

Eligibility: Students of arts and crafts, or design and social welfare. There is a preference for applicants from Bristol and south Wales.

Types of grants: Grants are available to help meet the educational costs of college students, vocational students and mature students and their children. Grants are given towards fees, books and equipment/instruments and range from £200 to £500 and are normally one-off.

Annual grant total: In 2006 the trust had assets of £848,000 and an income of £29,000, with a direct charitable expenditure of £17,000.

Applications: On a form available from the correspondent. Applications are considered in January, May and September.

Correspondent: Mrs R Fellows, The Secretary, c/o Bristol Guild, 68–70 Park Street, Bristol, BS1 5JY (0117 926 5548)

Other information: Grants are also made to organisations, usually for capital purposes or to meet start-up costs.

The Glamorgan Further Education Trust Fund

Eligibility: (i) Pupils who have for not less than two years at any time attended a county secondary school in the area of the former administrative county of Glamorgan (or Howell's Glamorgan County School, Cardiff, provided that the candidates attending the said school have lived in the former administrative county of Glamorgan for at least two years while a pupil at the school).

(ii) Female pupils who, in addition, have for not less than two years at any time attended any maintained primary school in the parishes of Llantrisant, Pontypridd, Pentyrch, Llanfabon, Llantwit Fardre, Eglwysilan and that part of the parish of Llanwonno comprising the former Ynysybwl ward of the former Mountain Ash urban district. There is a preference for such girls who while in attendance at any such school lived in the parish of Eglwysilan.

N.B. Applicants are not eligible for assistance if they are in receipt of a central government bursary or a mandatory or discretionary award, or are exempt from the payment of the tuition fee.

Types of grants: (a) Cash grants tenable at any teacher training college, university or other institution of further education (including professional and technical) approved by the council and governed by rules made by the council.

(b) Financial assistance, outfits, clothing, tools, instruments or books to assist those leaving school, university or other educational establishments to prepare for or enter a profession, trade or calling.

Annual grant total: In 2006/07 the trust had an income of £85,000 and a total expenditure of £185,000. Grants to individuals for educational purposes totalled £47,000.

Applications: On a form available from the correspondent. Applications should be submitted before 31 May each year for consideration in July/August.

Correspondent: Mrs Helen Lewis, Student/Pupil Support Section, Department for Education, Leisure and Lifelong Learning, 1st Floor, Aberafan House, Port Talbot SA13 1PJ (01639 763580)

The Gwent Further Education Trust Fund

Eligibility: People over 16 studying part-time who are resident in the former Gwent area (excluding Newport) and went to a Gwent secondary school.

Types of grants: Grants to help with school, college or university fees, books and equipment. Students on Income Support or Job Seekers Allowance can receive grants of about £360; employed students receive grants of around £60.

Annual grant total: About £10,000 each year is available for grants to individuals.

Applications: On a form available from the correspondent.

Correspondent: The Trustees, c/o Pupil & Student Services Section, Monmouthshire County Council, Education Department, County Hall, Cwmbran, Gwent NP44 2XH (01633 644507/644664; email: jemmacleverly@monmouthshire.gov.uk)

The Geoffrey Jones (Penreithin) Scholarship Fund

Eligibility: People who have lived in the following parishes or districts for at least 12 months: Penderyn, Ystradfellte Vaynor and Taff Fechan Valley, Merthyr Tydfil.

Types of grants: Grants to students in further or higher education (no upper age limit) to help with the cost of books, fees/living expenses and study or travel abroad.

Annual grant total: In 2007/08 the trust had an income of £16,000 and a total expenditure of approximately £4,000. About 25 grants are made each year totalling £2,000 to £3,000.

Applications: In writing to the correspondent, including details of any educational grant received. Applications are considered in September/October each year.

Correspondent: Mr Butler, 17–19 Cardiff Street, Aberdare, Rhondda Cynon Taff CF44 7DP (01685 885500; Fax: 01685 885535)

The Monmouthshire Further Education Trust Fund

Eligibility: Students on part-time courses who have attended a local comprehensive/secondary school and have lived in the Greater Gwent area, except Newport, that is, the council areas of Caerphilly (part), Torfaen, Blaenau Gwent and Monmouthshire.

Types of grants: One-off grants, although students can reapply in subsequent years, towards books, fees, travel and equipment. Grants range between £60 and £360, depending on student's circumstances. Full-time students receiving funding from another source are not funded.

Annual grant total: Around £10,000 is given each year in grants to individuals.

Applications: Application forms are available from the correspondent, for consideration throughout the year.

Correspondent: The Further Education Department, The School and Student Access Unit, Floor 5, Monmouthshire County Council, County Hall, Cwmbran, Gwent NP44 2XH

Caerphilly

The Rhymney Trust

Eligibility: People in need who live in Rhymney.

Types of grants: One-off grants ranging from £30 to £100 to school children and college students.

Annual grant total: About £1,500 a year. Between 27 and 35 grants are made each year.

Applications: In writing to the correspondent directly by the individual. Applications should be submitted in June for consideration in August.

Correspondent: D Brannan, 11 Forge Crescent, Rhymney, Gwent NP22 5PR (01685 843094)

Carmarthenshire

The Dorothy May Edwards Charity

Eligibility: Former pupils of Ysgol Pantycelyn School, Llandovery who are under 25 and are pursuing a course of higher education.

Types of grants: Grants of £15 to £125 to: provide outfits, clothing, tools, instruments or books on leaving school, university or other educational establishment; prepare for and to enter a profession, trade or calling; travel in this country or abroad to pursue education; study music or other art; or continue education at college or university or at any approved place of learning.

Annual grant total: In 2006/07 the trust had an income of £2,800 and a total expenditure of £800.

Applications: Application forms are available from the correspondent. These

should be completed and returned by 31 October.

Correspondent: Roger Jones, Director of Resources, Carmarthenshire County Council, County Hall, Carmarthen, Dyfed, SA31 1JP

The Elizabeth Evans Trust *see entry on page 73*

Correspondent: The Trust Secretary, c/o Ungoed Thomas and King, Gwynne House, 6 Quay Street, Carmarthen, SA31 3AD (email: hazelthorogood@ theelizabethevanstrust.co.uk; website: www.theelizabethevanstrust.co.uk)

The Minnie Morgans Scholarship

Eligibility: People under the age of 25 who have attended any of the secondary schools in Llanelli and who are studying drama and dramatic art at the University of Wales or any school of dramatic art approved by the trustees.

Types of grants: One-off grants usually of £1,000.

Annual grant total: In 2006/07 the charity had an income of £12,000 and a total expenditure of £15,000.

Applications: Application forms are available from the correspondent and should be returned by 31 October.

Correspondent: Roger Jones, Carmarthenshire County Council, County Hall, Carmathen, Dyfed, SA31 1JP

The Mary Elizabeth Morris Charity

Eligibility: Past and present pupils of Ysgol Rhys Prichard School and Ysgol Pantycelyn School, who are under 25.

Types of grants: Grants to: pupils transferring from Ysgol Rhys Pritchard; supplement existing grants of beneficiaries in further or higher education; help towards the cost of education, training, apprenticeships or education for those starting work; and help with the cost of educational travel at home or abroad.

Annual grant total: About £1,000.

Applications: Application forms are available from the correspondent and should be returned in either June (for primary school pupils) or by 31 October (for secondary school pupils).

Correspondent: Roger Jones, Director of Resources, Carmarthenshire County Council, County Hall, Carmarthen, Dyfed, SA31 1JP (01267 234567; Fax: 01267 221692)

The Robert Peel/Taliaris School Charity

Eligibility: People under the age of 25 years who at the time of application live in the ancient parish of Llandeilo Fawr and have done so for a minimum of two years. Preference is given to applicants who are members of or are connected with the Church in Wales. The ancient parish of Llandeilo Fawr was a very large parish extending from Capel Isaac and Taliaris in the north west down to the outskirts of Brynamman in the south east and including the township of Llandeilo.

Types of grants: Awards to promote the educational interests of individuals transferring to a recognised course of further education and also to assist school pupils in need.

Annual grant total: Income of around £700 per year.

Applications: On a form available from the correspondent to be returned by 31 October.

Correspondent: Roger Jones, The Old School, Llansteffan Road, Johnstown, Carmarthen, Dyfed, SA31 3LZ

City of Cardiff

The Cardiff Caledonian Society

Eligibility: People of Scottish nationality and their families, who live in Cardiff or the surrounding district and are in need.

Types of grants: Grants are made to college students, undergraduates, vocational students and mature students, including those towards fees, books and instruments and equipment. Grants are also made to people starting work.

Annual grant total: In 2006/07 the trust had an income of £9,500 and a total expenditure of £7,500.

Applications: In writing to the correspondent. Applications can be submitted directly by the individual or through a social worker, Citizens Advice or other welfare agency at any time. Applications are considered on a regular basis.

Correspondent: Mrs Cathy Rogers, 2 Llandinam Crescent, Cardiff, CF14 2RB (029 2062 3680)

Other information: The trust gives grants mainly to organisations.

The Cardiff Further Education Trust Fund

Eligibility: Young people who are resident in Cardiff and who attended a primary or secondary school in the city and are in need.

Types of grants: Grants in connection with the costs of further education.

Annual grant total: In 2006/07 the trust had assets of £23 million and an income of £158,000. Around £97,000 was given in charitable activities.

Applications: In writing to the correspondent.

Correspondent: Rick Zaple, Room 348, County Hall, Atlantic Wharf, Cardiff CF10 4UW (029 2087 2324)

The Howardian Educational Trust

Eligibility: Young people who are resident in Cardiff and who attended a primary or secondary school in the city and are in need.

Types of grants: Grants in connection with the costs of further education.

Annual grant total: In 2007/08 the trust had both an income and a total expenditure of around £1,000

Applications: In writing to the correspondent.

Correspondent: Rick Zaple, Room 348, County Hall, Atlantic Wharf, Cardiff CF10 4UW (029 2087 2324)

Monmouthshire

Llandenny Charities

Eligibility: Students in full-time higher education who live in the parish of Llandenny and have lived there for more than one year.

Types of grants: Recurrent.

Annual grant total: About £1,000 for educational and welfare purposes.

Applications: In writing to the correspondent, to be submitted directly by the individual. Applications should be submitted by 15 January for consideration in February.

Correspondent: Dr G K Russell, Forge Cottage, Llandenny, Usk, Monmouthshire NP15 1DL (01633 432536; email: gsrussell@btinternet.com)

Monmouth Charity

Eligibility: Further education students who live within an eight-mile radius of Monmouth.

Types of grants: One-off grants usually up to a maximum of £500.

Annual grant total: In 2006/07 the charity had both an income and expenditure of £11,000. Grants are made for both educational and welfare purposes.

Applications: The trust advertises in the local press each September/October and applications should be made in response to this advertisement for consideration in November. Emergency grants can be considered at any time. There is no application form. Applications can be submitted directly by the individual or through a social worker, Citizens Advice or other welfare agency.

Correspondent: A R Pirie, Pen-y-Bryn, Oakfield Road, Monmouth NP25 3JJ

The Monmouthshire Farm School Endowment

Eligibility: Further and higher education agriculture students (and those studying related subjects) living in the former county of Monmouthshire (as constituted in 1956). Preference is given to students who are under the age of 25.

Types of grants: Grants of between £500 and £1,000 to help with the costs of study at the Usk College of Agriculture or any other farm institute, school, university or department of agricultural education approved by the governors. Grants can be for books, equipment/instruments, fees, living expenses and educational outings in the UK.

Annual grant total: Between £10,000 and £20,000 a year.

Applications: On a form available from the correspondent which can be submitted at any time directly by the individual including an estimate of costs. Applications are considered in October and January.

Correspondent: Directorate of Lifelong Learning and Leisure, The School and Student Access Unit, Floor 5, Monmouthshire County Council, County Hall, Cwmbran, Gwent NP44 2XH

Other information: The trust has previously stated that owing to a shortage of applications, the trust deed is in the process of being revised in an attempt to widen the field of applications. However, the endowment remains open for applications.

The Monmouthshire Welsh Church Acts Fund

Eligibility: People of any age studying at school, university or any other place of study, who live in the boundaries of Monmouthshire County Council and their dependants. Grants are also made to people starting work.

Types of grants: Scholarships, bursaries, loans and maintenance allowances ranging from £50 to £500 for uniforms, other clothing, books, equipment, fees, childcare and travel in the UK and overseas for educational purposes. Grants include those for music or arts courses.

Annual grant total: In 2006/07 the fund had assets of £4.6 million and an income of £2.2 million. Grants to organisations and individuals totalled £157,000.

Applications: On a form available from the correspondent which can be submitted at any time, and must be signed by a county councillor. Applications can be made either directly by the individual, or through his or her school, and are usually considered in June, September, December and March.

Correspondent: Marie Rees, Management Accountancy, Monmouthshire County Council, County Hall, Cwmbran, Monmouthshire NP44 2XH

Other information: Following the reorganisation of local councils the funds from the Gwent Welsh Church Fund were divided and are now administered by five new councils. The above council is the only one which makes grants directly to individuals.

James Powell's Education Foundation

Eligibility: People who live in the ancient parish of Llantilio Crossenny and who are 16 years old and over. No grants to students who live outside this area.

Types of grants: Grants are given for books, equipment and other essentials for people starting work, and for students and pupils for maintenance and living expenses.

Annual grant total: In 2007 the foundation had an income of £6,100 and a total expenditure of £4,200.

Applications: In writing to the correspondent, by a parent of the applicant. Applications should be made by August for consideration in September.

Correspondent: D T Hayhurst, Rose Cottage Chapel, Llanvetherine, Abergavenny, Gwent, NP7 8PY

Neath Port Talbot

Elizabeth Jones' Charities

Eligibility: People under the age of 25 in further/higher education who live in the old borough of Port Talbot and are in need.

Types of grants: One-off grants ranging from £50 to £400, towards books and study abroad.

Annual grant total: In 2006/07 the trust had an income of £3,200 and a total expenditure of £3,700.

Applications: On a form available from the correspondent. Applications can be submitted directly by the individual.

Correspondent: Ken Tucker, 6 Glandwffryn Close, Port Talbot SA13 2UB (01639 766224)

Pembrokeshire

The Charity of Doctor Jones

Eligibility: People between 16 and 25 who live in Pembroke.

Types of grants: Help towards the cost of education, training, apprenticeship or equipment for students, schoolchildren and those starting work.

Annual grant total: In 2007 the charity had an income of £39,000 and a total expenditure of £18,000. About £3,000 is available each year for grants to individuals.

Applications: Application forms are available from the correspondent.

Correspondent: Cllr D M Davies, Gwaun Derw, Norgans Hill, Pembroke SA71 5EP (01646 682257)

Other information: The charity advertises locally when grants are available, usually twice each year.

Milford Haven Port Authority Scholarships

Eligibility: Undergraduates at British universities. Applicants must have resided at some time in Pembrokeshire and have spent the majority of their secondary education in a Pembrokeshire school. Students who have lived in Pembrokeshire but attended secondary schools in nearby counties are also eligible.

Types of grants: Scholarships of £1,000 each.

Annual grant total: Each year the scheme provides five awards of £1,000 each to undergraduates.

Applications: Application forms are available from the port authority and on its website. All communication should be marked 'Scholarship Scheme'.

Correspondent: The Secretary, Gorsewood Drive, Milford Haven, Pembrokeshire, SA73 3ER (01646 696157; Fax: 01646 696125; email: community@ mhpa.co.uk; website: www.mhpa.co.uk)

Other information: Each year a further grant of £2,000 is made to a postgraduate. The course of study must be at a British University and have some relevance to the activities of Milford Haven Port Authority.

Narberth Educational Charity

Eligibility: People who have lived in the community council areas of Narberth, Llawhaden, Llanddewi Velfrey, Lampeter Velfrey (including Tavernspite and Ludchurch), Templeton, Martletwy (including Lawrenny), Begelly, part of Jeffreyston, Minwere and Reynalton. Applicants must have lived there for at least two years and be aged under 25.

Types of grants: Grants ranging from £100 to £150 to help those at school and those transferring to a recognised course or further or higher education.

Annual grant total: About £1,500.

Applications: Application forms are available from the correspondent. They must be returned directly by the individual by August for consideration in November.

Correspondent: M R Lewis, Education Offices, Pembrokeshire County Council, County Hall, Haverfordwest, Pembrokeshire SA61 1TP

Other information: The charity also provides financial assistance for local organisations engaged in youth activities and the promotion of education for young people/children living in the catchment area.

The Tasker Milward and Picton Charity

Eligibility: Former pupils of the Sir Thomas Picton School or the Tasker Milward School in Haverfordwest, Pembrokeshire, who are under the age of 25 and are experiencing financial hardship or other circumstances which could affect their studies.

Types of grants: One-off and recurrent grants ranging from £100 to £1,000. Students in further or higher education can receive grants towards books, living expenses and study or travel abroad.

Annual grant total: In 2006/07 the trust had an income of £39,000 and made grants to students totalling £3,900, with £38,000 given in grants to schools.

Applications: On a form available from the correspondent. Applications should be made directly by the individual or through a school/college/educational welfare agency and should be received by 1st September although individual applications are accepted throughout the year. Applications are considered twice in the autumn term and once in the spring and summer terms.

Correspondent: T A L Davies, 3 Picton Close, Crundale, Haverfordwest, Pembrokeshire SA62 4EP

Swansea

The Swansea Foundation

Eligibility: People in education who live in Swansea. Preference is given to people who have attended one of the following schools or colleges: Bishop Gore Comprehensive School, Dynevor Comprehensive School, Swansea College and Swansea Institute of Higher Education.

Types of grants: One-off and recurrent grants according to need.

Annual grant total: Previously about £500.

Applications: In writing to the correspondent.

Correspondent: The Trustees, City & County of Swansea Council, County Hall, Oystermouth Road, Swansea, SA1 3SN

Torfaen

The Cwmbran Trust

Eligibility: People in need who live in the former urban area of Cwmbran, Gwent.

Types of grants: The trust gives one-off and recurrent grants for a wide variety of purposes. Previous grants of an educational nature have included funding for home-study courses and IT equipment Grants usually range between £125 and £2,500.

Annual grant total: In 2007 the trust had assets of £1.7 million and an income of £67,000. Grants to 18 individuals totalled £13,000 with an additional interest loan of £3,500 also awarded to one individual.

Applications: In writing to the correspondent. Applications can be submitted directly by the individual or through a social worker, Citizens Advice, welfare agency or other third party. Applications are usually considered in March, May, July, October and December.

Correspondent: K L Maddox, Arvinheritor HVBS (UK) Ltd, Grange Road, Cwmbran, Gwent NP44 3XU (01633 834040; Fax: 01633 834051; email: cwmbrantrust@ arvinmeritor.com)

Vale of Glamorgan

The Cowbridge with Llanblethian United Charities

Eligibility: People in need who live in the town of Cowbridge with Llanblethian.

Types of grants: Grants are towards clothing, fees, travel and maintenance for people preparing, entering or engaging in any profession, trade, occupation or service.

Annual grant total: In 2006/07 the charity had assets of £669,000 and an income of £30,000. Grants to individuals for educational purposes came to £1,000 and was given in student grants.

Applications: In writing to the correspondent. Applications can be submitted directly by the individual or through a school/college or educational welfare agency.

Correspondent: H G Phillips, 66 Broadway, Llanblethian, Cowbridge, Vale of Glamorgan CF71 7EW (01446 773287; email: unitedcharities@aol. com)

4. NORTH EAST

The Christina Aitchison Trust

Eligibility: Young people under the age of 25 years from north east or south west England.

Types of grants: One-off or recurrent grants for up to £300 to support young people in educational music, riding or sailing activities and other educational purposes. Donations are made in the form of books, equipment, fees, bursaries and fellowships.

Annual grant total: In 2006/07 the trust had an income of £1,800 and a total expenditure of £1,000.

Applications: On a form available from the correspondent, to be submitted in March or September for consideration in April or November.

Correspondent: R Massingberd-Mundy, c/o The Old Post Office, The Street, West Raynham, Fakenham, Norfolk NR21 7AD

Other information: Grants are also given to assist people who have an ophthalmic disease or who are terminally ill.

Lord Crewe's Charity

Eligibility: Necessitous clergy, their widows and dependants, who live in the dioceses of Durham and Newcastle. Grants may also be given more generally to people in need who live in the area.

Types of grants: The trust can give grants for a whole range of education needs up to and including first degrees.

Annual grant total: In 2007 the charity had assets of £28.4 million and an income of £960,000. Grants were awarded as follows:

Type	
Educational grants to clergy dependants	£147,000
Grants to clergy	£70,000
Miscellaneous charitable giving	£38,000

The level of grants in this financial year was lower than the charity anticipated due to a drop in applications.

Applications: On a form available from the correspondent.

Correspondent: Peter Church, Durham Cathedral, The Chapter Office, The College, Durham DH1 3EH (0191 375 1226; email: peter.church@ durhamcathedral.co.uk)

Hylton House Fund

Eligibility: People in the North East with cerebral palsy and related disabilities, and their families and carers. The priority 1 areas cover County Durham, Darlington, Gateshead, South Shields and Sunderland. Priority 2 areas are Hartlepool, Redcar, Cleveland, Middlesbrough and Stockton.

Types of grants: Grants of up to £500 towards: education, training and therapy, such as sound and light therapy for people with cerebral palsy to improve quality of life or funding towards further education courses; training and support for carers and self-help groups where no statutory support or provision is available); provision of aids and equipment, particularly specialist clothing, communication and mobility aids; travel costs, such as taxi and rail fares to attend a specific activity if no alternative transport is available; and respite support for an individual when the needs of the person requires them to either be accompanied by an employed carer or by visiting a specialist centre where full-time extensive care is provided.

Exclusions: No grants for: legal costs; ongoing education; medical treatment; decorating and/or refurbishment costs (unless the work is due to the nature of the applicant's disability); building adaptations; motor vehicle adaptations; motor insurance; deposits or running costs; televisions or videos; assessments, such as the costs involved in the Scope Living Options Schemes; or retrospective funding.

Annual grant total: In 2006/07 a total of £227,000 was given in grants to individuals. Grants are made for both educational and welfare purposes.

Applications: Applicants can either: use a form available from the correspondent or the website; or write to the correspondent including their name, address, relationship to beneficiary (if applying on somebody else's behalf), how the eligibility criteria is met, what the grant will be used for and why it is important, details of the course and the benefits it will bring (for educational grants), total costs, how much is being asked for, how any shortfall will be met, who else has been approached and details of who any cheque should be payable (usually a supplier or provider rather than directly to the applicant).

All applications must include a reference from a social worker or professional adviser in a related field, with a telephone number and the individual's permission for them to be contacted about an application.

Appeals are considered in January, April, July and October and needed to be received before the start of the month. They can be considered between these dates within a month of application if the need is urgent, but the applicant will need to request this and provide a reason why an exception to the usual policy needs to be made.

Correspondent: Grants Officer, Jordan House, Forster Business Centre, Finchale Road, Durham DH1 5HL (0191 383 0055; Fax: 0191 383 2969; email: info@ countydurhamfoundation.co.uk; website: www.countydurhamfoundation. co.uk)

The Northern Counties Children's Benevolent Society

Eligibility: Children in need through sickness, disability or other causes with a preference for those who live in the counties of Cheshire, Cleveland, Cumbria, Durham, Greater Manchester, Humberside, Lancashire, Merseyside, Northumberland, North Yorkshire, South Yorkshire, Tyne and Wear and West Yorkshire.

Types of grants: Both one-off and recurrent grants for education and clothing. The trust has previously stated that assistance takes the form of grants towards school fees, the cost of school clothing and equipment and, in a limited number of cases, the provision of special equipment of an educational or physical nature for disabled children. In almost every case, the need for assistance arises through the premature death of the major wage earner, or the break up of the family unit. Applications are treated in strict confidence and the financial circumstances of each applicant are fully and carefully considered by the trustees before an award is made.

Annual grant total: In 2007 the trust had assets of £1.5 million and an income of £71,000. Education and clothing grants totalled £105,000.

Applications: On a form available from the correspondent, for consideration in January, April, July or October.

Correspondent: Ms G Mackie, 29a Princes Road, Gosforth, Newcastle upon Tyne NE3 5TT (0191 236 5308)

The Northumberland Village Homes Trust

Eligibility: Young people under the age of 21 who live in Tyne and Wear, Durham, Cleveland or Northumberland.

Types of grants: One-off and recurrent grants according to need. Grants are given to promote the education and training of young people. Grants are available for a wide range of needs. In the past help has been given towards the costs of books, clothing and other essentials.

Exclusions: Grants are not given for gap year projects.

Annual grant total: In 2006/07 the trust had assets of £1.3 million generating an income of £54,000. Grants totalling £41,000 were made to organisations who work with people under 21. No grants were made to individuals during the year.

Applications: In writing to the correspondent. The trustees meet in November and applications should be submitted in September. No personal applications will be considered unless supported by an accompanying letter from the headteacher or an official from the local authority or other such body.

Correspondent: Derek McCoy, Clerk to the Trustees, Savages Solicitors, Maranar Building, 2nd Floor, 28–30 Mosley Street, Newcastle upon Tyne NE1 1DF (0191 221 2111; Fax: 0191 222 1712)

The Sir John Priestman Charity Trust

Eligibility: Clergy and their families in need who live in the historic counties of Durham and York (especially the county borough of Sunderland).

Types of grants: Grants to help towards the cost of school fees and for gap year activities including Christian mission.

Annual grant total: In 2007 the trust had assets of £10.1 million and an income of £369,000. Grants to clergy and their families totalled £17,000.

Applications: In writing to the correspondent. Applications are considered quarterly.

Correspondent: P W Taylor, McKenzie Bell, 19 John Street, Sunderland, Tyne & Wear SR1 1JG (0191 567 4857)

Other information: The trust also assists charities serving County Durham

(especially the Sunderland area) and helps maintain Church of England churches and buildings in the above area.

The Provincial Grand Charity

Eligibility: Children (including adopted and step-children) of present and deceased masons who live or lived in North Yorkshire and Humberside.

Types of grants: Grants for those at school, college or university towards school clothing, books, school fees and living expenses depending on the parental circumstances. Grants range from £100 to £3,000.

Annual grant total: In 2007 the fund had net assets of £965,000, an income of £148,000 and a total expenditure of £44,000. Grants totalled £30,000, of which £1,000 went to individuals.

Applications: In writing to the correspondent, to be considered at quarterly meetings. Applications must be supported by the relative who is a member of the masons.

Correspondent: The Trustees, Provincial Offices, Castlegate House, Castlegate, York YO1 9RP

Prowde's Educational Foundation

Eligibility: Boys and young men between the ages of 9 and 25 who live in Somerset or the North or East Ridings of Yorkshire. There is a preference for those who are descendants of the named persons in the will of the founder. There is also a preference for boys with serious family difficulties such that the child has to be educated away from home and for those with special education needs.

Types of grants: One-off grants to boys and men in further or higher education, including postgraduates, for fees, uniforms, other school clothing, books, equipment, instruments, fees and study or travel abroad. The average grant to an individual is £450.

Annual grant total: In 2006/07 the foundation had an income of £16,000 and a total expenditure of £17,000.

Applications: Applications can be submitted directly by the individual, parents or occasionally social workers, and should include a birth certificate and evidence of acceptance for a course. They should be submitted in May/June for consideration in July.

Correspondent: R G Powell, Administrative Trustee, Broad Eaves, Hawks Hill Close, Leatherhead, Surrey KT22 9DL (01372 374561)

The Sherburn House Educational Foundation

Eligibility: People aged between 16 and 21 who live in the pre-1972 boundaries of County Durham.

Types of grants: Grants of between £50 and £450 are available to students towards books, equipment, instruments and fees.

Annual grant total: About £2,000.

Applications: Applications should be made through the individual's school/college, educational welfare agency or a third party such as social services or a Citizens Advice. They are considered throughout the year.

Correspondent: Stephen P Hallett, Ramsey House, Sherburn Hospital, Sherburn House, Durham DH1 2SE (0191 372 2551; email: admin@sherburnhouse.org; website: www.sherburnhouse.org)

Viking Cares (Cash for Kids)

Eligibility: People who are 19 or under and either live or go to school in the East Yorkshire and Northern Lincolnshire area. This area extends to Mablethorpe in the South, York and Carlton in the West and Flamborough in the North.

Types of grants: Grants are made towards children who are sick, disabled or have learning disabilities.

Annual grant total: In 2006/07 the trust made 66 grants totalling £57,000 to groups and individuals.

Applications: On a form available from the correspondent. They are considered quarterly. Cheques are paid to a charity on the individual's behalf to ensure it is spent for the intended purpose.

Correspondent: Debbie Westlake, c/o Viking FM, Commercial Road, Hull HU1 2SG (01482 593193; email: debbie. westlake@vikingfm.co.uk; website: www. vikingfm.co.uk)

The Yorkshire Training Fund for Women

Eligibility: British women aged 16 or over who live in, or have connections to, Yorkshire and are in higher or further education.

Types of grants: One-off grants of generally about £50, but they can be up to £250, for women undertaking courses of study that should enable them to become self-sufficient financially. Grants are given towards books, equipment and instruments.

Exclusions: People on access courses are not eligible.

Annual grant total: About £1,500.

Applications: On a form available from the correspondent, to be submitted either by the individual or through a social worker, Citizens Advice or other welfare agency. Applicants should provide details of two referees and detailed information of their financial position. Completed forms should be returned by 1 May for the June meeting or by 1 November for the December meeting.

Correspondent: Mrs F M Slater, Hon. Secretary, 5 Bede Court, Wakefield WF1 3RW (01924 373077)

Other information: The trust states that 'there is a great deal of competition for the grants'.

County Durham

County Durham Foundation

Eligibility: Young people who live in the County Durham area.

Types of grants: Grants are made towards the cost of course fees, tuition fees, books, educational, sporting and musical equipment and travel costs. Bursaries are also awarded.

Annual grant total: In 2006/07 the foundation had assets of £6 million and an income of £2.3 million. Grants to individuals totalled £227,000. The foundation administers eight funds that give for both educational and welfare purposes.

Applications: Please visit the foundation's website for full details of grant schemes. Applications forms are also available to download from the foundation's website.

Correspondent: Mrs Gillian Stacey, Suite 2, Jordan House, Finchale Road, Durham, DH1 5HL (0191 383 0055; email: info@ countydurhamfoundation.co.uk; website: www.countydurhamfoundation. co.uk)

Other information: Grants are also made to organisations.

The Lady Dale Scholarship

Eligibility: Girls and young women from poorer families going from school to further and higher education and who have attended Branksome, Eastbourne, Haughton, Hummersknott, Hurworth or Longfield comprehensive schools – Darlington.

Types of grants: Scholarships for those going on to colleges of further education.

Annual grant total: In 2006/07 the trust had an income of £1,300. The trust usually gives only one or two scholarships per year.

Applications: In writing to the correspondent, to be submitted through the individual's school by early August, although preferably earlier.

Correspondent: Elaine Sayers, Clerk to the Trustees, Children's Services, Town Hall, Darlington DL1 5QT

The Darlington Education Fund

Eligibility: Persons under the age of 25 who attend or have attended Branksome, Eastbourne, Haughton, Hummersknott, Hurworth or Longfield comprehensive schools, or the Queen Elizabeth Sixth Form College – Darlington.

Types of grants: Grants are made for the following purposes:

- people at school/college/university
- people leaving any educational establishment to prepare for and enter a profession, trade or calling
- educational travel in this country and abroad and for people to study music or other arts.
- Financial assistance for clothing, training, travel, equipment, books and the like.

With the approval of the managing trustees, the award of exhibitions tenable at any secondary school, college of education, university or other institution of further education (including professional and technical) can also be made.

Students currently attending the Darlington College of Technology and who previously attended one of the above mentioned schools are also eligible to apply for grants. Except in exceptional circumstances, assistance will not be given towards the cost of travel expenses within the Darlington area.

Awards are made on a quarterly basis.

Annual grant total: In 2006/07 the trust had an income of £67,000, and a total expenditure of £7,100, all of which was given in grants to individuals.

Applications: Further information and an application form are available from the correspondent. Pupils still in attendance at any of the schools/college listed may discuss the matter with the headteacher in the first instance. Full details of the purpose for which the award is required and some indication of the cost involved should be given. The trustees meet once each term to consider applications.

Correspondent: Elaine Sayers, Clerk to the Trustees, Children's Services, Town Hall, Darlington DL1 5QT (01325 388814)

The Sedgefield District Relief-in-Need Charity

Eligibility: College, university, vocational and mature students who live in the parishes of Bishop Middleham, Bradbury, Fishburn, Mordon, Sedgefield and Trimdon in County Durham.

Types of grants: One-off grants are made to undergraduates and mature students for maintenance/living expenses.

Annual grant total: About £3,000 to individuals for welfare and educational purposes.

Applications: On a form available from the correspondent, to be submitted by 30 September each year.

Correspondent: R Smeeton, Clerk, 13 North Park Road, Sedgefield, County Durham, TS21 2AP (01740 620009)

Other information: This trust mostly provides relief-in-need grants to people of any age in the geographical area of benefit.

The Sedgefield Educational Foundation

Eligibility: People who normally live in the civil parishes of Sedgefield, Fishburn, Bradbury and Morden in County Durham and are aged between 18 and 25.

Types of grants: Recurrent grants during period of study. Grants to help with college, university or technical college courses or other vocational courses towards the cost of books and to help with fees/living expenses. The trustees normally only help with education higher than A-level and current policy is to limit aid to courses not available at schools. Grants range from £140 to £300 (depending on the applicant's circumstances).

Students seeking funds for study or travel abroad and mature students over 25 may be referred to the Sedgefield District Relief-in-Need Charities, to which welfare applications are also referred (see separate entry).

Annual grant total: About £3,000.

Applications: On a form available from the correspondent. Applications must be submitted by 30 September for consideration in October.

Correspondent: R Smeeton, Clerk, 13 North Park Road, Sedgefield, County Durham TS21 2AP (01740 620009)

Durham

The Johnston Educational Foundation

Eligibility: People under 25 who live or whose parents live in the city of Durham and who have attended one of the city's comprehensive schools for at least two years.

Types of grants: One-off and recurrent grants ranging from £50 to £1,000. Grants are made to students in further/higher education to help with the cost of books, equipment/instruments, fees, living expenses and study or travel abroad and to people starting work or entering a trade.

Annual grant total: In 2006/07 the trust had an income of £3,000 and a total expenditure of £4,000.

Applications: On a form available from the correspondent. Applications are considered in February, June and October and should be submitted directly by the individual.

Correspondent: Barry Piercy, Clerk to the Trustees, School and Governor Support Service, County Hall, Durham DH1 5UJ (0191 383 4596; Fax: 0191 383 4597; email: barry.piercy@durham.gov.uk)

Frosterley

The Frosterley Exhibition Foundation

Eligibility: People in full-time education, from secondary school age upwards, whose parents live in the parish of Frosterley. Preference is given to college and university students.

Types of grants: Grants are given towards books, uniforms and any other educational requirement deemed necessary.

Annual grant total: In 2006/07 the trust had an income of £2,400 and a total expenditure of £1,800.

Applications: In writing to the correspondent, to be submitted by the applicant's parent, to whom the cheque will be made. Applications should be submitted in August for consideration in September.

Correspondent: Miss Judith Bainbridge, Norton House, 6 Osborne Terrace, Frosterley, Bishop Auckland, County Durham DL13 2RD (01388 527668)

Stanhope

The Hartwell Educational Foundation

Eligibility: People aged between 11 and 21 who live in the civil parish of Stanhope. Eligibility is dependent on parental income.

Types of grants: Grants are primarily awarded on a recurrent basis to students going to college or university for help with fees/living expenses and books. Students from low-income families receive larger grants and one-off grants can also be given to younger pupils attending secondary school towards the cost of uniforms, other clothing, books, and so on.

Annual grant total: In 2006/07 the trust had an income of £1,100 and a total expenditure of £1,400. Previously grants have totalled around £1,000.

Applications: Applications should be made by the last Saturday in August, on a form available from the correspondent, for consideration in September/October. Applications can be made either directly by the individual or by a parent/guardian.

Correspondent: Mrs Dorothy Foster, Sowen Burn, Stanhope, County Durham DL13 2PP (01388 528577)

East Yorkshire

Joseph Boaz Charity

Eligibility: People from Hull and East Yorkshire who are in further or higher education, including mature students and postgraduates.

Types of grants: One-off grants of £250 to £500 are given towards books, equipment and instruments.

Exclusions: Grants are not given for course fees or living expenses.

Annual grant total: In 2007/08 the trust had an income of £17,000 and a total expenditure of £18,000. In previous years the trust has concentrated its giving to organisations, although applications are welcomed from individuals.

Applications: In writing to the correspondent to be submitted either directly by the individual or a parent/guardian, through a third party such as a teacher, or through an organisation such as a school or an educational welfare agency. Applications are considered in June and December.

Correspondent: P R Evans, Graham & Rosen Solicitors, 8 Parliament Street, Hull HU1 2BB (01482 323123; Fax: 01482 223542; email: pre@graham-rosen.co.uk)

Other information: Grants are also made to organisations.

The Joseph & Annie Cattle Trust

Eligibility: Schoolchildren who have dyslexia and live in Hull or the East Riding of Yorkshire area.

Types of grants: One-off grants of £200 to £500.

Annual grant total: In 2006/07 the trust had assets of £9.5 million and an income of £406,000. Grants to 49 individuals totalled £44,000.

Applications: In writing to the correspondent, only via a welfare organisation, for consideration on the third Monday of every month. Please note, if applicants approach the trust directly they will be referred to an organisation, such as Disability Rights Advisory Service or social services.

Correspondent: Roger Waudby, Administrator, Morpeth House, 114 Spring Bank, Hull HU3 1QJ (01482 211198; Fax: 01482 211198)

The Leonard Chamberlain Trust

Eligibility: People who live in Selby or the East Riding of Yorkshire and are in further or higher education.

Types of grants: Grants are given towards books.

Annual grant total: In 2007 grants were made totalling £3,700.

Applications: On a form available from the correspondent. They should be returned in August for consideration in September.

Correspondent: The Secretary, c/o 6 Manor Park, Preston, Hull HU12 8XE

The East Riding Director's Charity Fund

Eligibility: People who live in the East Riding of Yorkshire.

Types of grants: Grants for educational purposes including social and physical training. Assistance for clothing, tools, instruments, books and travel in the UK or abroad.

Annual grant total: In 2006/07 the trust had an income of £1,800 and a total expenditure of £1,600.

Applications: In writing to the correspondent.

Correspondent: Caroline White, East Riding of Yorkshire Council, County Hall, Cross Street, Beverley, North Humberside, HU17 9BA (01482 394263; email: louise.greef@eastriding.gov.uk)

Other information: Grants are also made to organisations.

The Hesslewood Children's Trust (Hull Seamen's & General Orphanage)

Eligibility: Young people under 25 who live or have firm family connections with the former county of Humberside and North Lincolnshire, with a preference for children of former seamen who served in the Merchant Navy. The trust also gives to former Hesslewood Scholars.

'Applicants must be in need, but must show their resolve to part fund themselves.' Preference is given to people with special educational needs.

Types of grants: One-off grants are given towards: books, school uniforms, educational outings and maintenance for schoolchildren; books for students in higher and further education; and equipment and instruments and clothing for people starting work.

Exclusions: Loans are not made.

Annual grant total: In 2006/07 the trust had assets of £2.8 million and an income of £108,000. Grants to individuals totalled approximately £25,000.

Applications: On a form available from the correspondent, accompanied by a letter from the tutor or an educational welfare organisation (or from medical and social services for a disability grant). Applications can be submitted by the individual, through their school, college or educational welfare agency, or by another third party such as the Citizens Advice bureau or health centre. Details of the applicant's and parental income must be included, along with an indication of the amount the applicant will contribute and a contact telephone number. Applications are considered in February, June and September.

Correspondent: Michael Mitchell, Graham & Rosen (Solicitors), 8 Parliament St, Hull, HU1 2BB (01482 323123; Fax: 01482 223542; email: law@graham-rosen.co.uk)

Other information: Grants are also made to organisations (£67,000 in 2006/07)

The Hook & Goole Charity

Eligibility: People aged 16 to 25 who are in further or higher education and have lived in the parish of Hook and the area of the former borough of Goole as constituted on 31 March 1974 within the last two years.

Types of grants: Grants of between £150 and £400 are given towards books, living expenses, educational outings and study or travel overseas.

Annual grant total: In 2006 the trust had an income of £13,000 and a total expenditure of £17,000.

Applications: On a form available from the correspondent. Applications should be submitted directly by the individual in July/August for consideration in September.

Correspondent: K G Barclay, 3–15 Gladstone Terrace, Goole, East Yorkshire DN14 5AH (01405 765661; email: ken.barclay@heptonstalls.co.uk)

Humberside Educational Trust

Eligibility: People aged 21 or under in the East Riding area of Yorkshire.

Types of grants: One-off grants of £500 to £750 are given to schoolchildren for maintenance and living expenses.

Annual grant total: In 2006/07 the trust had an income of approximately £5,000 with no expenditure. About four or five grants are given each year totalling £3,000.

Applications: In writing to the correspondent. The trustees usually meet in November, although applications are also considered at other times.

Correspondent: P S Bennett, Secretary of the Trust, Pocklington School, West Green, Pocklington, York YO42 2NJ (01759 321204; Fax: 01759 306366; email: bursar@pocklington.e-yorks.sch.uk)

The Nancie Reckitt Charity

Eligibility: People under 25 who have, or whose parents have, a minimum of five years' residency and are still living in the civil parishes of Patrington, Winestead and Rimswell in East Yorkshire.

Types of grants: Recurrent grants of £100 to £600 are given to people starting work

for clothing and equipment and to students in further or higher education for equipment, books and fees.

Annual grant total: In 2006/07 the trust had an income of £6,600 and a total expenditure of £6,000.

Applications: On a form available from the correspondent to be submitted directly by the individual. Applications from people starting work should be submitted in April for consideration in May. University and college students should apply in August for consideration in September. Claims for books, materials, tools and so on should have the cost substantiated by forwarding receipts.

Correspondent: Mrs M Stansfield, Clerk, Heath House, 19 Northside, Patrington, East Yorkshire, HU12 0PA (01964 630960)

The Sir Philip Reckitt Educational Trust Fund see entry on page 27

Correspondent: The Trustees, Charity's principal address: Wilberforce Court, High Street, Hull, HU1 1YJ (website: www.spret.org/)

Sir Henry Samman's Hull Chamber of Commerce Endowment Fund

Eligibility: Preference to young people of Hull and the former East Riding. Applicants should normally have reached the age of 18, and be studying, or planning to study, at degree level, although consideration will be given to those slightly under this age limit.

Types of grants: The fund provides scholarships to assist young people who wish to spend a period overseas to further their study of 'business methods or a foreign language' with a view to taking up a career in commerce or industry.

Annual grant total: In 2006 the fund had an income of £6,100 and a total expenditure of £600.

Applications: In writing to the correspondent.

Correspondent: Dr I Kelly, Secretary, Hull & Humber Chamber of Commerce, Industry & Shipping, 34–38 Beverley Road, Hull HU3 1YE (01482 324976)

Other information: The fund was set up in 1917 originally to encourage the study of Russian in a commercial context, but has since been extended.

The Sydney Smith Trust

Eligibility: Long-term residents of Kingston-upon-Hull and its immediate vicinity who are undertaking further, higher or vocational training or re-training, and are in need. Applicants must be under 35 and have attended secondary school in Hull.

Types of grants: One-off grants to people starting work and students in further/higher education, including mature students under 35, towards equipment and instruments.

Annual grant total: In 2006/07 the trust had an income of £5,000 and a total expenditure of £20,000. Grants are made to organisations and individuals.

Applications: In writing to the correspondent at any time. Details of schools attended, qualifications obtained and future plans are required.

Correspondent: The Trust Controller, HSBC Trust Company (UK) Ltd, Commercial Road, Southampton, SO15 1GX

Robert Towries Charity

Eligibility: People under 25 years old who live in Aldbrough and Burton Constable.

Types of grants: One-off grants for educational purposes.

Annual grant total: In 2006/07 the charity had an income of £8,000 and a total expenditure of £5,000. Grants usually total about £4,000 a year.

Applications: In writing to the correspondent directly by the individual.

Correspondent: Mrs P M Auty, 6 Willow Grove, Headlands Park, Aldbrough, Hull HU11 4SH (01964 527553)

Other information: Grants are also made for welfare purposes.

Ann Watson's Trust

Eligibility: People in need under the age of 25 who live in the former borough of Kingston-upon-Hull and the East Riding of Yorkshire.

Types of grants: One-off and recurrent grants according to need.

Annual grant total: In 2007 the trust had assets of £13 million and an income of £324,000. Educational grants to individuals were made totalling £61,000.

Applications: In writing to the correspondent at any time during the year. The trustees meet quarterly.

Correspondent: Karen Palmer, Flat 4, The College, 14 College Street, Sutton-on-Hull, Hull HU7 4UP (01482 709626; email: awatson@awatson.karoo.co.uk)

The Christopher Wharton Educational Foundation

Eligibility: People who live in the former parish of Stamford Bridge with Scoreby or the parish of Gate Helmsley. Applicants must be under 25 years old.

Types of grants: Grants of about £100 to help with further education, tools, instruments or apprenticeships not normally provided by the local education authorities.

Annual grant total: About £1,000.

Applications: In writing to the correspondent by 31 October.

Correspondent: Mrs E M Catterick, 25 High Catton Road, Stamford Bridge, York YO41 1DL

Barmby on the Marsh

The Blanchard's Educational Foundation

Eligibility: People under the age of 25 living in Barmby on the Marsh.

Types of grants: Grants are available for: (a) schoolchildren, including help with the cost of clothing, books and educational outings but not school fees or maintenance; (b) students in further or higher education including help with the cost of books and study or travel abroad, but not for fees/living expenses; (c) people starting work for books and equipment, but not clothing or travel; and (d) mature students (under 25) for books and travel, but not for fees or childcare expenses.

Annual grant total: In 2006/07 the foundation had an income of £2,400 and a total expenditure of £1,800.

Applications: In writing to the correspondent. Meetings are held in July and December.

Correspondent: John Burman, Clerk, Heptonstalls Solicitors, 7–15 Gladstone Terrace, Goole, East Yorkshire DN14 5AH (01405 765661; Fax: 01405 764201)

Beverley

The Christopher Eden Educational Foundation

Eligibility: People under the age of 25 who live in the town of Beverley and the villages in Beverley Rural Ward. People with special educational needs are given preference.

Types of grants: One-off grants of £50 to £400 are given to: (a) schoolchildren and students in higher education to help with books, equipment, clothing, travel, field trips, sports equipment and training and for studying music and the arts, but not for school fees or school uniforms; (b) people in further or higher education towards fees or to supplement existing grants, including grants to travel in connection with education and books; and (c) people starting work to help with the cost of books, equipment, clothing and travel.

Recurrent grants are occasionally given for the duration of the course, but no loans are available.

Annual grant total: In 2006 the trust had both an income and a total expenditure of £13,000.

Applications: On a form available from the correspondent. Applications for assistance with university or college costs should be submitted in September for consideration in October. Applications for any other purposes are considered in January, April, July and October. A parent/guardian should complete the application for those under 16. Applications must also include course details, education details, parents' income, applicant's income and outgoings and the reason why help is needed. Incomplete or incorrectly completed applications will not be considered and are not returned.

Correspondent: Mrs Judy Dickinson, 85 East Street, Leven, Beverley HU17 5NG (01964 542593; email: judydickinson@mac.com)

Other information: The charity has endowed a berth on a sail training schooner and selects a deserving young person for the berth each year.

The James Graves Educational Foundation

Eligibility: Students preferably under the age of 18 who live in the parish of St Martin, Beverley.

Types of grants: Grants to help towards the costs of books and other essentials for schoolchildren, particularly those with a church connection and with a specific emphasis on religious education. The maximum grant is £500.

Annual grant total: The trust has both an income and a total expenditure of around £2,000 consistently. About £1,500 is usually given in grants per annum.

Applications: In writing to the correspondent. Apparently not many suitable applications are received each year. Applications are considered twice yearly.

Correspondent: Mrs Joy Willson, The Parish Office, Beverley Minster, East Yorkshire HU17 0DP

The Wray Educational Trust

Eligibility: People aged 25 or under who have lived in the parish of Leven in Beverley for at least three years.

Types of grants: One-off grants are given to schoolchildren, people starting work and students in further or higher education towards books, equipment, instruments, fees, educational outings and study or travel abroad.

Annual grant total: About £5,000.

Applications: On a form available from the correspondent, who knows many of the people in the village and is always willing to discuss needs. Applications are considered in January, April, July and October.

Correspondent: Mrs J Dickinson, 85 East Street, Leven Beverley, North Humberside HU17 5NG (01964 542593)

Hedon

The Hedon Haven Trust

Eligibility: People at any stage or level of their education, undertaking study of any subject, who live in Hedon near Hull. Preference is given to children with special educational needs.

Types of grants: One-off grants ranging from £50 to £500 are given to: schoolchildren for educational outings in the UK and abroad; students in further or higher education towards study or travel abroad and maintenance/living expenses; and mature students for living expenses.

Annual grant total: In 2006/07 the trust had an income of £3,800 and a total expenditure of £2,800. Grants are made to organisations and individuals.

Applications: In writing to the correspondent at any time, enclosing an sae. Applications can be submitted directly by the individual or through the school/college or educational welfare agency.

Correspondent: Ian North, Secretary, Burnham House, Souttergate, Hedon, Hull HU12 8JS (01482 897105; Fax: 01482 897023; email: iannorth@lineone.net)

Horbury

The Daniel Gaskell & John Wray Foundation

Eligibility: People under 25 in full-time education who live in the former urban district council of Horbury.

Types of grants: Grants towards books, equipment, field trips, travel, course expenses for those at school, college or university. Grants tend to range from £25 to £150 depending on the number of suitable applications.

Annual grant total: In 2006 the trust had an income of £4,000 and a total expenditure of £2,000. About £1,500 is given annually in grants to individuals.

Applications: Applications should be made after advertisements are placed in the local press. The trustees meet annually in September, so applications should be received by the end of August.

Correspondent: Mrs M Gaunt, 22 Westfield Road, Horbury, Wakefield, West Yorkshire WF4 6HP (01924 263166)

Humbleton

Heron Educational Foundation

Eligibility: People living in the parish of Humbleton, under the age of 25.

Types of grants: Grants for clothing and books given on entering primary and secondary school, further education or university.

Annual grant total: In 2006/07 the trust had an income of £7,800 and a total expenditure of £5,800. Previously grants have totalled around £1,500

Applications: In writing to the correspondent.

Correspondent: Mrs Angela Greenwood, 2 Townend Villas, Humbleon, HU11 4NR

Kingston-upon-Hull

Alderman Ferries Charity

Eligibility: People aged 16 to 25 and live in the city of Kingston-upon-Hull.

Types of grants: One-off grants of about £300 to £500 each. Grants are given to college students and vocational students and apprentices for books, equipment, instruments, fees, maintenance and living expenses.

Annual grant total: In 2007 the trust had an income of £13,000 and a total expenditure of £12,000.

Applications: On a form available from the correspondent. Applications are available in September and should be submitted directly by the individual or a parent/guardian by 1 November for consideration at the beginning of December.

Correspondent: Mrs V Fisher, Trust Manager, Hull United Charities, Northumberland Court, Northumberland Avenue, Kingston-upon-Hull HU2 0LR (01482 324135; Fax: 01482 324135; email: office@hulluc.karoo.co.uk; website: beehive.thisishull.co.uk)

The Doctor A E Hart Trust

Eligibility: People who live within the city boundary of Kingston-upon-Hull (this does not include students who only live in Hull while at college). Applications are not encouraged from students under 18.

Types of grants: The trust was established for 'the promotion and encouragement of education for needy students'. Assistance may be given towards course fees, maintenance, study or travel overseas, text books, equipment and other essentials for schoolchildren, students, mature students and people starting work. Grants for childcare can also be given to mature students. One-off and recurrent grants are made ranging from £200 to £300, but not loans.

Exclusions: No grants to overseas students studying in Britain or for student exchanges.

Annual grant total: In 2006/07 the trust had assets of £618,000 and an income of £40,000. Educational grants were awarded to 63 individuals totalling approximately £16,000.

Applications: On an application form (seven pages long which must be photocopied four times by the applicant and stapled together) available from the correspondent from June onwards. One academic and one character reference must accompany the form. Applications for awards must be submitted in October each year and are usually considered in December or January. Only in the most exceptional circumstances (e.g. for a course starting in January and of which the applicant had no knowledge the previous June) can applications outside these dates be considered, provided they explain why they are applying at that time.

The grants available from this trust are relatively modest, and are most unlikely to have any significant bearing on an applicant's decision to embark on any given course. In any event, the amount of the award (if any) will not be known until January/February, by which time most courses will have already started. Grants are paid in cheques and applicants must have their own bank accounts.

Correspondent: John Bullock, Secretary, Williamsons Solicitors, Lowgate, Kingston-upon-Hull HU1 1EN (01482 323697; Fax: 01482 328132; email: admin@williamsons-solicitors.co.uk)

Kingston-upon-Hull Education Foundation

Eligibility: People over 13 who live, or whose parents live, in the city of Kingston-upon-Hull and either attend, or have attended, a school in the city.

Types of grants: Grants of £80 to £250 towards: (i) scholarships, bursaries or grants tenable at any school, university or other educational establishment approved by the trustees or (ii) financial assistance towards the cost of outfits, clothing, tools, instruments or books to assist such persons to pursue their education or to prepare for and enter a profession, trade, occupation or service on leaving school, university or other educational establishment.

Annual grant total: In 2006/07 the charity had both an income and a total expenditure of around £4,000.

Applications: On a form available from August from the correspondent. Applications are considered in November (closing date mid-October) and February (closing date mid-January). A letter of support from the applicant's class or course tutor, plus evidence of their progress and attendance on the course is needed before a grant is made.

Correspondent: K D Brown, Corporate Finance, 2nd Floor Treasury Building, Hanover Square, Guildhall Road, Kingston-upon-Hull, HU1 2AB

Newton on Derwent

Newton on Derwent Charity

Eligibility: Students in higher education who live in the parish of Newton on Derwent.

Types of grants: One-off grants towards fees, usually paid directly to the relevant institution.

Annual grant total: Educational grants usually total around £5,000 per annum.

Applications: In writing to the correspondent, for consideration throughout the year.

Correspondent: The Clerk to the Charity, Grays Solicitors, Duncombe Place, York YO1 7DY

Ottringham

The Ottringham Church Lands Charity

Eligibility: People in need who live in the parish of Ottringham.

Types of grants: Grants are made according to need.

Exclusions: No grants are given which would affect the applicant's state benefits.

Annual grant total: About £7,000.

Applications: In writing to the correspondent at any time. Applications can be submitted either directly by the individual, through a third party such as a social worker or teacher, or through an organisation such as Citizen's Advice or a school.

Correspondent: J R Hinchliffe, 'Hallgarth', Station Road, Ottringham, East Yorkshire HU12 0BJ (01964 622230)

Rawcliffe

The Rawcliffe Educational Foundation

Eligibility: People who live in the parish of Rawcliffe, who were educated at one of the local schools, and are aged between 16 and 25.

Types of grants: One-off and recurrent grants of up to £600 to assist young people remaining in full-time education beyond normal school leaving age. This includes help with the cost of books and fees/living expenses for students.

Exclusions: It does not include school fees or study or travel overseas.

Annual grant total: In 2006/07 the trust had an income of £16,000 and an expenditure of £6,700.

Applications: Applications should be made in writing, including the type and duration of the course to be studied.

Students must affirm that they are not in receipt of any salary. They are considered in September.

Correspondent: Julie Parrott, 26 Station Road, Rawcliffe, Goole, North Humberside DN14 8QR (01405 839637)

Riston

The Peter Nevill Charity

Eligibility: Young people under 25 who live, or who have a parent who lives, in the parish of Riston.

Types of grants: Grants of £50 to £200 are given towards books, clothing and other essentials for school-leavers taking up employment and for students in further or higher education. (Grants also made to Riston Church of England Primary School and village organisations serving young people.)

Annual grant total: Grants to individuals are made each year totalling about £1,000.

Applications: In writing to the correspondent.

Correspondent: Revd David Perry, The Vicarage, Skirlaugh, Hull HU11 5HE (01964 562259)

North Yorkshire

The Beckwith Bequest

Eligibility: People living or educated in the parishes of Easingwold and Husthwaite who are in need of financial assistance.

Types of grants: Cash grants of £100 to £150 for beneficiaries to help with books, equipment, clothing and travel. (Grants are also made towards the provision of facilities not normally provided by the local education authority for recreation, education, and social and physical training for those receiving education.)

Annual grant total: In 2006/07 the trust had an income of £10,000 and a total expenditure of £9,000.

Applications: In writing to the correspondent. Applications are considered at quarterly trustees' meetings.

Correspondent: P D Hannam, Solicitor, Hileys Solicitors, Market Place, Easingwold, York YO61 3AB (01347 821234)

Bedale Educational Foundation

Eligibility: People aged between 5 and 25 who live in the parishes of Aiskew, Bedale, Burrill, Cowling, Crakehall, Firby and Leeming Bar. Preference is given to people with special educational needs.

Types of grants: One-off grants in the range of £200 and £600 are given to school children and college students, including those towards books, fees maintenance/living expenses and excursions.

Annual grant total: In 2006/07 the trust had an income of £1,000.

Applications: On a form available from the correspondent, to be submitted at any time either directly by the individual or a parent.

Correspondent: P J Hirst, 18 Firby Road, Bedale, North Yorkshire, DL8 2AS (01677 423376; email: johnwinkle@awinkle.freeserve.co.uk)

Bedale Welfare Charity

Eligibility: People who live in Bedale and the immediate surrounding area.

Types of grants: One-off grants usually ranging from £50 to £5,000.

Annual grant total: In 2006/07 the trust had an income of £13,400 and a total expenditure of £18,500, most of which is distributed in relief-in-need grants and to organisations, although this does not exclude applications for educational purposes.

Applications: On a form available from the correspondent, to be submitted at any time either directly by the individual or through a third party such as a social worker or teacher.

Correspondent: John Winkle, 25 Burrill Road, Bedale, North Yorkshire, DL8 1ET (01677 424306; email: johnwinkle@awinkle.freeserve.co.uk)

Other information: Grants are also made to organisations.

The Gargrave Poor's Land Charity

Eligibility: People in need who live in Gargrave, Banknewton, Coniston Cold, Flasby, Eshton or Winterburn.

Types of grants: One-off and recurrent grants and loans are given to: schoolchildren for uniforms, clothing and outings; and students in further or higher education towards maintenance, fees and textbooks. Help is also available to students taking vocational further education courses and other vocational training.

Annual grant total: In 2006/07 the charity had assets of £370,000 and an income of £29,000. Grants totalled £18,000, of which £2,000 was given to individuals for educational purposes.

Applications: On a form available from the correspondent. Applications can be submitted at any time.

Correspondent: The Trustees, 10 Ivy House Gardens, Gargrave, Near Skipton, North Yorkshire, BD23 3SS

Other information: The charity also gives grants for relief-in-need purposes.

Reverend Matthew Hutchinson Trust (Gilling and Richmond)

Eligibility: People who live in the parishes of Gilling and Richmond in North Yorkshire.

Types of grants: Grants are given to school children for fees, equipment and excursions. Undergraduates, including mature students, can receive help towards books whilst vocational students can be supported for study/travel overseas.

Annual grant total: This charity has branches in both Gilling and Richmond, which are administered jointly, but have separate funding. In 2006 the combined income of the charities was £17,000 and their combined expenditure was £14,000. The combined grant total is usually about £10,000 a year.

Applications: In writing to the correspondent. Applications can be submitted directly by the individual or through a trustee, social worker, citizen's advice bureau or other welfare agency.

Correspondent: Mrs C Wiper, 3 Smithson Close, Moulton, Richmond, North Yorkshire, DL10 6QP (01325 377328; email: christinewiper@yahoo.co.uk)

Other information: Grants are also made to local schools and hospitals.

The Kirkby-in-Malhamdale Educational Foundation

Eligibility: People under 25 who have a parent or guardian living in one of the following parishes in the county of North Yorkshire: Airton, Calton, Hanlith, Kirkby Malham, Malham, Malham Moor, Otterburn and Scosthrop.

Types of grants: One-off grants of £100 to £200 to: schoolchildren for uniforms/clothing, study/travel overseas, books, equipment/instruments and excursions; college students, undergraduates and children with special educational needs for uniforms/clothing, fees, study/travel overseas, books, equipment/living expenses and excursions; and to people starting work for work clothes, fees, books and equipment/instruments.

Annual grant total: In 2007 the foundation had both an income and total expenditure of around £1,000.

Applications: In writing to the correspondent. Applications can be submitted either directly by the individual or through the individual's school/college or an educational welfare agency. Applications are considered three times per year.

Correspondent: C Pighills, Cross Stones, Airton, Skipton, North Yorkshire, BD23 4AP

The Nafferton Feoffee Charity Trust

Eligibility: People in need who live in the parish of All Saints Nafferton with St Mary's Wansford.

Types of grants: Bursaries are available to local students for things such as educational overseas trips.

Exclusions: The trust stated that the parish only consists of 3,000 people and every household receives a copy of a leaflet outlining the trust's work. People from outside this area are not eligible to apply.

Annual grant total: In 2007 the trust had an income of £13,000 and a total expenditure of £14,000. Grants were made totalling about £11,000.

Applications: In writing to the correspondent at any time, directly by the individual.

Correspondent: Margaret Buckton, South Cattleholmes, Wansford, Driffield, East Yorkshire YO25 8NW (01377 254293)

Other information: Grants are also made to organisations.

York Children's Trust

Eligibility: Children and young people under 25 who live within 20 miles of York.

Types of grants: One-off grants of between £100 to £300 and are awarded to schoolchildren for uniforms/clothing, equipment/instruments and excursions, college students for study/travel overseas, equipment/instruments, maintenance/living expenses and childcare, undergraduates for study/travel overseas, excursions and childcare, vocational students for uniforms/clothing, fees, study/travel overseas, excursions and childcare, mature students for childcare, and to people starting work and those with special educational needs for uniforms/clothing. Preference is given to schoolchildren with serious family difficulties so that the child has to be educated away from home and to people with special educational needs who have been referred by a paediatrician or educational psychiatrist.

Exclusions: Grants are not available for private education or postgraduate studies.

Annual grant total: In 2006 the trust had assets of £2.3 million, an income of £96,000 and made grants to individuals totalling £32,000.

Applications: Application forms are available from the correspondent and can be submitted directly by the individual or by the individual's school, college or educational welfare agency, or a third party such as a health visitor or social worker. Applications are considered in January, April, July and October, and should be received one month earlier.

Correspondent: The Clerk, c/o 29 Whinney Lane, Harrogate, North Yorkshire, HG2 9LS

Acaster

The Knowles Educational Foundation

Eligibility: People who live in the ancient parish of Acaster Malbis.

Types of grants: In the past grants have been given towards swimming lessons for small children, field trips and visits abroad for schoolchildren and students at college and university. Grants have also been given towards books, materials and cost of transport from place of study to lodgings.

Annual grant total: In 2007 the foundation had an income of around £3,800, and a total expenditure of £2,300.

Applications: In writing to the correspondent, including invoices for expenses. As each case is considered on its own merit the more information the applicant can supply, the better. Applications are considered in March, June and October.

Correspondent: J Jenkinson-Smith, The Granary, Mill Lane, Acaster Malbis, York, YO23 2UL (01904 706153)

Harrogate

The Haywra Crescent Educational Trust Fund

Eligibility: People who live in the Harrogate Borough Council area and are in any form of post-16 education.

Types of grants: One-off grants towards books, equipment or travel.

Annual grant total: In 2006/07 the trust had an income of £11,000 and a total expenditure of £10,000. The trust gives about 17% of its annual income to individuals and about 68% to organisations with the balance being used for further investment.

Applications: On a form available from the correspondent. Students in post-16 educational courses at secondary schools in Harrogate or at Harrogate College are expected to make their application through their institution. The deadline for applications is 30 November; they are considered in December.

Correspondent: The Student Support Manager, Continuing Education, North Yorkshire County Council, County Hall, Northallerton, North Yorkshire DL7 8AL

Kirkbymoorside

The John Stockton Educational Foundation

Eligibility: Students and apprentices aged 16 to 25 who live in certain parishes in the Kirkbymoorside area and have done so for at least two years.

Types of grants: Grants range from £30 to £60. Apprentices can receive help towards the cost of tools. Vocational students and students at university can receive grants towards books, fees, living expenses and study or travel abroad. Students may apply for three years.

Exclusions: Sixth form students do not qualify for grants.

Annual grant total: In 2007/08 the trust had an income of £780 and a total expenditure of £620.

Applications: On a form available from the correspondent, to be submitted by the first week of June or December. Applications can be made directly by the applicant or parent.

Correspondent: Mrs Elizabeth Mary Kendall, Clerk, The Sheilings, Chapel Street, Nawton, York YO62 7RE (01439 771575)

Lothersdale

Raygill Trust

Eligibility: Full-time students on a first degree or equivalent course at a university or college who live in the ecclesiastical parish of Lothersdale.

Types of grants: Grants to students in the first three years of their further education.

Annual grant total: In 2006/07 the trust had an income of £10,000 and a total expenditure of £11,000.

Applications: In writing to the correspondent. Applicants who do not send thank you letters will not be considered for future grants.

Correspondent: Roger Armstrong, Armstrong Wood & Bridgman, 12–16 North Street, Keighley, West Yorkshire BD21 3SE (01535 613660)

Newton upon Rawcliffe

Poad's Educational Foundation

Eligibility: People from a poor background who are under 25 and live in the ancient town of Newton upon Rawcliffe.

Types of grants: Grants towards course fees, travel, books, incidental expenses and maintenance costs. Grants are towards a broad range of educational needs including support for courses that are not formal and after-school swimming classes.

Annual grant total: Grants total about £1,500.

Applications: In writing to the correspondent by 25 March.

Correspondent: P J Lawrence, Secretary to the Trustees, c/o Pearsons & Ward, 2 Market Street, Malton, North Yorkshire YO17 7AS

Scarborough

The Scarborough Municipal Charities

Eligibility: People who live in the borough of Scarborough.

Types of grants: Support is given to college, vocational, mature student and undergraduates, including those for books, fees, uniforms, travel, equipment, maintenance/living expenses and excursions.

Annual grant total: In 2007 grants were made for both educational and welfare purposes totalling £14,000.

Applications: On a form available from the correspondent. Applications are considered quarterly. A sub-committee of three trustees interview each applicant.

Correspondent: Mrs E Greening, 42 Green Lane, Scarborough, YO12 6HT (01723 371063)

The Scarborough United Scholarships Foundation

Eligibility: People under 25 who live in the former borough of Scarborough and have attended school in the area for at least three years.

Types of grants: Grants range from £100 to £500 a year. Grants are usually given to those at Scarborough Sixth Form College, Yorkshire Coast College or a college of further education 'where a student is following a course which is a non-advanced course'.

Grants are also given to schoolchildren, college students, undergraduates, vocational students, mature students and to people starting work for uniforms/clothing, study/travel overseas, books, equipment/instruments and excursions.

Grants are occasionally given to second-degree students, and loans are sometimes obtainable.

Exclusions: No grants for fees.

Annual grant total: In 2006/07 the trust had an income of £8,100 and a total expenditure of £4,600.

Applications: The foundation mostly deals with the local colleges to ensure potential applicants are made aware of when and how to apply.

Correspondent: Anne Morley, 169 Scalby Road, Scarborough, North Yorkshire, YO12 6TB

Swaledale

Muker Educational Trust

Eligibility: People who live in the ecclesiastical parish of Swaledale.

Types of grants: The trust gives one-off and recurrent grants of £15 to £400 to schoolchildren for books, equipment/instruments and travel/study overseas and to college students, undergraduates, vocational students and mature students for fees, study/travel overseas, books and equipment/instruments.

Exclusions: Grants are not given for maintenance, clothing or living expenses.

Annual grant total: Previously around £2,000 to individuals.

Applications: On a form available from the correspondent. Replies are only given if an sae is enclosed. Applications are considered in November and should be submitted in October either directly by the individual or through an organisation such as a school or educational welfare agency.

Correspondent: Michael B McGarry, Secretary, c/o Johnsons Solicitors, Market Place, Hawes, North Yorkshire DL8 3QS

Wensleydale

Yorebridge Educational Foundation

Eligibility: Students under 25 years of age undertaking full-time courses of further education. Students or parents must live in Wensleydale, North Yorkshire.

Types of grants: One-off grants, typically of £200 a year, towards books, fees and living expenses.

Annual grant total: Grants to individuals total around £8,000.

Applications: Applications are considered in September/October each year and should be submitted in writing directly by the individual.

Correspondent: R W Tunstall, Treasurer, Kiln Hill, Hawes, North Yorkshire DL8 3RA

Other information: Grants are also made to organisations.

York

The Merchant Taylors of York Charity

Eligibility: People involved in education/training in the area of art and craft who live in Yorkshire, particularly in York and nearby.

Types of grants: On average about eight one-off grants are made ranging between £500 to £2,000 each.

Annual grant total: In 2006/07 the trust had assets of £362,000 and an income of £97,000. Grants were made totalling £4,000, of which £1,900 went to individuals in grants (£900) and student prizes (£1,000).

Applications: In writing to the correspondent. Applications are considered throughout the year.

Correspondent: Nevil Pearce, Chancellor, 104 The Mount, York YO4 1GR (01904 655626; email: n.pearce@ calvertsmith.co.uk)

Other information: Grants are also made for welfare purposes to 'decayed tailors' and people who worked in allied crafts.

The Micklegate Strays Charity

Eligibility: Freemen or dependants of freemen, under 25, of the city of York and who are now living in the Micklegate Strays ward. (This is now defined as the whole of the part of the city of York to the west of the River Ouse.) The applicant's parents must be living in the above area.

Types of grants: Grants of £30 a year are given to schoolchildren and people starting work for uniforms, clothing, books, equipment, instruments, fees, maintenance and living expenses. Grants are also given to students in further or higher education towards study or travel abroad.

Annual grant total: Previously about £600 a year for educational and welfare purposes.

Applications: Applications can be submitted directly by the individual or by a parent. They must include the date at which the parent became a freeman of the city and the address of the parent. Applications are considered twice a year.

Correspondent: The Clerk, PO Box 258, York, YO24 4ZD

Other information: The trust was created by the 1907 Micklegate Strays Act. The city of York agreed to pay the freemen £1,000 a year in perpetuity for extinguishing their rights over Micklegate Stray. This sum has been reduced due to the forced divestment of the trust government stock, following the Charities Act of 1992.

York City Charities

Eligibility: People in need who live within the pre-1996 York city boundaries (the area within the city walls).

Types of grants: This trust has three funds. Lady Hewley's Fund gives grants to mature students aged 21 or over for general purposes. The Advancement Branch gives grants to young people aged under 21 for general educational purposes, except school trips. There is also The Poor's Branch which has relief-in-need purposes.

Annual grant total: In 2006 the trust had assets of £1.1 million and an income of £211,000. Grants were made to individuals totalling £1,400.

Applications: In writing to the correspondent, to be submitted by a headteacher, doctor, occupational nurse, social worker, Citizen's Advice or other third party or welfare agency. Applications are considered throughout the year.

Correspondent: Mrs Carol Bell, 41 Avenue Road, Clifton, York YO30 6AY (01904 645131; Fax: 01904 645131; email: carol@forthergil15.freeserve.co.uk)

Northumberland

Coates Educational Foundation

Eligibility: People up to the age of 25 who live in the parishes of Ponteland, Stannington, Heddon-on-the-Wall, and the former district of Newburn. Pupils and former pupils of Coates Endowed Middle School are also supported.

Types of grants: One-off grants to help with the cost of books, clothing, educational outings, maintenance and fees for schoolchildren and students at college or university. People starting work can be helped with books, equipment/ instruments, clothing or travel.

Annual grant total: In 2006 the foundation had assets of £339,000 and an income of £27,000, with grants totalling £8,000

Applications: On a form available from the correspondent, to be submitted directly by the individual. Applications are considered in February and June.

Correspondent: P Jackson, Secretary, 184 Darras Road, Ponteland, Tyne & Wear NE20 9AF (0191 274 7074)

The Eleemosynary Charity of Giles Heron

Eligibility: People in need who live in the ancient parish of Simonburn.

Types of grants: One-off grants according to need. Recent grants have been given to help towards the cost of education, training, apprenticeship and equipment for those starting work and for educational visits abroad.

Annual grant total: In 2006/07 the charity had an income of £14,000 and a total expenditure of £8,000. Grants were made totalling £6,000, of which about £3,000 was given in individual awards, with the rest being donated to local organisations.

Applications: In writing to the correspondent directly by the individual.

Correspondent: George Benson, Chair, Brunton House, Wall, Hexham, Northumberland NE46 4EJ (01434 681203)

Other information: Individual grants are also made for welfare purposes.

The Rothbury Educational Trust

Eligibility: People aged 18 to 25 who live in the ancient parish of Rothbury, Thropton and Hepple. Applicants must be pursuing a full-time further education course at a technical college, university or similar establishment approved by the trustees.

Types of grants: Cash grants, usually of about £100.

Annual grant total: In 2006/07 the trust had an income of about £5,400 and an expenditure of £5,000.

Applications: In writing to the correspondent for consideration in late August/ early September. Grants are advertised in the local newspapers.

Correspondent: Mrs Susan Rogerson, 1 Gallow Law, Alwinton, Morpeth, Northumberland NE65 7BQ (01669 650390)

Allendale

Allendale Exhibition Endowment

Eligibility: People under 25 (on 31 September in year of application) and who live in the parishes of East and West Allendale.

Types of grants: Grants of £50 to £150 to: schoolchildren for educational outings in the UK or overseas; people starting work for books, equipment, instruments, maintenance, living expenses, educational outings in the UK and study or travel abroad; and students in further or higher education for all of the above as well as student exchanges.

Annual grant total: In 2006/07 the trust had an income of £5,700 and a total expenditure of £6,600.

Applications: On a form available from the correspondent. Applications should be submitted directly by the individual and the deadline is usually at the end of October. An advert is placed in the local paper, library and shops in mid-August.

Correspondent: G Ostler, Low House, Allendale, Hexham, Northumberland, NE47 9NX (01434 345229)

Blyth

The Blyth Valley Trust for Youth

Eligibility: People who live in the borough of Blyth Valley and are under 21.

Types of grants: Grants to assist people active in the fields of arts, music and physical recreation. Support can be given for uniforms/clothing, fees, books, equipment, instruments and awards for excellence. Applicants should be of amateur status and support may only be given to those who are able to identify specific 'Centres of Excellence' which they will be attending. Grants usually range from £50 to £250 and are one-off.

Annual grant total: In 2006/07 the trust had an income of £2,000 and a total expenditure of £1,200.

Applications: Application forms are available from the correspondent and can be submitted directly by the individual. Full details of the activity and references must be included on the form. The trust advises applicants to apply early (preferably before February each year) in time for the trustees' meeting, usually held in April.

Correspondent: D Earl, Civic Centre, Renwick Road, Blyth, Northumberland NE24 2BX (01670 542000; email: llittle@ blythvalley.gov.uk)

Haydon Bridge

Shaftoe Educational Foundation

Eligibility: Individuals in need who live in the parish of Haydon Bridge.

Types of grants: One-off and recurrent grants of at least £400. Grants are made to schoolchildren for fees and study or travel abroad, people starting work for equipment or instruments, and further and higher education and mature students for fees.

Annual grant total: In 2006/07 the trust had assets of £4.7 million and an income of £134,000. Grants totalled £67,000, of which £11,000 was distributed to 26 individuals.

Applications: In writing to the correspondent, for consideration in March, July and November. Initial telephone calls are welcomed. Applications can be made either directly by the individual or through the individual's school, college or educational welfare agency.

Correspondent: Richard A D Snowdon, Clerk, The Office, Shaftoe Terrace, Haydon Bridge, Hexham, NE47 6BW (01434 688871; email: shaftoe@fsmail.net)

Kirkwhelpington

The Kirkwhelpington Educational Charity

Eligibility: People who live in the civil parish of Kirkwhelpington who are under the age of 25, to promote education including social and physical training. (Grants are also given to schools and voluntary organisations in the parish who provide facilities for people under the age of 25.)

Types of grants: Individuals who have gone on to some form of training or further education after school have received help with items such as equipment, books, cost of transport and extra courses where these are not covered by Local Education Authority grants. Schoolchildren have received help with the cost of educational outings and special tuition. Grants are usually one-off and in the range of £50 and £300.

Annual grant total: In 2007 the trust had an income of £4,000 and a total expenditure of £3,000. About £1,000 is given annually in grants to individuals.

Applications: In writing to the correspondent including details of how the money is to be spent, other possible sources of grants and receipts of money spent where possible. Applications are usually considered in February, May and October.

Correspondent: Mrs H Cowan, 11 Meadowlands, Kirkwhelpington, Newcastle upon Tyne NE19 2RX

South Yorkshire

The Aston-Cum-Aughton Educational Foundation

Eligibility: Pupils in the area of Aston-Cum-Aughton and Swallownest with Fence, where needs cannot be met from official sources.

Types of grants: One-off and recurrent grants towards items the LEA cannot provide, such as books and other equipment.

Annual grant total: In 2006 the trust had an income of £4,400 and a total expenditure of £18,000.

Applications: In writing to the correspondent or to any trustee either by the individual or their headmaster. Applications are considered in March and September, but special cases will be considered throughout the year. Applications should include some details of what the grant is to be spent on and the total cost.

Correspondent: J Nuttall, 3 Rosegarth Avenue, Aston, Sheffield S26 2DB

The Bolsterstone Educational Charity

Eligibility: People aged between 16 and 25 who live in the parishes of St Mary's – Bolsterstone, St Matthias' – Stocksbridge and St John's – Deepcar.

Types of grants: Grants of between £50 and £200 are given towards books, equipment/instruments and study or travel abroad.

Exclusions: No grants are given to mature students or people starting work.

Annual grant total: In 2006/07 the trust had an income of £8,900 and a total expenditure of £6,600.

Applications: On a form available from the correspondent. They should be submitted directly by the individual for consideration at the start of March, July or November.

Correspondent: C A North, 5 Pennine View, Stocksbridge, Sheffield S36 1ER (0114 288 2757; Fax: 0114 288 7404; email: cliff.north@virgin.net)

The Elmhirst Trust

Eligibility: People who live in Barnsley, Doncaster and Rotherham, normally over the age of 30, seeking to develop their life in new directions and who are prevented from doing so by low income. Particular emphasis is given to those whose proposals benefit the community as a whole. Applicants may be undertaking vocational training or retraining in any subject, and must be in need of financial assistance to support them in their training. The trust strongly prefers to support people who have had little or no post-16 education and are involved in the voluntary sector to offer them a second chance of personal or vocational development.

Types of grants: One-off grants range from £100 to £850 which has previously been spent predominantly on fees but also on travel, books, equipment and childcare.

Annual grant total: In 2006/07 the trust had an income of £6,400 and a total expenditure of £3,300.

Applications: On a form available from the correspondent. 'A response, by telephone or post, is made to all applicants and where applications are considered an assessor visits the applicant. The trust attempts to maintain contact with beneficiaries during their course/activity and thereafter.'

Correspondent: John Butt, 2 Paddock Close, Staincross, Barnsley S75 6LH

The Robert Woods Exhibition Foundation

Eligibility: Students in higher education who live in the ecclesiastical parish of Kirk Sandall or Edenthorpe. Applicants must be resident in either parish at date of application.

Types of grants: Grants of £20 to £50 a year to help with the cost of books for first degree students.

Annual grant total: In 2007/08 the trust had both an income and a total expenditure of around £1,000, most of which was given in grants to individuals.

Applications: On a form available from local secondary schools or the correspondent. Applications must be submitted by 30 August, for consideration in September.

Correspondent: D M Telford, Clerk, 15 Woodford Road, Barnby Dun, Doncaster, DN3 1BN (01302 883496)

The Sheffield Bluecoat & Mount Pleasant Educational Foundation

Eligibility: People up to the age of 25 who live within a 20-mile radius of Sheffield Town Hall and have done so for at least 3 years.

Types of grants: One-off and recurrent grants towards artistic and sporting activities, educational travel, clothing, equipment and private school fees. Grants in 2006/07 ranged between £250 and £3,500.

Annual grant total: In 2006/07 the trust had assets of £1.5 million and an income of £72,000, with grants to individuals totalling £32,000.

Applications: In writing to the correspondent or through the school/ college or educational welfare agency. Applications are considered in April and September and should be submitted by March and August.

Correspondent: G J Smallman, c/o Wrigleys, Fountain Precinct, Balm Green, Sheffield S1 1JA (0114 267 5588; Fax: 0114 276 3176)

Other information: The fund also gives to organisations.

The Sheffield West Riding Charitable Society Trust

Eligibility: Clergy children at school and in further education in the diocese of Sheffield.

Types of grants: Only a small proportion of the grants are educational and are to help with the cost of books, clothing and other essentials.

Annual grant total: In 2007 the trust had an income and a total expenditure of £11,000. Around 20 grants are made each year.

Applications: On a form available from the correspondent.

Correspondent: Malcolm Fair, Diocesan Secretary, Diocesan Church House, 95–99 Effingham Street, Rotherham S65 1BL (01709 309100; email: malcolm.fair@ sheffield.anglican.org; website: www. sheffield.anglican.org)

Other information: Welfare grants are also made to the clergy, house-keepers and disadvantaged families in the diocese.

The Swann-Morton Foundation

Eligibility: Students who live in South Yorkshire.

Types of grants: One-off and recurrent grants according to need.

Annual grant total: In 2006/07 the trust had an income and a total expenditure of £45,000. The sum of £5,000 was given in student grants and electives.

Applications: In writing to the correspondent. In the past the trust has stated that applications have exceeded available funding.

Correspondent: The Administrator, Swann-Morton Ltd, Owlerton Green, Sheffield S6 2BJ

Armthorpe

Armthorpe Poors Estate Charity

Eligibility: People who are in need and live in Armthorpe.

Types of grants: One-off and recurrent grants of £50 minimum to schoolchildren who are in need for educational outings and to undergraduates for books.

Annual grant total: In 2006/07 the trust had an income of nearly £8,000 and a total expenditure of almost £6,000.

Applications: Contact the clerk by telephone who will advise if a letter of application is needed. Applicants outside of Armthorpe will be declined. Undergraduates are required to complete an application form, available from the correspondent, and return it by 31 August.

Correspondent: Frank Pratt, 32 Gurth Avenue, Edenthorpe, Doncaster DN3 2LW (01302 882806)

Other information: The trust gives to both individuals and organisations

Barnsley

The Shaw Lands Trust

Eligibility: People under 25 who live within the former county borough of Barnsley (as defined pre-1974) or are, or have for at least two years at any time been, in attendance at any county or voluntary aided school in the borough.

Types of grants: To provide scholarships/grants for university, school or other place of learning; assistance for purchase of clothing, tools, books and so on to help beneficiaries enter a profession, trade or calling; travel overseas to enable beneficiaries to further their education; assistance for provision of facilities of any kind not normally provided by the local education authority for recreation and social and physical training for beneficiaries who are receiving primary, secondary and further education; to assist in the study of music and other arts. Grants range from £200 to £750 and may be paid in three instalments.

Annual grant total: In 2006/07 the trust had assets of £1.3 million, with an income of £42,000. The trust made 10 grants to individuals totalling £13,000.

Applications: In writing to the correspondent. Applications are considered in September.

Correspondent: Jill Leece, 35 Church Street, Barnsley, South Yorkshire, S70 2AP (01226 213434)

Other information: Grants are also made to organisations.

Beighton

Beighton Relief-in-Need Charity

Eligibility: Students who live in the former parish of Beighton and are in need.

Types of grants: One-off grants according to need.

Annual grant total: Grants usually total around £9,000 per year.

Applications: In writing to the correspondent. Applications can be submitted directly by the individual or through a social worker, Citizens Advice, other welfare agency or a third party such as a relative, neighbour or trustee.

Correspondent: Michael Lowe, Elms Bungalow, Queens Road, Beighton, Sheffield S20 1AW (0114 2692875)

Other information: Grants are also made for relief in need purposes.

Bramley

The Bramley Poors' Allotment Trust

Eligibility: People in need who live in the ancient township of Bramley, especially people who are elderly, poor and sick.

Types of grants: One-off grants between £40 and £120

Annual grant total: In 2006/07 the trust had an income of £2,700 and a total expenditure of £2,400.

Applications: In writing to the correspondent. The trust likes applications to be submitted through a recognised referral agency (social worker, Citizens Advice, doctor, headmaster or minister). They are considered monthly.

Correspondent: Len Barnett, Mrs Marian Houseman, 9 Horton Rise, Rodley, Leeds, LS13 1PH (0113 2360115)

Epworth

Epworth Charities

Eligibility: People in need who live in Epworth.

Types of grants: One-off and recurrent grants in the range of £50 and £250. Grants are made to schoolchildren for equipment/instruments and college students, undergraduates, vocational students and mature students for books.

Annual grant total: This trust generally has an annual income of between £1,000 and £2,000 with total expenditure usually under £1,000.

Applications: In writing to the correspondent to be submitted directly by the individual. Applications are considered on an ongoing basis.

Correspondent: Mrs Margaret Draper, 16 Fern Croft, Epworth, Doncaster, South Yorkshire DN9 1GE (01427 873234; email: margaret.draper@btinternet.com)

Other information: Grants are also made for welfare purposes.

Sheffield

The Church Burgesses Educational Foundation

Eligibility: People up to the age of 25 whose parents have lived in Sheffield for the last three years.

Types of grants: Grants are given towards books, clothing and other essentials for schoolchildren. Grants are occasionally available for those at college or university, although no grants are made where a LEA grant is available. Postgraduates can only receive funding if there is a special need for retraining or education in a different subject. School fees are only paid where there is a sudden, unexpected hardship.

Special grants can also be made to individuals for gap year projects and overseas expeditions, helping churches and missions in the UK and abroad, attending summer schools and festivals, artistic and athletic activities and so on.

There is also a 'Music in the City' scheme which supported music tuition for over 140 individuals in 2006, and also covered funding for a student to attend an international violin competition in Versailles, France.

Annual grant total: In 2006 the foundation had assets of £365,000 and an income of £354,000. The foundation gave £126,000 in grants to individuals for a wide range of educational purposes. Approximately £83,000 was given for tertiary courses and in some cases the attendance of independent schools. A further £19,000 was given in special individual grants and £24,000 through the Instrumental Music Bursary Scheme.

Applications: In writing to the correspondent.

Correspondent: G J Smallman, Church Burgesses Educational Foundation, 3rd Floor Fountain Precinct, Balm Green,

Sheffield, S1 2JA (0114 267 5596; Fax: 0114 267 3176)

Other information: Grants are also made to organisations (£40,000, 2006)

The Sheffield Grammar School Exhibition Foundation

Eligibility: People who live in the city of Sheffield and have done so for at least three years (this excludes residency for educational purposes).

Types of grants: Grants can be given to people starting work for books, equipment, clothing or travel. Students in further or higher education may be helped with fees, living expenses, study or travel abroad and with the cost of books. Mature students may be provided with money to cover the costs of travel, fees, childcare or books. The trust will occasionally give towards schoolchildren's educational outings.

There is a preference for people who are attending or have attended King Edward VII School. Grants are also given for the benefit of the school.

Annual grant total: In 2006/07 the foundation had assets of £3.1 million and an income of £142,000. Grants to individuals totalled £74,000 with a further £19,000 going to organisations.

Applications: In writing to the correspondent. Applications are considered in March, July, October and December and should be submitted either directly by the individual or through their school, college or educational welfare agency.

Correspondent: G J Smallman, Clerk, c/o Wrigleys, Fountain Precinct, Balm Green, Sheffield S1 2JA

Teesside

The Captain John Vivian Nancarrow Fund

Eligibility: People under the age of 25 who live or work in Middlesbrough and who are or have at any time been in attendance at the following schools or colleges: Acklam Grange, Brackenhow/Kings Academy, Hall Garth, Kings Manor, Langbaurgh/Keldholme/Unity City Academy, Middlesbrough College and Teesside Tertiary College.

Types of grants: Grants are given for the following: attendance at any approved place of learning; clothing, equipment, and so on needed to prepare for, or enter, a trade or profession; educational travel scholarships; study of music and other arts; educational research; recreational and social and physical training; assistance in the event of sickness, disability and so on

to enable full benefit from educational facilities.

Exclusions: No grants where statutory funding is available or to people who have received a grant from Middlesbrough Council in the current financial year.

Annual grant total: In 2006/07 the trust had an income and a total expenditure of around £5,000.

Applications: Applications to these charities may be made directly by the individual or by recommendation, where appropriate, from a headteacher. Application forms are available from the correspondent.

Correspondent: Voluntary Sector Team, Middlesbrough Council, Children, Families & Learning, PO Box 69, Vancouver House, Gurney Street, Middlesbrough TS1 1EL (01642 728079 or 01642 728081)

Other information: In the case of educational research, assistance may also be provided to people over 25.

Guisborough

The Hutton Lowcross Educational Foundation

Eligibility: People under the age of 25 who live, or whose parents live, in the parish of Guisborough.

Types of grants: One-off and recurrent grants in the range of £50 to £500. Grants are given for the following: (i) attendance at any approved place of learning; (ii) clothing, equipment, etc. needed to prepare for, or enter, a career; (iii) educational travel at home or abroad; (iv) The study of music or the other arts; (v) educational research; and (vi) recreational, social and physical training.

Annual grant total: About £2,500 is distributed annually in grants to individuals.

Applications: On a form available from the correspondent to be submitted directly by the individual or a parent/guardian. Applications are considered in October each year.

Correspondent: M Sivills, Director of Children's Services, Student Finance Section, Redcar & Cleveland Borough Council, PO Box 83, Council Offices, Kirkleatham Street, Redcar (01642 444118; Fax: 01642 444251)

Hartlepool

The Preston Simpson Scholarship in Music

Eligibility: People aged 15 to 25 who were either born in Hartlepool or who have had at least one parent living in Hartlepool for the last five years.

Types of grants: Cash grants to help with the cost of the study of music at any school or college or towards instruments.

Annual grant total: About £1,000 is available each year.

Applications: On a form which is available from local schools and on request from the civic centre (see below). Grants are considered once a year, usually just before the start of the school summer holidays.

Correspondent: Alan McNab, Hartlepool Borough Council, Civic Centre, Victoria Road, Hartlepool TS24 8AY (01429 523763; email: alan.macnab@ hartlepool.gov.uk)

The Sterndale Scholarships in Music

Eligibility: Women aged between 15 and 25 on 31 July in the year of application who live in the borough of Hartlepool and have done so for at least three years prior to the application.

Types of grants: Scholarships (after audition) in music (vocal or instrumental) for those wishing to make use of their musical ability in their future career. The scholarships range from £150 to £800.

Annual grant total: About £3,000.

Applications: On forms available from the correspondent, Hartlepool secondary schools and sixth form colleges or through an advert placed in the local press.

Correspondent: Chief Financial Officer, Hartlepool Borough Council, Civic Centre, Victoria Road, Hartlepool, Cleveland TS24 8AY

Middlesbrough

Middlesbrough Educational Trust Fund

Eligibility: People under 25 who live or work in Middlesbrough.

Types of grants: Grants for the following: attendance at any approved place of learning (minimum period one year); the purchase of clothing, equipment or books to prepare for, or enter, a trade or profession; educational travel scholarships; assistance with the provision of facilities for recreation, sport and social and physical training for pupils and students; the study of music and other arts; educational research.

Exclusions: No grants where statutory funding is available or to people who have received a grant from Middlesbrough Council in the current financial year.

Annual grant total: Disposable funds of £2,400.

Applications: Applications to these charities may be made directly by the individual or by recommendation, where appropriate, from a headteacher.

Application forms are available from the correspondent.

Correspondent: The Voluntary Sector Team, Middlesbrough Council, Children, Families & Learning, PO Box 69, Vancouver House, Gurney Street, Middlesbrough TS1 1EL (01642 728079)

Thornaby-on-Tees

County Alderman Worsley JP Scholarships

Eligibility: Students at university or further education colleges who live in the former borough of Thornaby-on-Tees.

Types of grants: Recurrent grants to a usual maximum of £150 towards books, fees and equipment. Priority is given to families who have a low income.

Annual grant total: In 2007/08 the fund had an income of £5,400 and a total expenditure of £2,200.

Applications: On a form available from the correspondent from April, to be returned by 31 August for consideration in September/October. Applications should include two references.

Correspondent: Mrs A Metcalfe, Student Support, Stockton-on-Tees Borough Council, Education Leisure and Cultural Services, PO Box 228, Municipal Buildings, Church Road, Stockton-on-Tees TS18 1XE (01642 526609; Fax: 01642 393525; email: studentsupport@stockton.gov.uk)

Yarm

The Yarm Grammar School Trust

Eligibility: People under 25 years of age who live in the parish of Yarm.

Types of grants: Grants of around £100 are given to schoolchildren for uniforms and other school clothing, books, educational outings and study or travel abroad and to students in further or higher education for books, equipment, instruments, fees, living expenses, educational outings and study or travel abroad.

Annual grant total: About £3,000.

Applications: On a form available from the student support unit or the trust's website. Applications should be submitted directly by the individual by the end of May for consideration in July, or by the end of November for consideration in January.

Correspondent: Pupil Support, Stockton Borough Council, PO Box 228, Municipal Buildings, Church Road, Stockton-on-Tees TS18 1XE (email: schooladmissions@ stockton.gov.uk; website: www.stockton. gov.uk)

Tyne & Wear

The Cullercoats Educational Trust

Eligibility: People who live in the ecclesiastical parishes of St Paul – Whitley Bay and St George – Cullercoats.

Types of grants: Grants are made towards religious instruction in accordance with the doctrines of the Church of England and to promote the education, including social and physical training, of beneficiaries.

Annual grant total: In 2006/07 the fund had an income of £6,600 and a total expenditure of £7,200. Grants are made to individuals and organisations usually totalling about £5,000 each year.

Applications: By letter to the correspondent in February or August for consideration in March or September.

Correspondent: Donald J Kean, 40 Parkside Crescent, Tynemouth, Tyne and Wear NE30 4JR (0191 257 1765)

Charity of John McKie Elliott Deceased

Eligibility: People who are blind in Gateshead or Newcastle upon Tyne.

Types of grants: One-off and recurrent grants according to need.

Annual grant total: The trust has an annual income of just over £1,000 and generally about £550 available for grants each year. In recent years the trust has not always had any expenditure, however, the latest accounts show a total expenditure of £2,250.

Applications: In writing to the correspondent.

Correspondent: Roger Eager, 9 Beaumont Court, Whitley Bay, Tyne & Wear, NE25 9TZ (0191 2537079; email: eager6@ msn.com)

Other information: The trust gives educational grants and grants to individuals in need.

The Newcastle Dispensary Relief-in-Sickness Charity

Eligibility: People who are sick and in need and live in or near the city of Newcastle upon Tyne.

Types of grants: Grants are made up to a maximum of £200 per applicant. Recent grants have been given towards the cost of a nebuliser, a washing machine and spare bedding.

Exclusions: Grants to other agencies will not be considered, nor are grants given retrospectively.

Annual grant total: Previously about £500.

Applications: On a form available from the correspondent which should be submitted via a social worker, Citizen's Advice, or other welfare agency. Applications are considered when received.

Correspondent: Ian Humphreys, 25 Swallowdale Gardens, Newcastle-upon-Tyne, NE7 7TA

The Sunderland Orphanage & Educational Foundation

Eligibility: Young people under 25 who are resident in or around Sunderland who have a parent who is disabled or has died, or whose parents are divorced or legally separated.

Types of grants: (i) Maintenance payments and clothing for schoolchildren.

(ii) Help towards the cost of education, training, apprenticeship or equipment for those starting work.

(iii) Help with travel to pursue education, for the provision of athletic coaching and for the study of music and other arts.

Annual grant total: In 2006/07 the trust had an income of £24,000 and a total expenditure of £23,000.

Applications: Applications should be made in writing to the correspondent. They are considered every other month.

Correspondent: P W Taylor, McKenzie Bell, 19 John Street, Sunderland SR1 1JG (0191 567 4857)

Community Foundation Serving Tyne & Wear and Northumberland

Eligibility: People in need who live in Northumberland or Tyne and Wear.

Types of grants: The Community Foundation is essentially a local umbrella organisation of grant making trusts, which pools together money from various sources to maximise the interest levels on the investments. There are over 100 smaller funds administered by the foundation and only a handful support individuals. Information on funds is available from the foundation, or on its website.

Annual grant total: In 2006/07 the foundation had an income of £6.8 million and made grants totalling £7.6 million, of which £166,000 was distributed to 331 individuals for educational and welfare needs.

Applications: On a form available from the correspondent. The foundation is responsible for managing many different funds and will forward any application to the one most suitable, though it is important to note that several funds do have a separate application form and it is worth contacting the foundation prior to completing any submission. Applications can be made at any time and the foundation will generally reply within three months of receipt.

Correspondent: George Hepburn, Cale Cross, 156 Pilgrim Street, Newcastle upon Tyne, NE1 6SU (0191 222 0945; Fax: 0191 230 0689; email: general@ communityfoundation.org.uk; website: www.communityfoundation.org. uk)

Other information: More detailed information on this foundation can be found in DSC's *A Guide to the Major Trusts Volume 1*. Also see the foundation's website for more information on the application process and the different grant-making funds.

Houghton-le-Springs

The Kepier Exhibition Trust

Eligibility: Those attending higher education who live in the ancient parish of Houghton-le-Spring.

Types of grants: Cash grants, to a usual maximum of £200, to supplement existing grants. Current policy is to give a one-off grant, payable in the first term at the beneficiary's university, with a preference for students from poorer families.

Annual grant total: About £1,000.

Applications: On a form available from the correspondent from February, to be returned by first post on 1 May.

Correspondent: Mary Irwin, 5 Thistlecroft, Houghton le spring, DH5 8LT (0191 584 2198; email: maryirwin@talktalk.net)

Newcastle-upon-Tyne

The Newcastle upon Tyne Education Prize Fund

Eligibility: People under 25 who live in Newcastle upon Tyne and received a secondary school education in the city are eligible for mandatory or discretionary awards from Newcastle upon Tyne LEA.

Types of grants: Grants of between £100 and £200 to schoolchildren for equipment/ instruments, educational outings, study or travel abroad and to people in further education towards equipment/ instruments, educational outings, books and study or travel abroad.

Annual grant total: About £1,900.

Applications: In writing to the correspondent, to be considered at any time. Applications should include details of date of birth, secondary school attended and home address in the city.

Correspondent: Dave Baharie, Room 304, Civic Centre, Barras Bridge, Newcastle-upon-Tyne NE1 9PU

South Tyneside

Westoe Educational Charity

Eligibility: People under 25, resident in the Metropolitan Borough Council of South Tyneside (or have a parent resident) and are in financial need.

Types of grants: One-off and recurrent grants for schoolchildren, people with special educational needs, further/higher education students, vocational students, and people starting work towards uniforms/clothing, fees, study or travel abroad, books, equipment/instruments, maintenance/living expenses and excursions.

Exclusions: Grants are not made for musical instrument tuition.

Annual grant total: In 2006/07 the charity had an income and a total expenditure of £17,000.

Applications: In writing to the correspondent at any time although applications are usually considered in January.

Correspondent: Graham Fowler, South Tyneside MBC, Town Hall and Civic Offices, Westoe Road, South Shields, Tyne and Wear NE33 2RL

Sunderland

The George Hudson Charity

Eligibility: People under the age of 18 whose father has died or is unable to work and are living in Sunderland, with preference to children of seafarers.

Types of grants: The trust gives pocket money of £12 a month to children up to the age of 14 and £14 a month to older children. These children may also receive a grant towards clothing.

Annual grant total: In 2006/07 the charity had assets of £35,000 and an income of £31,000. Grants were made to 65 individuals totalling £20,000, of which £14,000 was spent on educational causes and the remaining £6,000 on clothing and footwear grants.

Applications: On a form available from: D G Goodfellow, Administrator, 54 John Street, Sunderland SR1 1QH. Applications are considered every other month.

Correspondent: P W Taylor, Messrs McKenzie Bell Solicitors, 19 John Street, Sunderland SR1 1JG

The Mayor's Fund for Necessitous Children

Eligibility: Children in need (under 16, occasionally under 19) who are in full-time education, live in the city of Sunderland and whose family are on a low income.

Types of grants: About £25 grants for provision of school footwear paid every six months.

Exclusions: No grants to asylum seekers.

Annual grant total: About £500.

Applications: Applicants must visit the civic centre and fill in a form with a member of staff. The decision is then posted at a later date. Proof of low income is necessary.

Correspondent: Children's Services Financial Manager, Sunderland City Council, Civic Centre, Sunderland SR2 7DN

West Yorkshire

Boston Spa School

Eligibility: People in need who live in Boston Spa, Collingham, Harewood, Alwoodley, Shadwell, Crossgates, Scholes, Barwichin Elmet, Bardsey, East Keswick, Whinmoor, Aberford, Thomer, Bramham, Clifford, Walton and Thorp Arch in the north east area of West Yorkshire.

Types of grants: One-off grants are usually given for expeditions and explorations or to students on higher education courses where no grants are available, such as postgraduate courses.

Annual grant total: In 2006 the trust had an income of £500. Grants have previously totalled around £1,000 although no recent accounts information was available.

Applications: In writing to the correspondent, to be considered in March, June and November.

Correspondent: Alun Rees, Boston Spa Comprehensive School, Clifford, Moor Road, Boston Spa, Wetherby, West Yorkshire LS23 6RW (01937 842915)

The Clayton, Taylor & Foster Charity

Eligibility: People in need who live in the city of Wakefield, Thornes with Alverthorpe and Wrenthorpe with Outwood, who are in full-time or higher education.

Types of grants: Small grants to a maximum of about £100 for a variety of educational purposes. As the main purpose of the charity is to administer grants to the over 60s within the area above, educational grants are only given if there are any surplus funds available.

Annual grant total: Previously grants have totalled about £1,000

Applications: In writing to writing to the correspondent, giving details of the project. Trustees meet in March, September and November.

Correspondent: Mrs Preston, Clerk to the Trustees, 16 Stopford Avenue, Wakefield WF2 6RJ (01924 258660)

Lady Elizabeth Hasting's Educational Foundation

Eligibility: Individuals in need who live in the parishes of Burton Salmon, Thorp Arch, Collingham with Harewood, Bardsey with East Keswick, Shadwell and Ledsham with Fairburn.

Types of grants: One-off and recurrent grants according to need, usually averaging between £500 and £600.

Exclusions: Applicants must reside in one of the above parishes to qualify for a grant.

Annual grant total: In 2006/07 the foundation had assets of £12 millions and an income of £407,000. Grants were made to 111 individuals totalling £62,000.

Applications: In writing to the correspondent. The trustees meet four times a year, although grants can be made between the meetings, on the agreement of two trustees.

Correspondent: E F V Waterson, Clerk, Carter Jonas, 82 Micklegate, York YO1 1LF

Other information: The trust is managed by, and derives its income from, Lady Elizabeth Hastings Estate Charity. The trust also gives yearly grants of £3,000 to designated local schools.

The Charity of Lady Mabel Florence Harriet Smith

Eligibility: Students in full-time attendance on a first degree course at a British university but who have not yet taken their final first degree examination at the date any awards are payable. Applicants must be ordinarily living in the former West Riding of Yorkshire as constituted on 31 March 1974.

Types of grants: Two grants of about £1,000 each are given towards travelling abroad to further education in a field of study which is the subject of the individual's full-time university course or a directly related field of study. Awards are tenable until 30 June of the year following the year of application.

Annual grant total: About £2,000.

Applications: On a form available from the correspondent. Applications are considered in May and should be submitted by 31 March, including a reference form a university tutor.

Correspondent: The Student Support Officer, Student Support Section, Education Offices, County Hall, Northallerton, North Yorkshire DL7 8AE

Other information: Further information on other trusts administered by North Yorkshire County Council can be obtained from the correspondent.

The Brian Strong Trust for Pudsey Young People

Eligibility: Young people aged between 16 and 21 who live in Calverley, Farsley or Pudsey. Preference is given to children from low-income families.

Types of grants: One-off grants of between £50 and £300 are given to people at school or in further or higher education for books, equipment, instruments, educational outings in the UK and overseas and student exchange. Grants are available to people with special educational needs and people starting work for the same purposes. Personal development, such as organised travel and music, is also supported.

Annual grant total: Income of about £600 a year.

Applications: On a form available from the correspondent. Applications should be submitted directly by the individual for consideration at any time.

Correspondent: Bridget Strong, 4 Burcot Road, Sheffield, S8 9FE

The Frank Wallis Scholarships

Eligibility: Students who have lived within the area of the former Clayton urban district council for at least three years.

Types of grants: Grants range from £50 to £100 and are given for any course of higher education to assist with the purchase of books and equipment.

Annual grant total: In 2007/08 the charity had an income of £580. No expenditure was recorded during the year.

Applications: In writing to the correspondent.

Correspondent: Deborah Beaumont, Britannia House, Hall Ings, Bradford BD1 1HX

Bradford

The Isaac Holden Scholarships

Eligibility: Male higher education students who have attended maintained schools within the area of the former City of Bradford County Borough Council for not less than three years.

Types of grants: Grants of £120 each.

Annual grant total: In 2006/07 the charity had an income of £1,400. No expenditure has been recorded in recent years.

Applications: In writing to the correspondent.

Correspondent: Deborah Beaumont, Britannia House, Hall Ings, Bradford BD1 1HX

Calderdale

The Community Foundation for Calderdale

Eligibility: Primary and secondary school pupils in Calderdale who are in need.

Types of grants: One-off grants (£100) and occasionally small loans are made for the costs of school trips, clothing, books or equipment and so on.

Annual grant total: In 2006/07 the foundation had assets of 37 million and an income of £3.6 million. £2.6 million was given in grants, of which £13,000 went to individuals, mostly for relief in need purposes.

Applications: Individuals must apply through a referring agency, such as Citizens Advice, on an application form available from the correspondent. Grants will only be awarded to individuals in the form of a cheque; cash is not given.

Correspondent: Grants Department, Community Foundation for Calderdale, Community Foundation House, 162A King Cross Road, Halifax, West Yorkshire, HX1 3LN (01422 349700; Fax: 01422 350017; email: enquiries@cffc. co.uk; website: www.cffc.co.uk)

Other information: The foundation also gives to organisations (£2.6 million in 2006/07).

Elland

The Brooksbank Educational Charity

Eligibility: People under the age of 25 who live in the former urban district of Elland (as constituted on 31 March 1974).

Types of grants: Grants for people who are moving from junior to secondary schools and to students going on to higher education. Grants are usually £30 per student.

Annual grant total: About £800.

Applications: Application forms are issued through the local junior schools; other students should apply direct to the correspondent. Juniors should apply in May, seniors in September. Trustees meet twice yearly, but can act rapidly in an emergency.

Correspondent: A D Blackburn, Clerk, Ryburn, 106 Victoria Road, Elland, Calderdale HX5 0QF (01422 372014)

Haworth

The Haworth Exhibition Endowment Trust

Eligibility: People who live, or whose parents lived, in the ancient township of

Haworth. Candidates must have attended one of the schools (including Oakbank) in the district of Haworth (including Oxenhope and Stanbury, but excluding Lees and Crossroads) for at least three years.

Types of grants: One-off grants ranging from £25 to £75 to people following A-levels and taking up further education, for books and equipment.

Annual grant total: In 2007/08 the trust had both an income and a total expenditure of approximately £700.

Applications: On an application form available from the town hall information desk following an advertisement in the local newspaper. The closing date for applications is 31 August. The trustees meet once a year in October.

Correspondent: Dr Andrew Collinson, 38 Gledhow Drive, Oxenhope, Keighley, West Yorkshire BD22 9SA

Keighley

Bowcocks Trust Fund for Keighley

Eligibility: People in need who live in the municipal borough of Keighley as constituted on 31 March 1974.

Types of grants: One-off grants according to need.

Annual grant total: In 2006/07 the trust had an income of £9,200 and a total expenditure of £9,600. Grants for education and welfare purposes totalled about £8,500. In previous years a majority of the grant total has gone into education grants.

Applications: Initial telephone calls are welcomed. Applications should be made in writing to the correspondent by a third party.

Correspondent: Mr P Vaux, Clerk, Old Mill House, 6 Dockroyd, Oakworth, Keighley, West Yorkshire BD22 7RH (01535 643 029)

Leeds

The Holbeck Mechanics Institute Trust Fund Scheme

Eligibility: People who live in the city of Leeds south of the River Aire. If no suitable applicant can be found from there, applications from other parts of Leeds will be considered.

Types of grants: Grants for those attending courses of further or higher education to assist with the costs of maintenance and travel but not fees. 'Normally, applications will not be considered where, on the basis of the appropriate regulations, a parental

contribution has been assessed or in situations where assistance is available from other sources.'

Annual grant total: Grants usually total around £500.

Applications: On a form available from the correspondent. Applications may be considered at any time.

Correspondent: The Clerk, Corporate Services Department, 2nd Floor West, Civic Hall, Leeds LS1 1JF

Kirke Charity

Eligibility: People in need who live in the ancient parishes of Adel, Arthington or Cookridge.

Types of grants: One-off grants of around £100.

Annual grant total: In 2006/07 the charity had an income of £8,000 and a total expenditure of £6,000. Grants were made totalling around £5,000.

Applications: Applications can be submitted directly by the individual or through a social worker, Citizens Advice or other welfare agency.

Correspondent: J A B Buchan, 8 St Helens Croft, Leeds LS16 8JY (01924 465860)

The Mitchell Memorial Fund

Eligibility: Students in higher/further education who live in Rawdon or Horsforth and do not receive assistance from Leeds City Council.

Types of grants: One-off and recurrent grants according to need.

Annual grant total: Income of about £1,500 per year.

Applications: On a form available from the correspondent.

Correspondent: Shafiq Ahmed Sattar, Leeds City Council, Civic Hall, Calverley Street, Leeds, LS1 1UR

Mirfield

The Mirfield Educational Charity

Eligibility: People under the age of 25 who live (or whose parents live) in the former urban district of Mirfield.

Types of grants: 'The policy of the trustees is to apply the income of the charity to schools, youth groups, Scouts, Guides etc. for the benefit of as many qualifying persons as possible rather than to individuals. Applications from individuals are not discouraged but the financial circumstances of the individual and, if applicable, his/her parents will be taken into account.'

Annual grant total: In 2006/07 the charity had assets of £1.4 million and an income of

£48,000. Grants totalled £44,000 of which about £1,000 went directly to individuals.

Applications: In writing to the correspondent. The trustees meet three times a year, in February, May and October.

Correspondent: M G Parkinson, 7 Kings Street, Mirfield WF14 8AW

Rawdon

The Rawdon & Laneshaw Bridge School Trust (Rawdon Endowment)

Eligibility: People under the age of 21 and living in the former urban district of Rawdon.

Types of grants: Grants for people at college or university (typically for books or equipment) and to needy students pursuing education at lower levels, and changing to higher levels of education.

Annual grant total: About £1,000.

Applications: In writing to the correspondent. Grants are awarded annually in October after applications have been invited in the local press during September.

Correspondent: Mrs A M Hargreaves, Park Dale, Layton Drive, Rawdon, Leeds LS19 6QY

Other information: The correspondent also administers the Charity of Francis Layton. This is for the advancement in life of deserving and necessitous Rawdon residents under the age of 21. It was formerly to assist with apprentice fees, but now tends to support other educational purposes. It gives one or two grants a year totalling £100.

Shipley

The Salt Foundation

Eligibility: People who live in the former urban district council of Shipley (Saltaire or Shipley).

Types of grants: The foundation supports local schools and individuals. One-off grants are given to: schoolchildren for books, equipment/instruments and educational outings in the UK; people starting work for equipment/instruments; and people in higher or further education, including mature students and postgraduates, for books, equipment/ instruments and study or travel overseas.

Annual grant total: In 2006/07 grants to organisations totalled £5,000. No grants have been made to individuals in recent years.

Applications: On a form available from the correspondent, it can be submitted either directly by the individual or through their school or college, an educational welfare agency or another third party. Applications should arrive in January or September for consideration in March and October.

Correspondent: Mrs M Davies, Clerk, 17 Springfield Road, Baildon, Shipley, West Yorkshire, BD17 5NA (01274 591 508; email: majoriedavies@ tiscali.co.uk)

Other information: The trustees' first responsibility is the upkeep of the foundation's properties in Saltaire.

Wakefield

Lady Bolles Foundation

Eligibility: People under 21 who live in the county borough of Wakefield, and who are in full-time education.

Types of grants: Grants are given to schoolchildren towards uniforms, other school clothing, fees and educational outings. Students in further and higher education can receive help towards books and fees.

Annual grant total: Grants total about £5,000 a year.

Applications: In writing to the correspondent, for consideration in February and October.

Correspondent: M E Atkinson, The Beaumont Partnership, 67 Westgate, Wakefield, West Yorkshire WF1 1BW (01924 291234; Fax: 01924 290350)

Feiweles Trust

Eligibility: Young artists at the beginning of their career.

Types of grants: One bursary is awarded per year to an artist/s near the beginning of their career, to allow them to work in short residencies in a variety of school contexts.

Annual grant total: Between £10,000 and £12,000 a year.

Applications: In writing to the correspondent, to be submitted directly by the individual. The deadline is January; applications are considered in February/ March.

Correspondent: The Trustees, c/o Yorkshire Sculpture Park, Bretton Hall, Bretton, Wakefield, West Yorkshire WF4 4LG (01924 830642; email: aducation@ysp.co.uk; website: www. ysp.co.uk)

5. NORTH WEST

The Bowland Charitable Trust

Eligibility: Young people in need in the north west of England.

Types of grants: One-off and recurrent grants towards educational character-forming activities for young people.

Annual grant total: In 2006 the trust had assets of £8 million and an income of £1.7 million. Grants made to four individuals totalled £8,000.

Applications: In writing to the correspondent, to be considered at any time.

Correspondent: Ms Carol Fahy, TDS House, Whitebirk Estate, Blackburn, Lancashire, BB1 5TH (01254 290433)

Cockshot Foundation

Eligibility: Children attending any institution in the counties of Cumbria, Lancashire and Greater Manchester.

Types of grants: Grants towards the furtherance of education (including social and physical training).

Annual grant total: In 2006/07 the foundation had an income of £18,000 and a total expenditure of £33,000. Grants are made for welfare and educational purposes.

Applications: In writing to the correspondent.

Correspondent: The Trustees, Belle Isle, Windermere, Cumbria, LA23 I BG (01539 447087; email: cockshotfoundation@belleisle.net)

Crabtree North West Charitable Trust

Eligibility: Young people up to the age of 18 in education in the North West.

Types of grants: One-off according to need.

Annual grant total: In 2006/07 the trust had an income of £20,000 and a total expenditure of £32,000. Grants to individuals have previously totalled around £5,000 to £10,000.

Applications: In writing to the correspondent.

Correspondent: Ian Currie, 3 Ralli Courts, West Riverside, Manchester M3 5FT (0161 831 1512)

Manchester Publicity Association Educational Trust

Eligibility: People aged 16 or over, living in Greater Manchester and the surrounding area, who are already working in or hoping to enter marketing or related occupations or who are studying marketing communications.

Types of grants: Grants ranging between £200 and £500 towards the cost of books or fees for education or training, usually to cover the second half of the year.

Annual grant total: Previously about £9,500.

Applications: On a form available from the correspondent. Applications must be supported by a tutor and are considered on demand.

Correspondent: Gordon Jones, Secretary, 38 Larkfield Close, Greenmount, Bury, Lancashire BL8 4QJ

The Northern Counties Children's Benevolent Society
see entry on page 117

Correspondent: Ms G Mackie, 29a Princes Road, Gosforth, Newcastle upon Tyne NE3 5TT (0191 236 5308)

The Bishop David Sheppard Anniversary Trust

Eligibility: People between the ages of 21 and 49 who live in the Anglican diocese of Liverpool (which includes Southport, Kirkby, Ormskirk, Skelmersdale, Wigan, St Helens, Warrington and Widnes) and who are doing second-chance learning at a college or training centre.

Types of grants: Grants are one-off, about £100 and are made to people in second-chance learning such as access courses and training. Priority is given to those who are unemployed or who have difficulty in finding the money for books, equipment, or uniforms. Grants can be for training purposes to enable applicants to get a job, for example, in order to obtain a HGV licence.

Exclusions: No grants to students who have had no break from their education (or schoolchildren), to people with good vocational qualifications or on degree courses, or to organisations. Grants cannot be given for fees, travel or childcare.

Annual grant total: About £8,000.

Applications: On a form available from the administrator to be submitted directly by the individual at any time. Applications are usually considered in March, May, September and December.

Correspondent: Mrs Jen Stratford, Administrator, St James' House, 20 St James Road, Liverpool, L1 7BY

Winwick Educational Foundation

Eligibility: Children and young people under the age of 25 who live in the parishes of Winwick, Newton St Peter's, Newton All Saints, Emmanuel Wargrave, St John's Earlestown, Lowton St Mary's and Lowton St Luke's.

Types of grants: One-off or recurrent grants for books, equipment and fees. Grants range from £75 to £100.

Annual grant total: About £1,000.

Applications: On a form available from the correspondent. Applications should be submitted in February and March for consideration in April. They can be made directly by the individual or through a third party such as the individual's school, college or educational welfare agency.

Correspondent: A Brown, Clerk, Forshaws Davies Ridgway, 17–21 Palmyra Square South, Warrington WA1 1BW (01925 654221; email: alastair.brown@fdrlaw.co.uk)

World Friendship

Eligibility: Overseas students studying at universities in the diocese of Liverpool. Preference is given to people in the final year of their course. Students from an EU country, or who are intending to stay in the UK at the end of their course, are not usually supported.

Types of grants: One-off grants towards relieving unexpected hardships which have arisen since the start of the course.

Exclusions: Grants are not given to those whose place of study is outside the diocese of Liverpool.

Annual grant total: In 2006 the trust had an income of £12,000 and a total expenditure of £10,000.

Applications: On a form available from the individual's institution. For details of the relevant contact, or to download a form, applicants should view the trust's website.

Correspondent: D E Evans, 19 Carlton Road, Southport, Merseyside, PR8 2PG (website: www.worldfriendship. merseyside.org)

Cheshire

The Sir Thomas Moulson Trust

Eligibility: Students under 25 who live in the villages of Huxley, Hargrave, Tarvin, Kelsall and Ashton in Cheshire.

Types of grants: One-off grants ranging from £100 to £500 to students in further/ higher education towards books, fees/ living expenses and study or travel abroad.

Annual grant total: About £500 to individuals with further monies distributed to organisations.

Applications: In writing to the correspondent. Applications should be submitted directly by the individual and are usually considered in September.

Correspondent: Mrs Julie Turner, Meadow Barn, Cow Lane, Hargrave, Chester CH3 7RU

The Thornton-Le-Moors Education Foundation

Eligibility: People under 25 in full-time education who live in the ancient parish of Thornton-Le-Moors which includes the following villages: Dunham Hill, Elton, Hapsford, Ince and Thornton-Le-Moors.

Types of grants: The trust gives grants mostly to students going to university for books and also to the local youth groups, mainly the guides, brownies, scouts and cubs.

Annual grant total: About £500.

Applications: In writing to the correspondent. Trustees meet twice a year, usually in April and November.

Correspondent: R F Edwards, Trustee, Jesmin, 4 School Lane, Elton, Chester CH2 4LN (01928 725188)

The Verdin Trust Fund

Eligibility: People who live in Northwich and surrounding districts.

Types of grants: Most of the trust's funds are given in the form of prizes to local schools, Young Farmers' Associations and courses, gap years and so on.

Annual grant total: This trust has about £2,000 a year to distribute in grants.

Applications: In writing to the correspondent.

Correspondent: J E Richards, Rose Cottage, 2 Vale Royal Drive, Whitegate, Northwich, Cheshire CW8 2BA

Other information: Grants are also made to organisations.

The Wrenbury Consolidated Charities

Eligibility: People in need who live in the parishes of Chorley, Sound, Broomhall, Newhall, Wrenbury and Dodcott-cum-Wilkesley.

Types of grants: Payments on St Marks' (25 April) and St Thomas' (21 December) days to pensioners and students. Grants are also given for one-off necessities.

Annual grant total: About £7,000.

Applications: In writing to the correspondent either directly by the individual or through another third party on behalf of the individual. The Vicar of Wrenbury and the parish council can give details of the six nominated trustees who can help with applications. Applications are considered in December and March.

Correspondent: Helen Smith, Eagle Hall Cottage, Smeatonwood, Wrenbury, North Nantwich CW5 8HD

Other information: Grants are also given to churches, the village hall and for welfare purposes.

Alsager

The Alsager Educational Foundation

Eligibility: People who live in the urban district of Alsager.

Types of grants: One-off and recurrent grants are given to schoolchildren, college students, undergraduates, vocational students and to individuals with special educational needs for study/travel overseas, books, instruments/equipment and excursions, and also to schoolchildren for uniforms and clothing.

In 2006 grants given ranged from £150 to £1,000 and were awarded for veterinary training, legal practice training and musical instruments and tuition.

Exclusions: Postgraduates and people who do not have a permanent home address in Alsager will not be supported.

Annual grant total: In 2006 a total of £4,500 was given in grants to individuals.

Applications: In writing to the correspondent directly by the individual. Applications are considered four times per year.

Correspondent: Mrs C Lovatt, Secretary, 6 Pikemere Road, Alsager, Stoke-on-Trent ST7 2SB (01270 873680)

Audlem

Audlem Educational Foundation

Eligibility: People in need who live in the ancient parish of Audlem and are under 25 years of age. Preference is given to people who are attending, or have attended a maintained school for at least two years.

Types of grants: One-off and recurrent grants according to need.

Annual grant total: In 2006/07 the trust had an income of £14,000 and a total expenditure of £16,000

Applications: In writing to the correspondent.

Correspondent: Richard Wilkinson, Cheshire County Council, Education Department, County Hall, Chester, CH1 1SQ (01244 602505)

Chester

The Chester Municipal Charities – Owen Jones Educational Foundation

Eligibility: Young people under 25 years of age (i) whose fathers are (or if dead, were at the date of death) a freeman of the City of Chester and a member of one of the City Companies 20 beneficiaries or, (ii) who attend or have attended a school in Chester and who live in the city. Priority is given to those in category (i).

Types of grants: One-off grants of between £100 and £800 are given to schoolchildren for help with uniforms and other school clothing, and to students in further/higher education for books, living expenses and equipment/instruments.

Annual grant total: About £40,000.

Applications: On a form available from the correspondent. Applications should be submitted directly by the individual for consideration in September and October.

Correspondent: Birch Cullimore Solicitors, 20 White Friars, Chester CH1 1XS (01244 321066)

Congleton

The Congleton Town Trust

Eligibility: People in need who live in the town of Congleton (this does not include the other two towns which have constituted the borough of Congleton since 1975).

Types of grants: The principal aim of the trust is to give grants to individuals in need or to organisations which provide relief, services or facilities to those in need. The trustees will, however, consider a grant towards education or training if the applicant is in need. Support can be given in the form of books, tools or in cash towards tuition fees or maintenance.

Annual grant total: In 2007 the trust had an income of £24,000 and a total expenditure of £22,000.

Applications: On a form available from the correspondent, to be submitted directly by the individual or a family member. Applications are considered quarterly, on the second Monday in March, June, September and December.

Correspondent: Ms J Money, Clerk, c/o Congleton Town Hall, High Street, Congleton CW12 1BN (01260 291156)

Other information: The trust also administers several smaller trusts, and has taken over the finances of the William Barlow Skelland Charity for the Poor which has recently been wound up.

Knutsford

Knutsford Educational Foundation

Eligibility: People who live in the urban district of Knutsford and are on courses of higher education or training. There is a minimum age of 18 and maximum age of 24 by 31 August in the year in which the application is being considered.

Types of grants: Grants to help with the cost of books, fees and living expenses, study or travel abroad and assistance with entering a profession or trade. Usually a full grant is only given once to each applicant, although on occasions, a half grant can be made to second-time applicants.

Exclusions: No grants for student exchanges.

Annual grant total: About £1,500.

Applications: On a form available from the correspondent. Completed application forms must be submitted by 24 December. Grants are issued in January.

Correspondent: S D Armstrong, Clerk, Hague Lambert Solicitors, 131 King Street, Knutsford, Cheshire WA16 6EJ (01565 652411)

Warrington

The Police-Aided Children's Relief-in-Need Fund

Eligibility: Children of pre-school or primary school age living in the borough of Warrington and whose families are in financial or physical need. Applications from students of secondary school age and over will be considered in exceptional circumstances.

Types of grants: Vouchers to help with the cost of clothing and footwear. Vouchers are only redeemable at selected retailers in the borough.

Annual grant total: In 2006/07 the fund had an income of £6,800 and a total expenditure of £9,400.

Applications: On a form available from the correspondent.

Correspondent: The Administrator, Warrington Council For Voluntary Services, The Gateway, 89 Sankey St, Warrington, WA1 1SR

Widnes

The Widnes Educational Foundation

Eligibility: People under the age of 25 who have either lived in the borough of Widnes for at least three years or who have attended college there for at least three years.

Types of grants: The foundation mainly focuses on giving grants to help with educational trips and visits. Cash grants can also be given for books and educational outings for those at school. Very occasionally small grants are given to help with school/college fees or to supplement existing grants.

Annual grant total: About £500.

Applications: On a form available from the correspondent. Applications must be supported by a third party, such as senior teachers.

Correspondent: Miss Wendy Jefferies, Halton Borough Council, Municipal Buildings, Kingsway, Widnes, Cheshire WA8 7QF

Wilmslow

The Lindow Workhouse Trust

Eligibility: Children with special educational needs who live in the ancient parish of Wilmslow.

Types of grants: One-off grants of amounts up to £500.

Annual grant total: About £8,000 for welfare and educational purposes.

Applications: In writing to the correspondent at any time. Applications can be submitted either directly by the individual or a family member, through a third party such as a social worker or teacher, or through an organisation such as Citizen's Advice or a school.

Correspondent: Jacquie Bilsborough, 15 Hazelwood Road, Wilmslow, Cheshire, SK9 2QA

Cumbria

The Barton Educational Foundation

Eligibility: People who live in Barton, Yanwath, Pooley Bridge, Martindale or Patterdale.

Types of grants: Recurrent grants ranging between £25 and £100 to students at colleges and universities for help with books, fees and living expenses. Help with the costs of books for school children is also occasionally provided.

Annual grant total: In 2007 the foundation had both an income and total expenditure of £1,200

Applications: Directly by the individual on a form available from the correspondent. Applications are considered in October.

Correspondent: A Wright, 15 Church Croft, Pooley Bridge, Penrith, Cumbria, CA10 2NL (01768486312)

The Brow Edge Foundation

Eligibility: People in need who live in the area of Haverthwaite and Backbarrow, aged between 16 and 25.

Types of grants: Grants for full and part-time students and those starting apprenticeships. Preference will be given to applications for one-off grants.

Annual grant total: In 2007 the foundation had an income of £1,900 and an expenditure of £2,100.

Applications: In writing to the correspondent, directly by the individual. Applicants must state the type of course of study or apprenticeship they are about to undertake. Applications are usually considered in September.

Correspondent: Robert William Hutton, 20 Ainslie Street, Ulverston, Cumbria LA12 7JE (01229 585888; email: gordon@421.co.uk)

The Burton-in-Kendal Educational Foundation

Eligibility: People aged between 16 and 25 years who live in the parishes of Burton, Beetham, Arnside, Storth and Meathop, Ulpha, Holme, Preston and Patrick and are in need of financial assistance. Applicants must have attended a county or voluntary primary school for no less than two years.

Types of grants: Grants ranging between about £10 and £60 a year are made to schoolchildren, college students, undergraduates and vocational students towards fees, study/travel abroad, books, equipment/instruments and maintenance/living expenses. Grants are also made to people with special educational needs.

Annual grant total: In 2006/07 the trust had an income of £2,800 and an expenditure of £2,600.

Applications: On a form available from the correspondent, which should be submitted directly by the individual. Applications are considered in May and October/November and should be received by April and September respectively.

Correspondent: Mrs E M Falkingham, Clerk to the Governors, 7 Hollowrayne, Burton-in-Kendal, Cumbria LA6 1NS (01524 782302; email: liz.falk21@tiscali.co.uk)

The Cartmel Old Grammar School Foundation

Eligibility: People between the ages of 18 and 25 who live in the parishes of Cartmel Fell, Broughton East, Grange-over-Sands, Lower Holker, Staveley, Lower Allithwaite, Upper Allithwaite and that part of the parish of Haverthwaite east of the River Leven.

Types of grants: Cash grants of about £85, usually for up to three years, for students in higher education to help with books, fees/living expenses or study or travel abroad. Help is also given for those studying music and the arts in special cases.

Annual grant total: In 2007/08 the foundation had an income and a total expenditure of around £10,000.

Applications: On a form available from the correspondent, including schools attended, qualifications and place of higher education. Applications are considered in October/November.

Correspondent: Anthony William Coles, Clerk, 2 Rowan Side, Grange-over-Sands, Cumbria LA11 7EQ (01539 534348)

The Mary Grave Trust

Eligibility: People in need aged between 11 and 21 who were born in the former county of Cumberland (excluding those whose parents were resident in Carlisle). Applicants must live, study or have studied (for at least two years, in secondary/further education) in one of the following areas, listed in order of priority: (i) the former boroughs of Workington or Maryport, or (ii) the former borough of Whitehaven, (iii) elsewhere in the former county of Cumberland.

Students in sixth forms, further education colleges, universities and higher education colleges or in the gaps between these stages can all be considered as can those at work, in training or involved through youth organisation activities.

Activities should usually be based abroad but can take place within the UK, providing that they involve a residential element away from home and are beyond the boundaries of Cumbria.

Types of grants: Grants up to about £1,000 to assist in travel overseas which is of educational value.

The trust offers bursaries in two principal areas:

● Activities organised by a school or college, whereupon students/pupils can apply for funding through a teacher or lecturer. The trust states that a major venture in this field is the Educational Cruise which takes place every two years (October 2008, 2010 etc), and can usually take up a large proportion of funding.

● The trust is also keen to encourage applications from post-GCSE students for activities such as field-work trips, work-experience visits and specialist study bursaries for art and music schools, and from further and higher education students for gap year activities and outward bound courses such as Raleigh International.

Exclusions: Funding cannot be given to employees of British Steel or the National Coal Board.

Annual grant total: In 2006/07 the trust had assets of £1.8 million and an income of £60,000. Grants were awarded totalling £45,000, of which 31 grants were given to educational cruise applicants and 69 grants were awarded to independent applicants.

Applications: On a form available from the correspondent, submitted through the individual's school or college or directly by the individual. The trustees require a copy of the applicant's birth certificate and information about his/her financial circumstances. Applications should be received by 30 April, 30 September and 31 January.

Correspondent: The Secretary, Cumbria Community Foundation, Dovenby Hall, Dovenby, Cockermouth, CA13 0PN (01900 825760; email: enquiries@ cumbriafoundation.org)

The Greysouthen Educational Charity

Eligibility: People under 24 who live in Greysouthen or Eaglesfield.

Types of grants: Help with the cost of books, clothing, educational outings, fees and other essentials for schoolchildren. Grants are also available for those at college or university towards books, fees/living expenses, childcare costs and study

or travel abroad. Grants for people starting work will be made for books, equipment/instruments, clothing and travel.

Annual grant total: The trust has both an income and a total expenditure of approximately £2,000 a year consistently.

Applications: In writing to the correspondent either directly by the individual or through his/her school, college or an educational welfare agency. Applications are considered in July/August.

Correspondent: John Chipps, Brunlea, Greysouthen, Cockermouth, Cumbria CA13 0UA (01900 825235)

Kelsick's Educational Foundation

Eligibility: Young people, under the age of 25, who were born or who have lived in Ambleside, Grasmere, Langdale or part of Troutbeck (the Lakes Parish) for at least four years. There is a preference for children/students with special needs.

Types of grants: Grants are given to: (i) schoolchildren towards equipment and educational outings, including study or travel abroad; (ii) students in further or higher education to help with books, equipment, computer hardware and software, maintenance/living expenses, educational outings and study or travel abroad; and (iii) vocational students to help with the cost of books and equipment.

Grants are one-off and recurrent and range from £25 to £3,000.

Exclusions: No grants are made towards maintenance

Annual grant total: In 2006/07 the trust had assets of £5.5 million and an income of £303,000. Grants to individuals totalled £63,000, which were broken down as follows:

● Primary £3,000

● Secondary and further £9,000

● Higher £49,000.

Applications: On a form available from the correspondent for consideration in February, May, August and November, although applications are accepted at any time. Applicants must list detailed costs (with receipts) of the items required. Applications should be submitted directly by the individual, or by a parent/guardian if the applicant is under 18.

Correspondent: P G Frost, Clerk, Kelsick Centre, St Mary's Lane, Ambleside, Cumbria LA22 9DG (015394 31289; Fax: 015394 31292; email: john@kelsick.plus.com; website: www.kelsick.org.uk/)

Lamonby Educational Trust

Eligibility: People who live in the Lamonby area who are under the age of 25.

Types of grants: One-off grants in the range of £20 and £200 to schoolchildren, college students, undergraduates, vocational students including those for clothing/uniforms, study/travel abroad, books, equipment/instruments and excursion. Grants are also made to people starting work and people with special educational needs.

Annual grant total: In 2006/07 the trust had an income of £2,100 and a total expenditure of £2,200.

Applications: On a form available from the correspondent. Applications are considered in October and May.

Correspondent: Lynne Miller, Arbour House, Lamonby, Penrith, Cumbria CA11 9SS (01768 484385)

Silecroft School Educational Charity

Eligibility: People under 25 who were born in the parishes of Whicham, Millom, Millom Without and Ulpha and are moving away from home to continue their education.

Types of grants: Recurrent grants are given for a wide range of educational needs for people at university or college, from books, clothing, equipment and other supplementary awards to foreign travel and other educational visits. However, the trust does not give grants for travel to and from the applicant's place of residence.

Exclusions: Grants are not given for schoolchildren, people starting work or to students who have not moved away from home to continue their education.

Annual grant total: About £2,000.

Applications: On a form available from the correspondent, to be submitted in September for consideration in November. Applications can be made either directly by the individual, or through their school, college or educational welfare agency.

Correspondent: Janet Pinney, Riber, Main Street, Silecroft, Millom, Cumbria LA18 4NU

The Wiggonby School Trust

Eligibility: People who have left school, are under 25 and live in the parishes of Aikton, Beaumont and Burgh-by-Sands, or are former pupils of Wiggonby School.

Types of grants: Grants, usually of around £200, for people engaged in further education or training, including help with fees/living expenses, books, equipment and so on. People starting work may also receive help.

Annual grant total: In 2006/07 the trust had an income and a total expenditure of £24,000.

Applications: Applications are invited annually in answer to an advertisement placed in the Cumberland News in August. They can be made on a form available from the correspondent and are considered in September. Information required includes

place of further study and qualification aimed for.

Correspondent: Mrs M Fleming, Flemsyam, Aikton, Wigton, Cumbria, CA7 0JA

Barrow-in-Furness

The Billincoat Charity

Eligibility: People under 21 who live in the borough of Barrow-in-Furness.

Types of grants: One-off grants towards the cost of education, training, apprenticeship or equipment for those starting work; and books, equipment/ instruments, fees, educational outings in the UK and study or travel abroad for schoolchildren and people in further and higher education. Schoolchildren can also be supported for uniforms or other school clothing.

Annual grant total: In 2006/07 the trust had an income of £8,000 and a total expenditure of £2,200.

Applications: On an application form available from the correspondent to be submitted in December and June for consideration in January and July. Applications can be submitted by the individual or through their school, college, social services or probation service and so on.

Correspondent: Kenneth J Fisher, Glenside House, Springfield Road, Ulverston, Cumbria LA12 0EJ (01229 583437)

Carlisle

The Carlisle Educational Charity

Eligibility: People (or whose parents) who live in the area of Carlisle city (i.e. north and north east Cumbria), aged under 25.

Types of grants: Grants of £50 to £400 are given to: (i) students due to attend full time courses at a university or institution of further education; (ii) graduates undertaking, or wishing to undertake higher studies or obtaining professional qualifications; (iii) students who have to travel in the UK or abroad as part of their course.

Grants are for general educational costs, such as books and equipment.

Annual grant total: In 2006/07 the trust had an income of around £8,000 and a total expenditure of around £7,000.

Applications: On a form available from the correspondent. Applications are considered in March and October and should be submitted by February and September respectively.

Correspondent: Angela Brown, The Civic Centre, Carlisle CA3 8QG (01228 817268; Fax: 01228 817048; email: angelab@carlisle. gov.uk; website: www.carlisle.gov.uk)

Crosby Ravensworth

The Crosby Ravensworth Relief-in-Need Charities

Eligibility: People in need who have lived in the ancient parish of Crosby Ravensworth for at least 12 months.

Types of grants: One-off and recurrent grants. As well as relief-in-need grants, funds can also be given to local students entering university if they have been educated in the parish.

Annual grant total: In 2007 the trust had an income of £11,000 and a total expenditure of £9,000.

Applications: In writing to the correspondent submitted directly by the individual including details of the applicant's financial situation. Applications are considered in February, May and October.

Correspondent: G Bowness, Ravenseat, Crosby Ravensworth, Penrith, Cumbria CA10 3JB (01931 715382; email: gordonbowness@aol.com)

Egton-cum-Newland

Egton Parish Lands Trust

Eligibility: Children and young people in need living in the parish of Egton-cum-Newland. Particular favour is given to parents on low incomes whose children wish to go on educational trips.

Types of grants: One-off and recurrent grants of £100 to £1,000 to schoolchildren for equipment/instruments and excursions and to college and university students for books.

Annual grant total: In 2006/07 the trust had an income of £12,000 and a total expenditure of £7,000. Previously grants have been awarded mostly to organisations.

Applications: In writing to the correspondent. Applications should be submitted in April and October for consideration in May and November. They can be made either by the individual or through his/her school, college or welfare agency, or other third party.

Correspondent: Mrs J Ireland, Clerk, Threeways, Pennybridge, Ulverston, Cumbria LA12 7RX (01229 861405)

Sedbergh

Robinson's Educational Foundation

Eligibility: People below the age of 25 who live in the parish of Sedbergh, with a preference for people who live in Howgill.

Types of grants: One-off grants from £15 to £1,000 are given for a wide range of educational needs not covered by the local education authority. Grants can be given to schoolchildren towards music lessons. Students in further/higher education can receive help for books, fees/living expenses or study or travel abroad.

Annual grant total: In 2006/07 the foundation had an income of £8,900 and a total expenditure of £4,900.

Applications: In writing to the correspondent, either directly by the individual or through a social worker, Citizens Advice, other welfare agency or other third party. Applications are considered in September.

Correspondent: A M Reid, Milne Moser Solicitors, 100 Highgate, Kendal, Cumbria LA9 4HE (01539 729786)

Greater Manchester

The Barrack Hill Educational Charity

Eligibility: People under the age of 21 who live or whose parents live in Bredbury and Romiley.

Types of grants: One-off grants to assist towards educational expenses. Students in full-time and part-time education can receive grants towards books, study or travel abroad and equipment; people in vocational training can be helped with tools, uniform, equipment and so on; and schoolchildren can be given grants towards school uniforms, other school clothing and equipment or instruments.

Annual grant total: In 2006/07 the trust had an income of £8,200 and a total expenditure of £7,400.

Applications: On a form available from the correspondent, usually made available from local libraries towards the end of the school year. Applications are considered in September and October.

Correspondent: J H Asquith, 24 Links Road, Romiley, Stockport, Cheshire, SK6 4HU (0161 430 3583)

The Dorothy Bulkeley & Cheadle Lads' Charity

Eligibility: People under the age of 25 living in the former district of Cheadle and Gatley (as constituted on 30 April 1974) or people who are or who have attended school in the above district.

Types of grants: Grants are given for general educational purposes to schoolchildren, students in further/higher education, vocational and mature students and people starting work. This can include assistance for professional training, apprenticeships and schooling costs. Grants usually range from £500 to £1,000 and are usually given to two or three individuals each year.

Annual grant total: About £1,000.

Applications: On a form available from the correspondent. Applications are considered in November.

Correspondent: Dr Peter Martin Dooley, Secretary, 48 Chorlton Drive, Cheadle, Cheshire SK8 2BG (0161 491 1816; email: p.m.dooley@salford.ac.uk)

The Ann Butterworth & Daniel Bayley Charity

Eligibility: Children and young people aged 25 and under who are of the Protestant religion and live in Manchester.

Types of grants: Grants towards the cost of education, training apprenticeships and so on, including for books, equipment, clothing, uniforms and travel. School and university/college fees are not met.

Annual grant total: In 2006/07 the charity had an income of £3,000. Grants usually total £800.

Applications: The charity stated that it receives more applications than it can possibly support

Correspondent: The Trust Administrator, Gaddum Centre, Gaddum House, 6 Great Jackson Street, Manchester M15 4AX (0161 834 6069; Fax: 0161 839 8573)

The Darbishire House Trust

Eligibility: Women who were born in, reside in or work(ed) in Greater Manchester. Preference is given to professional women who are retraining.

Types of grants: Grants towards the costs of education and retraining, including for books, equipment, clothing, uniforms and travel. A one-off contribution to fees may be considered.

Annual grant total: In 2006/07 the trust had an income of £800 and a total expenditure of £700.

Applications: On a form available from the correspondent which must be completed by a sponsor from an educational establishment.

Correspondent: Ms Shirley Adams, Gaddum Centre, Gaddum House, 6 Great Jackson Street, Manchester M15 4AX (0161 834 6069; Fax: 0161 839 8573; email: sma@gaddumcentre.co.uk)

The Greater Manchester Educational Trust

Eligibility: Young people aged 11 to 18 living within the former Greater Manchester boundary who are attending certain independent schools in the area and have been placed in the top 25% of the entrance exams.

Types of grants: Grants are made for school fees to allow children from low-income families the opportunity of an independent school education. Grants are also available to families who have temporarily fallen on hard times.

Annual grant total: In 2006/07 the trust had assets of £3.5 million and an income of £191,000. Grants were made to 310 pupils totalling just over £1 million.

Applications: On recommendation of the individual's school, including details of income.

Correspondent: The Secretary, Natwest Bank PLC, Trust and Estate Services, 5th Floor, Trinity Quay 2, Avon Street, Bristol BS2 0PT (0117 940 3283; Fax: 0117 940 3275)

Community Foundation for Greater Manchester

Eligibility: People in need who live in Greater Manchester.

Types of grants: Grants are usually one-off. Funds for individuals have included those from the Greater Manchester Sports Fund and the Joshua Short Foundation, for parents of pre-school children who are have autism and live in the borough of Stockport.

Annual grant total: In 2006/07 the foundation had assets of £2.6 million and an income of £5.3 million. Grants to organisations totalled £3.7 million.

Applications: Please visit the foundation's website or contact the foundation for details of grant funds that are appropriate for individuals to apply for.

Correspondent: The Grants Team, Beswick House, Beswick Row, Manchester, M4 4LA (0161 214 0953 (Grants Hotline: 0161 214 0951); Fax: 0161 214 0941; website: www.communityfoundation.co.uk)

Other information: The Community Foundation for Greater Manchester manages a portfolio of grants for a variety of purposes which are mostly for organisations, but there are a select few which are for individuals.

Mynshull's Educational Foundation

Eligibility: Children and young people aged 25 and under who are at school, university or college, on an apprenticeship or attending another educational/training course, except postgraduates. Applicants must be resident or have been born in the city of Manchester and the following adjoining districts: Reddish, Audenshaw, Failsworth, Chadderton, Middleton, Prestwich, Old City of Salford, Stretford, Sale, Cheadle, Heaton Moor, Heaton Mersey and Heaton Chapel.

Types of grants: Grants towards the costs of education, training, apprenticeship and so on, including books, equipment, clothing, uniforms, travel and so on.

Exclusions: School and university/college fees are not usually met.

Annual grant total: About £9,000.

Applications: On a form available from the correspondent which must be completed by a sponsor from the educational establishment.

Correspondent: The Trust Administrator, Gaddum Centre, Gaddum House, 6 Great Jackson Street, Manchester M15 4AX

The Pratt Charity

Eligibility: Women over 60 who live in or near Manchester and have done so for a period of not less than five years.

Types of grants: Grants are given towards education, health and relief of poverty, distress and sickness.

Annual grant total: About £1,000 per year.

Applications: In writing to the correspondent via a social worker.

Correspondent: Anne Hosker, Gaddum Centre, Gaddum House, 6 Great Jackson Street, Manchester M15 4AX (0161 834 6069; email: amh@ gaddumcentre.co.uk)

The Rochdale Ancient Parish Educational Trust

Eligibility: People, preferably but not exclusively under 25, who live in Rochdale, Littleborough, Milnrow, Wardle, Todmorden, Saddleworth and Whitworth and who attend or have attended a school in the area of the ancient parish. Preference is given to schoolchildren with serious family difficulties who have to be educated away from home, and people with special educational needs.

Types of grants: One-off grants to schoolchildren and further and higher education students, including mature students and postgraduates, towards the cost of uniforms or other school clothing, books, equipment/instruments, fees, educational outings in the UK, study or travel abroad and student exchanges. Further and higher education students can

also receive help with maintenance/living expenses and childcare costs. People starting work can also receive financial assistance. Grants are for up to £1,000 each.

Exclusions: No grants to students studying at a level they already hold a qualification in (such as a second degree course) or to people who have received assistance from either the Hopwood Hall College Access Fund or The Rochdale Educational Trust.

Annual grant total: In 2006/07 the trust had an income of £19,000 and a total expenditure of £20,000.

Applications: On a form available from the correspondent; applications can be submitted directly by the individual or through the school/college or educational welfare agency, and are considered in January, March, July and September.

Correspondent: The Clerk, Rochdale Metropolitan Borough Council, Finance Services, PO Box 530, Rochdale, Lancashire, OL16 9DJ

Other information: The trust also has to maintain several cottages that it owns.

Seamon's Moss Educational Foundation

Eligibility: People aged under 25 who live in the ancient townships of Dunham Massey, Bowden and Altrincham.

Types of grants: One-off grants up to a maximum of £250 each.

Exclusions: People must reside in the ancient townships of Dunham Massey, Bowden and Altrincham.

Annual grant total: In 2006/07 the trust had an income of £1,900 and a total expenditure of £840. Grants are made to schools as well as to individuals.

Applications: In writing to the correspondent. Applications should be submitted directly by the individual and are considered in August. Ineligible applications will not be responded to.

Correspondent: R Drake, Secretary, 32 Riddings Court, Timperley, Altrincham, Cheshire WA15 6BG (0161 969 7772)

The Stockport Educational Foundation

Eligibility: People under 25 who live in Stockport and the surrounding area.

Types of grants: Schoolchildren may receive grants for educational outings or school fees. Students in further/higher education can be supported for books, fees/living expenses and study or travel abroad.

Annual grant total: Previously about £1,500.

Applications: In writing to the correspondent, providing the applicant's date of birth, address, educational career to date, course details and costs and financial

situation and resources. Applications are usually considered in April and October.

Correspondent: Anthony Roberts, 32 Sevenoaks Avenue, Stockport, Cheshire, SK4 4AW

Billinge

John Eddleston's Charity

Eligibility: Persons under the age of 25 years in need of financial assistance who live in, or whose parents live in, the parish of Billinge.

Types of grants: One-off grants for educational purposes including social and physical training.

Annual grant total: In 2006 the trust had assets of £1.8 million and an income of £63,000. Previously grants to individuals have totalled around £1,000 a year.

Applications: In writing to the correspondent by the end of March. The annual meeting of the trustees takes place after the end of March.

Correspondent: Graham Bartlett, Parkinson Commercial Property Consultants, 10 Bridgeman Terrace, Wigan, Lancashire, WN1 1SX (01942 7401800)

Other information: The trust gives to both individuals and organisations.

Bolton

The Chadwick Educational Foundation

Eligibility: Schoolchildren and students, under 25 years of age, living in Bolton and, who are in need.

Types of grants: One-off grants of £100 to £250 for text books, uniforms, equipment/ instruments, educational outings in the UK and study or travel abroad. The foundation prefers to support the promotion of education in the principles of the Church of England.

Annual grant total: In 2006 the trust had assets of £50,000 and an income of £103,000. The trust made grants totalling around £3,000 to four individuals.

Applications: Application forms available from the correspondent, to be submitted by the individual in July for consideration in September. Proof of parental income is essential.

Correspondent: Diane Abbott, Secretary, R P Smith & Co, 71 Chorley Old Road, Bolton, Lancashire, BL1 3JA (01204 534421)

The James Eden Foundation

Eligibility: Students in or entering full-time further education at universities or colleges, aged under 25, who are residents of the metropolitan borough of Bolton. Preference is given to people who have lost either or both parents, or whose parents are separated or divorced.

Types of grants: Cash grants of between £400 and £1,500 are given to assist college students and undergraduates with fees, books, equipment/instruments, maintenance/living expenses, educational outings in the UK and study or travel overseas. Parental income is taken into account in awarding grants.

Annual grant total: In 2006/07 the trust had both an income and a total expenditure of approximately £18,000.

Applications: On a form available from the correspondent, to be returned by the individual before September for consideration in October. If an individual has applied previously the trustees are particularly interested to know about his or her progress.

Correspondent: Mrs D P Abbott, R P Smith & Co, 71 Chorley Old Road, Bolton BL1 3AJ (01204 534421; Fax: 01204 535475; email: info@rpsmith. co.uk)

Golborne

The Golborne Charities

Eligibility: People in need who live in the parish of Golborne as it was in 1892.

Types of grants: One-off grants for equipment such as books, school uniforms and instruments, or for excursions. Grants are usually of between £50 and £80, but occasionally of up to £250. They are usually cash payments, but are occasionally in kind.

Exclusions: Loans or grants for the payments of rates are not made. Grants are not repeated in less than two years.

Annual grant total: The trust has both an income and expenditure of around £5,000 consistently, with the majority of expenditure given for welfare purposes and a few grants given for educational purposes.

Applications: In writing to the correspondent through a third party such as a social worker or a teacher, or via a trustee. Applications are considered at three-monthly intervals. Grant recipients tend to be known by at least one trustee.

Correspondent: Paul Gleave, 56 Nook Lane, Golborne, Warrington WA3 3JQ

Other information: Grants are also given to charitable organisations in the area of benefit, and for relief-of-need purposes.

Leigh

The Leigh Educational Endowment

Eligibility: People under the age of 25 who live in the former borough of Leigh, are going on to higher education and have achieved high A-level results.

Types of grants: Grants for students attaining good examination results and proceeding with further training to help with fees and living expenses, books and equipment. Grants are between £250 and £500 per year per student.

Annual grant total: Around £5,000 to about 20 individuals each year.

Applications: Applications should be submitted in September after A-level results are released for consideration in October. Applications must be submitted through the individual's college, which submits a list of suitable applicants for the trustees to choose from.

Correspondent: The Director of Education, Education Department, Progress House, Westwood Park Drive, Wigan WN3 4HH (website: www. wiganmbc.gov.uk)

Rochdale

The Heywood Educational Trust

Eligibility: People who live in the Heywood area or the village of Birch or those attending or who have previously attended a school in the area.

Types of grants: One-off grants for schoolchildren and further and higher education students, including mature students, to help with uniforms or other school clothing, books, equipment/ instruments, fees, educational outings in the UK, study or travel abroad and student exchanges.

Annual grant total: In 2006/07 the trust had an income of £2,000 and total expenditure of £500.

Applications: By the individual on a form available from the correspondent for consideration in February and September. Applications should include confirmation that the student is on the course, and details of academic record, family income, previous awards, LEA awards and student loans.

Correspondent: Committee Services Officer, Rochdale Metropolitan Borough Council, PO Box 39, Rochdale OL16 1LQ

The Middleton Educational Trust

Eligibility: People who live or attend or have attended a school in the area of the former borough of Middleton, Rochdale.

Types of grants: Cash grants for schoolchildren with books, equipment/ instruments, uniforms and other school clothing, educational outings in the UK, study or travel abroad and student exchanges. Grants to students in further and higher education, including mature students, postgraduates and foreign students, also include assistance for fees, maintenance/living expenses and childcare. People starting work can also receive financial assistance. Grants are one-off and are up to £300.

Annual grant total: Up to £5,000 a year.

Applications: On a form available from the correspondent. Applications can be submitted directly by the individual or through the individual's school/college/ educational welfare agency and they are considered twice yearly in April and September.

Correspondent: Michael Garraway, Committee Services, Town Hall, Rochdale OL16 1AB

The Rochdale Educational Trust

Eligibility: People who live, have lived or are studying in the old county borough of Rochdale (excluding Wardle, Milnrow and Littleborough).

Types of grants: Grants to schoolchildren further and higher education students including mature students and postgraduates, and people starting work towards the cost of uniforms or other school clothing, books, equipment/ instruments, fees, maintenance/living expenses, educational outings in the UK, study or travel abroad or student exchanges. Grants range from £50 to £1,500.

Annual grant total: In 2006/07 the trust had both an income of £8,100 and total expenditure of almost £10,000.

Applications: On a form available from the correspondent or as a download from www.rochdale.gov.uk. Applications can be submitted directly by the individual, through the individual's school/college/ educational agency or through another third party such as a social worker. Applications are considered in March, July, September and December.

Correspondent: Rebecca Tomlinson, Rochdale Metropolitan Borough Council, PO Box 530, Floor 7, Telegraph House, Rochdale, OL16 9DJ (website: www. rochdale.gov.uk)

Sale

The Sale Educational Foundation

Eligibility: People who have attended/are attending a secondary school in the former borough of Sale, and whose parents have lived in the borough for at least two years prior to the application.

Types of grants: Grants to students undertaking/about to undertake further or higher education, which may be used for books, equipment and travel. The award is £250 a year for up to three years per student.

All grants are in addition to any award made available by the local education authority.

Annual grant total: In 2006/07 the charity had an income and a total expenditure of £6,700.

Applications: On a form available from the correspondent.

Correspondent: P E F Ribbon, Hon. Secretary, 84 Ashton Lane, Sale M33 6WS

Salford

The Salford Foundation Trust

Eligibility: People in residence in the area of Salford of between 5 and 25 years of age. Priority will be given to applicants who have resided in Salford for a minimum of three years.

Types of grants: The trust will consider requests to fund opportunities that will enable a young person to learn and/or develop new skills or take part in a character building experience or activity. Examples of this could be an item of equipment, an activity or a training course. The trust is keen to hear about the impact the opportunity will have on the applicant and what they hope to achieve from it.

Exclusions: 'Funding will not be considered for the following: driving lessons, childcare costs, higher education course fees, living expenses, remedial intervention i.e. therapies (speech/language/occupational etc), retrospective funding. No consideration will be made on opportunities that have a political or religious focus or should be financed by statutory services.'

Annual grant total: In 2006/07 the trust had an income of £43,000 and made 31 grants totalling £8,300.

Applications: Application forms are available from the trust and can be submitted directly by the individual, a family member, a third party such as a teacher or social worker or through an organisation such as a Citizens Advice or school.

Correspondent: Grants Administrator, 1st Floor, Charles House, Albert Street, Eccles, Manchester, M30 0PW (0161 787 3834; Fax: 0161 787 8555; email: mail@ salfordfoundationtrust.org.uk; website: www.salfordfoundationtrust.org. uk)

Stockport

Sir Ralph Pendlebury's Charity for Orphans

Eligibility: People who have been orphaned and live, or whose parents lived, in the borough of Stockport for at least two years.

Types of grants: Grants for schoolchildren towards the cost of clothing, holidays and books. Grants can be for £5 or £6 a week and recipients also receive a clothing allowance twice a year. The main priority is for relief-in-need (About £16,000 a year).

Annual grant total: Previously about £1,400 a year for educational purposes.

Applications: In writing to the correspondent.

Correspondent: S M Tattersall, Carlyle House, 107–109 Wellington Road South, Stockport, SK1 3TL

Tameside

The Ashton-under-Lyne United Scholarship Fund (The Heginbottom & Tetlow and William Kelsall Grants)

Eligibility: People under the age of 25 who have attended a secondary school in the former borough of Ashton under Lyne or who live, or whose parents live, in the former borough and who will not have any award or grant other than a local education authority or state grant. Applications from residents in Audenshaw, Denton and the area of the former Limehurst Rural District Council will also be considered.

Types of grants: Grants for those who will be attending university, teacher training college or an institution of full-time technical education.

Annual grant total: In 2007/08 the trust had an income of £5,200 and had a total expenditure of £4,700.

Applications: On a form available from the correspondent to be submitted directly by the individual by 30 September for consideration in October.

Correspondent: Scott Littlewood, Finance Officer, Tameside Metropolitan Borough Council, Education and Cultural Services, Council Offices, Wellington Road, Ashton under Lyne OL6 6DL (0161 342 2878; Fax: 0161 342 2619)

Other information: Various grants are administered under this fund. The above refers to The Heginbottom & Tetlow Grants and William Kelsall Grants. There are also two smaller trusts: Thomas Taylor Grant to those studying full-time for a degree or diploma in electrical engineering; and J B Reyner Grants to those attending approved colleges of music.

The Dowson Trust and Peter Green Endowment Trust Fund

Eligibility: People aged under 25 who live in the former borough of Hyde.

Types of grants: Grants to those undertaking approved courses at universities or teacher training colleges.

Annual grant total: The trust has had both an income and expenditure of approximately £600 since 2001.

Applications: In writing to the correspondent. Applications should be submitted by the individual by 30 September for consideration in October.

Correspondent: The Director of Education & Cultural Services, Tameside Metropolitan Borough Council, Room 223, Council Offices, Wellington Road, Ashton Under Lyne OL6 6DL (0161 342 2878; Fax: 0161 342 2619)

Timperley

The Timperley Educational Foundation

Eligibility: Pupils, students or apprentices under the age of 21 and in need, who have a parent resident in the parish of Timperley. Assistance is also given to educational establishments and youth organisations within the parish.

Types of grants: One-off and recurrent grants to meet general expenses for students in further/higher education, including those being instructed in the doctrines of the Church of England. Schoolchildren may receive assistance on the recommendation of the headteacher only.

Annual grant total: In 2007 the foundation had an income of £9,600 and a total expenditure of £9,200. Grants are made to individuals and organisations.

Applications: On a form available from the correspondent, either directly by the individual or, more usually, through the individual's parent/guardian, school, college or educational welfare agency. Applications are usually considered in August prior to the academic year for which support is needed, although this is not always essential. Application forms for new university entrants, however, must be received by 31 August.

Correspondent: P Turner, Clerk to the Trustees, 103 Sylvan Avenue, Timperley, Altrincham, Cheshire WA15 6AD (0161 969 3919)

Tottington

The Margaret Ann Smith Charity

Eligibility: People who live in the urban district of Tottington, as defined on 23 June 1964.

Types of grants: Grants of about £200 to help towards the cost of overseas exchange visits. There is an emphasis on Commonwealth countries.

Annual grant total: About £1,500.

Applications: In writing to the correspondent. Applications should be submitted directly by the individual or through the individual's school/college or an educational welfare agency.

Correspondent: The Clerk, Woodcock & Sons, West View, Princess Street, Haslingden, Rossendale, Lancashire BB4 6NW

Isle of Man

The Manx Marine Society

Eligibility: Young Manx people under 18 who wish to attend sea school or become a cadet.

Types of grants: One-off grants for people about to start a career at sea towards uniforms, books, equipment/instruments and fees.

Annual grant total: About £5,000.

Applications: In writing to the correspondent. Applications are considered at any time and can be submitted by the individual or through the school/college or educational welfare agency.

Correspondent: Capt. R K Cringle, Cooil Cam Farm, St Marks, Ballasalla, Isle of Man IM9 3AG

Lancashire

The Baines Charity

Eligibility: People in need who live in the ancient townships of Carleton, Hardhorn-cum-Newton, Marton, Poulton and Thornton.

Types of grants: One-off grants ranging from £100 to £250. 'Each case is discussed in its merits.'

Annual grant total: In 2007 the charity had an income of £21,000 and a total expenditure of £14,000. Grants are made for welfare and educational purposes.

Applications: On a form available from the correspondent, either directly by the individual, or through a social worker, Citizens Advice or other welfare agency. Applications are considered upon receipt.

Correspondent: Duncan Waddilove, 2 The Chase, Normoss Road, Blackpool, Lancashire FY3 0BF (01253 893459)

The Educational Foundation of John Farrington

Eligibility: People under the age of 25 who live, or have a parent who has lived for at least two years, in any of the following areas: the parish of Ribbleton in the borough of Preston, the parishes of Goosnargh, Grimsargh, Haighton, Longridge, Whittingham and part of Fulwood. Residents in the Ribbleton area will be given preference over the residents in other areas. There is a preference for people with special educational needs.

Types of grants: Help with the cost of books and educational outings for people at school. People starting work can receive grants towards equipment/instruments, fees, childcare and educational outings in the UK. Students in further or higher education may be given help towards books and equipment or instruments. Grants range from £25 to £250.

Grants are also made to help people to develop leadership qualities and social awareness, towards, for instance, leadership courses, community development activities, camping expeditions or any other 'suitable' activity.

Exclusions: Grants are not given where the applicant is already in receipt of a local authority grant. Nor are they intended to cover night-school fees for courses which do not lead to some form of educational progression in a young persons career.

Annual grant total: In 2006/07 the trust had an income of £2,500 and a total expenditure of £600.

Applications: In writing to the correspondent for consideration in March and October. The foundation has a leaflet outlining the format and contents of any application letter. Applications can be either made by the individual or through a school, college, educational welfare agency or other third party.

Correspondent: D V Johnson, 51 The Pastures, Grimsargh, Preston, PR2 5JW (01772 701328)

Fort Foundation

Eligibility: Young people in Pendle Borough and district, especially those undertaking courses in engineering.

Types of grants: One-off grants of £50 to £1,000 to schoolchildren, college students, undergraduates and vocational students for uniforms/clothing, study/travel overseas, books and equipment/ instruments and excursions.

Exclusions: Grants are not made for fees.

Annual grant total: In 2006/07 the trust had assets of £33,000 and a total expenditure of £84,000. Grants to individuals totalled £3,500, with approximately £2,000 given for educational purposes. A further £1,500 was given in welfare grants.

Applications: In writing to the correspondent, directly by the individual. Applications are considered at any time.

Correspondent: E S Fort, Trustee, Fort Vale Engineering Ltd, Parkfield Works, Brunswick Street, Nelson, Lancashire BB9 0SG (01282 440000; Fax: 01282 440046)

Other information: Grants are also made to organisations and small groups, for example, scouts/guides (2006/07 £50,000).

The Harris Charity

Eligibility: People in need under 25 who live in Lancashire, with a preference for the Preston district, who are in further or higher education.

Types of grants: One-off grants of £250 to £1,000 for equipment/instruments, tools, materials and so on.

Exclusions: No grants are available to cover the cost of fees or living expenses.

Annual grant total: In 2006/07 the trust had assets of £3.1 million and an income of £151,000 and a total expenditure of £104,000, of which £6,700 was given in grants to individuals and a further £12,000 given in five loans.

Applications: In writing to the correspondent with information about financial income and outgoings. Applications are considered during the three months after 31 March and 30 September and can be submitted directly by the individual or through a school/ college or educational welfare agency.

Correspondent: P R Metcalf, Richard House, 9 Winckley Square, Preston PR1 3HP (01772 821021; Fax: 01772 259441)

Other information: The charity also supports charitable institutions that benefit individuals, recreation and leisure and the training and education of individuals (£51,000 in 2006/07).

The Khaleque & Sarifun Memorial Trust

Eligibility: People who live in Lancashire (including overseas students studying there).

Types of grants: Grants are made to schoolchildren, further and higher education students and postgraduates towards the cost of uniforms or other school clothing, books, equipment/ instruments and maintenance/living expenses. Foreign students in further and higher education in the UK can also be supported. Grants range from £50 to £1,100.

Annual grant total: The trust gives grants totalling around £1,000.

Applications: In writing to the correspondent directly by the individual with a supporting letter from the individual's school or college. Applications should be submitted in October for consideration in November.

Correspondent: Dr A Zaman, Craigmoor, 121 Manor Road, Darwen, Lancashire, BB3 2SN

Peter Lathom's Charity

Eligibility: People in need living in West Lancashire.

Types of grants: Cash grants according to need.

Annual grant total: In 2007 grants were made to individuals totalling £6,000.

Applications: On a form available from the correspondent, to be submitted by 30 September. Awards in all cases are based on financial need as applications always exceed distributable income.

Correspondent: Mark Abbott, c/o The Kennedy Partnership, 15 Railway Road, Ormskirk, Lancashire L39 2DW (01695 575271)

John Parkinson Charity

Eligibility: People starting work and further and higher education students in need aged under 25 who live in the parishes of Goosnargh, Whittingham and part of Barton.

Types of grants: One-off grants of up to £150 for tools, books, outfits or payment of fees towards entering a profession, trade, occupation or service. People who have to travel outside Lancashire to attend an interview for a further education course or a job interview can receive grants towards travel expenses and living expenses. Students in further or higher education can be given help towards books.

Annual grant total: In 2006 the charity had an income of £5,700 and a total expenditure of £1,500.

Applications: On a form available from the correspondent, to be submitted by the individual's parent or guardian. Applications are considered in May and November.

Correspondent: J Ward, Longtons Farm, Ashley Lane, Goosnargh, Preston, PR3 2EE

The Peel Foundation Scholarship Fund

Eligibility: People in need aged 18 to 25 who live in and around Blackburn. This area is defined as: the borough of Blackburn, the whole borough except the civil parish of North Turton; the borough of Hyndburn, those parts of the former urban districts of Rishton and Oswaldtwistle which are close to the boundary with Blackburn; and the Ribble Valley borough, the civil parishes of Balderstone, Billington, Clayton-le-Dale, Dinckley, Mellor, Osbaldeston, Ramsgreave, Salesbury and Wilpshire.

Types of grants: Awards of £500 to students entering university or other institutions of higher education for first or second degree courses. Candidates must begin their course in the term following the award of scholarships (usually in September), unless excused by the trustees for sufficient cause. Grants are for general student expenses.

Annual grant total: About £2,500.

Applications: On a form available from the correspondent. Candidates must be nominated by the headteacher or principal of the school or college and applicants are called for an interview. Applications are considered in July and August and should be submitted in April and May.

Correspondent: Mrs Catherine Oldroyd, Barnfield, Billinge End Road, Blackburn, BB2 6QB

Superintendent Gerald Richardson Memorial Youth Trust

Eligibility: People under 25 who live within 15 miles of Blackpool Town Hall. There is a preference for people who are physically or mentally disabled.

Types of grants: One-off and recurrent grants are made, typically in the range of £50 to £250. Grants can be made to schoolchildren and further and higher education students to attend character-building courses or training courses in the arts or sports. Grants can also be made to cover the cost of equipment for outdoor courses.

Annual grant total: In 2006/07 the trust had an income of £15,000 and a total expenditure of £11,000. Grants are made to schools, youth organisations and individuals.

Applications: In writing to the correspondent, giving details of the individual's age, the cost of the course and so on. Applications should be submitted at least two months before the amount being requested is required. They are considered bimonthly from September and can be submitted either directly by the individual, or via a third party such as a school/college welfare agency or carer.

Correspondent: D H Leatham, 2 Paddock Drive, Blackpool FY3 9TZ (01253 762090)

Shaw Charities

Eligibility: People in need who live in Rivington, Anglezarke, Heath Charnock and Anderton.

Types of grants: Grants to students on first degree courses for books.

Annual grant total: In 2006/07 the charities had an income of £3,600 and a total expenditure of £3,500.

Applications: On a form available from the correspondent to be submitted for consideration in March and November.

Correspondent: Mrs E Woodrow, 99 Rawlinson Lane, Heath Charnock, Chorley, Lancashire PR7 4DE (01257 480515; email: woodrows@ tinyworld.co.uk)

Other information: The charities also make grants for relief of need.

Tunstall Educational Trust

Eligibility: Young people under 25 living in Burrow, Tunstall and Cansfield.

Types of grants: One-off and recurrent grants according to need. The trust mainly makes travel grants.

Annual grant total: In 2007 the charity had an income of £5,200 and a total expenditure of £4,300. The trust makes grants to individuals and organisations.

Applications: In writing to the correspondent. Trustees meet in June and November to consider applications.

Correspondent: Joyce Crackles, Mill Farm, Burrow, Carnforth, Lancashire, LA6 2RJ (015242 74239)

Bickerstaffe

Bickerstaffe Education Trust

Eligibility: Mainly children and young people resident in the parish of Bickerstaffe or attending Bickerstaffe Voluntary Controlled School.

Types of grants: Grants given according to need

Annual grant total: In 2006/07 the trust had an income of £4,300 and a total expenditure of £6,300.

Applications: In writing to the correspondent.

Correspondent: M W Rimmer, Trustee, Primrose Cottage, Hall Lane, Bickerstaffe, Ormskirk, Lancashire, L39 0EH

Other information: Grants are also made to organisations.

Blackpool

The Blackpool Children's Clothing Fund

Eligibility: Children aged 4 to 16 who live in the Blackpool area and attend an educational establishment there.

Types of grants: Help with providing school clothing for children whose parents cannot afford it. The fund does not give cash grants but letters of authorisation which can be exchanged at designated retailers.

Annual grant total: In 2006/07 the trust had an income of £2,100 and a total expenditure of £6,000.

Applications: In writing to the correspondent, by an education social work service on behalf of the applicant. Individuals in need identified by the local education authority are also considered.

Correspondent: Mr Alan Rydeheard, 96 West Park Drive, Blackpool, FY3 9HU (01253 736812)

The Swallowdale Children's Trust

Eligibility: People who live in the Blackpool area who are under the age of 25. Orphans are given preference.

Types of grants: One-off grants are given to: schoolchildren, college students, undergraduates, vocational students and people starting work, including those for clothes/uniforms, fees, study/travel abroad and equipment/instruments.

Annual grant total: In 2006/07 the trust had assets of £1 million and an income of £32,000. There were 123 relief-in-need grants made during the year totalling £16,000. A further £2,700 was given in 5 educational grants.

Applications: On a form available from the correspondent, with the financial details of the individual or family. Applications must be made through a social worker or teacher. They are considered six times per year.

Correspondent: The Secretary, 145 Mayfield Road, St Annes on Sea, FY8 2DS

Burnley

The Edward Stocks Massey Bequest Fund

Eligibility: People who live in the borough of Burnley.

Types of grants: Whilst consideration will be given to applications for financial assistance with education courses, this is not seen as the primary purpose of the fund which is to assist individuals and voluntary organisations to promote education and projects in the arts, sciences and general cultural activities.

Exclusions: No assistance will be given to applicants in receipt of a mandatory award from their LEA. Other sources of funding must have been explored.

Annual grant total: In 2006/07 the trust had assets of £1.2 million and an income of £40,000. Grants were made totalling £64,000 including £8,000 to individuals.

Applications: On a form available from the correspondent, either directly by the individual or by the secretary or treasurer of an organisation. Applications are considered in April/May.

Correspondent: Saima Afzaal, Burnley Borough Council, Town Hall, Manchester Road, Burnley BB11 1JA

Darwen

The W M & B W Lloyd Trust

Eligibility: People in need who live in the old borough of Darwen in Lancashire. Preference is given to single parents.

Types of grants: One-off and recurrent grants according to need. Grants are made to schoolchildren, college students, undergraduates, vocational students and mature students, including those for uniforms/clothing, books, study/travel abroad, equipment/instruments, excursions and awards for excellence.

Annual grant total: In 2007/08 the trust had an income of £90,000 and made grants totalling £97,000 to individuals and organisations.

Applications: In writing to the correspondent to be submitted either directly by the individual or through a relevant third party. Applications are considered quarterly in March, June, September and December.

Correspondent: The Secretary, The Lloyd Charity Committee, 10 Borough Road, Darwen, Lancashire BB3 1PL (01254 702111)

Leyland

The Balshaw's Educational Foundation

Eligibility: People living in the parish of Leyland.

Types of grants: Help with educational needs including the cost of books, clothing and other essentials for schoolchildren. Grants may also be available for those at college or university.

Annual grant total: In 2006 the trust had an income of £1,900 and a total expenditure of £1,700

Applications: In writing to the correspondent.

Correspondent: J G Demack, 11 Pendlebury Close, Longton, Preston PR4 5YT (01772 612556)

Littleborough

Alexander and Amelia Harvey Scholarship Fund

Eligibility: Students in need under 25 who live or whose parents live in the former urban district of Littleborough.

Types of grants: One-off grants, for instance towards clothing, tools, books, living expenses, fees and overseas travel.

Annual grant total: In 2007 the trust had an income of £1,600 and a total expenditure of £1,300. Previously grants to individuals have totalled around £1,000

Applications: In writing to the correspondent during August and September, for consideration in October. Applications can be submitted either directly by the individual, or through a school/college or educational welfare agency.

Correspondent: Mrs Patricia White, 29 Howarth Street, Littleborough OL15 9DW (01706 378360)

Lowton

The Lowton Charities

Eligibility: People in need who live in the parishes of St Luke's and St Mary's in Lowton.

Types of grants: Help with the cost of books, clothing and other essentials for schoolchildren. Grants are also available for those at college or university.

Exclusions: Grants are not given to postgraduates.

Annual grant total: Grants total about £4,000 a year. About half of grants are given at Christmas for relief-in-need purposes and the rest throughout the year.

Applications: Usually through the rectors of the parishes or other trustees.

Correspondent: J B Davies, Secretary, 10 Tarvin Close, Lowton, Warrington WA3 2NX (01942 678108)

Over Kellett

Thomas Wither's Charity

Eligibility: People under 25 who live in the parish of Over Kellett.

Types of grants: Grants are given to people starting work and apprentices.

Exclusions: Applications from outside the area of Over Kellett will not be considered.

Annual grant total: In 2007 the trust had an income of £5,800 and a total expenditure of £4,300.

Applications: On a form available from the correspondent, which should be submitted on or before 1 May or 1 November each year.

Correspondent: D J Mills, Clerk, 51 Greenways, Over Kellett, Carnforth, Lancashire LA6 1DE (01524 732194)

Preston

The Roper Educational Foundation

Eligibility: People aged 11 to 25, who live in St. Wilfrid's Parish, Preston or who have, for not less than two years at any time, attended a school in the parish.

Types of grants: The trust will consider supporting any educational need, at any educational level.

Annual grant total: In 2007 the foundation had assets of £655,000 with an income of £63,000 and an expenditure of £48,000. The foundation gave bursaries to individuals totalling £1,500.

Applications: On a form available from the correspondent. Applications should be submitted directly by the individual. They are considered in February, July and October.

Correspondent: Mark Belderbos, Blackhurst, Swainson, Goodier, 10 Chapel Street, Preston, PR1 8AY (01772 253841; Fax: 01772 201713; email: mjb@bsglaw.co.uk)

Other information: Grants are also made to voluntary aided Roman Catholic schools in the county borough of Preston.

Rishton

The George Lawes Memorial Fund

Eligibility: People under the age of 21 who live in the township of Rishton.

Types of grants: One-off grants to help schoolchildren and further and higher education students, including mature students, with books, equipment, clothing/uniforms, fees, maintenance/living expenses, educational outings in the UK and study or travel abroad.

Annual grant total: About £500 a year.

Applications: In writing to the correspondent directly by the individual. Applications should be submitted around November/December for consideration in December.

Correspondent: The Trustees, Scaithcliff House, Ormerod Street, Accrington, Lancashire BB5 0PF

Merseyside

The Girls' Welfare Fund

Eligibility: Girls and young women, usually those aged between 15 and 25 years, who were born in Merseyside. Applications from outside this area will not be acknowledged. Preference will be given to those who are pursuing vocational or further education courses rather than other academic courses.

Types of grants: Both one-off and recurrent grants for leisure and creative activities, sports, welfare and the relief of poverty. Grants may be given to schoolchildren and students for uniforms/clothing, college students and undergraduates for uniforms/clothing, study/travel overseas and books, vocational students for uniforms/clothing, books and equipment/instruments and to people starting work for clothing and equipment/instruments. The fund is particularly interested in helping individual girls and young women of poor or deferred education to establish themselves and gain independence. Grants range from £100 to £1,000.

Exclusions: Grants are not made to charities that request funds to pass on and give to individuals.

Annual grant total: In 2007 the fund had both an income and total expenditure of £6,700.

Applications: In writing to the correspondent or by email. Applications can be submitted directly by the individual or through a social worker, Citizens Advice, other welfare agency or college/educational establishment. Applications are considered quarterly in March, June, September and December, and should include full information about the college, course and particular circumstances.

Correspondent: Mrs S M O'Leary, West Hey, Dawstone Road, Heswall, Wirral CH60 4RP (email: gwf_charity@hotmail.com)

Other information: The trust also gives grants to individuals in need and organisations helping girls and young women in Merseyside.

The Holt Education Trust

Eligibility: People in need who are studying on a course of higher education and have lived for most of their life on Merseyside and still have a home there.

The trust concentrates on first degree level courses; academic subjects are given preference. Some grants are given to students reading medicine who have already obtained another first degree.

Most awards are given for full-time study, although applicants who can only study part-time because of family circumstances will be considered.

Types of grants: Grants are single payments ranging from £50 to £300 to help with college or university fees, books, equipment, study trips and, increasingly, with childcare, accommodation and travel.

Annual grant total: Previously grants to individuals have totalled between £10,000 and £12,000.

Applications: On a form available from the correspondent. Applications should be made by those who have already started the relevant course and must be accompanied by a reference from the tutor. They should be submitted before the meetings held in February, July and November. Applications must include details of previous education, family circumstances, funding for the present course and the reason for seeking help.

Correspondent: Roger Morris, Secretary, Holt Education Trust, India Buildings, Water Street, Liverpool L2 0RB (0151 473 4693)

Other information: An explanatory leaflet available from the trust describes current policy in detail as the criteria for applications can vary from year to year. These can be obtained from the correspondent.

The Sheila Kay Fund

Eligibility: People in need living in Merseyside who have a background in the voluntary sector.

Types of grants: One-off and recurrent grants are made ranging between £50 to £300 for people engaged in social, youth and community work (paid or voluntary) who cannot afford the relevant education or training. Priority is given to those who have left school with few, if any, qualifications, and people from minority communities who have experienced difficulties in entering education. Any of the costs of education, including childcare, travel expenses and books, can be considered.

The trust helps people at a wide variety if educational stages, including Higher Education in social work and youth work, Access courses, GNVQ's, GSE's, counselling qualifications, introductory courses to Maths, English and IT, and Community courses such as Credit Union, Playwork and Capacity Building.

Exclusions: No grants for postgraduates.

Annual grant total: In 2006/07 the fund had both an income and a total expenditure of around £80,000, of which £77,000 was distributed in educational grants.

Applications: Applications should be made at least six weeks before the grant is required. Exemptions from this may be made in emergencies. Application forms are available from the correspondent. Applications are considered all year round.

Correspondent: Peter Clark, 60 Duke Street, Liverpool L1 5AA (0151 707 4304; Fax: 0151 707 4305; email: enquiries@skfunding.org.uk)

Other information: As the basic aim of the fund is to promote opportunities for the development of skills for community activists, it also offers education advice.

'Help is also extended to community groups who may want to attend a conference (such as credit unions), or who manage community projects where new legislation has necessitated training for their volunteers, or who wish to stage training events for their local community.'

Community Foundation for Merseyside

Eligibility: People in need who live in Merseyside.

Types of grants: Usually one-off.

Annual grant total: In 2006/07 the foundation had assets of £1.8 million and an income of £6 million. Grants to organisations totalled £4.6 million.

Applications: Please visit the foundation's website or contact the foundation directly for full details of what might be available for individuals.

Correspondent: Mrs Sue Langfeld, C/o Alliance And Leicester, Bridle Road, Bootle, Liverpool, G1R 0AA (0151 966 4604; email: info@cfmerseyside.org.uk; website: www.cfmerseysde.org.uk)

Other information: The foundation administers funds for a variety of purposes, which are mostly for organisations; however there may be a select few that give to individuals.

The John James Rowe Foundation

Eligibility: Girls aged 10 to 24 who live in Merseyside and: (i) have lost one or both parents; (ii) whose parents are separated; or (iii) whose home life is especially difficult.

Types of grants: Assistance is given for those at secondary school, college, university or other institutions of higher education. Grants are made for equipment, clothing, tools, instruments and books to help prepare for, or assist entry into, a profession, trade or calling. Maximum grant is £200. Single payment grants only are given.

Annual grant total: Grants total about £15,000 per year.

Applications: In writing to the correspondent for consideration at any time.

Correspondent: The Clerk, PSS, 18 Seel Street, Liverpool L1 4BE

The Rushworth Trust *see entry on page 72*

Correspondent: The Grants Team, Liverpool Charity and Voluntary Services, 151 Dale Street, Liverpool, L2 2AH

Great Crosby

The Halsall Educational Foundation

Eligibility: Girls who are leaving sixth form education and entering higher education and live or whose parents live in the ancient township of Great Crosby.

Types of grants: One-off towards books, stethoscopes and so on.

Exclusions: Grants are made only to girls living in the ancient township of Great Crosby.

Annual grant total: Small grants to individuals and an annual grant to Halsall School total about £1,000 each year.

Applications: In writing to the correspondent. Applications should be submitted between March and 31 May, including a sae, for consideration in August and September.

Correspondent: Ms Zorina Annette Jones, 8a Cambridge Avenue, Crosby, Merseyside, L23 7XW (0151 924 6082)

Liverpool

The Liverpool Council of Education

Eligibility: Sixth form pupils of Liverpool schools studying for A-levels.

Types of grants: Grants of £50 to £350 for pupils to study overseas or advance their education in other ways.

Annual grant total: Previously about £10,000 each year.

Applications: The correspondent writes to the headteachers of every school with a sixth form in Liverpool at the beginning of each school year, giving details of the trust. Applications should be made in writing and must be supported by a letter of recommendation from the headteacher. The closing date for applications is the last week in January.

Correspondent: Cathy Williams, Revenues and Benefits Service, PO Box 2014, Liverpool, L69 2UT

The Liverpool Friends Scholarship Foundation

Eligibility: Young people in need, who live in Liverpool and are aged between 12 and 18.

Types of grants: There are two types of education grants: (i) Ackworth

Scholarships are given to people attending Friends' School, Ackworth; (ii) General Scholarships are given to people attending any secondary school provided by the Liverpool Education Authority or any other secondary school approved by the governors. The holders of scholarships (and their parents) must be of 'narrow means' and of 'good moral character'.

Exclusions: No grants for private school fees, other than for Friends' School, Ackworth.

Annual grant total: About £1,500.

Applications: In writing to the correspondent, including details of education to date and means. Applicants are personally interviewed.

Correspondent: James Taylor, 21 St Anthony's Road, Blundellsands, Liverpool L23 8TN (0151 236 8211)

The Melling with Cunscough Educational Charity

Eligibility: People in further or higher education who live in the parish of Melling. Priority is given to people under 25, with funds only available to others after these needs have been met.

Types of grants: One-off grants are given to: (i) schoolchildren for help with books, educational outings and maintenance; (ii) people starting work for books, equipment instruments and clothing; (iii) students in further/higher education for books and fees; and (iv) mature students for books and fees.

Annual grant total: Grants total around £4,000.

Applications: In writing to the correspondent, to be submitted by the individual at any time.

Correspondent: Bert Dowell, 29 Woodland Road, Melling, Liverpool L31 1EB (0151 547 3142)

Sefton

The Joseph Harley Bequest

Eligibility: People under 25 who live in Formby.

Types of grants: Grants of up to £250 towards the cost of art, drama, dance, music, natural science, and physical, mental and spiritual training. Grants are only awarded for projects for which assistance is not available from public funds.

Annual grant total: The trust has previously had an income of around £3,000. Grants usually total about £1,500.

Applications: On a form available from the correspondent. The trustees usually meet twice yearly in July and February.

Correspondent: Director of Children's Services, Sefton Borough Council,

Education Department, Bootle Town Hall, Oriel Road, Bootle, Liverpool L20 7AE (0151 934 3361)

Other information: The following trusts, which each have between about £200 and £400 in total to be given in grants, are also administered by Sefton Borough Council. For further information please contact the Director of Finance.

(i) The Thomas Davies Scholarship

People under the age of 25 who live in Bootle and are studying engineering and electricity, towards college and university fees.

(ii) The Simon Mahon Memorial Scholarships

Male students over school leaving age who, or whose parents, have lived in Bootle for at least two years, towards full-time further or higher education.

(iii) The Kate Rimmer Trust

People who live in Southport who were educated at a school within the former county borough boundary are eligible to receive grants towards university fees or to supplement existing grants.

(iv) The Matthew Turbitt Trust Fund

People who live in Southport who were educated at a school within the former county borough boundary. Grants to help with university fees or to supplement existing grants.

St Helens

The Rainford Trust

Eligibility: People in need who are normally resident in the borough of St Helens.

Types of grants: One-off and recurrent grants ranging from £100 to £750 are paid directly to the college or other third party organisation. Grants can be for schoolchildren for equipment/instruments, fees, maintenance/living expenses and educational outings in the UK. Further and higher education students and mature students can receive grants for books, equipment/instruments, fees, childcare and educational outings in the UK.

Annual grant total: In 2006/07 the trust had an income of £220,000 and a total expenditure of £160,000. Around £1,000 to £2,000 is given to individuals each year. Grants are mostly made to organisations.

Applications: In writing to the correspondent, for consideration throughout the year. Applications can be made directly by the individual, or through his or her school, college or educational welfare agency. The trust sends out a questionnaire, if appropriate, after the application has been made.

Correspondent: William H Simm, Secretary, c/o Pilkington plc, Prescot Road, St Helens, Merseyside WA10 3TT

(01744 20574; email: rainfordtrust@ btconnect.com)

Wirral

The Lower Bebington School Lands Foundation

Eligibility: People over 18 who live in Lower Bebington; other candidates cannot be considered.

Types of grants: Recurrent grants ranging from £200 to £300 for students in higher/ further education to help with the cost of books and fees/living expenses, and for mature students towards books, travel and fees.

Annual grant total: About £1,000.

Applications: By August each year, on a form available from the correspondent. Applications may be considered at other times if funds are available. Each application is considered on its merit.

Correspondent: S R Lancelyn Green, Poulton Hall, Bebington, Wirral, CH63 9LN

The Thomas Robinson Charity

Eligibility: People in need who live in Higher Bebington.

Types of grants: One-off grants in the range of £50 to £500.

Annual grant total: About £1,000.

Applications: In writing to: The Vicar, Christ Church Vicarage, King's Road, Higher Bebington, Wirral CH43 8LX. Applications can be submitted directly by the individual or a family member, through a social worker, or a relevant third party such as Citizen's Advice or a school. They are considered at any time.

Correspondent: Charles F Van Ingen, 1 Blakeley Brow, Wirral, Merseyside CH63 0PS

6. MIDLANDS

The Beacon Centre for the Blind

Eligibility: People who are registered blind or partially sighted and live in the metropolitan boroughs of Dudley (except Halesowen and Stourbridge), Sandwell and Wolverhampton, and part of the South Staffordshire District Council area.

Types of grants: One-off grants up to a maximum of £250 for specific items or improvements to the home.

Annual grant total: In 2006/07 the trust had assets of £4 million, an income of £2.3 million and a total expenditure of £2.2 million. In previous years a small number of grants have been made to individuals.

Applications: In writing to the correspondent stating the degree of vision and age of the applicant, and their monthly income and expenditure. Applications can be submitted through a social worker or a school and are considered throughout the year.

Correspondent: Chief Executive, Beacon Centre for the Blind, Wolverhampton Road East, Wolverhampton WV4 6AZ (01902 880111; Fax: 01902 886795; email: enquiries@beacon4blind.co.uk; website: www.beacon4blind.co.uk)

The Birmingham & Three Counties Trust for Nurses

Eligibility: Nurses on any statutory register, who have practiced or practice in the city of Birmingham and the counties of Staffordshire, Warwickshire and Worcestershire.

Types of grants: One-off grants up to £300 per annum to nurses taking post-registration courses (post-basic nurse training or back-to-nursing course). Grants are made towards books, travel and/or fees.

Annual grant total: In 2006/07 the trust had assets of £338,000 and an income of £16,000. There were two holiday and educational grants made totalling £800.

Applications: On a form available from the correspondent to be submitted directly by the individual. Applications are considered at any time.

Correspondent: Mrs Ruth Adams, Hon. Secretary, 26 Whitnash Road, Leamington Spa, Warwickshire CV31 2HL (01926 743660; email: ruthmadams_45@msn.com)

Other information: Grants were made to 62 individuals totalling £18,000. The majority of grants were made tor welfare purposes.

Burton Breweries Charitable Trust

Eligibility: Children and young people aged 11 to 25 who are involved in activities which build character and develop/improve skills or qualifications. People will only be considered who live, or are in full-time education, in Burton and the East Staffordshire and South Derbyshire district (including a small area of north west Leicestershire). 'The trustees recognise that some individuals are disadvantaged, through no fault of their own, and priority support will be given to undertake training which leads to personal development for such individuals to help them manage their lives more effectively.'

Types of grants: One-off grants ranging from £100 to £500. Grants are only given for extra curricular activities.

Exclusions: No support for education where there is provision by the state and grants will not be made for higher or university education.

Annual grant total: In 2006/07 the trust had assets of £1 million and an income of £39,000. Grants to 27 individuals totalled £4,000, which included £7,000 in total support costs.

Applications: In writing to the correspondent. Awards for the benefit of individuals will not be made direct but will be made, in general, via organisations with a significant youth membership and will normally take the form of a one-off sponsorship for a person nominated by the organisation to the trustees.

The trustees meet in February, June and October and applications should be sent by January, May and September. A copy of the trust's guidelines are available on request.

All applicants are requested to view the website and the current terms and conditions before applying for support.

Correspondent: Brian Edward Keates, Secretary to the Trustees, Gretton House, Waterside Court, Third Avenue, Centrum 100, Burton-on-Trent, Staffordshire DE14 2WQ (01283 740600; Fax: 01283 511899; email: info@burtonbctrust.co.uk; website: www.burtonbctrust.co.uk)

Other information: Grants are also made to organisations.

The Francis Bernard Caunt Education Trust

Eligibility: People aged between 16 and 25 who are, or whose parents or guardians are, resident within a 12 mile radius of Newark on Trent Parish Church to pursue further or higher education.

Types of grants: Grants and loans.

Annual grant total: In 2006/07 the trust had assets of £1.3 million, an income of £51,000 and made grants totalling £30,000.

Applications: In writing to the correspondent.

Correspondent: J D Kitchen, Larken & Co. , 10 Lombard Street, Newark, Nottinghamshire, NG24 1XE

The Charities of Susanna Cole & Others

Eligibility: Quakers in need who live in parts of Worcestershire and most of Warwickshire and are 'a member or attender of one of the constituent meetings of the Warwickshire Monthly Meeting of the Society of Friends'. Preference is given to younger children (for education).

Types of grants: One-off and recurrent grants for education or re-training.

Annual grant total: In 2007 the charity had an income of £13,000 and a total expenditure of £8,400. Grants are made for welfare and educational purposes.

Applications: In writing to the correspondent via the overseer of the applicant's Quaker meeting. Applications should be received by early March and October for consideration later in the same months.

Correspondent: The Secretary, 19 Oak Tree House, 152 Oak Tree Lane,

Bournville, Birmingham, B30 1TU
(0121 471 4064)

Melton Mowbray Building Society Charitable Foundation

Eligibility: People in need who live in Leicestershire, Lincolnshire, Nottinghamshire and Rutland.

Types of grants: One-off grants, for example, to schoolchildren for books, equipment/instruments and excursions, to college students and undergraduates for books and to vocational students for study/travel abroad. Other requests will be considered.

Exclusions: No grants are made for circular appeals, for projects of a high capital nature or tuition fees.

Annual grant total: About £3,000 in relief-in-need and educational grants.

Applications: In writing to the correspondent to be submitted either directly by the individual or a family member, through a third party such as a social worker or teacher, or through an organisation such as Citizens Advice or a school. Applications should include details of the cash value sought, the nature of the expense, the reason for application and the location of the applicant. Applications are considered at meetings held on a quarterly basis.

Correspondent: Miss M D Swainston, Leicester Road, Melton Mowbray, LE13 0D3 (01664 414141; Fax: 01664 414040; email: m.swainston@mmbs.co.uk)

Other information: Grants may also be given to organisations for education, disability, medical needs and safer communities.

Thomas Monke's Charity

Eligibility: Young individuals between the ages of 17 and 21 who live in Austrey in Warwickshire and Mersham, Shenton and Whitwick in Leicestershire.

Types of grants: One-off and recurrent grants in the range of £100 to £500 to college students, undergraduates, vocational students and people starting work for books and equipment/instruments. Vocational students and people starting work can receive grants for fees.

Exclusions: Expeditions, scholarships and university course fees are not funded.

Annual grant total: About £1,500 to individuals for educational and welfare purposes.

Applications: Application forms are available from the correspondent and should be submitted directly by the individual before 31 March, in time for the trustees' yearly meeting held in April.

Correspondent: C P Kitto, Steward, 20 St John Street, Lichfield, Staffordshire

WS13 6PD (01543 262491; Fax: 01543 254986)

The Newfield Charitable Trust

Eligibility: Girls and women (under 30) who are in need of care and assistance and live in Coventry or Leamington Spa.

Types of grants: Grants towards school uniforms and other school clothing, educational trips, books and childcare costs. Most grants are under £500.

Exclusions: No grants for postgraduate education.

Annual grant total: In 2006/07 the trust had assets of £1.4 million, an income of £53,000 and made grants totalling £34,000.

Applications: Write to the correspondent for an application form. Applications are accepted from individuals or third parties e.g. schools, social services, Citizens Advice etc. A letter of support/reference from someone not a friend or relative of the applicant (i.e. school, social services etc.) may be required. Details of income/expenditure and personal circumstances should also be given.

Applications are considered eight times a year.

Correspondent: D J Dumbleton, Clerk, Rotherham & Co. Solicitors, 8–9 The Quadrant, Coventry CV1 2EG (024 7622 7331; Fax: 024 7622 1293; email: d.dumbleton@rotherham-solicitors.co.uk)

The Norton Foundation

Eligibility: Young people under 25 who live in Birmingham or Warwickshire and are in need of care, rehabilitation or aid of any kind, 'particularly as a result of delinquency, deprivation, maltreatment or neglect or who are in danger of lapsing or relapsing into delinquency'.

Types of grants: One-off grants of up to £500. Recent grants have been given to school children and further and higher education students for school clothing, books, equipment, instruments, fees, maintenance and living expenses and educational outings in the UK.

Annual grant total: In 2006/07 the trust had assets of £4.2 million and an income of £160,000. Grants were made totalling £81,000, of which £28,000 was given in individual grants, £21,000 was awarded in discretionary grants and the remaining £31,000 was given to institutions. Grants to individuals were distributed as follows:

Type	No.	
Clothing	91	£8,000
Education and training	48	£7,000
Household	103	£13,000
Holidays	4	£1,000

Applications: By letter which should contain all the information required as detailed in the guidance notes for applicants. Guidance notes are available

from the correspondent or the website. Applications must be submitted through a social worker, citizens advice bureau, probation service, school or other welfare agency. They are considered quarterly.

Correspondent: The Correspondent, PO Box 10282, Redditch, Worcestershire B97 9ZA (01527 544446; email: correspondent@nortonfoundation.org; website: www.nortonfoundation.org)

Sir John Sumner's Trust *see entry on page 83*

see entry on page 83

Correspondent: The Secretary to the Trustees, No. 1 Colmore Square, Birmingham, B4 6AA

The Anthony & Gwendoline Wylde Memorial Charity

Eligibility: People in need with a preference for residents of Stourbridge (West Midlands) and Kinver (Staffordshire).

Types of grants: One-off grants in the range of £50 and £500 are given to college students and undergraduates for clothing, fees, books, equipment/instruments, maintenance/living expenses and excursions.

Exclusions: No grants towards bills or debts.

Annual grant total: In 2006/07 the charity had assets of £951,000, an income of £45,000 and made grants totalling £37,000. Donations are made to organisations and individuals.

Applications: In writing to the correspondent. Applications can be submitted directly by the individual or a family member and are considered on an ongoing basis.

Correspondent: Mr D J Nightingale, Clerk, Blythe House, 134 High Street, Brierley Hill, West Midlands DY5 3BG (01384 342100)

Derbyshire

Coke's Educational Charity

Eligibility: People under 25 who live in the parishes of Alkmonton, Hollington, Hungry Bently, Longford and Rodsley.

Types of grants: One-off and recurrent grants for educational purposes.

Annual grant total: In 2006 the trust had an income of £3,200 and a total expenditure of £3,600. Grants in previous years have totalled about £2,000.

Applications: In writing to the correspondent.

Correspondent: E R Hill, Clerk to the Trustees, Old Orchard, Longford

shbourne, Derbyshire DE6 3DR
)1335 330472)

The Dronfield Relief-in-Need Charity

Eligibility: People under 25 who live in the ecclesiastical parishes of Dronfield, Holmesfield, Unstone and West Handley.

Types of grants: One-off grants up to a value of £100 are given, including those for social and physical training.

Annual grant total: This charity gives around £1,000 in grants each year.

Applications: In writing to the correspondent though a social worker, doctor, member of the clergy of any denomination, a local councillor, Citizens Advice or other welfare agency. The applicants should ensure they are receiving all practical/financial assistance they are entitled to from statutory sources.

Correspondent: Dr A N Bethell, Ramshaw Lodge, Crow Lane, Unstone, Dronfield, Derbyshire S18 4AL (01246 413276)

Other information: Grants are also given to local organisations.

The Hallowes & Hope Educational Foundation

Eligibility: People under 25 who live in the ecclesiastical parishes of Mugginton and Kedleston. Preference is given to people with serious family difficulties or special educational needs.

Types of grants: One-off grants of up to £300 for (i) books and educational outings for schoolchildren; (ii) books, fees and living expenses for students in further/higher education; and (iii) books, equipment, clothing and travel for people starting work.

Annual grant total: Approximately £1,000 is available each year.

Applications: Applications should include details of need and can be submitted to the correspondent by the individual, through a school/college or educational welfare agency or other third party or parent and are usually considered in December or when necessary.

Correspondent: A J Naylor, Rock House Farm, Dalbury Lees, Ashbourne, Derbyshire DE6 5BS (01332 824277)

Hilton Educational Foundation

Eligibility: Young people aged under 25 in further or higher education who live, or whose parents live, in Hilton and Marston on Dove.

Types of grants: One-off grants, usually £100 to £150, towards books and/or equipment needed for studies.

Annual grant total: In 2007 the foundation had an income of £8,800 and a total expenditure of £11,800. Previously grants have been divided as follows: £1,000

to schools, £350 to the playgroup and £3,700 to individuals.

Applications: In writing to the correspondent directly by the individual. Applications should be submitted in March and October, for consideration in the same month.

Correspondent: Sue Cornish, 6 Willow Brook Close, Hilton, Derby, DE65 5JE

The Risley Educational Foundation

Eligibility: People under 25 who live in the parishes of Breaston, Church Wilne, Dale Abbey, Draycott, Hopwell, Risley, Sandiacre or Stanton-by-Dale.

Types of grants: Grants of £150 for books, equipment, educational travel and promoting the instruction of Church of England doctrines. People on music and arts courses can be supported. Grants are also given to schools.

Annual grant total: In 2006/07 the foundation had net assets of £720,000, an income of £51,000 and a total expenditure of £31,000. The foundation gave scholarships and grants to individuals totalling £13,000.

Applications: On a form available from the correspondent. Applications are considered on a quarterly basis.

Correspondent: The Clerk to the Trustees, 27 The Chase, Little Eaton, Derby, DE21 5AS

Scargill's Educational Foundation

Eligibility: People under the age of 25 who live in the parishes of West Hallam, Dale Abbey, Mapperley and Stanley (including Stanley Common).

Types of grants: The main beneficiary of the charity is Scargill Church of England Primary School. Priority is also given to three other schools in the area. After that, help is available for groups and also for individuals for the following purposes:

(i) Grants, usually up to about £45, for sixth form pupils to help with books, equipment, clothing or travel.

(ii) Grants, usually up to about £175, to help with school, college or university fees or to supplement existing grants.

(iii) Grants to help with the cost of books and educational outings for schoolchildren.

(iv) For the study of music and other arts and for educational travel.

Annual grant total: Around £8,000 to £10,000 is given in educational grants to individuals each year.

Applications: On a form available from the correspondent. The foundation places advertisements in August, and the formal closing date is 29 September, although

applications after this date will be considered if funds permit.

Correspondent: S F Marshall, Clerk, 10-11 St James Court, Friar Gate, Derby DE1 1BT (01332 291431; email: stephen. marshall@robinsons-solicitors.co.uk)

The Stanton Charitable Trust

Eligibility: People at any stage or level of their education, undertaking study of any subject who are in need and live near Staveley Works in Chesterfield, Derbyshire, namely Staveley, Brimington, Barrowhill, Hollingwold and Inkersall.

Types of grants: Grants can be given towards maintenance/living expenses, equipment/instruments and excursions.

Annual grant total: This trust has an annual income of around £2,000.

Applications: In writing either directly by the individual or a family member, or through an organisation such as Citizens Advice or a school. Applications should state the specific amount for a specific item.

Correspondent: Clive Turner, Saint-Gobain Pipelines plc, Lows Lane, Stanton-by-Dale, Ilkeston, DE7 4QU

Other information: Grants are also made to schools, churches, scouts, guides and local fundraising events.

Ault Hucknall

The Hardwick Educational Charity

Eligibility: People aged between 16 and 24, inclusive, whose parent(s) live in the civil parish of Ault Hucknall.

Types of grants: Help with the cost of books for students in further/higher education and with the cost of books, equipment and instruments for people starting work.

Exclusions: Grants are not available for student exchanges, maintenance, fees or mature students.

Annual grant total: Both income and expenditure usually total around £1,200 a year, most of which is allocated to grants.

Applications: In writing to the correspondent. Applications are considered in April and October.

Correspondent: Mrs C E Hitch, Stainsby Mill Farm, Heath, Chesterfield, Derbyshire S44 5RW

Buxton

The Bingham Trust

Eligibility: People in need, primarily those who live in Buxton. Most applicants from outside Buxton are rejected unless there is a Buxton connection.

Types of grants: One-off grants ranging from £200 to £1,000. Grants are made to individuals for a wide variety of needs, including further education.

Exclusions: No grants are made for higher education study.

Annual grant total: In 2006/07 the trust had assets of £2.4 million and an income of £101,000. The trust gave approximately £8,000 in grants to individuals.

Applications: In writing to the correspondent in March, June, September or December for consideration in the following months. Applications should be submitted through a third party such as a social worker, Citizens Advice, doctor or minister.

Correspondent: R Horne, Trustee, Blinder House, Flagg, Buxton, Derbyshire SK17 9QG (01298 83328; email: binghamtrust@aol.com)

Other information: The trust also gives to organisations (£66,000).

Derby

The Derby City Charity

Eligibility: People under 25 who live in the city of Derby and are in need.

Types of grants: Grants for education, training, apprenticeships, and for equipment for those starting work.

Exclusions: Assistance is not given where other funds are available or towards books or fees for pupils and students if the LEA already has a scheme covering such items.

Annual grant total: In 2006/07 the charity had both an income and expenditure of approximately £4,000. About £2,000 is given in grants each year. At least 5% of the trust's grant total must be used for educational purposes; the rest is used for welfare grants.

Applications: On a form available from the correspondent, on written request.

Correspondent: The Director of Corporate Services, Derby City Council, The Council House, Corporation Street, Derby DE1 2FS (01332 293111)

Holmesfield

The Holmesfield Educational Foundation

Eligibility: People living in the parish of Holmesfield, under the age of 25.

Types of grants: Probably help with the cost of books, clothing and other essentials for schoolchildren. Grants may also be available for those at college or university.

Annual grant total: In 2006 the trust had both an income and a total expenditure of

approximately £4,000. Grants to individuals usually total about £2,500.

Applications: In writing to the correspondent.

Correspondent: Mrs Doreen Bertram, 88 Main Road, Holmesfield, Dronfield, Derbyshire S18 7WT

Matlock

The Ernest Bailey Charity

Eligibility: People in need who live in Matlock (this includes Bonsall, Darley Dale, South Darley, Tansley, Matlock Bath and Cromford).

Types of grants: Most applications have been from local groups, but individuals in need and those with educational needs are also supported. Educational grants are one-off and generally of around £100 to £200. Grants are given to students in further/higher education towards books, fees, living expenses and study or travel abroad. Mature students can apply towards books, travel, fees or childcare. People with special educational needs are considered. Each application is considered on its merits.

Annual grant total: In 2006/07 the trust had an income of £7,600 and a total expenditure of £8,100.

Applications: On a form available from the correspondent. Applications can be submitted directly by the individual and/or can be supported by a relevant professional. They should be returned by the end of September for consideration and award in October. Applications should include costings (total amount required, funds raised and funds promised). Previous beneficiaries may apply again, with account being taken of assistance given in the past.

Correspondent: Head of Corporate Services, Derbyshire Dales District Council, Town Hall, Matlock, Derbyshire DE4 3NN (01629 761100; email: brian.evans@derbyshiredales.gov.uk)

Spondon

The Spondon Relief-in-Need Charity

Eligibility: People in education who live in the ancient parish of Spondon within the city of Derby.

Types of grants: Grants of amounts up to £500 are made to schoolchildren, college students, undergraduates and mature students, including those towards uniforms/clothing, study/travel abroad, books, equipment/instruments, excursions, awards for excellence and childcare.

Exclusions: This grant is not intended to supplement an LEA grant.

Annual grant total: In 2007 the trust had an income of £23,000 and a total expenditure of £13,000. Grants are made for educational and welfare purposes.

Applications: On a form available from the correspondent to be submitted either directly by the individual or a family member, through a third party such as a social worker or through an organisation such as Citizens Advice or a school. Each form must be accompanied by a letter of support from a sponsor such as a doctor, health authority official, social worker, city councillor, clergyman, headteacher, school liaison officer, youth leader or probation officer. The sponsor must justify the applicant's need. The latter is particularly important. The applicant should provide as much information on the form as possible. It is better to ask for a visit by a trustee if possible.

The trustees meet quarterly.

Correspondent: Richard J Pooles, Secretary and Treasurer, PO Box 5073, Spondon, Derby, DE21 7ZJ (01332 669879; email: info@spondonreliefinneedcharity.org; website: www.spondonreliefinneedcharity.org/)

West Hallam

The Foundation of Ann Powtrell

Eligibility: Students under the age of 25 who live, or whose parents live, in the parish of West Hallam.

Types of grants: Grants of up to £250 have been given for apprentices and educational trips, for instance, Duke of Edinburgh Awards and a trip to a world scout jamboree in Chile.

Annual grant total: In 2006/07 the trust had an income of £13,000 and a total expenditure of £8,300. Grants are made to organisations and individuals.

Applications: In writing to the correspondent.

Correspondent: Peter Briggs, 12 High Lane East, West Hallam, Ilkeston, Derbyshire DE7 6HW

Herefordshire

The Hereford Society for Aiding the Industrious

Eligibility: People in need who live in Herefordshire, with preference for Hereford City and its immediate environs. Applicants may be undertaking primary, secondary, further or higher education, non-vocational training or vocational training or re-training, in most subjects.

Types of grants: Normally one-off grants ranging between £50 and £1,000 and interest-free loans occasionally. Grants can be made towards: schoolchildren for educational outings; people starting work towards books and equipment/instruments; students in further/higher education towards books, fees and living expenses; and mature students towards books, travel, fees and childcare. Grants are rarely given towards gap year expeditions.

Annual grant total: In 2006/07 the trust had assets of £98,000 and an income of £123,000. Grants to individuals totalled £3,700, of which approximately £1,000 was spent on Christmas gifts for elderly residents and £2,700 was spent on 12 educational grants ranging from £70 to £600.

Applications: In writing to the correspondent. If eligible, an application form will be sent and the applicant will probably be asked to attend an interview. Grants are rarely given directly to the applicant; instead they are given to the bookseller, college and so on. The trust has stated that applications should be 'precise' and 'honest'. Applications are considered every month.

Correspondent: R M Cunningham, 8 Venns Close, Bath Street, Hereford HR1 2HH (01432 274014)

Other information: The trust also makes grants to organisations.

The Herefordshire Community Foundation

Eligibility: People in need who live in Herefordshire.

Types of grants: One-off and recurrent grants according to need.

Annual grant total: In 2006/07 the foundation had assets of £169,000 and both an income and a total expenditure of approximately £419,000. About £6,000 is given a year to individuals.

Applications: In writing to the correspondent.

Correspondent: David Barclay, Director, The Fred Bulmer Centre, Wall Street, Hereford, HR4 9HP (01432 272550)

Other information: Grants are also made to organisations (£366,000 in 2006/07).

The Herefordshire Educational Charity

Eligibility: People under the age of 25 who live in Herefordshire.

Types of grants: Grants in the range of £100 – £150 to school pupils and students in colleges, universities and so on, to help with books, equipment, clothing or travel. Help is also available towards the cost of education, training, apprenticeship, books or equipment for those starting work.

Annual grant total: The charity usually gives between £1,000 and £2,000 a year in grants to individuals.

Applications: On a form available from the correspondent.

Correspondent: Andrea Franklin, Herefordshire Council, Legal Department, 35 Hafod Road, Hereford, HR1 1SH

Jarvis Educational Foundation

Eligibility: People who live the parishes of Staunton-on-Wye, Bredwardine and Letton in Herefordshire.

Types of grants: One-off grants can be given: to individuals at secondary school, university or college where education authority support is not available, to provide outfits, clothing, tools, instruments or books to help people enter a trade, profession or calling on leaving education; and to enable such people to travel to pursue their education. Grants can range from £100 to £1,000.

Annual grant total: In 2006 the foundation had assets of £770,000 and an income of £35,000. Grants to individuals totalled only £1,500, as the accounts stated that the foundation is still allocating the majority of its expenditure to a local school. It was also commented in previous accounts that the trust was preparing to review its assets in order to increase the funding available in donations in future years.

Applications: In writing to the correspondent for consideration at any time.

Correspondent: The Charity Clerk, 4 Church Street, Hay-on-Wye, Hereford, HR3 5DQ (01497 821023; email: bettymchay@hotmail.com)

The Emma Russell Educational Foundation

Eligibility: People under 25 who live in the parishes of Ledbury Rural and Wellington Heath.

Types of grants: Grants to help people with expenses at university and those undertaking apprenticeships and training generally.

Annual grant total: About £700 is distributed each year.

Applications: On a form available from the correspondent. Awards are made in October.

Correspondent: W H Masefield, Clerk, The Knapp, The Homend, Ledbury, HR8 1AP

Bosbury

Bosbury Educational Foundation

Eligibility: Young people leaving school who live in the parish of Bosbury and have done so for at least three years.

Types of grants: Grants of up to £250 towards books are given to young people 'on leaving school' going on to further education. Students undertaking university courses of three years or longer are invited to apply for a further grant in their final year. Grants may also be given towards school uniform for children in need.

Exclusions: Only applications from people living in the parish of Bosbury will be considered.

Annual grant total: In 2006 the trust had an income of £12,000 and a total expenditure of £21,000.

Applications: In writing to the correspondent, including details of the course. Applications should be submitted directly by the individual and are considered at any time.

Correspondent: Mrs Susan Sharples, Little Croft, Bosbury, Ledbury, Herefordshire HR8 1QA

Other information: The parish of Bosbury consists of around 500 people. In previous years the trust has stated that it is being inundated by applications from outside the parish which cannot be considered due to the deeds of the trust, and these applications will not be acknowledged.

Hereford

The Hereford Municipal Charities

Eligibility: People in need who live in the city of Hereford.

Types of grants: One-off grants of up to £200. Grants are given to help with the cost of education and starting work.

Exclusions: No grants towards debts or nursery fees.

Annual grant total: In 2007 the trust had assets of £3 million and an income of £147,000. Grants to individuals totalled approximately £20,000, of which £18,000 was given for relief-in-need purposes and a further £1,400 was given in educational grants. About 75 grants are made each year.

Applications: On a form available from the correspondent to be submitted directly by the individual or through a relevant third party. Applications are considered monthly.

Correspondent: Lance Marshall, Clerk to the Trustees, 147 St Owen Street, Hereford HR1 2JR

Other information: Most of the charity's expenditure is allocated to the running of its almshouses (£99,000 in 2006/07).

Middleton-on-the-Hill

The Middleton-on-the-Hill Parish Charity

Eligibility: People living in the parish of Middleton-on-the-Hill.

Types of grants: One-off and recurrent grants for both welfare and educational purposes.

Annual grant total: About £1,000 a year is given in grants.

Applications: In writing to the correspondent.

Correspondent: Clare Halls, Secretary, Highlands, Leysters, Leominster, Herefordshire HR6 0HP

North Canon

The Norton Canon Parochial Charities

Eligibility: Young people who live in the parish of Norton Canon.

Types of grants: Grants have been given towards books and educational outings for schoolchildren, books, fees/living expenses and study or travel abroad for students in further or higher education and equipment/instruments, books, clothing and travel for people starting work.

Annual grant total: Grants total around £4,600 a year for educational and welfare purposes.

Applications: In writing to the correspondent at any time.

Correspondent: Mrs M L Gittins, Ivy Cottage, Norton Canon, Hereford HR4 7BQ (01544 318984)

Ross

The Minett & Skyrme Charity Trust

Eligibility: People in need under 25 who live in Ross-on-Wye or in Ross rural parish.

Types of grants: One-off or recurrent grants according to need. The trust's aim is to provide ' special benefits of any kind not normally provided by the education authority for any school substantially serving the area of benefit'. Grants are given to schoolchildren towards books and educational outings; people starting work towards books, equipment/instruments, clothing and travel expenses; and students

in further/higher education (including mature students) towards books, fees/living expenses and study or travel overseas.

Annual grant total: Previously around £6,000.

Applications: In writing to the correspondent directly by the individual. Applications must include details of age, address, how much the grant is for, what it is for and why it is needed. Applications must arrive in time for consideration in April or October.

Correspondent: Mrs Gina Lane, Clerk, Brampton Rise, Greytree, Ross-on-Wye, Herefordshire HR9 7HY (01989 563262)

The Ross Educational Foundation

Eligibility: People under 25 who live in (or whose parents live in) the urban district of Ross and the civil parish of Ross Rural only.

Types of grants: One-off and recurrent grants for those at school to help with equipment/instruments, excursions and study or travel abroad and to vocational students and further and higher education students for books, excursions equipment/instruments and study or travel abroad. Grants range from £25 to £120.

Exclusions: Accommodation costs and day-to-day travel expenses will not be considered.

Annual grant total: About £1,000.

Applications: On a form available from the correspondent to be submitted directly by the individual. Grants should be submitted in February and August for consideration in April and October respectively.

Correspondent: Mrs M Bickerton, Secretary, 3 Silver Birches, Ross-on-Wye, Herefordshire HR9 7UX

Leicestershire & Rutland

The Dixie Educational Foundation

Eligibility: People under 25 who live or whose parents/guardians live, or have at any time lived, in the area of the former district of Market Bosworth Rural District Council for a period of not less than two years.

Types of grants: One-off grants in the range of £75 and £150 for clothing, books, equipment, instruments, educational outings in the UK or study or travel abroad.

Annual grant total: In 2007/08 the foundation had an income of £87,000 and a total expenditure of £76,000. Grants totalling £20,000 were awarded to individuals for educational purposes.

Applications: In writing to the correspondent. Applications can be submitted directly by the individual, through the individual's school, college or educational welfare agency, or through a parent or guardian. Applicants must give their date of birth, residential qualification and brief details of educational background and present course of study or apprenticeship together with details and costs of items against which a grant is sought. Applications must be received at least two weeks before each of the termly meetings which are held on the first Friday of March, June and November.

Correspondent: P Dungworth, Clerk to the Trustees, Children and Young People's Service, County Hall, Glenfield, Leicester LE3 8RF (Fax: 0116 265 6634; email: education@leics.gov.uk)

Other information: The foundation also supports local organisations (£49,000 in 2005/06).

The Leicestershire Coal Industry Welfare Trust Fund

Eligibility: Redundant or retired mineworkers (and their dependants) from the British coal mining industry in Leicestershire, who have not taken up other full-time work.

Types of grants: Grants are given for education, relief-in-need, health and to organisations linked with the mining industry.

Annual grant total: In 2007 the trust had an income of £12,000 and a total expenditure of £21,000. Grants are made to individuals and organisations.

Applications: In writing to the correspondent, including details of mining connections, residence in Leicestershire and dependence on the mineworker (in the case of children).

Correspondent: Peter Smith, Trustee, NUM, Springboard Centre, 18 Mantle Lane, Coalville, Leicestershire LE67 3DW

The Thomas Rawlins Educational Foundation

Eligibility: People under 25 years of age living in Quorn, Woodhouse, Woodhouse Eaves and Barrow upon Soar only (preference is given to the first three villages).

Types of grants: (i) Grants, usually between £50 to £250, for school pupils, to help with books, equipment, school uniform, maintenance or fees, but not other school clothing or educational outings. (ii) Grants, up to about £250, for students in further and higher education, help with books, equipment, instruments, study or travel abroad or fees, but not for student exchange or for foreign students studying in the UK. (iii) Help towards the cost of books, equipment and instruments, travel and clothing for people starting work.

Annual grant total: About £2,000.

Applications: On a form available from the correspondent, including details of the parent/guardian's financial position. Applications can be submitted through a parent or guardian at any time.

Correspondent: Geoffrey Gibson, 2 Wallis Close, Thurcaston, Leicestershire LE7 7JS (0116 235 0946)

The Harry James Riddleston Charity of Leicester

Eligibility: People aged 21 to 34 who live in Leicestershire or Rutland.

Types of grants: 'The prime purpose of this charity is to set up young persons over the age of 21 and under 35 years in business or to further an existing career which can include grants for further education.' The standard award is not a grant but an interest-free loan.

Annual grant total: Loans totalling £78,000 were advanced during 2007.

Applications: On a form available from the correspondent, to be submitted directly by the individual. Applications are considered in February, May, August and November.

Correspondent: Mrs M E Bass, Clerk, 44 High Street, Market Harborough, Leicestershire, LE16 8ST (01858 463322)

The Rutland Trust

Eligibility: People, usually under 35, in need who live in Rutland and are at any level or stage of their education.

Types of grants: One-off grants ranging between £50 and £400. There are no restrictions on how the grants may be spent. In the past, grants have been made towards music and school trips for needy young people, for European exchange trips, and for young people to take part in educational, missionary and life-experience programmes overseas. Grants may also be spent on books, equipment, fees, bursaries, fellowships and study visits.

Annual grant total: In 2007 the trust had an income of £11,000 and a total expenditure of £10,000. Grants are made to organisations as well as to individuals for welfare and educational purposes.

Applications: An initial telephone call is recommended.

Correspondent: Richard Adams, Clerk, 35 Trent Road, Oakham, Rutland, LE15 6HE (01572 756706; email: adams@ apair.wanadoo.co.uk)

The Marc Smith Educational Charity

Eligibility: Students (usually under 25) living in the ancient parishes of Claybrook Magna, Claybrook Parva and Ullesthorpe.

Types of grants: Help towards the cost of education, training, apprenticeship or equipment for those starting work. A clothing grant is given to pupils moving from the village schools to the high school. Grants are also given to students in further or higher education.

Annual grant total: In 2006 the trust had an income of around £11,000 and a total expenditure of £12,000.

Applications: Applications for clothing grants should be in writing and they are considered in May. Further education applications are considered in September, and should be submitted at a meeting which applicants are invited to through local advertisements near to the time of the meeting.

Correspondent: Mrs Diana Jones, Secretary, Marc Smith Foundation, 21 Highcroft, Husbands Bosworth, Lutterworth, Leicestershire, LE17 6LF (01858 880741)

Sir Thomas White Loan Charity

Eligibility: People aged between 18 and 34 who have lived in Leicestershire or Rutland for a minimum of five years

Types of grants: Interest-free loans (present maximum of £12,000) to help with starting businesses. Loans up to £5,000 are also given to people with a degree who wish to do further study.

Annual grant total: In 2007 the charity had assets of £2.9 million and an income of £209,000. During the year £391,000 was loaned to 50 borrowers.

Applications: In writing to the correspondent, including a business plan. The trustees meet in February, May, August and November.

Correspondent: Mrs Wendy Faulkner, Charnwood Court, 5b Newalk, Leicester LE1 6TE (0116 204 6620; email: wf@ stwcharity.co.uk; website: www.stwcharity. co.uk)

The Wyvernian Foundation

Eligibility: People who live in the city or county of Leicester (i.e. those who have been permanently or ordinarily resident in the city or county for at least three years, excluding those temporarily resident whilst undertaking a period of study).

Types of grants: One-off and recurrent grants, generally for those in further and higher education (including mature students), towards the cost of fees/living expenses, study or travel overseas, and possibly books and equipment where they are an integral part of the course. Childcare

expenses may be given. Grants range from £50 to £300.

Exclusions: Grants are not given to those in private education.

Annual grant total: About £1,500.

Applications: An application form must be obtained by sending an sae to the correspondent. Applications should be completed by the applicant and supported by the sponsor. An sae and CV should also be included. They should be submitted by early February, May, August and December each year for consideration in the following months.

Correspondent: A R York, 6 Magnolia Close, Leicester, Leicester LE2 8PS

Other information: The foundation makes grants to individuals including loans.

Ashby-de-la-Zouch

The Mary Smith Scholarship Fund

Eligibility: People under 25 who live in Ashby-de-la-Zouch.

Types of grants: Maintenance allowances and bursaries for any place of learning that is approved by the governors. Help is given towards the cost of books; educational outings; maintenance; study/travel broad; student exchange; equipment/instruments; protective clothing; and childcare (mature students only). Grants are also given to enable people to prepare for, or to assist entry into, a profession, trade or calling. Grants can be given to study music or the arts, or to travel abroad to pursue education.

Annual grant total: About £2,500 to £3,000 a year.

Applications: On a form available from the correspondent to be considered in April.

Correspondent: The Headteacher's PA, Ashby School, Nottingham Road, Ashby-de-la-Zouch, Leicestershire, LE65 1DT (01530 413748; Fax: 01530 560665; email: admin@ashbyschool.org.uk; website: www.ashbyschool.org.uk)

Cossington

Revd John Babington's Charity

Eligibility: People in need in the parish of Cossington.

Types of grants: One-off and recurrent grants according to need.

Annual grant total: In 2006 the trust had assets of £424,000, an income of £28,000 and a total expenditure of £42,000. Grants of about £3,400 were made to individuals.

Applications: In writing to: Smith-Woolley, Collingham, Newark, Nottinghamshire NG23 7LG.

Correspondent: G Dickie, Chair, Old Manor House, Main Street, Cossington, Leicestershire LE7 4UU (01509 812340)

Great Glen

Great Glen Town Charity

Eligibility: People who live in the parish of Great Glen who are in need.

Types of grants: One-off and recurrent grants, for example, to people going to university, people starting work and people undertaking voluntary work in their gap year. The charity also has a welfare branch which distributes grants at Christmas to older residents at a rate of £15 per individual and £30 per couple.

Annual grant total: In 2007 the trust gave approximately £1,500 in grants to individuals, including £400 to a student taking part in voluntary work abroad and £1,100 in Christmas gifts to older residents. A further £2,000 was given to a local church project.

Applications: In writing to the correspondent. Applications from outside the beneficial area will not be acknowledged.

Correspondent: Mrs H M Hill, Secretary, 35 Ashby Rise, Great Glen, Leicester, Leicestershire LE8 9GB

Groby

Thomas Herbert Smith's Trust Fund

Eligibility: People who live in the parish of Groby in Leicestershire.

Types of grants: One-off and recurrent grants ranging from £100 to £500.

Annual grant total: In 2006/07 the trust had an income of £20,000 and a total expenditure of £8,900. Grants are made to organisations and individuals.

Applications: On a form available from the correspondent, for consideration throughout the year. Applications can be submitted either directly by the individual, or through a social worker, Citizens Advice or other third party.

Correspondent: A R York, 6 Magnolia Close, Leicester, LE2 8PS

Keyham

Keyham Educational Foundation

Eligibility: People up to 25 who live in the parish of Keyham, Leicestershire, who are in need. People who have strong family connections with the parish can also be considered.

Types of grants: One-off grants ranging between £100 and £1,000.

Annual grant total: In 2007 the foundation had a total expenditure of £5,000.

Applications: In writing to the correspondent, to be submitted directly by the individual, for consideration in March and October. Urgent applications can be considered at other times. If the applicant does not live in Keyham, information about their connection with residents should be provided with the application.

Correspondent: D B Whitcomb, Chair, Tanglewood, Snows Lane, Leicester, Leicestershire LE7 9JS

Other information: If funds are available, grants are made to groups which benefit the parish.

Leicester

Alderman Newton's Educational Foundation

Eligibility: People under 25 years of age who live (or people who have one parent who lives) in the city of Leicester.

Types of grants: Grants are given towards the cost of school uniforms, other school clothing, books, equipment/instruments, fees, educational outings and study or travel overseas.

Annual grant total: In 2006/07 the trust had assets of £3.1 million, an income of £122,000 and gave grants to organisations and individuals totalling £84,000. Please note, the amount given in grants varies each year.

Applications: On an application form, available from the correspondent and from the Leicester Charity Link website. Applications can be submitted directly by the individual.

Correspondent: P Griffiths, Leicester Charity Link, 20a Millstone Lane, Leicester, LE1 5JN (0116 222 2200; website: www.charity-link.org/anef.htm)

The W P B Pearson Bequest

Eligibility: Pupils who have received their early education at council or denominational schools in the city of Leicester and who proceed to a training college for teachers or to any university or college of higher education.

Types of grants: A non-recurrent award of £30 to £50 to each eligible student to help with college or university fees, to supplement existing grants, or to help those on teacher training courses.

Annual grant total: The charity had an income of around £1,000 a year.

Applications: Any secondary school in the city of Leicester may write to the correspondent with the names and addresses of recommended students whom

they consider meet the criteria. Applications can also be made directly in writing to the correspondent.

Correspondent: The Clerk, Children and Young People's Department, Malborough House, 38 Welford Road, Leicester LE 7A

Loughborough

The Dawson & Fowler Foundation

Eligibility: People who have lived in the borough of Loughborough (including Hathern) for a period of not less than three years and are aged between 11 and 25 years.

Types of grants: The trust provide funding for three principal causes, clothing grants, grants to state schools and other grants for courses.

Grants are awarded for pupils aged year 7 to 10 for school uniforms, with a maximum value of £50, which can be re-applied for every 12 months

Funds are available to allocated schools which are used at the discretion of the headteacher to support pupils known to be in genuine need. Grants can be used towards the costs of text books and equipment (including musical instruments) for their exclusive use. Help can also be given for educational visits, residential courses, conference attendance and interview expenses. The grant should not be more than **50%** and is capped at £200 (for the Endowed Schools: £500) although this limit could be exceeded with the permission of the Trustees. Schools currently active under this scheme and the funding they received during the year are

- Loughborough Grammar School and Loughborough High School (£6000) £4100 for 5 pupils
- Burleigh College (£2000) £3560 for 23 pupils
- Woodbrook Vale High (£1250) £1270 for 18 pupils
- Limehurst High (£1250) £1011 for 19 pupils.
- De Lisle RC (£1000) nil
- Our Lady's Convent (£1000) nil.
- Garendon High (£1250) £70 for 4 pupils
- The Rawlins College (£1000) nil

Other Grants

The trustees will consider applications from students in higher education, apprentices, young people involved in Scouting, Guiding, sports activities and the Duke of Edinburgh Award Scheme. Where these are school based, they may be funded from the lump sum. Young people who join voluntary organisations that require a uniform can also be helped with its provision.

Exclusions: No grants are given for accommodation, subsistence, day to day travelling costs, tuition, examination fees or crèche costs. Applications from groups of students or classes of pupils cannot be considered.

Annual grant total: In 2007 the trust had assets of £600,000 and an income of £121,000. The trust makes grants solely to individuals, however a portion of these grants are distributed to pupils through allocated schools. During the year grants totalled £17,000, which was broken down into the following categories:

- Scholarships & Grants to Endowed Schools: £5,100
- Grants to State Schools: £5,600
- Other Grants for Courses: £1,000
- Clothing Grants: £5,000

It should be noted that Scholarships to Endowed Schools has now finished.

Applications: On a form available from the correspondent or a school office. The trustees only meet quarterly so applications should be made well in advance to avoid disappointment.

Correspondent: The Clerk to the Trustees, c/o PO Box 73, Loughborough, Leicestershire LE11 0GA

Other information: The aim of the foundation is to support young people aged 11 to 25 in the county of Loughborough through educational grants. Whilst most applications for funding are received via a third-party such as a teacher or mentor, some requests are starting to arrive independently through applicants using the internet and directories to find the foundation. The trustees would like to encourage such independent applications, as the funds allocated to schools aren't always exhausted and often there is funding left over for independent applicants.

John Storer's Educational Foundation

Eligibility: People under the age of 25 at any stage or level of their education, undertaking study of any subject and living in the old borough of Loughborough who are in need.

Types of grants: One-off grants in the form of scholarships, bursaries or maintenance allowances for employment training, further education, educational travel, musical or physical training.

Annual grant total: About £5,000.

Applications: In writing to the correspondent.

Correspondent: The Clerk, 20 Churchgate, Loughborough, Leicestershire LE11 1UD

Oadby

The Oadby Educational Foundation

Eligibility: People with a home address within the former urban district of Oadby and were educated in Oadby.

Types of grants: One-off grants in the range of £50 and £200 are made to schoolchildren, college students and undergraduates, including those towards uniforms/clothing, study/travel abroad and equipment/instruments.

(ii) People of any age can receive one-off grants towards expeditions and voluntary work such as Operation Raleigh or Voluntary Service Overseas.

Grants are in the range of £50 and £200.

Annual grant total: About £12,000 to individuals, mostly for educational purposes.

Applications: On a form available from the correspondent. They should be submitted either through the individual's school, college or educational welfare agency, or directly by the individual. They are considered on the second Friday in March, June and October (the deadline for grants to undergraduates is 1 October). Applicants must have a home address in the parish of Oadby.

Correspondent: Rodger Moodie, Hon. Secretary, 26 Richmond Way, Oadby, Leicestershire LE2 5TR (0116 271 6279)

Other information: Grants are also made to organisations.

Peatling Parva

Richard Bradgate's Charity

Eligibility: People living in the parish of Peatling Parva only.

Types of grants: Help for students in further and higher education towards books or help with fees/living expenses or for people starting work for books and equipment/instruments.

Annual grant total: Grants total about £1,000 a year.

Applications: In writing to the correspondent. Applications are usually considered in October/November.

Correspondent: Dr Brian Higginson, The Old Rectory, Main Street, Peatling Parva, Leicester LE17 5QA (0116 247 8240)

Smisby

The Smisby Parochial Charity

Eligibility: People in need who live in Smisby.

Types of grants: Grants are given to schoolchildren, people starting work,

further and higher education students, mature students and postgraduates towards books and equipment. Grants are in the range of £10 and £500.

Annual grant total: About £1,500 to individuals, mostly for welfare purposes.

Applications: In writing to the correspondent.

Correspondent: Mrs S Heap, Clerk, Cedar Lawns, Forties Lane, Smisby, Ashby-De-La-Zouch, Leicestershire LE65 2SN (01530 414179)

Wigston

The Norton, Salisbury & Brailsford Educational Foundation

Eligibility: People under the age of 25 who live in Wigston.

Types of grants: One-off grants towards the cost of books, tools, equipment and travel, including travel abroad.

Annual grant total: About £1,000.

Applications: On a form available from the correspondent. Applications are considered three times a year, usually in March, September and November.

Correspondent: The Clerk to the Trustees, Oadby and Wigston Borough Council, Station Road, Wigston, Leicester LE18 2DR

Wymeswold

The Wymeswold Parochial Charities

Eligibility: People in need who have lived in Wymeswold for the last two years.

Types of grants: One-off grants are given for educational and relief-in-need purposes.

Annual grant total: Grants total about £4,000 a year.

Applications: In writing to the correspondent at any time.

Correspondent: The Trustees, 26 Church Street, Wymeswold, Loughborough LE12 6TX

Lincolnshire

The Alenson & Erskine Educational Foundation

Eligibility: People who live in the parishes of Wrangle, Old Leake and New Leake and are under 25. Applications are only considered from local people who have received at least five years education in the parish.

Types of grants: Grants vary and are given to: (i) school leavers to help with books, equipment, clothing or travel; (ii) college or university students to help with fees or to supplement existing grants, but not to travel or study abroad.

Schoolchildren, other than those with special education needs, are only considered if family difficulties are serious.

Annual grant total: In 2006 the trust had an income of £3,700 and a total expenditure of £7,000. The trust has previously stated that the grant total varies from year to year.

Applications: In writing to the correspondent. Applicants can only claim for what they have bought and not what they would like to buy and so must submit receipts with the application, which are usually considered in October/November.

Correspondent: Margaret Barnett, 29 Saddlers Way, Fishtoft, Boston, Lincolnshire PE21 0BB

Allen's Charity (Apprenticing Branch)

Eligibility: Young people who live in Long Sutton and Sutton Bridge.

Types of grants: Grants for apprentices.

Annual grant total: In 2006 the trust had an income of £3,800 and a total expenditure of £3,200.

Applications: On a form available from the correspondent. The scheme is advertised in the local press and is promoted by local employers.

Correspondent: K Savage, Lenton Lodge, 4 Armitage Close, Holbeach, Spalding, Lincolnshire PE12 7HR

Cowell and Porrill

Eligibility: People under 25 who live or whose parent(s) live in the parishes of Benington and Leverton, at any level or stage of their education and undertaking the study of any subject.

Types of grants: Grants of £250 to £600 for general educational needs.

Annual grant total: In 2007 the trust had an income of £10,000 and a total expenditure of £16,000. Grants have previously totalled £7,000 a year.

Applications: On a form available from the correspondent, to be submitted by the end of July for consideration in September each year. Applications should be submitted directly by the individual.

Correspondent: R J Hooton, 33 Glen Drive, Boston, Lincolnshire PE21 7QB (01205 310088; Fax: 01205 311282)

Gainsborough Educational Charity

Eligibility: People of at least secondary school age and under 25 who live, or whose parents live, in the former urban district council area of Gainsborough or the parishes of Thonock, Morton and Lea and are in need.

Types of grants: Grants are given to schoolchildren, further and higher education students, postgraduates and people starting work, including those for uniforms/other school clothing, books, equipment/instruments, fees, educational outings in the UK and study or travel abroad. Grants can also be made for the study of music or other arts.

Annual grant total: In 2006/07 the charity had both an income and a total expenditure of around £6,000. In previous years grants have totalled about £4,000.

Applications: On a form available from the correspondent for consideration in March and November; applications can be submitted directly by the individual up to three weeks prior to this. References are required.

Correspondent: Mrs Maria Bradley, Clerk to the Trustees, Burton & Dyson Solicitors, 22 Market Place, Gainsborough, Lincolnshire DN21 2BZ (01427 610761; Fax: 01427 616866; email: law@burtondyson.co.uk)

The Hesslewood Children's Trust (Hull Seamen's & General Orphanage) see entry on page 120

see entry on page 120

Correspondent: Michael Mitchell, Graham & Rosen (Solicitors), 8 Parliament St, Hull, HU1 2BB (01482 323123; Fax: 01482 223542; email: law@graham-rosen.co.uk)

The Kirton-in-Lindsey Exhibition Endowment

Eligibility: People who live in Kirton-in-Lindsey, Hibaldstow, Redbourne or Manton, Messingham, Blyborough or Waddingham, Grayingham, Northorpe or Scotter and Scotton and have attended one of the following primary schools for at least two years: Kirton-in-Lindsey, Scotter, Messingham, Waddingham or Hibaldstow.

Types of grants: Grants to help with the cost of books and other essentials for schoolchildren/mature students going on to college, university or teacher training.

Annual grant total: In 2007/08 the trust had both an income and expenditure of around £3,000. Grants to individuals usually total about £2,500 each year.

Applications: On a form available from the correspondent to be submitted before 1 September.

Correspondent: Mrs P Hoey, 6 Queen Street, Kirton-in-Lindsey, Gainsborough, Lincolnshire DN21 4NS

Kitchings Educational Charity

Eligibility: People under 25 who live in Bardney, Bucknall, Southrey or Tupholm

Types of grants: Grants to further and higher education students to assist with books, equipment/instruments, fees and other educational expenses.

Exclusions: No support is given to students who choose to take A-levels (or equivalent) at college when they could tak the same course at their school.

Annual grant total: In 2007/08 the trust had an income of £7,400 and a total expenditure of £7,600. Grants normally total about £4,000.

Applications: In writing to the correspondent. Applications can be submitted either through the individual's school, college, educational welfare agenc or directly by the individual. They are considered in October and should be received by the end of September.

Correspondent: Mrs M Sankey, 50 Statio Road, Barnley, Lincolnshire, LN3 5UB

The Kitchings General Charity

Eligibility: Students, especially mature (over 25 years of age), part-time, and vocational students, living in the parish c Bardney (covers Stainfield, Apley, Tupholme and Bucknall).

Types of grants: Grants are given to schoolchildren for playgroup fees and excursions and further and students for books. Grants are in the range of £200 an £500.

Annual grant total: Grants usually total around £10,000 per year, which includes welfare and educational grants and widow pensions.

Applications: In writing to the correspondent giving details of age, cours name, college and brief description of education to date. Applications are considered in May, October and January.

Correspondent: Mrs J Smith, Secretary, 42 Abbey Road, Bardney, Lincoln LN3 5XA (01526 398505)

The Kochan Trust

Eligibility: People living in Lincolnshire who are in need of financial assistance fo their study of the creative arts, music or veterinary medicine.

Types of grants: One-off grants according to need, e.g. towards concerts or instruments for students of the creative arts and music, or towards research projects or general course expenses for veterinary students.

Annual grant total: In 2007/08 the trust had assets of £788,000 and a total income of £38,000. Grants to individuals totalled £11,000 and were given mostly to veterinary students.

Applications: In writing to the correspondent initially, either directly by the individual or through the individual's school/college/educational welfare agency, with brief details about who you are and what you would like the grant for. An application form is then sent out. Applications are considered January, April, July and November.

Correspondent: Revd R Massingberd-Mundy, Secretary to the Trustees, The Old Post Office, West Raynham, Fakenham, Norfolk NR21 7AD (01328 838611; Fax: 01328 838698)

The Mapletoft Scholarship Foundation

Eligibility: People who have attended primary school in the parishes of North Thoresby, Grainsby and Waite, for not less than two years.

Types of grants: Grants up to about £150 to help with further/higher education books and fees/living expenses or to supplement existing grants. Travel grants are also available. Grants are recurrent.

Annual grant total: Annual income of around £3,000.

Applications: Applications should be received not later than 30 September for consideration in November.

Correspondent: P M Purves, Solicitor, The Old Vicarage, Church Street, Louth, Lincolnshire, LN11 9DE

Sir Thomas Middlecott's Exhibition Foundation

Eligibility: Students who live in the parishes of Algarkirk, Fosdyke, Frampton, Kirton, Sutterton and Wyberton, who are in further/higher education and are aged under 25. Applicants must have attended a maintained primary school in the area for at least two years.

Types of grants: Grants are given to students in further/higher education towards books, and equipment/instruments.

Annual grant total: In 2006/07 the trust had an income of £32,000 and a total expenditure of £31,000. Grants were made to individuals totalling around £12,000.

Applications: On a form available from the correspondent, or from the foundation's website, to be submitted directly by the individual. Applications are considered in October and should be submitted by the end of September.

Correspondent: Frank J Wilson, Clerk to the Board of Governors, 57a Bourne Road, Spalding, Lincolnshire PE11 1JR (01775 766117; Fax: 01775 766117; email: info@middlecotttrust.org.uk; website: www.middlecotttrust.org.uk)

Mary Parnham's Lenton Charity

Eligibility: People under 23 who live in parishes of Lenton, Keisby and Osgodby.

Types of grants: Help with the cost of books, clothing and other essentials for schoolchildren. Help may also be available for those at college or university and those undertaking apprenticeships or other professional training. Preference is given to people with special educational needs and to schoolchildren with serious family difficulties so the child has to be educated away from home.

Annual grant total: The charity has an income of around £500 a year. No expenditure has been recorded in recent years.

Applications: The charity has previously stated that it is trying to build up its asset fund so that it 'will continue to survive'.

Correspondent: F P J Grenfell, Lenton House, Ingoldsby Road, Lenton, Grantham, Lincolnshire NG33 4HB

Phillips Charity

Eligibility: People living in the parishes of Long Sutton, Little Sutton and Sutton Bridge, aged between 11 and 20.

Types of grants: Grants of up to £200 are given: (i) to schoolchildren for books, equipment, clothing or travel; (ii) to students in further/ higher education towards the cost of books and travel or study overseas; and (iii) for help with the study of music and the other arts, as well as for overseas study.

Exclusions: Grants are not given for school fees or maintenance, student fees/living expenses or for people starting work.

Annual grant total: In 2007 the trust had an income of £3,800 and a total expenditure of £2,800. Around £2,500 a year is given in grants to individuals.

Applications: On a form available from the correspondent. They are considered at trustees' meetings usually held in July and September.

Correspondent: K Savage, Clerk, Lenton Lodge, 94 Wignals Gate, Holbeach, Spalding, Lincolnshire PE12 7HR (01406 490157)

The Pike & Eure Educational Foundation

Eligibility: Young people between the ages of 16 and 25 who are in need and live in the parishes of Washingborough and Heighington in Lincolnshire.

Types of grants: One-off grants for students in further or higher education towards books, equipment/instruments, travelling scholarships, maintenance allowances and extra-curricular classes.

Exclusions: People starting work are not eligible.

Annual grant total: In 2007 the income totalled £3,800 with an expenditure of £4,000.

Applications: On a form available from the correspondent, submitted directly by the individual, with information about the nature of the course, location, and the occupation of the parent(s). Applications should be submitted in early August for consideration in October.

Correspondent: Mrs Susan Smith, Clerk to the Trustees, Susan Smith, 18 Oxford Close, Washingborough, Lincoln LN4 1DT (01522 792406)

The Educational Foundation of Philip & Sarah Stanford

Eligibility: People under 25 who live in the ancient parishes of Aylesby, Barnoldby-le-Beck, Bradley, Irby-upon-Humber and Laceby.

Types of grants: Grants of £60 to £100 towards books, clothing or equipment/instruments for college students and undergraduates.

Exclusions: Grants are not given for subjects and courses available in schools, nor for help with student fees, travel or living expenses.

Annual grant total: In 2007 the foundation had an income of £10,000 and a total expenditure of £6,000.

Applications: On a form available from the correspondent, submitted directly by the individual, including reasons for the application and plans for the future. The closing date is 1 October each year. Applications must be in the applicant's own handwriting.

Correspondent: Mrs E Hine, Clerk, 86 Brigsley Road, Waltham, Grimsby, South Humberside, DN37 0LA

The Sutton St James United Charities

Eligibility: People under 25 who are in need and live in the parish of Sutton St James and the surrounding area.

Types of grants: (i) Grants, of up to £100, to all pupils living in the village at age 11 when transferring to secondary schools, to help with books, equipment, clothing etc.

(ii) Grants, of up to £100, to help students taking A-levels and further education courses.

(iii) Grants, of up to £600 a year, to students over 18 at university to help with general expenses and to supplement existing grants.

Help is also given to people entering a trade or profession.

Annual grant total: In 2006/07 the charities had an income of £14,000 and a total expenditure of £10,000. This was divided between education and relief-in-need grants.

Applications: On a form available from the correspondent. Applications are considered in April/May for primary school children and December/January for A-level and university students.

Correspondent: K Savage, Clerk, Lenton Lodge, 94 Wignals Gate, Holbeach, Spalding, Lincolnshire PE12 7HR (01406 490157; email: keithsavage@ btinternet.com)

Dame Margaret Thorold's Apprenticing Charity

Eligibility: People aged 18 to 25, who live in the ancient parishes of Sedgebrook, Marston and Cranwell.

Types of grants: Small cash grants to assist students in further or higher education, especially vocational training. Grants may be recurrent or one-off and are towards books, fees/living expenses or study/travel abroad.

Annual grant total: About £1,500.

Applications: Applications should be submitted in writing by the individual or parent/guardian or through the school/ college/educational welfare agency, by mid-January for consideration in February. If appropriate, a letter of support from the employer or place of training should be included with the application.

Correspondent: T S Kelway, Clerk, Tallents, 3 Middlegate, Newark, Nottinghamshire NG24 1AQ (01636 671881)

Viking Cares (Cash for Kids)
see entry on page 118

Correspondent: Debbie Westlake, c/o Viking FM, Commercial Road, Hull HU1 2SG (01482 593193; email: debbie. westlake@vikingfm.co.uk; website: www. vikingfm.co.uk)

Barkston

The Barkston Educational Foundation

Eligibility: People under 25 who live or whose parents live in the parish of Barkston.

Types of grants: One-off and recurrent grants for educational purposes, according to need.

Annual grant total: In 2006/07 the trust had an income of £6,200 and a total expenditure of £5,500.

Applications: In writing to the correspondent.

Correspondent: T S Kelway, Clerk, Tallents, 3 Middlegate, Newark, Nottinghamshire NG24 1AQ (01636 671881; email: tim.kelway@tallents. co.uk)

Boston

The Sutterton Education Trust

Eligibility: People in need who live in parishes of Sutterton or Ambellhill in Boston.

Types of grants: Grants of between £50 and £200 are available for: (i) uniforms, school clothing, books and educational outings for schoolchildren; (ii) books, fees, living expenses, study or travel aboard for students in further/ higher education, but not overseas students or student exchange; and (iii) books, travel and fees for mature students, but not childcare. Each case is considered individually.

Annual grant total: About £2,500.

Applications: In writing to the correspondent.

Correspondent: Mrs D P McCumiskey, 6 Hillside Gardens, Wittering, Peterborough, PE8 6DX

Corby Glenn

The Willoughby Memorial Trust

Eligibility: People under 25 who live in the Corby Glen area of Lincolnshire.

Types of grants: One-off grants are available to schoolchildren for help with books, fees and educational outings and to students in further/higher education for help with books and fees.

Annual grant total: In 2007 the trust had assets of £781,000 and an income of £39,000. After funding its own projects, a total of £1,800 was given in grants.

Applications: On a form available from the correspondent, to be submitted by the individual's headteacher.

Correspondent: Timothy Paul Clarke, Grimsthorpe House, Grimsthorpe, Bourne, Lincolnshire PE10 0LY (01778 951205)

Other information: This trust mainly give grants to schools and organisations, although it budgets a small amount each year for grants to individuals.

Deeping

The Deeping St James United Charities

Eligibility: College and university students from the parish of St James, Deeping.

Types of grants: All young university (or equivalent) students are given an annual grant towards the cost of their studies for three years. The grant may be used for books or equipment needed for study towards a degree or vocational qualification, such as scissors for hairdressing or knives for a chef, for example.

In order to qualify, applicants should normally be aged 18 to 25 years, be studying for their first degree or college qualification and be resident in Deeping S James (including Frognall).

Annual grant total: In 2006 the trust had assets of £2.5 million and an income of £1.3 million. Grants were made totalling £21,000. A total of £5,200 was given in grants to individuals for educational purposes. Of this amount, £2,600 was distributed through book grants to 40 individuals, with the remaining funds given to both local schools and individual to enable children to attend residential centres and take part if music lessons.

Applications: A PDF form can be downloaded from the website and returned by post or in person to The Institute. Applicants starting Higher Education during the autumn term should apply for their grant as soon as a place has been awarded and their entry qualifications confirmed.

Correspondent: R Moulsher, The Institute, 38 Church Street, Deeping St James, Lincolnshire, PE6 8HD (01778 344707/380754/345890; email: clerk@dsjunitedcharities.org.uk; website: www.dsjunitedcharities.org.uk)

Other information: This trust also gives grants to individuals for relief-in-need purposes and to local organisations.

Dorrington

Dorrington Welfare Charity

Eligibility: People under the age of 25 who have lived in the village of Dorrington for at least a year.

Types of grants: Traditionally one-off grants of have been made in amounts of up to £200.

Annual grant total: Grants usually total around £1,000 per year.

Applications: In writing to the correspondent or any trustee directly by the individual. Applications are considered at any time.

Correspondent: Mrs Susan Tong, Penneshaw Farm, Sleaford Road, Dorrington, Lincoln LN4 3PU (01526 833395; email: susantong@ btinternet.com)

Fleet

The Deacon & Fairfax Educational Foundation

Eligibility: People who live in the parish of Fleet (Lincolnshire), aged between 16 and 25 and attending further education.

Types of grants: Grants are given to further and higher education students, including those for clothing, books, equipment/instruments and fees.

Annual grant total: In 2006/07 the trust had both an income and expenditure of around £3,000.

Applications: In writing to the correspondent directly by the individual. Applications are considered in October and should be received in August or September.

Correspondent: Mrs Jill Harrington, Coubro Chambers, 11 West End, Holbeam, Lincolnshire PE12 7LW (01406 426739)

Other information: Grants are also made to schools in the area.

Frampton

The Frampton Educational Foundation

Eligibility: People in higher education who have lived in the ancient parish of Frampton for at least five years.

Types of grants: One-off and recurrent grants according to need.

Annual grant total: In 2006/07 the foundation had both an income and expenditure of around £6,000. Previously grants to individuals have totalled around £3,000.

Applications: In writing to the correspondent. Applications are considered in early October and students must reapply each year.

Correspondent: The Clerk, Moore Thompson, Broad Street, Spalding, Lincolnshire, PE11 1TB (01775 711333)

Gainsborough

The Tyler Educational Foundation

Eligibility: People under 21 who live in Morton and Thornock and are in financial need, with a preference for Church of England.

Types of grants: Grants for educational purposes.

Annual grant total: In 2007 the foundation had an income of £9,000 and a total expenditure of £1,000.

Applications: In writing to the correspondent.

Correspondent: Mrs E M Bradley, 22 Market Place, Gainsborough, Lincolnshire, DN21 2BZ (01427 010761)

Holbeach

The Farmer Educational Foundation

Eligibility: People who live in the parish of Holbeach, South Lincolnshire, and are above the statutory school-leaving age.

Types of grants: Grants, to a usual maximum of about £100, to help students in higher/further education and to assist schools serving Holbeach with projects.

Annual grant total: In 2006/07 the trust had an income of £23,000 and a total expenditure of £18,000.

Applications: On a form available from Holbeach Library, to be submitted by the individual at the end of August. Applications are considered in September.

Correspondent: M J H Griffin, Hurdletree Farm, Hurdletree Bank, Whaplode, Spalding, Lincolnshire PE12 6SS (01406 540424; email: hurdletree@aol.com)

Other information: Grants were made to eight schools totalling £10,000.

Horncastle

George Jobson's Trust

Eligibility: Young people in need who attend or have attended schools in Horncastle or live in the parish of Horncastle.

Types of grants: Recurrent grants of between £50 and £500 for general education costs.

Exclusions: No grants are given to postgraduate students.

Annual grant total: In 2006/07 the trust had an income of £38,000 and a total expenditure of £22,000, almost all of which was spent in grants to individuals.

Applications: On a form available from the correspondent. Applications can be submitted directly by the individual or through a social worker, Citizens Advice or other welfare agency.

Correspondent: The Clerk, c/o Messrs Chattertons Solicitors, 30 Avenue Road, Grantham, Lincolnshire, NG31 6TH

Kesteven

The Kesteven Children in Need

Eligibility: Children/young people up to the age of 16 who live in Kesteven.

Types of grants: Grants of up to £500 towards books, clothing and educational outings.

Annual grant total: In 2006/07 the trust had an income of £24,000 and a total expenditure of £15,000. Grants usually total around £1,000 a year.

Applications: Generally through local social workers, health visitors, teachers and education officers. Information should include the family situation, the age of the child and his/her special needs. Applications are considered throughout the year.

Correspondent: Mrs Jane Howard, Nocton Rise, Sleaford Road, Nocton, Lincoln LN4 2AF (01522 791217; email: alex@emhoward.co.uk)

Lincoln

The Leeke Church Schools & Educational Foundation

Eligibility: People between 16 and 24 years who live, or whose parents live, in the city of Lincoln. People studying in Lincoln with a home address elsewhere are ineligible.

Types of grants: One-off and recurrent grants in the range of £150 to £500 each term. Grants are given to: schoolchildren for educational outings in the UK, study or travel abroad and student exchanges; and further and higher education students for uniforms, books, equipment/instruments, fees, educational outings in the UK, study or travel abroad and student exchanges. Grants are not given for private education – there must be a financial need.

Annual grant total: In 2006/07 the foundation gave £33,000 to individuals and £10,000 to schools.

Applications: On a form available from the correspondent to be submitted by the individual for consideration at any time. Educational costs should be listed, and either the real amount given, or a fair estimate.

Correspondent: Mrs C Goddard, Clerk and Grants Officer, 5 Woburn Avenue, Lincoln, LN1 3HJ

Lindsey

The Joseph Nickerson Charitable Foundation

Eligibility: Young people in further education in the old county of Lindsey. Beneficiaries are usually aged 18 or over and are studying at university.

Types of grants: Recurrent grants of about £900 a year, donated in three tranches.

Annual grant total: About £8,000 to individuals for educational purposes.

Applications: In writing to the correspondent. Applications for grants starting in September should be made by 30 June for consideration in July.

Correspondent: Eric White, Estate Office, Rothwell, Market Rasen, Lincolnshire LN7 6BJ

Moulton

The Moulton Poors' Lands Charity

Eligibility: People in need, generally older people, who live in the civil parish of Moulton.

Types of grants: Mainly relief-in-need grants, very occasional education grants are available.

Annual grant total: In 2007 the charity has an income of £39,000 and a total expenditure of £42,000. Previously grants to individuals and organisations have totalled around £15,000.

Applications: In writing to the correspondent, usually through a trustee. Applications are considered in April and December.

Correspondent: R W Lewis, Clerk for the Charity, Maples & Son, 23 New Road, Spalding, Lincolnshire PE11 1DH

Navenby

The Navenby Towns Farm Trust

Eligibility: University students and young people doing their A-levels who are in need and live in the village of Navenby.

Types of grants: Recurrent grants while at university, but only following reapplication every year.

Exclusions: No grants can be given outside the village.

Annual grant total: About £9,000 to individuals and organisations.

Applications: On a form available from the correspondent, the post office, or Smith and Willows the newsagents. Applications are considered in September. Unsolicited applications are not responded to.

Correspondent: The Secretary, 17 North Lane, Navenby, Lincoln LN5 0EH

North Lincolnshire

The Withington Education Trust

Eligibility: People under the age of 21 who live in the area of the new North Lincolnshire Council.

Types of grants: Grants to help with fees/living expenses, travel and other education needs, but not normally books or equipment. Grants to assist with non-formal education such as music and ballet are also given. Grants range from £50 to £300.

Exclusions: Grants towards fees for private schooling are not given.

Annual grant total: About £1,500.

Applications: In writing at any time, preferably supported by the school or college. Applications are considered once per term.

Correspondent: John Irving, Treasurer and Secretary, Education Office, North Lincolnshire Council, PO Box 35, Brigg, South Humberside, DN20 8XJ

Potterhanworth

The Christ's Hospital Endowment at Potterhanworth

Eligibility: People under the age of 25 who live, or whose parent(s) live, in the parish of Potterhanworth, Lincolnshire.

Types of grants: Grants are available for the cost of educational visits for schoolchildren and towards fees for extra-curricular activities such as music, the arts and social and physical training. A block grant only is given to further education students.

Exclusions: Grants are not given for other costs for schoolchildren such as books or for school fees, nor for people starting work, other than for equipment.

Annual grant total: In 2006/07 the trust had an income of £27,000. Grants to individuals totalled £13,000, with £1,200 awarded to further education students, and the remaining funds granted to educational visits, tuition and primary school leavers.

Applications: In writing to the correspondent, either by the individual, his/her parents, or through the individual's school, college or university. Applications are considered once a year in November and must include valid receipts where applicable. Applications must be received before 31 October.

Correspondent: Mrs Y Woodcock, The Conifers, Barff Road, Potterhanworth, Lincoln LN4 2DU (01522 790942)

Quadring

The Cowley & Brown School Foundation

Eligibility: People under 25 who live in the ancient parish of Quadring.

Types of grants: Grants towards the cost of books, clothing and other essentials for schoolchildren. Help may also be available for students at college or university.

Annual grant total: In 2007 the foundation had an income of £4,200 and a total expenditure of £3,800.

Applications: In writing to the correspondent. Applications are considered in July and November.

Correspondent: K J Watts, Clerk, 99 Hawthorne Bank, Spalding, Lincolnshire PE11 1JQ (01775 760911)

Scunthorpe

The James R Heslam Settlement

Eligibility: People in need who live in Scunthorpe.

Types of grants: One-off and recurrent grants or loans to help with maintenance/living expenses, books and essential equipment for education purposes for students in further or higher education, including vocational and mature students.

Annual grant total: In 2006/07 the trust had an income of £2,200 and a total expenditure of £2,700.

Applications: In writing to the correspondent. Applications must include a cv and details of the applicant's financial situation.

Correspondent: R J H Sumpter, c/o Syme Bains Broomer, 2 Park Square, Laneham Street, Scunthorpe DN15 6JH (01724 281616)

South Holland

The Moulton Harrox Educational Foundation

Eligibility: People up to 25 who live in the South Holland district council area.

Types of grants: Grants for school pupils and college students, including mature students, to help with books, equipment, fees, clothing, educational outings and study or travel abroad. Preference is given to schoolchildren with serious family difficulties so the child has to educated away from home, and to people with special education needs.

One-off and recurrent grants according to need. Individuals must reapply in order to receive the grant in the following year.

Annual grant total: About £500 to individuals with further monies distributed to schools.

Applications: On a form available from the correspondent. Applications should be submitted before 31 August for consideration in September.

Correspondent: R W Lewis, Clerk for the Charity, Maples & Son Solicitors, 23 New Road, Spalding, Lincolnshire PE11 1DH (01775 722261; Fax: 01775 767525)

The Spalding Relief-in-Need Charity

Eligibility: People in need who live in the area covered by South Holland District Council with priority to residents of the parishes of Spalding, Cowbit, Deeping St Nicholas, Pinchbeck and Weston.

Types of grants: One-off grants in the range of £100 to £400. Normally payments are made directly to suppliers.

Annual grant total: In 2006 the charity had assets of £515,000 and an income of £27,000. Grants to individuals totalled £31,000.

Applications: On a form available from the charity. Applications can be submitted directly by the individual or assisted if appropriate by a social worker, teacher, school, Citizens Advice, other welfare agency or third party. Grants are considered on a weekly basis.

Correspondent: R A Knipe, Clerk and Solicitor, Dembleby House, 12 Broad Street, Spalding, Lincolnshire PE11 1ES (01775 768774)

Other information: Grants can also be made to organisations.

Stickford

The Stickford Relief-in-Need Charity

Eligibility: Schoolchildren in need who live in the parish of Stickford.

Types of grants: School clothing grants. Grants are also made for welfare purposes.

Annual grant total: Previously about £15,000.

Applications: In writing to the correspondent. Applications should be submitted directly by the individual and are considered all year.

Correspondent: Mrs K L Bunting, Clerk, The Old Vicarage, Church Road, Stickford, Boston, Lincolnshire PE22 8EP

Sutton Bridge

Sutton Bridge Power Fund

Eligibility: Adults living, and children living or attending schools, in Sutton Bridge, Lincolnshire (very clearly defined boundaries which incorporate Waldpole Cross Keys, Norfolk, Tydd St Giles, Cambridgeshire, Sutton Bridge, Tydd St Mary, Lincolnshire).

Types of grants: One-off and recurrent grants according to need.

Annual grant total: Each year £15,000 is made available for grants to individuals.

Applications: In writing to the correspondent.

Correspondent: The Executive Committee, EDF Energy, 40 Grosvenor Place, London SW1X 7EN

Sutton St Edmund

The Sutton St Edmund Charities United Educational Foundation

Eligibility: Children or young persons who live in the ancient parish of Sutton St Edmund.

Types of grants: Recurrent grants are given to further and higher education students for books, equipment/instruments, fees and maintenance/living expenses. The amount given in individual grants is dependent on the number of applicants and the amount of available income.

Annual grant total: About £1,500.

Applications: In writing to the correspondent either directly by the individual, or through a parent or guardian including details of the course attended i.e. A-level, NVQ, degree, and so on. Applications should be submitted by mid-February each year and grants are paid in April.

Correspondent: K Savage, Lenton Lodge, 94 Wignals Gate, Holbeach, Spalding, Lincolnshire PE12 7HR (01406 490157)

Waddingham

James Thompson Educational Charity

Eligibility: People under 25 who live in the parish of Waddingham and are in need.

Types of grants: One-off and recurrent grants ranging from £50 to £250. Grants are given to: schoolchildren towards school uniform, other school clothing, books, equipment/instruments and educational outings; and vocational students and students in further and higher education towards clothing, books, other equipment, fees/living expenses and study/travel overseas or in the UK.

Exclusions: No grants to children below primary school age.

Annual grant total: In 2006/07 the trust had an income of £3,500 and a total expenditure of £3,100.

Applications: In writing to the correspondent, either directly by the individual or by their parent or guardian, stating who requires the grant and why, the educational establishment attended and the course being studied. Applications are usually considered in September and should be received in the preceding month.

Correspondent: B Milton, Clerk to the Trustees, South View, Moor Road, Snitterby, Gainsborough, Lincolnshire DN21 4TT (01673 818314)

Other information: Grants are also given to schools which serve the parish.

Northampton-shire

Arnold's Education Foundation

Eligibility: People in need who are under 25 and live in the parishes of Stony Stratford, Buckinghamshire; Nether Heyford, Upper Heyford, Stowe-Nine-Churches, Weedon Bec, Northamptonshire; and the ancient parish of St Giles, Northampton. Preference for members of the Church of England.

Types of grants: One-off and recurrent grants for educational purposes (including social and physical training). Grants are made: for schoolchildren towards the cost of clothing, books, educational outings, maintenance and school fees; towards the cost of books, fees/living expenses, travel exchange and study or travel abroad for students in further or higher education; and towards books, equipment/instruments, clothing and travel for people starting work. Grants range from £200 to £500.

Annual grant total: In 2006 the trust had an income of £13,000 and a total expenditure of £7,300.

Applications: On a form available by writing to the correspondent. Applications are considered in April and October.

Correspondent: Miss Jane Forsyth, c/o Messrs Wilson Browne, Solicitors, 60 Gold Street, Northampton NN1 1RS (01604 628131)

The Hervey & Elizabeth Ekins Educational Charity

Eligibility: People who (i) have lived in the borough of Northampton or the parish of Great Doddington for not less than three years; (ii) attended a maintained school in Northampton for not less than one year and (iii) attended an Anglican church on a regular basis. Applicants should be under 25 (or in exceptional cases under 30). No grants to non-Anglicans.

Types of grants: Grants are given to schoolchildren, students in further or higher education and to people starting work towards books, equipment and educational outings in the UK and overseas. Grants are also given for music tuition fees.

Grants average around £200, but in exceptional circumstances can be for as much as £500. Other grants are given to a school for larger projects.

There is a preference for those entering the ministry of the Church of England.

Exclusions: Grants are not given for school fees.

Annual grant total: In 2006/07 the charity had assets of £1.1 million and an income of

£36,000. Grants to individuals totalled £12,000.

Applications: In writing to the correspondent directly by the individual, including details of school and church attended. Applications are considered in January, March, May, September and November.

Correspondent: Mrs Elizabeth Fisher, 'The Pines' 36 Lower Street, Great Doddington, NN29 7TL (01933 224369)

The Horne Foundation

Eligibility: Schoolchildren and students in need who live in Northamptonshire.

Types of grants: Bursaries are made towards living expenses, course fees and so on, to a maximum of £5,000.

Annual grant total: In 2006/07, the foundation had assets of £7.2 million and an income of £226,000. Grants were made to 37 students totalling £65,000.

Applications: The bursary scheme is run in conjunction with the local council, and bursaries to schoolchildren are made on the recommendation of schools. If the applicant is at school, he or she should therefore apply through the head teacher of the school. Students can apply to the trust directly, in writing. Applications are considered twice a year.

Correspondent: Mrs R M Harwood, PO Box 468, Church Stowe, Northampton, NN7 4WL (email: hornefoundation@ fsmail.net)

The Isham Educational Foundation

Eligibility: People under 25 who live in the ancient parish of Lamport and Hanging Houghton.

Types of grants: One-off and recurrent grants of between £50 and £1,000 are given to: (i) school pupils, to help with books, equipment, clothing, travel or school fees but not for maintenance; (ii) students in further/ higher education towards fees or to supplement existing grants; and (iii) those leaving school, college or university to prepare for or enter a trade, profession or calling.

Preference is given to schoolchildren with serious family difficulties so the child has to be educated away from home.

'In the allocation of all benefits the trustees shall have regard to the principles of the Church of England.'

Annual grant total: In 2007 the trust had an income of £2,200 and a total expenditure of £1,500. About £1,000 is given in grants each year.

Applications: In writing to the correspondent. Applications can be submitted by the individual or by parents and are considered in July and November.

Correspondent: David Surtees-Dawson, 10 Church Street, Brigstock, Kettering, Northamptonshire NN14 3EX

The Dorothy Johnson Charitable Trust

Eligibility: People under 25 who were born and are living, have lived or were educated at some time in Northamptonshire.

Types of grants: One-off and recurrent grants in the range of £100 and £500. Grants are made to schoolchildren, college students, undergraduates, vocational students and people with special educational needs, towards clothing/ uniforms, fees, study/travel abroad, books, equipment/instruments, maintenance/ living expenses and excursions.

Annual grant total: In 2006/07 the trust had an income of £22,000 and a total expenditure of £23,000.

Applications: In writing to the correspondent. Applications are considered three times a year.

Correspondent: Miss Z B Silins, Clerk, DNG Dove Naish, Eagle House, 28 Billing Road, Northampton NN1 5AJ (01604 657200; Fax: 01604 232251; email: zinaida.silins@dovenaish.co.uk)

The Kettering Charities (Apprenticing)

Eligibility: People over 16 who live in the town of Kettering or Barton Seagrave and are in training or further education.

Types of grants: Grants are one-off and given for general educational needs such as books and equipment. They are given towards students in further and higher education, vocational and mature students, people starting work and people with special educational needs. In 2006/07 the average level of grant was £250.

Annual grant total: In 2006/07 the charity had an income of £2,600.

Applications: Applications should be made by the individual, their parent or guardian or through the individual's school, college or educational welfare agency for consideration in November and February. Details of the applicant's financial situation must be included. Grants are subject to the parents' income if the applicant is under 21, otherwise they are subject to the applicant's income.

Correspondent: Mrs Anne Ireson, Kettering Borough Council, Municipal Offices, Bowling Green Road, Kettering NN15 7QX (email: anneireson@kettering. gov.uk)

Other information: 'The Trustees are keen to encourage applications from mature students, as well as school leavers and students in higher education, to reflect the national trend for more mature students entering higher education.'

Parson Latham's Educational Foundation

Eligibility: Children 12 aged years and upwards who have lived in the urban district of Oundle and Ashton since birth or have been resident for at least 5 years and have attended a local school. The foundation will consider giving grants to mature students, although prefers to support people under 25.

Types of grants: One-off and recurrent grants of £100 to £250 are given to: (i) Schoolchildren for uniforms/other school clothing, books, equipment/instruments, fees and educational outings in the UK; (ii) People starting apprenticeships for equipment/instruments; (iii) Further education students for clothing, books, equipment/instruments, fees and maintenance/living expenses; (iv) Higher education students for fees, books and maintenance/living expenses; (v) Mature and vocational students for books and fees.

Exclusions: No grants are given to overseas students studying in the UK or for student exchange.

Annual grant total: In 2006/07 the trust had an income of £3,900 and a total expenditure of £3,200.

Applications: On a form available from the correspondent or the local tourist information centre. Applications to be submitted directly by the individual before 20 August for consideration in September. Applications should include: parental annual income; details of whether the applicant will be living at home or at college; and the number and ages of all dependant children.

Correspondent: Mrs M E Slater, Clerk to the Trustees, 24 North Street, Oundle, Peterborough PE8 4AL (01832 273872)

The Foundation of Thomas Roe

Eligibility: People in need who are under 25 and live in the parishes of Scaldwell and Brixworth, Northamptonshire.

Types of grants: One-off grants of £50 to £150 to schoolchildren, students in further or higher education and people starting work for school uniform, school clothing, books, educational outings in the UK, study or travel abroad, maintenance, fees, living expenses and equipment/ instruments.

Annual grant total: About £1,000.

Applications: On a form available from the correspondent to be considered in March and September each year.

Correspondent: Mrs U Morris, Highfield Grange, Highfield Park, Creaton, Northampton NN6 8NT (email: ursula@ enta.net)

Sir Thomas White's Loan Fund

Eligibility: People who live within the extended borough of Northampton.

Types of grants: (i) Nine-year interest-free loans to people aged between 21 and 34 for education and new businesses (and home improvements). (ii) Grants to young people aged between 16 and 25 attending school, college or university.

The fund was originally set up for the provision of tools for people setting up in a trade or profession.

Annual grant total: In 2007 the fund had in assets of £3.2 million and an income of £240,000. Grants totalled £80,000.

Applications: Apply in writing for a form in November, following a public notice advertising the grants.

Correspondent: Clerk to the Trustees, Hewitsons, 7 Spencer Parade, Northampton NN1 5AB (01604 233233; email: angelamoon@hewitsons.com)

The Wilson Foundation

Eligibility: Young people in Northamptonshire, with a particular emphasis on the underprivileged or disadvantaged.

Types of grants: Scholarships and 'character building' trips/expeditions.

Annual grant total: About £70,000.

Applications: An application form can be downloaded from the foundation's website.

Correspondent: The Trustees, The Maltings, Tithe Farm, Moulton Road, Holcot, Northamptonshire, NN6 9SH 01604 782240; email: info@thewilsonfoundation.co.uk; website: www.thewilsonfoundation.co.uk)

Other information: Grants are made to organisations and individuals.

Blakesley

The Blakesley Parochial Charities

Eligibility: People in need who live in Blakesley.

Types of grants: One-off and recurrent grants according to need.

Annual grant total: In 2006/07 the charities had an income of £5,600 and a total expenditure of £4,600.

Applications: In writing to the correspondent. Applications are considered in September.

Correspondent: Patricia Paterson, Secretary, Quinbury Cottage, 35 Quinbury End, Blakesley, Towcester, Northamptonshire NN12 8RF (01327 860517; email: derekjlucas@tiscali.co.uk)

Brackley

The Brackley United Feoffee Charity

Eligibility: People under the age of 25 who live in the parish of Brackley.

Types of grants: One-off grants in the range of £100 and £1,000 to: schoolchildren for uniforms/clothing, study/travel abroad, books, equipment/instruments, excursions and childcare; college students and undergraduates for study/travel abroad, books and excursions; and to people with special educational needs for excursions and childcare.

Previous educational grants (2006/07) have included funding for educational trips to developing countries, music lessons, purchasing of musical instrument and contributions towards fees to attend a musical college.

Annual grant total: In 2006/07 the trust had an income of £26,000. Grants to individuals totalled £11,000, with £2,000 going to educational causes.

Applications: In writing to the correspondent either directly by the individual or through the individual's school, college or educational welfare agency. Trustees meet every three to four months.

Correspondent: Mrs R Hedges, 7 Easthill Close, Brackley, Northamptonshire NN13 7BS (01280 702420)

Brington

The Chauntry Estate

Eligibility: People who live in the parish of Brington. Applicants must have lived in the parish for at least five years.

Types of grants: One-off grants for payment of uniforms for children transferring to secondary schools, books and equipment for students in further/higher education or apprentices, and assistance towards items of school equipment not provided by LEA. Grants are also available for mature students.

Annual grant total: In 2006/07 the trust had an income of £8,500 and a total expenditure of £5,600.

Applications: In writing to the correspondent. Ineligible applications are not acknowledged.

Correspondent: Rita Tank, Walnut Tree Cottage, Main Street, Great Brington, Northampton NN7 4JA (01604 770809; Fax: 01604 771003)

Burton Latimer

The Burton Latimer United Educational Foundation

Eligibility: People who live in Burton Latimer (people who live in other parts, or outside, the borough of Kettering are not eligible).

Types of grants: A general grant is made to students in further or higher education, usually to be used for books; grants to people undertaking training with low earnings to be used at their discretion; and a few grants to schoolchildren towards the cost of field study courses for GCSE work.

Grants are also made to mature students undertaking full or part-time training, in the latter case dependent on their income.

Annual grant total: Around £3,000 a year.

Applications: Application forms are available and must be submitted directly by the individual. Applications are usually considered in October. Applications unrelated to educational needs will not be considered.

Correspondent: Mrs C A Chennell, Clerk, 32 Alexandra Street, Burton Latimer, Kettering, Northamptonshire NN15 5SF

Other information: Grants are also given to the three primary schools in the town.

Byfield

The Byfield Poors Allotment

Eligibility: People in need who live in the parish of Byfield.

Types of grants: Grants are given to undergraduates for books and study/travel overseas.

Annual grant total: Grants generally total around £1,000 a year for both welfare and education.

Applications: On a form available from the correspondent. Applications can be made directly by the individual or a relevant third party. They can be submitted at any time for consideration in March, June, September and December.

Correspondent: Ms Delith Jones, 15 Banbury Lane, Byfield, Daventry, Northamptonshire, NN11 6UX (01327 261405)

Other information: The charity also makes grants for welfare purposes.

Chipping Warden

Relief in Need Charity of Reverend William Smart

Eligibility: People in need who live in the parish of Chipping Warden, Northamptonshire. Preference is given to elderly people and young people in education.

Types of grants: One-off grants according to need.

Annual grant total: In 2007 the charity had an income of £3,000 and a total expenditure of £4,000. Grants usually total about £3,000 a year.

Applications: In writing to the correspondent either directly by the individual or by another third party such as a social worker. Applications are considered at any time.

Correspondent: N J Galletly, 3 Allens Orchard, Chipping Warden, Banbury, Oxfordshire OX17 1LX (01295 660365)

East Farndon

The United Charities of East Farndon

Eligibility: Students in need who live in East Farndon.

Types of grants: One-off grants of up to £50 for people starting work, schoolchildren and college students. Grants given include those for books, equipment and instruments, as well as to schoolchildren for excursions.

Annual grant total: In 2007 the charities had both an income and a total expenditure of £2,600.

Applications: In writing to the correspondent directly by the individual or a family member for consideration as they are received.

Correspondent: C L Fraser, Linden Lea, Main Street, Market Harborough, Northamptonshire LE16 9SJ (01858 464218; email: fraser-cameron@hotmail.com)

Harringworth

The Harringworth Parochial Charities

Eligibility: Students under 25 who live in Harringworth.

Types of grants: One-off grants of between £50 and £300 are given to schoolchildren, students in further/higher education and vocational students for books and equipment/instruments.

Exclusions: No grants for school fees or clothing.

Annual grant total: In 2006/07 the charities had an income of £2,600 and a total expenditure of £2,100.

Applications: In writing to the correspondent, either directly by the individual or through the individual's school/college/educational welfare agency. Applications should be submitted in February for consideration in March.

Correspondent: A C Scholes, Lindisfarne, Wakerley Road, Harringworth, Northamptonshire NN17 3AH (01572 747257)

Isham

The Isham Apprenticing and Educational Charity

Eligibility: Young people under the age of 25 who live in the parish of Isham, Northamptonshire.

Types of grants: Help with (a) the cost of books, clothing, educational outings, maintenance and school fees for schoolchildren and (b) books, equipment/instruments, clothing and travel for people starting work.

Annual grant total: In 2007 the trust had an income of £2,200 and a total expenditure of £600.

Applications: Directly by the individual or their parent/guardian in writing to the correspondent. Applications are considered regularly.

Correspondent: A S Turner, 36b South Street, Isham, Kettering, Northamptonshire NN14 1HP (01536 722500)

Middleton Cheney

Middleton Cheney United Charities

Eligibility: People who live in Middleton Cheney.

Types of grants: One-off grants are available to schoolchildren for equipment/instruments, and to students in higher and further education, including mature students, for books and study or travel abroad. Grants are in the range of £100 to £200.

Annual grant total: About £900 in educational grants.

Applications: In writing to the correspondent. Applications should be submitted directly by the individual and are considered four times a year.

Correspondent: Nigel Watts, 1 Chacombe Road, Middleton Cheney, Banbury, Oxfordshire OX17 2QS

Northampton

The Beckett's & Sergeant's Educational Foundation

Eligibility: People under 25 who either: (a) live in the borough of Northampton and are attending or have attended a school or further education institution in the borough for at least two years; or (b) are

attending or have attended for at least two years All Saints Middle School or Beckett & Sergeants School.

Types of grants: Grants can be given for wide range of educational purposes, including: educational trips; supplementing existing grants; purchasing books and equipment and studying music or the arts.

Annual grant total: In 2007 the trust had assets of £3.5 million and an income of £219,000. Grants to individuals totalled £49,000.

Applications: A written request should be made to obtain an application form. Applications are considered four times a year.

Correspondent: Clerk to the Grants Committee, Hewitsons, 7 Spencer Parade Northampton NN1 5AB (01604 233233; email: gillevans@hewitsons.com)

Other information: Grants may also be given to other Church of England school and organisations that are connected with the Church of England (£233,000).

The Blue Coat Educational Charity

Eligibility: People in need who are under 25 years old and live in the borough of Northampton.

Types of grants: One-off and recurrent grants to schoolchildren and students for a wide range of educational purposes, including the costs of school clothing, educational outings, books, school fees and study/travel abroad or student exchange. People starting work may also receive help towards equipment/instruments. Grants range from £100 to £400.

Exclusions: No support for mature students or for overseas students studying in Britain.

Annual grant total: In 2007/08 the trust had an income of £8,100 and a total expenditure of £10,000.

Applications: Application forms are available by writing to the correspondent, they are usually considered in February, July and November.

Correspondent: W G Gee, c/o Wilson Browne solicitors, 4 Grange Park Court, Roman Way, Northampton, NN4 5EA (01604 401237)

Ringstead

The Ringstead Gift

Eligibility: People up to the age of 25 whose parents live in the parish of Ringstead.

Types of grants: One-off grants in kind to schoolchildren, college students, undergraduates and vocational students, including those for uniforms/clothing,

udy/travel abroad, books and equipment/
instruments.

Annual grant total: About £1,000 a year
for educational and welfare purposes.

Applications: In writing to the
correspondent, to be submitted either
directly by the individual or a family
member, through a third party such as a
social worker or teacher or through an
organisation such as Citizens Advice or a
school. Applications are considered in June
and November and should be submitted at
least two weeks prior to this.

Correspondent: Mrs D Pentelow,
0 Carlow Street, Ringstead, Kettering,
Northamptonshire NN14 4DN

Scaldwell

The Scaldwell Charity

Eligibility: People in need who live in the
parish of Scaldwell.

Types of grants: Help with the cost of
books, clothing and other essentials for
schoolchildren; books, fees and travel
expenses for students in further or higher
education; books, equipment and clothing
for people starting work; and books, travel
and fees for mature students.

Annual grant total: In 2006 the charity
had an income of £3,100 and a total
expenditure of £1,900.

Applications: In writing to the
correspondent, including details of
financial circumstances. Applications are
considered in March, July and November.

Correspondent: James Kearns, Clerk to the
Trustees, Wilson Browne Solicitors, Manor
House, 12 Market Street, Higham Ferrers,
Rushden, Northamptonshire NN10 8BT
01933 410000; email: jkearns@
wilsonbrowne.co.uk)

Towcester

The Sponne & Bickerstaffe Charity

Eligibility: People in need who live in the
civil parish of Towcester.

Types of grants: Grants of £50 to £250 are
given to schoolchildren for uniforms,
clothing and excursions, to college
students for books and to mature students
for childcare.

Annual grant total: About £3,000 for
welfare and educational purposes.

Applications: In writing to the
correspondent, through a social worker,
Citizens Advice or other welfare agency.
Applications are considered on the third
Wednesday of every month.

Correspondent: Sue Joice, Moorfield,
Buckingham Way, Towcester,

Northamptonshire NN12 6PE
(01327 351206)

Welton

The Welton Town Lands Trust

Eligibility: Students in higher education
who are in need and have lived in the
village of Welton for at least two years.

Types of grants: One-off grants of up to
£75 to assist students in higher education
for the cost of books, equipment and so
on.

Exclusions: Grants are not made to school
aged children unless they have a mental or
physical disability or to individuals
pursuing a hobby.

Annual grant total: In 2007/08 the trust
had both an income and expenditure of
£4,000. Grants were made to individuals
totalling £2,000, of which £700 was given
in educational grants and £1,400 was
distributed in welfare awards.

Applications: By application form
available on-line to the correspondent.
Applications are considered on 1 March
and distributed in the same month. Only
one application is allowed per financial
year. The details of the trust are usually
well publicised within the village.

Correspondent: Deborah Taylor, 1 The
Ridgeway, Welton, Daventry NN11 5LQ
(01327 310439; email: dtadmin@
btinternet.com)

Other information: The trust also makes
grants to local schools and churches
(£2,000 in 2007/08).

Nottinghamshire

The Bristowe Trust

Eligibility: Pupils or former pupils of
schools within the administrative area of
the former county council of
Nottinghamshire (excluding the city of
Nottingham) who are aged between 16 and
21.

Types of grants: Grants averaging £100
towards the cost of educational visits
abroad.

Annual grant total: In 2006/07 the trust
had an income of £1,100 and a total
expenditure of £3,300.

Applications: In writing to the
correspondent at any time. Applicants will
be interviewed by the trust.

Correspondent: David Litchfield, Student
Awards Section, Nottinghamshire County
Council, County Hall, Loughborough
Road, West Bridgford, Nottingham
NG2 7QP (0115 977 3223)

The Midland Orphanage Fund

Eligibility: Girls between 4 and 25 years,
living in Nottinghamshire. Preference is
given to young girls and those who have
lost one or both parents, or who are
dependent on one parent. Girls must
normally be of school or college age
(although consideration may be given to
pre-school children in terms of items such
as educational play equipment).

Types of grants: One-off grants to a usual
maximum of £250 each to cover the cost of
meeting specific needs regarding the
education and maintenance of applicants.
Grants are given to schoolchildren, college
students and undergraduates, including
those towards clothing/uniforms, fees,
study/travel abroad, books, equipment/
instruments, maintenance/living expenses,
excursions and awards for excellence.

Exclusions: Grants cannot be given for
domestic appliances, household goods, to
fund areas that should be funded by
government, to boys, to girls who live
outside the Nottingham area, pre-school
children, organisations or families whose
income is not very low.

Annual grant total: Up to £1,000.

Applications: On a form available from
the correspondent to be submitted at any
time, either directly by the individual,
through a third party such as a teacher or
through the individual's school/college/
educational welfare agency. Applications
are considered quarterly.

Correspondent: Barbara Ricks, 30 Cyprus
Road, Nottingham NG3 5EB
(0115 9603135)

Nottingham Gordon Memorial Trust for Boys & Girls

Eligibility: Children and young people
aged up to 25 who are in need and live in
Nottingham and the area immediately
around the city.

Types of grants: Grants are given to
schoolchildren and further and higher
education students including those for
books, equipment, maintenance/living
expenses, educational outings in the UK
and study or travel abroad. Grants are also
given for school uniforms/other school
clothing.

Annual grant total: Around £3,000 per
year is given in educational grants.

Applications: On a form available from
the correspondent to be submitted through
the individual's school, college,
educational welfare agency, health visitor,
social worker or probation officer.
Individuals, supported by a reference from
their school/college, can also apply directly.
Applications are considered all year round.

Correspondent: Mrs Colleen Douglas,
Cumberland Court, 80 Mount Street,
Nottingham NG1 6HH

Other information: The trust also supports organisations in the Nottingham area.

The Nottingham Roosevelt Memorial Travelling Scholarship

Eligibility: People between the ages of 21 and 30 who are engaged in industry, commerce or 'the professions' and live or work in Nottingham and Nottinghamshire.

Types of grants: Grants to help with the cost of visiting the USA for up to three months to investigate a topic of the applicant's and/or employer's choice. The value of each scholarship can be up to about £3,000, plus return flight tickets to New York. 'Scholars are expected to travel widely throughout the USA and learn about the American way of life – an ambassadorial role.'

Exclusions: Grants are not given to students.

Annual grant total: In 2007 the trust had an income of £3,200 and a total expenditure of £11,000.

Applications: Detailed guidelines and application forms can be downloaded from the trust's website.

Correspondent: The Hon. Secretary, PO Box 119, Nottingham, NG3 5NA (website: www.rooseveltscholarship.org)

The Puri Foundation

Eligibility: Individuals in need living in Nottinghamshire who are from India (particularly the towns of Mullan Pur near Chandigarh and Ambala). Employees/past employees of Melton Medes Group LTD, Blugilt Holdings or Melham Inc and their dependants, who are in need, are also eligible.

The trust wants to support people who have exhausted state support and other avenues, in other words to be a 'last resort'. Eligible people can receive help at any stage of their education, including postgraduates and mature students.

Types of grants: One-off and recurrent grants according to need. The maximum donation is usually between £150 and £200.

Annual grant total: In 2006/07 the foundation had assets of £3.3 million and an income of £575,000. Grants mostly to organisations totalled £672,000.

Applications: In writing to the correspondent, either directly by the individual or through a social worker.

Correspondent: Nathu Ram Puri, Environment House, 6 Union Road, Nottingham NG3 1FH (0115 901 3000)

Arnold

The Arnold Educational Foundation

Eligibility: People who live in the ancient parish of Arnold, under the age of 25.

Types of grants: Primarily help for those at college or university, for example, for equipment or books. Help with the cost of books, clothing and other essentials for schoolchildren is given, but only in special circumstances.

Annual grant total: In 2006/07 the trust had an income of £18,000 and total expenditure of £16,000. In previous years about 100 grants totalling around £15,000 were made.

Applications: In writing to the correspondent. An application form should be completed by those requesting grants for further education. Grants are given post-expenditure on receiving the receipts for items purchased.

Correspondent: B W West, 73 Arnot Hill Road, Arnold, Nottingham NG5 6LN (0115 920 6656)

Bingham

The Bingham Trust Scheme

Eligibility: People under the age of 21 living in Bingham.

Types of grants: Grants in the range of £50 and £150 to help with expenses incurred in the course of education, religious and physical welfare and so on. They are made in January and early July each year.

Annual grant total: In 2006/07 the trust had an income of £3,800 and a total expenditure of £1,300.

Applications: Application forms are available from: Mrs R Pingula, 74 Nottingham Road, Bingham, Nottinghamshire NG13 8AW. They can be submitted directly by the individual or a family member by 30 April and 31 October each year.

Correspondent: Gillian M Bailey, 20 Tithby Road, Bingham, Nottingham NG13 8GN (01949 838673)

Bingham United Charities

Eligibility: People in need who live in the parish of Bingham.

Types of grants: One-off grants in the range of £50 and £300. Grants are given for a range of educational purposes including school uniforms, books, school trips, Duke of Edinburgh expeditions and music lessons.

Exclusions: Grants are not given to the same person twice.

Annual grant total: In 2006/07 the trust had an income of £8,800 and a total expenditure of £7,200.

Applications: In writing to the correspondent, preferably directly by the individual; alternatively, they can be submitted through a social worker, Citizens Advice or other welfare agency. Applications are considered on the second Tuesday in alternate months, commencing in May. Details of the purpose of the grant and other grants being sought should be included.

Correspondent: Claire Pegg, c/o Bingham Town Council, The Old Court House, Church Street, Bingham, Nottinghamshire NG13 8AL (01949 831445)

Other information: Grants are also given to organisations and individuals for educational purposes.

Carlton in Lindrick

The Christopher Johnson & the Green Charity

Eligibility: School children in need who live in the village of Carlton in Lindrick.

Types of grants: One-off grants ranging from £10 to £250 for school trips, books and so on.

Annual grant total: Grants usually total about £2,000 each year and are given for educational and welfare purposes.

Applications: In writing to the correspondent either directly by the individual, via a third party such as a social worker, doctor or district nurse or through a citizens advice bureau or other welfare agency. Applications are considered throughout the year.

Correspondent: C E R Towle, Hon. Secretary and Treasurer, 135 Windsor Road, Carlton in Lindrick, Worksop, Nottinghamshire S81 9DH (01909 731069 email: robin@towle.screaming.net)

Collingham

William and Mary Hart Foundation *see entry on page 43*

Correspondent: David Marshall, 2 Keats Drive, Hucknall, Nottingham, NG15 6TE (0115 963 5428)

Mansfield

Faith Clerkson's Exhibition Foundation

Eligibility: Boys and girls of school leaving age upwards who have for at least two years lived in the borough of Mansfield or

he urban district of Mansfield
Woodhouse.

Types of grants: Small cash grants, with no
fixed maximum limit, to help students and
others leaving school who are undertaking
full-time education, with the cost of books,
equipment, clothing and travel.

Exclusions: No grants for fees.

Annual grant total: In 2006/07 the
foundation had an income of £7,700 and a
total expenditure of £1,800.

Applications: In writing to the
correspondent, including proof of income
and details of any other grant applied for.
Applications are considered in early June
and early October.

Correspondent: C P McKay, 67 Clumber
Avenue, Beeston, Nottingham NG9 4BH

North Muskham

The Mary Woolhouse Foundation

Eligibility: People under 25 who live in the
parish of North Muskham and Bathley.

Types of grants: One-off grants are given
to schoolchildren and college students
towards books and equipment/
instruments.

Annual grant total: In 2006 it had both an
income and a total expenditure of £10,000.
Grants are made to individuals and local
schools.

Applications: In writing to the
correspondent. Applications should be
submitted directly by the individual and
are considered at any time.

Correspondent: Mrs S M White,
5 Waterside, North Muskham, Newark,
Nottinghamshire, NG23 6FD
(01636 704409)

Nottingham

The Audrey Harrison Heron Memorial Fund

Eligibility: Girls and women who live in
the city of Nottingham and are under the
age of 25.

Types of grants: Grants of between £50
and £2,000 to help with books, equipment,
clothing or travel, school, college or
university fees or to supplement existing
grants. Grants can be one-off or recurrent.

Annual grant total: In 2007/08 the trust
had both an income and a total
expenditure of around £4,000.

Applications: On a form available from
the correspondent. Applications can be
submitted directly by the individual,
through the individual's school/college/
educational welfare agency or other third
party, and are considered all year round.

Correspondent: The Manager, Natwest
Trust and Estate Services, 153 Preston
Road, Brighton BN1 6PD (0602 417536)

The Haywood Scholarships

Eligibility: First year higher education
students who are members of the Church
of England and have lived in the city of
Nottingham for at least six years before the
date of application. The applicant should
be studying science, maths or technological
subjects

Types of grants: Cash grants not exceeding
£100.

Exclusions: Grants are not given for
students intending to follow a teaching
course.

Annual grant total: In 2006/07 the trust
had an income of £1,400. Grants have
previously totalled around £900 a year.

Applications: In writing to the
correspondent. Students satisfying the
basic eligibility conditions are sent the
necessary forms direct. Applications are
judged in accordance with a basic means
test of parental income.

Correspondent: Student Awards Section,
Nottingham City Council, PO Box 7167,
Nottingham NG1 4WD (0115 915 4994)

The Peveril Exhibition Endowment Fund

Eligibility: Applicants who (or whose
parents) live within the city of
Nottingham, aged 11 to 24. There is a
minimum residential qualification period
within the city of two years and the trustees
will give preference to applicants who
originate from, or who have long-term ties
with, the Nottingham area rather than to
those who are merely living there whilst
completing an educational course locally.

Types of grants: One-off and recurrent
grants tenable at any secondary school,
college of education, university or other
institution of further (including
professional and technical) education
approved by the trustees. Grants available
up to £1,000. Larger grants may be given in
exceptional circumstances.

Annual grant total: In 2006/07 the fund
had an income of £7,000 and a total
expenditure of £6,500.

Applications: At any time on a form
available from the correspondent.
Applications should be submitted directly
by the individual; parents will be requested
to complete a means-test form if the
applicant is still a dependant. Applications
are considered all year around.

Correspondent: A B Palfreman, Clerk,
84 Friar Lane, Nottingham NG1 6ED
(0115 947 2541; Fax: 0115 947 3636;
email: apalfreman@fraserbrown.com)

Tuxford

Read's Exhibition Foundation

Eligibility: Children and young people,
including university students, who have
lived in and attended a school in the parish
of Tuxford.

Types of grants: Mainly help for students
in further or higher education. Help is also
given towards the cost of education,
training, apprenticeship or equipment for
those starting work and towards essentials
for schoolchildren.

Annual grant total: In 2006/07 the
foundation had an income of £5,600 and a
total expenditure of £9,800. Grants are
made to organisations and individuals.

Applications: In writing to the
correspondent. Invoices for school
equipment must be submitted on
application before any grant is issued.
Applications can be considered at any
time.

Correspondent: A A Hill, Sandy Acre,
Eagle Road, Spalford, Newark NG23 7HA
(01522 778250)

Warsop

The Warsop United Charities

Eligibility: People in need who live in the
urban district of Warsop (Warsop, Church
Warsop, Warsop Vale, Meden Vale, Spion
Kop and Skoonholme).

Types of grants: Grants for those at
school, college or university.

Annual grant total: Previously about
£5,000.

Applications: In writing to the
correspondent. Trustees meet three or four
times a year.

Correspondent: Mrs J R Simmons,
Newquay, Clumber Street, Warsop,
Mansfield, Nottinghamshire, NG20 0LX

Other information: Grants are also made
for relief-in-need purposes.

Shropshire

The Atherton Trust

Eligibility: People in need who live in the
parishes of Pontesbury and Hanwood and
the villages of Annscroft and Hook-a-Gate
in the county of Shropshire.

Types of grants: One-off grants given
towards fees, living expenses or study or
travel abroad for students in further and
higher education and towards equipment
or instruments for people starting work.

Annual grant total: In 2006/07 the trust had an income of £6,000 and a total expenditure of £3,300. Generally the trust gives around £900 annually to individuals for educational purposes.

Applications: On a form available from the correspondent, which can be submitted directly by the individual. Applications are considered quarterly in February, May, August and November.

Correspondent: The Secretary, Whittingham Riddell LLP, Belmont House, Shrewsbury Business Park, Shrewsbury SY2 6LG (01743 273273; Fax: 01743 273274; email: rtt@whittinghamriddell.co.uk)

Other information: The trust also supports organisations that give, or agree to give when required, support and services to people who need aid by loss of sight, limb or health by accident or inevitable causes.

Bowdler's Educational Foundation

Eligibility: People under the age of 25 who live in the county of Shropshire, but with a first priority for those living in the Shrewsbury area.

Types of grants: Grants, to a maximum of £100 to £200, for: (i) school pupils, to help with books, equipment, clothing or travel; (ii) help with school, college or university fees or to supplement existing grants; and (iii) help towards the cost of education, training, apprenticeship or equipment for those starting work.

Annual grant total: In 2006 the trust had an income of £2,500 and a total expenditure of £2,300.

Applications: On a form available from the correspondent.

Correspondent: T Collard, Clerk to the Trustees, c/o Legal Services, Shropshire County Council, The Shire Hall, Abbey Foregate, Shrewsbury SY2 6ND (01743 252756; email: tim.collard@shropshire-cc.gov.uk)

The Careswell Foundation

Eligibility: People under the age of 25 who live in Shropshire and have attended certain schools in the county, namely Shrewsbury School, Bridgnorth Endowed School, Adam's Grammar School (Newport), Idsall School (Shifnal), Thomas Adam's School (Wem) and the school or schools of secondary education by which Donnington, Shropshire is served.

Types of grants: Cash grants, to a usual maximum of about £150 a year for three years, to help with the cost of books and equipment, to be used at college or university or other establishments of further education.

Annual grant total: In 2006/07 the trust had an income of £12,000 and a total expenditure of £11,000.

Applications: On a form supplied by the headteacher of the relevant school to be submitted in August or September for consideration in October.

Correspondent: Mrs B A Marshall, 24 The Crescent, Shrewsbury SY1 1 TJ (01743 351332; Fax: 01743 351844; email: solicitors@turnbullgarrard.co.uk)

The Clungunford Educational Foundation

Eligibility: People under the age of 25 who live in the parish of Clungunford, the part of the parish of Onibury that used to be in Clungunford, and the former hamlet of Broome in the parish of Hopesay.

Types of grants: Help with the cost of books, clothing and other essentials for schoolchildren. Help is also available for students at college or university, and towards books, equipment, clothing and travel for people starting work. Grants range from £20 to £200.

Annual grant total: In 2007 the foundation had an income of £1,300 and a total expenditure of £1,700. Grants usually total about £1,000.

Applications: In writing to the correspondent or any trustee. An information sheet is distributed to each household in the parish at two or three-year intervals and to all newcomers.

Correspondent: Mrs B W Sheaman, Rose Cottage, Hopton Heath, Craven Arms, Shropshire SY7 0QD

Millington's Charity

Eligibility: Preference for people who live in Shropshire. Applicants must be residents or have been educated in Shropshire, be aged between 15 and 24, and should be members, or their parents/guardian must be members, of the Church of England.

Types of grants: One-off grants ranging from £100 to £400 to help with incidental expenses associated with college or university attendance where there is a special need; to supplement existing grants; or to assist with funding a specific educational project. Grants are given towards the cost of books, equipment/instruments, maintenance/living expenses and study or travel abroad. Grants can also be awarded to people starting work.

Exclusions: Grants are not normally given towards fees.

Annual grant total: About £3,000 a year.

Applications: Applications should be made on forms available from the correspondent upon written request. Details of parental income irrespective of the age of the applicant are obligatory. Decisions and awards are made at

quarterly meetings in early March, June, September and December.

Correspondent: J W Rouse, Clerk to the Trustees, Houlston Cottage, Myddle, Shropshire SY4 3RD (01939 290898; Fax: 01939 290898; email: johnwrouse@btinternet.com)

The Shrewsbury Municipal Charity

Eligibility: People in need who live, work or study in the borough of Shrewsbury and Atcham. Usually, 60% of the disposable income is for education/training of people under 25 years of age; the balance is for general relief of need.

Types of grants: One-off grants of £50 to £250 to assist with educational and vocational needs.

Annual grant total: About £500.

Applications: In writing to the correspondent, either directly by the individual or through a social worker, Citizens Advice, welfare agency or other third party. Applications are considered in January, May, and September, but emergencies can be considered at any time. Please include details of any other charities that have been contacted for assistance.

Correspondent: John Goldsworthy, 21 Eastwood Road, Shrewsbury SY3 8ES

The Shropshire Youth Foundation

Eligibility: People under the age of 25 years who live in Shropshire.

Types of grants: One-off grants, typically of £200, towards education through leisure time activities, such as voluntary service overseas and expeditions, may be given on occasions, so as to develop the physical, mental and spiritual capacities of individuals.

Exclusions: No grants are made towards educational courses.

Annual grant total: About £6,000 in grants to individuals and organisations.

Applications: Application forms are available from the foundation. The trustees meet twice yearly in June/July and January/February.

Correspondent: D E Wise, Honorary Secretary, The Shirehall, Abbey Foregate, Shrewsbury, Shropshire SY2 6ND (01743 252726; email: david.wise@shropshire-cc.gov.uk)

The Walker Trust

Eligibility: People who live in Shropshire.

Types of grants: Grants for people in further and higher education, especially medical and veterinary students, where no local authority grant or student loan is available. Assistance to A-level students is